latest edh 01/13

# Modern Britain

'Admirable balance, allowing the reader to see the issues involved and draw informed conclusions . . . extremely competently done and wholly reliable as a source of information.'

Sidney Pollard, University of Sheffield

*Modern Britain* focuses on two major periods of British history; the interwar period and postwar Britain. The authors compare and contrast developments in the two periods, dealing with the themes of:

- growth and welfare
- industry
- labour
- social policy
- the economy

Combining a narrative with a conceptual and analytic approach, *Modern Britain* provides an end-of-century review of progress and decline, and an essential background to current polemics and major issues of concern. Clearly structured and written, this is an invaluable textbook for students of twentieth-century British history.

**Sean Glynn** is a Senior Research Fellow at London Guildhall University. He is the author of *Interwar Britain* (1976) and several other books on modern economic history. **Alan Booth** is Senior Lecturer in Economic History at the University of Exeter. He is the author of *British Economic Policy 1931–1949* (1989) and co-editor with Sean Glynn of *The Road to Full Employment* (1986).

WITHDRAWN BOOK SALO WANDSWORTH

D0242516

# Modern Britain

## An economic and social history

Sean Glynn and Alan Booth

WANDSWORTH PUBLIC LIBRARIES

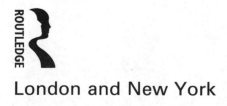

London and New York

First published 1996
by Routledge
11 New Fetter Lane, London EC4P 4EE

Simultaneously published in the USA and Canada
by Routledge
29 West 35th Street, New York, NY 10001

© 1996 Sean Glynn and Alan Booth

Typeset in Palatino by
J&L Composition Ltd, Filey, North Yorkshire

Printed and bound in Great Britain by
Clays Ltd, St. Ives PLC

All rights reserved. No part of this book may be reprinted
or reproduced or utilized in any form or by any electronic,
mechanical, or other means, now known or hereafter
invented, including photocopying and recording, or in any
information storage or retrieval system, without permission
in writing from the publishers.

*British Library Cataloguing in Publication Data*
A catalogue record for this book is available from the British Library

*Library of Congress Cataloguing in Publication Data*
A catalogue record for this book has been requested

ISBN 0–415–10472–6
   0–415–10473–4 (pbk)

500052378

# Contents

# List of figures

# List of tables

# Chapter 1

# Introduction

On almost any reckoning, the 1914–18 war marks a major watershed between the comparatively stable nineteenth-century world system, focused on British hegemony, and the shifting fortunes of the twentieth century. For historians it may be said that the twentieth century commences in 1914. This book deals with British economic and social experience between the First World War and the present. It is essentially an introduction to modern British economic and social history designed principally for first year university and college students and those without a substantial background in the subject and will also be of use to students at Advanced Level GCE.

In a short work of this kind it is inevitable that coverage of detailed developments has had to be heavily circumscribed and we seek to focus on themes rather than giving a blow by blow account of eventualities. In terms of chronology we have taken the two world wars as historical dividing lines. Part I of the book considers developments up to the end of the Second World War and Part II deals with the period since. Within these broad sub-periods we examine the main features of economic and social development under a number of headings which are intended to inject a more orderly and analytical approach to the examination of change than a simple chronological catalogue might.

There is now a formidable body of literature on twentieth-century economic and social history which is still growing at a rapid rate. In the past two decades there has been a flood of a new writing on twentieth-century Britain. Much of the textbook literature, particularly on the period since 1945, is for advanced and specialist students and this book seeks to fill a gap in general literature. Any exercise in contemporary history gives hostages to fortune and runs the risk of soon being superseded while the pitfalls of writing recent history are well known and have been much discussed there is, nevertheless, an undoubted importance in seeking to understand the developments which have shaped our present and we hope that what follows will make some contribution to future interpretation as well as present understanding.

## RELATIVE ECONOMIC DECLINE

By the end of the First World War, three great empires (Ottoman, Austrian, Russian) had collapsed, the map of Europe was being redrawn, and the United States had clearly superseded Britain as the world's leading economic and financial power. Nevertheless, Britain's relative decline was a protracted process which did not depend simply upon economic developments. It is inevitable that one of the themes of a book of this kind should be this question of decline which is an endless issue in modern British economic historiography. Ironically, Britain's loss of position in the world order has taken place against a background of by far the most dramatic improvement in material standards in any comparable period of history. Our theme, therefore, is one of decline and progress. In the absence of relative decline Britain's material and social progress since 1914 would surely be regarded as something truly remarkable. Unfortunately Britain's phenomenal material and social progress in the twentieth century has been tarnished by better performance elsewhere. By the end of the twentieth century Britain had been overtaken in terms of real GDP per capita by most industrial nations and had fallen badly behind the leaders. In the dramatic words of Sidney Pollard (1982: 3): 'Britain is no longer counted amongst the economically advanced nations of the world. A wide gap separates her from the rest of industrialised Europe. The difference as measured in national product per head between Britain and say, Germany, is now as wide as the difference between Britain and the Continent of Africa.' In fact, Britain may not have slipped quite so badly as this well-known but controversial comparison suggests; but other measures, in terms of 'purchasing power parities' (see below pp. 189–90), tell an essentially similar if less dramatic story.

Much of this relative decline has taken place since 1950 and it was only in the 1960s and later that the British people became painfully aware of the drift. However, the beginnings of comparative deficiencies in economic performance can be detected from the late nineteenth century and the causes have been traced to the nature of the Industrial Revolution in the late eighteenth and early nineteenth centuries (Crafts 1985). Throughout the first half of the twentieth century war and depression disguised and retarded the process of relative decline to some extent but in the long post-Second World War boom Britain lagged well behind other countries in the league tables of economic growth rates which began to attract so much attention. By the late 1960s it was no longer possible to explain these differences in terms of postwar recovery or catching up. It was concluded that Britain had a long-run tendency to grow less rapidly than virtually all other industrial nations. It is possible that during the 1980s Britain began to experience a process of relative acceleration against other industrial economies such as Germany but we cannot be sure of this without the benefits of perspective. In dealing with very recent history there are serious problems in distinguishing trend from cycle and these can only be definitively resolved in the longer run.

Was British relative decline inevitable? The answer must surely be in the affirmative up to a point. In retrospect much of the British hegemony was based upon what might be termed exceptional and essentially fortuitous short-run circumstances. Geographical position and short-run military (primarily naval) supremacy enabled Britain to capture the 'lion's share' of imperial territory and influence. The world was finite and much of it was already British by the time other nations took up the challenge (Kennedy 1988). Similarly, a financial and commercial system with Britain as its hub was created during conditions of quasi-monopoly. The Industrial Revolution which had made this imperial, financial and commercial strength possible, was based upon exceptional and highly unusual circumstances. The industrial base was suprisingly narrow, depending heavily on a relatively small group of so-called 'old staple' industries of which cotton, wool, coal, iron and steel, shipbuilding, railways and engineering were the base. Prowess in these areas was established through the development of a craft-based production system with the majority of workers receiving no formal education beyond basic literacy and no technical education other than on-the-job experience (Sanderson 1988). The essential feature of the Industrial Revolution had involved the early creation of an industrial work-force, and a rapid running down of agriculture, at low levels of income and productivity (Crafts 1985). In the century before 1914 the British balance of payments became increasingly dependent upon invisible overseas earnings and visible exports covered visible imports in only four highly exceptional years in the century before 1939. Thus British supremacy owed much to highly exceptional, short-run circumstances, both at home and abroad. While industrial leadership played a critical role, the industrial system and base was far from being the whole explanation and was, in any event, both weak and, in the long-run was to prove inadequate (Kirby 1981).

In the late nineteenth century British hegemony was challenged. Meanwhile, on the domestic front moves towards democratisation created political, social and economic pressures for change. Industrialisation before 1914 had enabled Britain to support a much larger population without a fall in living standards but the standard of life for the majority failed to match aspirations, and by the late nineteenth-century problems of extensive poverty and unemployment and poor living conditions had begun to attract increasing attention (Harris 1972; Stedman Jones 1971). Any understanding of Britain's relative decline must address the failure to meet these external and internal challenges. There were, of course, degrees of success and the essential questions are first, could Britain, having gained economic leadership have maintained it, or retained it longer? Second, could British living standards have remained in the vanguard of the industrial world? These are, of course, counterfactual questions which may never be answered in a totally satisfactory way. They are, nevertheless, essential reference points for modern economic history.

## EXPLAINING RELATIVE ECONOMIC DECLINE

Unfortunately there has been both confusion and disagreement about the nature, extent and causes of Britain's relative decline. Definitions and explanations have varied enormously, reflecting different interests and ideologies as well as current fashions in economic and social theory. As a result, generalisation is both difficult and hazardous. In what follows we do not attempt a full and systematic review of all the explanations offered since that would be impossible in the space available and, in any event, inconclusive since there is no consensus. Nor do we attempt the comparative international investigation which is arguably a necessary feature of a full explanation.

There is a measure of agreement that British decline is based on a comparative industrial failure, in terms of relative efficiency, but much disagreement and confusion on its origins and causes. Some commentators have stressed the supply side, giving particular attention to the quality and management of labour and the supply and deployment of capital inputs. But attention has also been given to the configuration and development of market demand and the influence of this on production systems and possibilities. Others have stressed the importance of influences from outside industry including, in particular, the role of institutions, government, economic policies and elite culture. Insofar as relative economic decline was not inevitable, it can be attributed to decision-making processes or to institutional failure. Either wrong decisions were made or industrial efficiency was not the first priority in resource allocation.

It is increasingly asserted that Britain failed to make sufficient effort to improve labour quality and management skills through investment in human capital (Crafts and Thomas 1986; Gospel 1992; Sanderson 1988). Attention has also been given to the failure to increase and sustain investment in manufacturing industry (Pollard 1982). Neglect of the manufacturing base has been emphasised, both in terms of an anti-industrial elite culture (Wiener 1981), and the excessive burden of government spending (Bacon and Eltis 1976). It has been suggested that British industry may have become focused on areas with less potential, in particular, empire and Third World markets, rather than First World markets including Europe (Cain and Hopkins 1993a). The domestic market may have suffered from a highly uneven income distribution and consumer demand constraint, leading to a haemorrhage of capital into overseas investment (Hobson 1896; Glynn and Booth 1983a). Thus we already have a bewildering variety of possible lines of explanation involving alternative resource deployments. Others have suggested that there was both institutional and market failure (Elbaum and Lazonick 1986; Olson 1982). All of these, and other views, contain important insights and observations, but all have been questioned, and no particular view seems to have gained general acceptance (Coates 1994).

With foreign commentators, in particular, the British Empire has often been given a central role in Britain's rise to prominence and loss of empire has been seen as the major influence in subsequent decline. While the formal colonial empire may have enriched and provided an outlet for British individuals, its social benefits appear to have been relatively minor and it played a relatively small part in the main process of British income generation (Cain and Hopkins 1993a). From the later decades of the nineteenth century British industry and finance appears to have become geared into relationships with third world and imperial markets rather than seeking to integrate into and compete with First World systems. In the twentieth century British political leaders continued to pursue great power status and this may have had damaging consequences for industry, particularly in the period after the Second World War. Heavy outlays on military and other government expenditure may have been a source of balance of payments weakness as well as a diversion of R & D effort from more orthodox channels. Also, the pursuit of imperialist or great power objectives appears to have been a major influence on Britain's failure to play a leading part in European integration (Young 1993; Chalmers 1985).

Economists and economic historians have given a great deal of attention to differences in income levels between nations (Maddison 1987). The general conclusion is that development cannot commence until a backward country acquires certain minimal levels of economic organisation, educational attainment, and political and social stability. By the late nineteenth century several countries possessed this basis for development which combined with the 'economic advantages of relative backwardness'. The latter included a greater awareness in more backward nations of the need for change on the part of both governments and individuals, the ability to borrow from leaders through transfers of capital, technology and methods of organisation and the opportunity of transferring labour from less efficient sectors, including agriculture, and thus improving productivity. In some cases these advantages were augmented by social upheavals resulting from disruptive events such as war or revolution which, subsequently, allowed more rapid change to take place (Gerschenkron 1962; Feinstein 1990b).

The logical outcome of theories of this kind should, of course, be longrun convergence. To what extent does this fit the British experience? Britain was unique in having the first 'Industrial Revolution' which occurred spontaneously as a result of fortuitous circumstances (Mokyr 1985; Crafts 1985). However, a group of other nations were never very far behind and it is surely inconceivable that a small offshore island with only 2 per cent of world land and population and a narrow resource base would continue to dominate economic and industrial development for very long. In particular, the transfer of organisation and technology between leader nations was a comparatively easy matter. From the late nineteenth century other nations began to exploit the economic advantages of backwardness, generating higher rates of economic growth than Britain. In Europe it had long been British policy to prevent the emergence of a dominant continental influence through balance of power diplomacy and limited indulgence in warfare. However, with the unification of Germany in the 1860s this strategy began to fail. Meanwhile, across the Atlantic another great continental power was emerging. The German challenge produced two world wars in which Britain was a major participant. These depleted British resources while serving only to delay rather than prevent the German advance. In the event, it was the United States which replaced Britain as world leader and this process was accelerated by two world wars focused on Europe (Kennedy 1988).

The USA had higher income levels than Britain even before industrialisation. This reflected superior natural endowments and abundant resources in relation to population. By 1900 the USA was beginning to challenge Britain as an industrial power. Productivity levels in the USA during the next 30 years raced ahead of Britain so that by the 1920s US industrial workers may have produced twice as much per head as British. It could be argued, therefore, that at an early stage in the present century Britain was beginning to acquire some of the economic advantages of backwardness. By the 1960s these began to be enhanced in relation to other nations, but Britain's relative economic decline continued, particularly in terms of comparative industrial productivity, and this was reflected in declining relative income levels (Crafts 1988).

Thus it may be suggested that arguments in terms of the advantages of relative economic backwardness and consequent convergence appear to have some relevance, but even allowing for overshoot and short-run policy failure, they do not at present appear to provide a full and convincing explanation for Britain's relative economic decline. Alternative explanations must rely either upon resource constraints or upon the development and deployment of resources being in some way inadequate. In turn the latter implies either institutional or market failure or failure on the part of government to remove barriers to modernisation and change.

It is agreed by most commentators that Britain's balance of payments weakness and relatively slow growth emanates from an inadequate and comparatively inefficient industrial base. However, during the 1980s there was some support, particularly at government level, for the idea that Britain could succeed as a service economy and it became fashionable to deride concern about de-industrialisation (Conservative Party 1992). Wiener has interpreted industrial failure as being the consequence of an anti-industrial culture (Wiener 1981). Olson, on the other hand, has suggested that in more stable societies vested interests tend to accumulate with the effect of creating barriers to rapid economic change (Olson 1982). Societies which are disrupted by revolution or war, particularly where there is occupation and or defeat, have fewer disadvantages in generating rapid economic change.

Approaches of this kind may provide partial explanations of short- and medium-term relative decline, although it seems likely that, in the long-run, cultural and institutional barriers to change in advanced economies are likely to be overcome by the relative advantages and pressures for change which result from backwardness. There can be little doubt that such pressures now exist in British society and act as an influence on both government and other decision-making.

## ECONOMIC CHANGE

In the chapters that follow, the process of economic change in Britain during this century is outlined and examined in some detail. Economic growth, as conventionally defined and measured in terms of the increase in real GDP per head, has been a major focus of attention since the emergence of national income accounting in the 1940s. Britain's combination of historically fast but relatively slow growth since 1900 (an average long-run growth rate of about $2-2\frac{1}{2}$ per cent per annum) has generally been seen as below what could have been achieved and thus major opportunities for enhanced production have been lost. Nevertheless, in the present century almost the entire population has come to expect to be fully satisfied in terms of the basic material needs such as food, clothing and shelter, and remaining deficiencies in these areas became qualitative rather than quantitative. While problems of supply were largely solved, those of distribution were not, and this was illustrated at the end of our period by the egregious example of people living in cardboard boxes in parts of central London.

By 1914 the proportion of employment in agriculture and manufacturing had reached peak levels and subsequent employment growth was in services. This configuration reflected income and productivity effects, but from the 1970s there was increasing concern about 'deindustrialisation' and, in the 1980s, Britain became a regular net importer of manufactured goods for the first time since the Middle Ages. In the seven years before 1914 Britain had a large current account surplus and more new capital was invested abroad than at home. The strength and reliability of sterling at this time went without question. From the end of the First World War there were persistent balance of payments weaknesses although these were partially concealed by heavy unemployment in the interwar years. The 'financial Dunkirk' which Keynes predicted after the Second World War was, in the event, less dire than expected but the ongoing weakness on external account was to prove not only an intractable problem but, in reality, the essential manifestation of modern economic failure. The persistent decline in the relative value of sterling matched the diminution in Britain's influence and prestige.

Nevertheless, the economy continued to deliver and Britain retained its place as one of the world's richer nations. Living standards remained at First World levels and there was a good deal of economic success blended with the indifference and failure. Britain continued to make a major contribution to international advances in technology and lifestyles and some leading British companies continued to play a significant and successful international role. On the conventional definition, living standards by the late 1930s were almost double the pre-First World War level. After the Second World War standards doubled again. In terms of distribution of income and wealth there was considerable change between 1914 and about 1950, largely as a result of fiscal and welfare innovations and the emergence, after 1940, of full employment. These moves towards less inequality, from a highly inequitable start, appear to have been thrown into reverse during the 1980s. In the 1990s it was being claimed that inequalities in income distribution had reverted to late nineteenth century patterns and that the extent of poverty was increasing. Emerging relative deprivation could be seen as another indication of economic and social failure (George and Miller 1994).

It can be asserted with no fear of contradiction that the quality of life in Britain has improved since 1914 and that the economic growth which has been achieved has been largely worthwhile. Nevertheless, by the late twentieth century there were major concerns about the sustainability of the economic system and its depletion and destruction of finite resources. Some major environmental sins had been inherited from the nineteenth century and these have been augmented, not least through the development of the internal combustion engine (Simmons 1993).

## SOCIAL CHANGE

Britain entered the 1990s with an enhanced awareness of its relative backwardness but without any clear or emergent consensus regarding possible solutions. In turn, this reflected social and political problems and pressures which had been evident since the late nineteenth century.

It was suggested earlier that Britain's former hegemony was based upon unusual domestic, as well as international circumstances, and that these were challenged internally by democratisation. The nineteenth-century system had been based upon a largely uneducated work-force which sold its labour in free market circumstances, accepting in return low material standards, gross inequalities and a general absence of state welfare. Late nineteenth-century Britain can be characterised as a 'one-third two-thirds' society in which only a minority enjoyed acceptable lifetime material standards and security. For the majority poverty was a constant threat and a likely condition, especially in childhood, during family creation and in old age. By the end of the twentieth century Britain had become a 'two-thirds one-third' society, with poverty still existing and posing a serious threat, but to a minority. This transition was achieved through many difficulties and vicissitudes but against a background of fundamental political stability (Lowe 1993; Digby 1989; Crowther 1988; Thane 1982).

Against this background of fundamental stability and continuity the twentieth century has seen a remarkable pattern of change. This has included the conduct of two cataclysmic world wars, the establishment of a welfare state and the evolution of a modern democratic society. In 1914 the majority of working class people (85 per cent of the British population) lived a life which can only be described as very circumscribed and deprived by modern standards (Gourvish 1979). Women were totally disenfranchised and largely confined to a subordinate role and the majority of men failed to exercise the vote in any meaningful way. Social deference was extreme by late twentieth-century standards and aspirations were low. By the end of the First World War important new attitudes had begun to emerge (Burke 1982). These tendencies were blunted by interwar unemployment but by the end of the 1930s certain regions and groups in British society were moving towards consumer affluence. After the Second World War sustained growth and the establishment of the welfare state produced Harold Macmillan's 'affluent society'. These changes were accompanied by dramatic and far reaching developments in the role of the state in British economic and social life. By the 1970s it became fashionable to blame poor economic performance on the 'excessive' burden of state expenditure and the political and economic compromises inherent in the postwar consensus (Barnett 1986). At the same time, working class aspirations for better material standards, as represented by the trade unions, were increasingly seen as a baleful influence.

By the early twentieth century a distinct and clearly identifiable working class sub-group and culture had emerged in Britain and included perhaps three quarters of the population. In the interwar years this was consolidated through the emergence of popular forms of consumption, leisure and entertainment including sports, radio and cinema (Jones 1986). After the Second World War this culture seems to have moved towards a peak, at least in terms of intellectual mythology, before beginning to weaken in response to changing economic circumstances and social attitudes. By the 1990s it was widely recognised that there had been some significant changes in such basic institutions as the family, in gender relations, sexual attitudes and social status (Hamnett *et al*. 1989). At the same time, there were important continuities in the causes and extent of relative poverty and the importance of employment in determining social attitudes and maintaining cohesion. There were also significant regional changes with the North, along with Wales, Scotland and Ireland tending to diminish in relative demographic and economic importance as the industrial centre of gravity shifted to the Midlands and the South East. Yet Britain remained a segmented society with important class and racial dimensions and attitudes and there were times when these were expressed in terms of conflict and dissent. Social and economic failure was frequently analysed in terms of class and it could only have been a British Prime Minister who, towards the end of the century, declared that there was 'no such thing as society'. Despite the attention given to social change, and new attitudes in terms of class, race and gender, social continuities continued to dominate. The vast majority of British people remained nominally Christian, white and lived in family or heterosexual pair-bonded circumstances. The majority continued to be working class and this was reflected in the structure of employment, though the proportion of blue-collar workers fell. On the available evidence it can be argued that social continuity has been more important than social change but that economic change has presented challenges to social structure and attitudes. In particular, the situation in the labour market and the resulting structure and nature of employment had major social consequences. By the late twentieth century unemployment had once again become an important agent promoting social change (Glynn 1991).

It is clear, therefore, that Britain's failure in the international context has been mirrored by domestic pressures and a corresponding impression of domestic failure at least since the 1960s. The British system has failed to satisfy rising materialist aspirations, despite changes in social structure and organisation and a greatly enhanced role for government. At the same time, economic change has created major social pressures. It is a matter for debate to what extent international decline is the result of domestic change and to what extent the disappointment in the latter is the result of the former. Have the British people expected too much and made too many demands on the system, giving rise to international failure? Or was the system inherently inadequate for twentieth century circumstances? This is an issue which cannot easily be resolved.

In the chapters which follow we explore the vicissitudes of historical change and seek also to highlight the fundamentals of continuity. In general we have sought to avoid the pitfalls of partisanship, as far as possible, by giving both sides of the argument. While we have from time to time suggested conclusions, we believe that these should be left to the reader, and strong lessons have not been emphasised. What is very clear is that history is a retrospective view and things can look very different in retrospect. We are aware that some of our most critical readers will be those with substantial personal experience of the twentieth century. Above all we hope that what follows will contribute to the understanding and further study of modern Britain

# Part I

# Interwar Britain

# Chapter 2

# Growth and living standards

## IMPRESSIONS OF ECONOMIC PERFORMANCE

British interwar economic performance has been viewed in both opti-
mistic and pessimistic terms. For contemporary observers the divisions
were largely regional. J.B. Priestley (1934) discerned four Englands: the
nineteenth-century England of the industrial North; the England of the
Dole which could be said to have included most of the industrial North
as well as extending into Wales, Scotland and Northern Ireland; the
traditional rural England of the southern counties and finally twentieth-
century England of the bustling home counties, of bypasses and housing
estates and suburban villas and cocktail bars gleaming with chromium
trim (quoted in Mowat 1955: 480–90). More recently, historians have
pieced together much more quantitative information on interwar economic performance but without reaching consensus. Opinions have
included the highly optimistic views of Aldcroft (1967) who saw the
period as one of greatly enhanced growth performance and entrepreneurial rejuvenation and Alford (1972: 82) who is more pessimistic, in
part because of the heavy unemployment which prevailed.

The impression of stagnation, decay and poverty alongside growth,
innovation and prosperity combines with a more powerful sense of
major disruption and discontinuity resulting from two world wars and
world depression. Above all there is the feeling that unemployment
during the period wasted lives and product, constituting an economic
disaster and a social and human tragedy: in the 1920s and 1930s 'the
workshop of the world was on short time' (Mowat 1955: 281). By the
1940s there was a general presumption that the interwar years had been
a cruel economic waste.

It is, in fact, very difficult to fit the interwar years easily into the long-
run themes of British economic historiography. It is clear that during the
second half of the nineteenth century British economic growth began to
slow in absolute terms and also in comparison with leading industrial
nations. During the early twentieth century the economy became stag-

nant. It is also beyond much doubt that after the Second World War growth accelerated to levels which had not occurred on a regular basis before, although British performance remained weak in international comparisons. Accordingly, there are three major possibilities for the interwar years. First, that the period marks a continuation of the slow-down which had commenced during the late nineteenth century. Second, that the period saw the beginnings of the process of faster and better sustained growth which characterises the long postwar boom. Third, the interwar period was unique and characterised by the major disruptions of war, depression and mass unemployment.

In fact, it is impossible to select any of these three possibilities to the exclusion of others. Each provides insights into interwar economic performance. During what might be termed the 'normal' years, when there was peace and a degree of economic buoyancy, the economy clearly had dualistic aspects. On the one hand the old staple industries were beginning to enter a phase of very noticeable terminal decline which marked the end of the Victorian economy. Meanwhile, new industries and areas of growth in the economy were beginning to emerge as harbingers of rapid postwar acceleration. Although the real breakthrough into higher growth appears to have come, at least in statistical terms, around 1950, some of the groundwork occurred in the interwar years and there is clear evidence of productivity improvements. Thus the concept of the 'dual economy' captures some important quali-tative changes which were taking place in the interwar economy. Unfor-tunately, the conventional quantitative measures of aggregate economic growth obscure some of these changes, making summary judgement difficult.

The most detailed study of the topic has suggested that the long-run pattern of British economic growth is best described as U-shaped: with a decline in the growth rate to a low point at some time before or around the First World War, then acceleration to 1973, with the interwar years as the turning point (Matthews *et al*. 1982: 5). The downturn of 1919–21 was 'the greatest setback to real GDP that the country had experienced since the industrial revolution. On the other hand, those years marked also the beginning of a phase of increase in the rate of growth of productivity that persisted for the next half century' (Matthews *et al*. 1982: 5–6).

## THE GROWTH RECORD

The conventional economist's definition of economic growth is the rate of change in Gross National Product (or a related aggregate) per head. Gross Domestic Product can be defined as the total production of goods and services in the economy in a year. Gross National Product is GDP plus income from abroad. Calculating total output or GNP is complex and there are many problems which can only be solved in arbitrary ways. Calculations may be made on the basis of income, output or expenditure. Unpaid work such as that carried out by housewives has to be totally excluded; double counting has to be avoided; all product has to be converted to a monetary value. In service industries, in particular, there are problems in estimating output. Usually output is assumed to equal the incomes generated in the industry. Thus, in effect, output of a school is assumed to equal the incomes of the teachers and others employed in running it. While there are major problems in estimating GNP for any single year, additional difficulties arise in attempting to construct a consistent and comparable series for a number of years. Historical estimates encounter problems of qualitative change over time which make quantification even more difficult, as well as inadequacies and inconsistencies in quantitative records or data. Also, prices change creating exceptionally difficult conceptual and empirical problems which can be solved only by arbitrary judgements.

Also, GNP may not be a very good measure of human welfare. Measured output will, for example, include weapons of destruction as well as products which are required to combat the unwanted effects of growth. On the other hand, materials which are destroyed in the process of production and pollution and other adverse influences on the environment and quality of life are not measured or allowed for. In the last twenty years a vigorous 'anti-growth' literature has developed and there are a number of alternative approaches some of which take account of environmental issues. So far at least, most economists and historians have continued to use the conventional measures in the belief that, despite their limitations they remain the best available indicators of growth and welfare. They are not, of course, the only indicators and the interwar years, in particular, with their sad record of unemployment and poverty, clearly carry the message that growth is not the whole story.

British national income statistics were first developed in the 1930s by Colin Clark and were greatly improved by economists and statisticians working in the wartime civil service (Chapter 8). The great explosion of interest in economic growth in the 1950s stimulated attempts to estimate retrospectively British national income before 1939 and Feinstein (1972b) produced a continuous series for the UK covering the period 1855–1965. The margin of error in Feinstein's estimates is only 5 per cent up to 1929, and subsequently much less (Feinstein 1972a: 20).

Once national annual estimates for GNP and related variables are available, and some means of allowing for price changes between different years has been adopted, we are left with a series for *real GNP*. This can be divided by population to give *real GNP per capita*. The change in this aggregate is the conventional definition of economic growth. These

*Table 2.1* British trade cycles, 1918–38

| Peaks | Troughs |
| --- | --- |
| October 1918 | April 1919 |
| March 1920 | June 1921 |
| November 1924 | July 1926 |
| March 1927 | September 1928 |
| July 1929 | August 1932 |
| September 1937 | September 1938 |

*Source*: Aldcroft 1970: 29.

annual figures will vary enormously from year to year. In some interwar years the change in GNP was negative while in others it exceeded 5 per cent. The problem for the historian is to ascertain what is typical. There are cyclical variations in the economy and these may have a major influence on measurement. If we measure growth during a cyclical upswing this will give us an exaggerated impression while measuring through a downswing will do the opposite. It is now widely accepted that measurement must be between years which have reasonably comparable levels of economic activity and, in practice, this means measuring from peak to peak (though allowance may have to be made for differing intensity of cyclical peaks – see Chapter 10).

In the interwar years Aldcroft has identified five cycles between 1918 and 1938 (see Table 2.1).

Most of the interwar cycles were of short duration compared with the classic or Juglar cycle of the late nineteenth century, but the downturns of 1920–21 and 1929–32 were severe. The latter was followed by a long and vigorous upswing lasting five years.

In measuring interwar growth rates we can, in theory, select any of the peaks listed above, but these peaks had very different rates of unemployment and thus did not have comparable levels of economic activity. There are, moreover, statistical problems relating to the period 1918–21: this was a period of postwar adjustment in which the length of the average working week fell from fifty-four hours to forty-eight. In 1921 twenty-six counties of Ireland were separated from the United Kingdom and this represented a break in statistical series. For these and other reasons growth in the interwar period is usually measured across the peaks 1924–29 and 1929–37. While more convenient and reliable this yardstick does have the effect of excluding eight or nine years from the period. Over the period 1924–37 growth in GDP averaged 2.2 per cent per annum and GDP per head grew at an average rate of 1.8 per cent per annum.

The interwar years were preceded by a period of very slow or negative growth and abysmal productivity performance at least on the basis of

*Table 2.2* British growth rates, 1760–1973 (average annual percentage)

|           | GDP  | GDP per head |
|-----------|------|--------------|
| 1760–1800 | 1.1  | 0.3          |
| 1800–30   | 2.7  | 1.3          |
| 1830–60   | 2.5  | 1.1          |
| 1856–73   | 2.2  | 1.4          |
| 1873–1913 | 1.8  | 0.9          |
| 1913–24   | −0.1 | −0.6         |
| 1924–37   | 2.2  | 1.8          |
| 1937–51   | 1.8  | 1.3          |
| 1951–73   | 2.8  | 2.3          |

*Source*: Matthews *et al.* 1982: 498.

available measures. It is far from clear why the economy should have performed so badly during the Edwardian years, but Britain was not unique, and there appears to have been an international slowdown at this time. Interwar growth does not appear to have been spectacular by the standards of the mid-nineteenth or the later twentieth centuries but it followed half a century of very poor performance.

International comparisons are notoriously difficult for reasons of inadequacies and variations in data. The rate of growth in Britain has tended to be lower by approximately one-third than in most other industrial nations since 1870 (see Chapter 10). In general it can be said that Britain tended to lag behind other major industrial countries in the 1920s but made some relative gains in the 1930s. Britain recovered relatively quickly from the First World War compared with other European powers but was badly affected by the downturn of 1921. It is widely assumed that in the 1920s the economy was slowed by exporting difficulties and deflationary policies, including the return to gold in 1925. Unlike certain economies, Britain failed to experience a strong boom in the later 1920s. Nevertheless, British growth rates over the decade as a whole matched those throughout much of Europe. The 1930s depression was relatively mild in Britain and recovery to the pre-depression level was quicker than elsewhere, with few exceptions. Indeed some countries including France and the United States failed to recover fully during the remainder of the 1930s. The 1930s are comparable to the 1980s in that in each period Britain recorded higher growth rates than many other industrial nations in adverse world circumstances. (OECD 1991). However, it would be wrong to make much of these very modest reversals in long-run relative decline. Indeed, the underlying picture in terms of productivity trends saw Britain lagging throughout the entire interwar period.

British productivity levels in 1913 were still very high by international

Table 2.3 Growth rates of real output per worker employed, 1873–1951 (% per annum)

|  | UK | USA | France | Germany | Japan |
|---|---|---|---|---|---|
| 1873–99 | 1.2 | 1.9 | 1.3 | 1.5 | 1.1 |
| 1899–1913 | 0.5 | 1.3 | 1.6 | 1.6 | 1.8 |
| 1913–24 | 0.3 | 1.7 | 0.8 | −0.9 | 3.2 |
| 1924–37 | 1.0 | 1.4 | 1.4 | 3.0 | 2.7 |
| 1937–51 | 1.0 | 2.3 | 1.7 | 1.0 | −1.3 |

Source: Matthews et al. 1982: 31.

Table 2.4 Real GDP per hour worked: comparisons with the UK in selected years

|  | UK | USA | France | Germany | Japan |
|---|---|---|---|---|---|
| 1870 | 100 | 90 | 49 | 53 | 17 |
| 1890 | 100 | 105 | 50 | 58 | 19 |
| 1913 | 100 | 125 | 62 | 70 | 23 |
| 1929 | 100 | 146 | 71 | 69 | 31 |
| 1938 | 100 | 143 | 84 | 78 | 36 |
| 1950 | 100 | 171 | 71 | 57 | 24 |

Source: Feinstein 1988: 4

standards. German and French productivity was about two-thirds of the British level and Japanese was only one quarter (Feinstein, 1988: 4). Only the United States exceeded the British level, by about 25 per cent, and this reflected superior natural resources and capital equipment. In the 1920s British productivity growth lagged badly behind that of other leading nations and by 1929 American productivity had climbed to 50 per cent above the British level. In the 1930s the United States stagnated in productivity terms but France, Germany and Japan continued to narrow the productivity gap. By 1950 the impact of war had led to further relative gains by the USA but France, Germany and Japan had fallen back before rising again rapidly in the 1950s and 1960s (Table 10.2 below). This supports the well-established view that from the late nineteenth century other leading industrial nations tended to grow considerably faster than Britain, both in terms of total output and productivity, except during crisis periods resulting from war and world depression. As a result, Britain was gradually overhauled by a succession of international rivals.

Britain's secular tendency towards relatively slow growth appears to have been a feature of British industrialisation from the beginning. Crafts has shown that, even during the classic Industrial Revolution period, growth rates were modest and productivity performance, overall, was remarkably slow. Rapid growth was confined to a small group of industries namely cotton, worsted, wool, iron, canals, railways and shipping. These 'old staple' industries had begun to decelerate long before the interwar period, but remained mainstays of the economy until the Second World War (Crafts 1985).

## GROWTH ACCOUNTING

In recent years it has become fashionable to examine economic growth in terms of a model which views output as the result of inputs of the factors of production (land, labour and capital) and of the increased productivity of those inputs (Crafts 1981: 6). Growth (or the change in GNP) is seen as being the result of growth in Total Factor Inputs (TFI) plus growth of Total Factor Productivity (TFP). Thus, GNP = TFI + TFP. The formula for growth is usually expressed as follows:

$$\Delta Y = \frac{\alpha \Delta K}{K} + \frac{\beta \Delta L}{L} + r^*$$

Where $\Delta$ indicates the amount of change in a particular variable, so that $\Delta Y$ equals the change in output or growth. $K$ and $L$ represent capital and labour respectively. Land is also a factor of production but is of relative insignificance by this period. $\alpha$ and $\beta$ are the shares of profits and wages in total income and $r^*$ is the 'residual', that is growth which is not accounted for in terms of increased factor inputs. The 'residual' may also be termed 'Total Factor Productivity', although

> It includes any contribution that may arise from increasing returns to scale and from effects of technical progress and advances in knowledge, of shifts in resources between sectors, and of changes in the extent of obstacles to more efficient use of resources (for example, restrictive practices on the part of management or trade unions). It will also reflect any errors in the measurement of inputs and output, and in the specification of the relationship between them.
>
> (Matthews *et al.* 1982: 15)

Growth accounting is a convenient way of approaching growth questions although it is certainly not beyond criticism and it contains a number of problems. Of course, this is not the only way of dividing up and analysing growth. Inevitably the emphasis is placed upon supply rather than demand influences and this may be especially misleading in relation to the interwar years when there is strong evidence of deficient demand. Also, there are problems of measurement and, inevitably, assumptions which can be questioned. In the words of Alford:

The severe limitations of the technique become clear when account is taken of the conditions which would have to hold in order to render the results accurate. (Totally homogenous capital and labour markets; constant returns to scale over all ranges of output; marginal productivity pricing for all factors; continuously variable relationships between factors of time; land as an insignificant input.) Quite apart from these constraints there are more familiar problems associated with compound growth calculations: the weighting of capital and labour is on the crude basis of their respective shares in gross domestic income; the technique of weighting from year to year is, as always, a compromise between different types of index; compound rates of change are constant over a given period and, therefore, may not adequately reflect sharp movements within the period.

(Alford 1988: 16–17)

Nevertheless, the method has become well established and in dealing with the interwar period it does serve to highlight some important aspects of growth as well as emphasising certain important contrasts with other periods. In particular, it shows that the pattern of interwar growth was in many ways quite different from that which prevailed after 1951.

Taking the four peacetime periods between 1856 and 1973, Matthews *et al.* estimate the following for growth of inputs and total factor productivity.

It will be seen that, allowing for margins of error, there is a broad similarity in growth of net output in each of the main peacetime periods since the mid-nineteenth century: it is 'almost as if the range of two to two and a half per cent per annum had been meted out to the British economy by divine grace – or, in the eyes of many critics, by divine retribution' (Von Tunzelmann 1981: 241). However, as the table shows, this apparent stability conceals some major changes in the components of growth.

The second column shows that during 1924–37 there was a very sharp rise in labour input compared with other periods. This was mainly the

*Table 2.5* Growth rates of net output, inputs and total factor productivity, 1856–1973 (% per annum)

|  | Net output | Labour inputs | Capital inputs | Total factor productivity |
|---|---|---|---|---|
| 1856–73 | 2.2 | 0.0 | 1.7 | 1.5 |
| 1873–1913 | 1.8 | 0.9 | 1.8 | 0.5 |
| 1924–37 | 2.2 | 1.5 | 2.0 | 0.6 |
| 1951–73 | 2.6 | −0.5 | 3.9 | 2.2 |

*Note*: labour inputs are in man hours and capital inputs are net.
*Source*: Matthews *et al.* 1982: 208, 210.

result of the rising proportion of the population which was of working age. In the previous period labour inputs had fallen very sharply as the result of the reduction in the average working week and the onset of mass unemployment between the end of the war and 1921. Capital inputs reflect both the size of input and the degree of utilisation. In the interwar period investment and savings were relatively low but the intensity of utilisation of capital appears to have increased (Matthews *et al.* 1982: 120, 151–4). British capital assets tended to stagnate in aggregate during the period 1913–51 because of the rundown of overseas assets during war and the exceptionally low savings level throughout. Some fifteen per cent of overseas assets were lost during the First World War and a further twenty five per cent during the second. The low savings ratio in interwar Britain is attributable to inadequate demand and heavy unemployment. After the Second World War with full employment savings and investment rose to new and unprecedented levels.

On this basis the most important single source of growth between 1924 and 1937 is additional labour input while capital input and growth in total factor productivity are approximately equal and rather disappointing, especially in comparison with the period since 1945. These results suggest strongly that the characteristics of the late Victorian and Edwardian economies continued into the interwar period and that total factor productivity performance remained relatively poor between 1870 and 1939. The improvement in growth rates during the interwar period is largely attributable to changes in age structure and a greater intensity of capital utilisation rather than increased investment or higher rates of productivity growth.

Growth in TFP was low by post-Second World War standards but improved over the level attained in the period 1873–1913. There were important changes in productivity, perhaps amounting to a breakthrough in manufacturing. Applying the growth accounting approach to manufacturing reveals that during the interwar years manufacturing

Table 2.6 Growth of output, inputs and TFP: manufacturing, 1873–1973 (% per annum)

|  | Output | Labour input | Capital input | Total factor productivity |
|---|---|---|---|---|
| 1873–1913 | 2.0 | 0.8 | 2.6 | 0.6 |
| 1924–37 | 3.2 | 1.4 | 1.0 | 1.9 |
| 1937–51 | 2.5 | 1.0 | 2.9 | 0.9 |
| 1951–64 | 3.2 | 0.2 | 3.3 | 2.0 |
| 1964–73 | 3.0 | −1.6 | 3.3 | 3.1 |

Source: Matthews *et al.* 1982: 228–9.

output and productivity rose sharply to levels comparable with the post-Second World War years.

This was achieved partly through a relatively high level of labour input but in spite of an exceptionally low input of capital.

Once again it appears that interwar growth has dualistic aspects which may be concealed if growth is examined simply in aggregate. It also has to be pointed out that a focus on growth serves to obscure the fact that the interwar economy was operating at what might be seen as a relatively low absolute level; with at least 10 per cent of the insured work-force unemployed, interwar Britain produced much less than it might have done with fuller employment. While the relationship between unemployment and productivity remains obscure, clearly, a continuation of the modest growth rates of the late nineteenth century through the first two decades of the twentieth century together with fuller employment would have left the interwar economy operating at much higher levels of output.

There are considerable differences in TFP between sectors and also important differences between the 1920s and 1930s (Matthews *et al.* 1982: Appendix M, 608–11). Agriculture, mining, construction and transport were the best performers in 1924–9, while commerce and manufacturing did better in 1929–37. Manufacturing was by far the largest contributor to TFP growth in the interwar period followed by transport and agriculture. Overall there was better performance in TFP in 1924–9 than in 1929–37, but this was not the case in manufacturing, where most industries did better in 1929–37 than in 1924–9. In the 1930s TFP improved only in manufacturing and public utilities and this may reflect the influence of the 1930s depression. The possibility exists of a peculiar relationship between manufacturing productivity and unemployment. Labour shakeouts in the early 1920s and again in the early 1930s appear to have been translated into lasting improvements in manufacturing productivity. In the service industries the response appears to have been different with a more sluggish response to changes in the labour market and adverse productivity effects, notably in commerce where TFP fell absolutely between 1924 and 1937, almost certainly because labour crowded into low productivity work in the face of general unemployment (Matthews *et al.* 1982: 233).

In summary it can be said that there was a marked improvement in TFP in the interwar period which was evident from the 1920s and there was no overall improvement in the 1930s. This enhanced performance was partially masked by the effects of unemployment. Productivity performance was however well below the achievements recorded after 1945, even if allowance is made for unemployment effects. The improved growth performance of the interwar years resulted more from TFI, and especially labour inputs, than from TFP improvement. After the Second

World War a very different situation emerged with greatly enhanced contributions from TFP and capital input while crude labour input contracted.

## THE STANDARD OF LIVING

Our discussion of growth so far has dealt with national aggregates which ignore some important issues affecting living standards. These include wealth and income distribution, regional disparities and the external account.

As we have seen, the annual average growth rate of GDP was 2.2 per cent and growth of GDP per capita averaged 1.8 per cent from 1924 to 1937. These figures do not include external transactions. During this period net income from abroad was zero but the favourable movement of the terms of trade (average import prices compared with average export prices) added 0.3 per cent per annum to GDP per capita, giving an overall increase in real disposable income per capita of approximately 2.0 per cent per annum (Matthews et al. 1982: 498). In the interwar period disposable income per head appears to have grown faster than in any previous period and this followed a decline during 1913–24. It was not until after 1950 that this rate of growth in real disposable income per head was exceeded.

Although the terms of trade improvement appears to have had a relatively small impact upon income growth in aggregate terms it almost certainly had a more important influence on living standards. As a major exporter of manufactured goods and importer of primary products, Britain gained from the sharp relative decline of prices for primary products. If the ratio of British export to import prices in 1913 is assumed to be 100, by the 1920s the index averaged 127 and rose to 138 in the 1930s (Lewis 1949: 202). These gains were, to some extent, offset by losses resulting from reduced income in the primary producing countries which damaged British export industries and contributed to economic stagnation and unemployment. Nevertheless, cheaper imports, especially of food, made a substantial contribution to improved living standards. This influence must have increased down the social scale as the proportion of income spent on food increased. A contemporary survey suggested that, in 1935, out of an average weekly income per head of £1.50, a total of 45p was spent on food (Boyd-Orr 1936: Appendix V, table II). For a nation spending nearly one third of its income on food the fall in imported food prices, by 40 per cent or more during the early 1930s, helped to sustain spending which was the central feature in recovery from depression.

One of the most convenient ways of attempting to quantify living standards is to compare prices, or the 'cost of living' with money wages or earnings. Combining the two will give an index for *real* wages. Obviously there may be differences between wage rates and actual earnings and some allowance has to be made for unemployment. Average weekly wage rates fell sharply between 1920 and 1923, on average by about 25 per cent. After that there was hardly any change in average rates until the late 1930s when they rose slightly. Prices also fell sharply during the early 1920s, but not as much as wages, so there was a slight fall in real wages until the mid-1920s. However, prices fell sharply again during the early 1930s, while money wages were almost maintained, and the result was a rise in real wages of up to 12 per cent. Overall, the improvement in real wages was very modest by post-1945 standards and we must also remember that between 10 and 23 per cent of insured workers failed to benefit in particular years because they were unemployed. Real GDP per head improved much more than real wages and, once again, this seems to emphasise the importance of changing age structure. Fewer children meant that a higher proportion of the population could either work or claim unemployment benefits and within families wages had to support a smaller number of people.

We have also seen that in the interwar years the savings ratio, that is the proportion of national income not consumed, fell. While this resulted

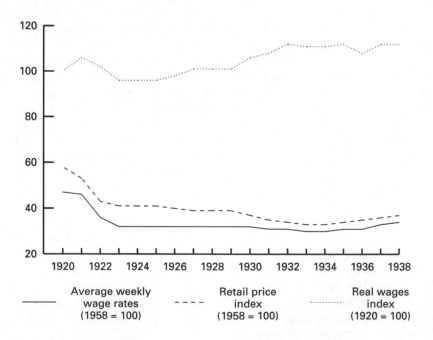

*Figure 2.1* Wage rates, retail prices and real wages, 1920–38
*Source*: LCS, *Key Statistics*: Table E; 8.

*Table 2.7* Population age groups and dependency ratios, 1913 and 1939 (million)

|  | 0–14 (1) | 15–64 (2) | 65+ (3) | Total (4) | Dependency ratio (per cent) (1) + (3) as percentage of (4) |
|---|---|---|---|---|---|
| 1913 | 13.88 | 29.13 | 2.66 | 45.67 | 36 |
| 1939 | 10.30 | 33.21 | 4.25 | 47.76 | 30 |

*Source*: Calculated from Feinstein 1972: Table 56, T123.

in a lower rate of investment it allowed the propensity to consume to increase. It is not clear why savings fell, but in part this was the result of changes in income distribution and, perhaps also, the result of deficient demand and unemployment. The share of wages in national income tended to increase and the share of profits fell. Inevitably the unemployed tended to have a high propensity to consume and unemployed people were compelled to spend available savings. At the same time, a depressed economy reduced retained profits in business which could be used for investment purposes.

In terms of the income scale British society has been compared to a group of people on a moving staircase. While the staircase as a whole moves upwards the relative position of the people on it remains largely unchanged. In the interwar period the staircase moved upwards as real incomes, on average, increased. On the whole the relative positions of different income groups did not change much but there was a slight shift towards greater income equality. The top end of society became less rich and the middle became slightly better off in relative terms. There has been a well-established long-run trend towards greater income equality in Britain during much of the twentieth century (Diamond 1979). However, this has mainly taken the form of levelling down with redistribution from the very rich to middle-income groups. The tendency towards greater equality, indicated by a diminishing Gini coefficient, has come from the relatively faster growth of middle-order incomes, reflecting changes in the occupational structure with an increase in salaried staff and white collar workers. In the interwar years the share of income going to the top 5 per cent declined from 44 per cent in 1913 to 30 per cent in 1939. However, the bottom 40 per cent does not appear to have made any significant gains in relative terms.

With wealth also there was a slight movement towards greater equality, but distribution remained highly inequitable and much more so than the distribution of income. The overwhelming majority of people had no significant wealth at all and, in 1913, it is estimated that 70 per cent of the total wealth of Britain was owned by 1 per cent of the population. By 1930 the wealthy 1 per cent owned only 55 per cent of total wealth (Atkinson and Harrison 1978: 139).

Lower-income groups gained from the increase in direct taxation of incomes and wealth which commenced during the Edwardian period and gained momentum from wartime needs and fiscal changes. Average wage earners on about £3.00 per week were well below the income tax threshold of £5.00 per week and only the very wealthy were inconvenienced by estate duties. (The latter could be avoided by *inter vivos* transfers.) To some extent the progressive nature of direct taxation was offset by indirect taxes, mainly customs and excise duties, which hit working-class consumption and especially beer and tobacco. The sharp increase in state expenditure over the pre-1914 period also tended to benefit the lower-income groups through the receipt of pensions and social security benefits.

As we have seen, there were important improvements in productivity during the interwar years, especially in manufacturing, and these were translated into income improvements. Overall, however, the rate of growth in TFP was relatively disappointing and other influences were more important in generating income growth. Changing age structure and reduced family size appears to have been the largest single factor, but the improvement in the terms of trade along with a range of distributional changes were also important. It appears, therefore, that the connections between growth on a narrow definition and living standards are complex and somewhat tenuous. Demographic and political influences were at least as important in raising growth and improving distribution as strictly economic factors and it is clear that growth is far from being the whole story. Absolute real income levels failed to recover to pre-First World War standards until the late 1920s. After that there was marked improvement but some of this could be seen as a catching-up exercise as productivity improved. Throughout the period incomes remained at levels which were insufficient to ensure the full employment of available resources, although the export industries continued to complain that they were cost constrained by high wage levels.

## THE QUALITY OF LIFE

It is increasingly argued that the conventional measures of economic growth fail to provide a useful indication of the quality of life. This may be less true of the interwar period than of more recent times because quantitative changes were probably matched by qualitative improvements. As noted above, personal consumption grew much more than real wages between the wars. The quality of life appears to have improved as the margin between wages and the cost of basic necessities widened; working hours became shorter, the market began to supply more leisure activity and entertainment on a commercial basis and the home became more tolerable and attractive as a centre for consumption

(Stevenson 1984: Ch. 4). It is possible to cite a whole range of new consumer developments which emerged during the interwar years, ranging from radio, cinema and mass circulation daily newspapers to Kellogg's Corn Flakes, Bisto and Ovaltine. In his somewhat discredited stage theory of history W.W. Rostow concludes that the 'age of high mass consumption' arrived in Britain during the 1930s, at which point, there would be 'expansion of consumption levels beyond basic food, shelter and clothing, not only to better food, shelter and clothing but into the range of mass consumption or durable consumers' goods and services, which the mature economies of the twentieth century can provide' (Rostow 1971: 74). However, Western Europe lagged at least two decades behind the USA in this development and Rostow is by no means certain about the British arrival during the 1930s. He suggests that the Great West Road, the rise of Coventry, and the Morris works at Oxford were symptoms of the new consumerism but unemployment and low wages meant that consumer durables such as motor vehicles, washing machines and other new amenities remained middle class luxuries. For the bulk of the population the new consumer goods and services remained confined to relatively minor and cheap items. It is impossible to know how much access to electric lighting, radio, a daily newspaper or regular cinema attendance (mainly female) enhanced the quality of life. To some extent these replaced earlier consumer and leisure activities such as beer drinking (heavily male) and the chapel. However, the fact that other activities were replaced may be taken to indicate a preference.

The growing commercialisation of sport and leisure activity reflects a number of developments including higher disposable incomes, the shorter working week and the emergence of Saturday afternoon as a leisure period. Jones (1986) concludes that the interwar years were a crucial period in the development of modern forms of leisure in Britain. Again, it is clear that smaller family size played a crucial role, as home life became less cramped and constrained and new leisure forms developed, the home was seen in a new light. Formal holidays became more common and holidays with pay provisions spread rapidly in the 1930s with the spur of legislation in 1938. A range of new products including durables such as washing machines and vacuum cleaners began to relieve the burden of running the home and radio and newspapers may have made it a more pleasant place to be. For women, in particular, the fall in family size and the new range of products represented one of the most important liberating influences since the Industrial Revolution and there is no doubt that housewives were the vanguard of the new consumerism. However, the spread of these new developments varied very greatly in both vertical and horizontal scales. It was in London and the South East that new consumer and leisure patterns spread most rapidly, while the depressed areas, because of poverty and unemployment, remained relatively unaffected. The middle classes were best placed to benefit. Improvements were also reflected in demographic trends discussed in Chapter 3.

During the interwar period the number of salary earners grew by 50 per cent and by 1939 about 15 per cent of workers were in this category. Most of these earned in excess of £250 per annum, a figure which is usually assumed to represent the threshold of middle-class status (Seers 1951: 34). The burgeoning middle class was a product of the growth in clerical, commercial and administrative employment. It could be said that the middle class became more differentiated and expanded 'down-market', but these were the groups, in particular, who benefited most from the growing consumerism and moved, with enthusiasm to new durables and homes. This new 'cut-price' affluence (Stevenson 1984: 130) was reflected in the expansion of the car market from 140,000 vehicles on the road in 1914 to 3 million in 1939. By 1931 an Austin Seven or a Ford Eight could be bought for a little over £100, which was about a third of a year's salary for a teacher. The cost of housing also fell and the affordability of mortgages rose. Domestic service continued as a major form of employment with over 1.4 million so employed in 1931. One in five households still had at least one domestic servant in 1931. For many middle-class families the interwar years were a time of relative privilege and access to amenities which later became devalued through mass availability. After 1940 with the sharp decline of domestic service and the sharp rise in progressive taxation, things were never quite the same again.

## POVERTY

Historians are generally agreed that absolute poverty had diminished in the decades before 1914 and that it continued to diminish during the interwar period. Nevertheless, sufficient poverty remained for it to continue to be a major issue for concern. The vogue for social investigation of poverty which had developed during the late Victorian years continued in the interwar period and may have been given a new momentum and focus as a result of the emergence of heavy and sustained unemployment. A series of poverty surveys, both official and unofficial, provide substantial detail of interwar poverty and the sufferings of the unemployed became a subject for literary and journalistic discourse as well as a subject for sober academic books and journals (Whiteside 1987).

While the overwhelming evidence supports the thesis of a general long-term diminution of poverty, the abiding folk memory of the interwar years remains one of social suffering. This paradox arises in part because of unemployment and the fact that poverty affected new sections of the population and also because of the increasing popular attention and concern which interwar poverty attracted. It may also be the case that recent attention to economic aggregates has deflected attention and some important areas of suffering notably through ill health, stress, poor diet and inadequate housing, have been to some degree overlooked. Also, the official or governmental line tended to be that the British poor and unemployed were relatively well treated so that the political emphasis tended to minimise poverty (Macnicol 1980; Webster 1982 and 1985).

The most important interwar surveys of poverty included A.L. Bowley and M. Hogg, *Has Poverty Diminished?* (1925); H. Llewellyn Smith (ed.), *The New Survey of London Life and Labour* (1934); B.S. Rowntree, *The Human Needs of Labour* (1937); *Poverty and Progress* (1941); H. Tout, *The Standard of Living in Bristol* (1938); and D. Caradog Jones (ed.), *The Social Survey of Merseyside* (1934) but this list could be considerably extended and a long catalogue of works on poverty could be added (Stevenson 1977). All of these surveys adopted the device pioneered by Booth and Rowntree in the late nineteenth century of applying a 'poverty line' based upon the simplest human needs in terms of food, clothing and shelter. While Booth and Rowntree had defined poverty in terms of customary standards, the interwar surveys attempted to apply more scientific principles taking account, for example, of recent research into dietary needs.

Rowntree's 1936 survey of York made comparisons with his earlier survey of 1899 possible and it was clear that between the two surveys there had been substantial improvements both in real incomes and the quality of life. Rowntree concluded:

> The economic condition of the workers is better by thirty per cent than in 1899, though working hours are shorter. Housing is immeasurably better, health is better, education is better. Cheap means of transport, the provision of public libraries and cheap books, the wireless, the cinema and other places of entertainment, have placed within the reach of everyone forms of recreation unknown forty years ago . . . but if instead of looking backward we look forward, then we see how far the standard of living of many workers falls short of any standard which could be regarded, even for the time being, as satisfactory . . . there is no cause for satisfaction in the fact that in a country so rich as England, over thirty per cent of the workers in a typical provincial city should have incomes so small that it is beyond their means to live even at the stringently economical level adopted as a minimum in this survey, nor in the fact that almost half the children of working class parents spend the first five years of their lives in poverty and that almost a third of them live below the poverty line for ten years or more.
>
> (Rowntree 1941: 99)

In 1899, on the basis of a very strict poverty line, Rowntree had found about thirty per cent of the working population in York living in poverty. Half of these were in what he termed 'primary poverty', with not enough to maintain basic physical health. For his 1936 survey Rowntree found it necessary to define a new poverty line, revised according to changes in conditions. He concluded that poverty was only half as widespread as in 1899. The main element in the new definition of poverty was a minimum allowance for food based upon the report of a committee appointed in 1933 by the British Medical Association. Rowntree calculated that the typical family consisting of husband, wife and three dependent children required forty three shillings and six pence (£2.17p) per week, of which just half would be spent on food (rent excluded). He was well aware that on this income, according to prevailing standards, a family of five could only be maintained adequately if the utmost stringency was applied. There was no margin for luxuries or emergencies or bad housekeeping. However, on this basis, 31 per cent of the working population surveyed were living in some degree of poverty and, once again, about half of these were classified as being in 'primary poverty' with incomes which were inadequate in relation to basic physical needs. About 18 per cent of the total population of York were living in some degree of poverty. (We should of course, remember that 1936 was a good year in terms of the economic cycle.) The other surveys suggested a less extensive degree of poverty. The London survey indicated that about 10 per cent of working-class families were below its poverty line; for Merseyside the figure was 16 per cent; Herbert Tout's figure for Bristol was about 10 per cent and the 1924 survey of five towns by Bowley and Hogg indicated 11 per cent. The London survey covered the area first investigated by Charles Booth in the 1880s. While poverty had certainly diminished it was found that the rate of decline had been slowed by the persistent housing shortage which the poor faced and the departure from the area of the more prosperous families. As a result, East London remained an area where there was persistent poverty. Nevertheless, the survey found that poverty was only one third as extensive as indicated by Booth. Out of a total population of 2.4 million, 284,000 (12 per cent) were living in poverty as defined by Booth (Llewellyn Smith 1934: 6).

Table 2.8, based on Rowntree's Survey, compares his poverty lines with other indicators.

The principal causes of poverty were, in general, much the same in the interwar years as in 1899 and have remained so ever since. In simple terms poverty resulted from having either no income or low income in relation to needs (see Table 2.9). Children, the disabled, sick or elderly and the unemployed were likely to fall into poverty without the support of others. It was also the case, however, that many of the employed

*Table 2.8* Minimum needs 1936 (excluding rent)

| | |
|---|---|
| 1 man (working) | £1.28 |
| 1 woman (working) | £1.08 |
| couple | £1.59 |
| couple plus 1 child | £1.90 |
| couple plus 2 children | £2.06 |
| couple plus 3 children | £2.17 |
| couple plus 4 children | £2.44 |
| Plus 17p for food and 5p for other items per additional child. | |

*Source*: Rowntree 1941: 28.

*Table 2.9* Poverty, wages and benefits in the 1930s (couple plus 3 children, rent 50p per week)

| | |
|---|---|
| Rowntree human needs 1936 | £2.67 (employed) |
| | £2.51 (unemployed) |
| Average wage | £3.00 |
| Typical miner's wage | £2.25 |
| Unemployment insurance | £1.75 |
| Unemployment assistance, 1936 | £2.10 |
| Rowntree 1899 poverty line at 1936 prices | £1.56 |
| Bristol survey poverty line 1937 | £2.38 |
| Average spending of working-class households, 1938 (excluding unemployed) | £4.25 |

*Source*: Glynn and Oxborrow 1976: 43.

found their incomes were inadequate and this was especially the case where there were large families to support. The market system did not relate income to needs and the wage spectrum fell well below most poverty lines when family needs were taken into account.

British working-class life consisted of a series of income peaks and troughs. Poverty was most likely to affect the young, the middle-aged and the elderly in what Rowntree referred to as the 'three crises' of poverty. The greatest risk of living in poverty came during childhood. This was followed by a period of comparative affluence once employment commenced, usually at the age of 14. Manual labour earnings tended to peak when physical vigour was at its greatest and young adults without dependants were the most affluent members of the working class. At marriage most women ceased employment and children usually arrived in the early years of marriage. Poverty was quite likely again during the child-rearing period, especially if there were more than two or three children. Once the children commenced employment, or departed the home, the situation improved and there was another comparatively affluent period in later middle age providing

*Table 2.10* Proportion of working-class population in primary poverty due to various causes (York 1899 and 1936, per cent)

|  | 1899 | 1936 |
|---|---|---|
| Death of chief wage-earner | 2.42 | 0.61 |
| Illness of chief wage-earner | 0.79 | 1.60 |
| Unemployment | 0.36 | 3.04 |
| Irregularity of work | 0.44 | 0.40 |
| Largeness of family | 3.43 | 0.54 |
| In regular work but low wages | 8.03 | 0.63 |

*Source*: Rowntree 1941: 116.

health and employment were maintained. This was followed by old age when poverty again became possible if savings were inadequate and there was a lack of support from relatives. The old age pension alone was insufficient to keep pensioners out of poverty.

In York in 1899 Rowntree had found that low wages were the most important single cause of poverty followed by family size and death of the main wage-earner. In 1936 the chief cause was unemployment, followed by illness and old age (see Table 2.10).

There is no doubt that children bore a disproportionate burden of poverty. According to Rowntree the majority of working-class children in York spent at least part of their childhood in poverty. In Bristol, Tout found 'one working class child in every five comes from a home where income is inadequate to provide a base minimum standard, according to the austere Survey rules. It means that in these homes there is not enough income to provide the minimum diets prescribed by the British Medical Association' (Tout 1938: 40). If we remember that York and Bristol were relatively prosperous cities it becomes clear that most British children during the interwar years had some experience of poverty and an alarmingly high proportion lived in circumstances so basic that physical stature and health may have been adversely affected. There can be little doubt that experiencing or witnessing poverty at first hand was an important formative influence upon British working-class attitudes and the events and changes of the 1940s must be seen against this background.

## CONCLUSIONS

During the interwar period life experience for most British people appears to have improved in both quantitative and qualitative terms. Nevertheless, at the end of the period the majority experience remained both mean and constrained by modern standards. While sections of the population, including the middle classes and better-paid workers with fewer dependants, gained a glimpse of a new level of affluence, most people were only touched by this in relatively trivial ways. Higher wages and smaller families were the main influences in the diminution of poverty but this was partially offset by the rise in unemployment and its impact in the old industrial areas which had been relatively prosperous before 1920. Poverty remained an important part of the interwar experience affecting most people's lives either directly or indirectly.

# Chapter 3

# Society and politics

## POPULATION SIZE AND DISTRIBUTION

During the early twentieth century Britain was approaching the end of a 'demographic transition' from the high birth and death rates typical of pre-industrial society to the modern situation of low birth and death rates and relatively slow population growth. Population in England, at least, continued to grow, but at much slower rates than during the nineteenth century. In Wales, Scotland and Northern Ireland the population total tended to stagnate (see Table 3.1).

Population growth results from an excess of births over deaths and/or from net migration. After 1920 both birth and death rates continued on downward trends which had been evident since the late nineteenth century. After a brief postwar baby boom, the birth rate fell faster than the death rate and the rate of natural increase fell by the 1930s to levels which caused some alarm. There was considerable net emigration during the 1920s but the flow was reversed from 1930 as British citizens returned from abroad, refugees fled Continental Europe and modest inflows continued from the Irish Republic (Ermisch 1983).

Population grew by about 2 million in the 1920s and 1.8 million in the 1930s (see Table 3.2). This represented a sharp fall in growth compared

*Table 3.1* Population of Great Britain and Ireland, 1901–51 (millions)

|      | England and Wales | Scotland | Ireland | |
|------|------|------|------|------|
| 1901 | 32.5 | 4.5 | | 4.6 |
| 1911 | 36.0 | 4.8 | | 4.4 |
| 1921 | 37.0 | 4.9 | 1.3[a] | 3.0[b](1926) |
| 1931 | 40.0 | 4.8 | 1.3[a](1937) | 3.0[b](1936) |
| 1951 | 43.8 | 5.1 | 1.4[a] | 3.0[b] |

*Notes*: (a) = Northern Ireland; (b) = Republic of Ireland
*Source*: Mitchell and Deane 1962: 6–7.

Table 3.2 Population increase in Great Britain, 1921–41 (millions)

|  | Natural increase | Net migration | Population increase |
| --- | --- | --- | --- |
| 1921–31 | 2.6 | −0.6 | 2.0 |
| 1931–41 | 1.2 | 0.7 | 1.8 |

Source: Glynn and Oxborrow 1976: 189.

with the first decade of the twentieth century, which recorded a natural increase of 4.6 million. Of course, by the interwar period the exceptionally high number of births recorded in the Edwardian period was being reflected in an increased work-force. Indeed, as a result of demographic changes, the interwar period experienced an unusually high ratio of workers, or potential workers, to dependants. Unfortunately, because of heavy unemployment, much of this enhanced potential was wasted.

Historians have tended to downgrade the demographic effects of the First World War. War service casualties are estimated at 610,000 and few British families escaped tragedy. More than a quarter of all males aged between 12 and 25 in 1914 were killed. Also, there was injury on a massive scale and 2.5 million men were officially classified as disabled after the war (Winter 1986a). However, it has been suggested that if prewar rates of emigration had continued this might have reduced the young male population even more than war deaths.

Fertility had been declining since the 1860s and the decline appears to have accelerated during and after the First World War. Live births per married women fell from 5.7 for marriages in the 1860s to 2.19 for the late 1920s (Cmd 7695 1949). There was a further fall in the 1930s and by the mid-1930s the replacement rate was less than unity. The reasons for declining fertility have been much discussed but still remain to some extent unclear. By the 1930s some form of birth control was being used in 80 per cent of marriages where there was risk of pregnancy, although this usually involved natural or 'non appliance' methods (Mitchison 1977). At the same time, artificial means were gaining wider acceptance in medical and other circles and were being more widely publicised in the interwar years. New efforts were made to give birth control a more wholesome image by linking it with marital fulfilment and planned family formation, notably in the work of the feminist writer and birth control pioneer Marie Stopes and the Family Planning Association.

The decline in family size of the late nineteenth century had been largely a middle-class affair. By the 1920s the fall had spread to the working class although some work groups such as miners and farm labourers continued to have large families. The willingness to limit births appears to some extent to have been related to the costs (material and non-material) of child bearing and rearing. The factors which may have had some influence in declining fertility include the decline of the family as an economic and social unit, a rise in the norms of child rearing, the declining value of child labour, the changing status of women and declining mortality so that more children survived. Economic insecurities in the 1930s, in terms of employment, may have intensified the downward trend in fertility. The decline in family size is a complicated social phenomenon which cannot be readily attributed to a single cause or motivation. Declining fertility occurred in most of the world's industrial economies at about the same time. What can be said is that where couples became aware that it was possible to have smaller families than would have occurred naturally, and where the means of family limitation were morally and financially acceptable, the majority clearly preferred to have smaller families. Indeed, by the end of the 1930s large families were beginning to be seen not only as social anomalies but as a source of social problems.

Average household size did not fall as much as completed family size but there was a decline from 4.36 in 1911 to 3.19 in 1951. Changing family and household size undoubtedly had an impact on life experience for the majority of the population and it seems likely that the result was a significant but unquantifiable improvement in the quality of life. This combined and interacted with other influences pushing in the same direction.

Mortality also fell, continuing a trend from the 1860s onwards. This is usually attributed to improvements in nutrition, housing, dress and environment rather than to advances in medicine, but public health improvements played some part. Infectious diseases, notably tuberculosis, were the major cause of death in nineteenth-century Britain and improved resistance reduced mortality. Death rates for older age groups (45+) fell less than for the population as a whole so that, while life expectancy at birth grew enormously, there was less improvement after middle age. Infant mortality had improved dramatically from 154 per thousand births in 1900 to 60 in 1930, but this remained high by modern standards. In the interwar period death rates for people in middle life fell almost to modern levels and this can be largely attributed to better living standards. For infants and older age groups there remained much scope for improvement and this had to await advances in medicine and in the system of medical care. Also, there remained some significant horizontal and vertical variations in mortality with, for example, mortality rates well above the national average in some older industrial centres and regions and a tendency for rates to increase sharply down the social scale.

It has been argued that after 1920 the internal mobility of the British population was lower than in previous decades (Lee 1977). This may seem remarkable in view of the high regional differentials in employment and it should be said that internal migration is not easy to define and measure objectively (Baines 1985). Certainly by the 1920s there was only limited scope for further rural–urban drift. Frielander and Roshier (1966) have shown that vestiges of the rural–urban drift of the nineteenth century survived into the middle years of the twentieth in the form of movement, usually of single people, from villages to cities. However, this was heavily exceeded by movement, usually of recently married couples, from large cities to medium-sized towns. There was a fairly continuous flow from North to South. The population of Wales, Scotland and Ireland tended to stagnate and there were individual years of decline. Much of the external emigration in the 1920s appears to have been from these areas, especially Scotland. The share of national population in the South East, including London, had been rising for many decades but after 1920 this accelerated and the Midlands also began to increase its share. All other regions had a declining share of population, although absolute increases were recorded in most. These changes clearly reflect economic circumstances, including industrial contraction in some regions and expansion in others.

## SOCIAL ORDER AND STRUCTURE

It is possible to suggest that in the first half of the twentieth century there were strong signs of increasing social tension in Britain and class conflict appeared to become more violent, harsh and intense than in the late Victorian period. Politics, ostensibly at least, became organised on social class lines, the threat of revolution troubled the Cabinet in 1919, industrial relations were in turmoil between 1911 and 1926, and the general strike was seen by some as a threat to the constitution. Despite these outward signs of conflict and instability, British society through the early twentieth century exhibited a remarkable stability and cohesion despite the strains of two world wars, depression and heavy unemployment. In fact, the only real rupture was the separation of 26 counties of Ireland to form the Irish Free State and this was essentially a national and political rather than a social change.

At the end of the nineteenth century, in the world's oldest industrial society, the very modest increase in living standards which industrialisation had brought had been purchased at the cost of long, intense, disciplined and sustained work activity, often in very unpleasant and sometimes hazardous working conditions and strict personal and social disciplines. Also, industrialisation compelled society, or large sections of it, to accept the human consequences of urban concentration in the form of cramped and often inadequate living conditions with related environmental problems. One of the major problems facing British society was to make urban and industrial life for the masses more acceptable. By the standards of today the majority of British people at the beginning of this century lived drab and narrow lives which were largely dominated by arduous monotony. In return they acquired a modest security and marginally better standards than their parents.

Although there are some grounds for suggesting that in the twentieth century social divisions have diminished and that this process was accelerated by two world wars, the fact remains that British society was and remained enormously differentiated with a complexity of hierarchy and status differentials and glaring inequalities in income and wealth (Halsey 1972; 1978). It is clear that there were important divisions within particular social groups as well as between them and there is no simple and generally accepted way of describing social structure (Roberts 1971). Usually, however, social classifications are defined and presented in terms of occupations.

In 1914 British society was dominated numerically by manual workers and their families who made up about 75 per cent of the population (Carr-Saunders 1937) covering a wide range from farm workers at the bottom end of the earnings range to skilled industrial workers at the top. More than half of the manual work-force had some degree of skilled or semi-skilled status. In the interwar period the average wage was approximately £3.00 per week, with adult male manual wages ranging from about £1.50 to £4.50. Most of the remainder of the work-force were employed in routine non-manual work and this merged into 'white-collar' activity which sometimes enjoyed a higher status if not higher rewards. This area tended to expand over time and manual labour declined to about 70 per cent of the work-force by the end of the 1930s. The lower middle class included some professional groups such as schoolteachers, 'white-collar' higher grades and some of the self-employed. In the interwar years the average family could manage what was regarded as a middle-class existence on about £5 a week, but not all who aspired to the status earned sufficient to finance it. The upper middle classes, which consisted mainly of professional groups such as lawyers and doctors and better-off business proprietors, numbered approximately one million or about 2–3 per cent of the population by 1920. This group usually had income over £20 per week, or about seven times the average wage, or more. In relative terms, at least, they appear to have enjoyed an exceptionally good position in the interwar period.

Finally, at the top of the scale was a tiny but highly influential elite which owned more than 90 per cent of British capital assets, including enormous investments overseas. This elite had switched the basis of its wealth during the nineteenth century from landownership to industry, commerce and finance. This process was accelerated by the First World War, but most of the old wealthy survived and landowning families, in general, found new ways of retaining and increasing capital assets (Rubinstein 1981 and 1986). The British elite was sufficiently open to ensure political survival but sufficiently exclusive to restrict its ranks to very small numbers. Although British society by the early twentieth century was overwhelmingly dominated, numerically, by an urbanised working class, control over almost all non-human resources was owned by a tiny, very wealthy and highly privileged minority. Apart from the extension of the franchise in 1867 and 1884, capitalism and the controlling elite had made few concessions. Important signs of change came with the Liberal reforms of 1906–12 when the burden of taxation began to shift from the poorest sections of society.

Social stratification and inequality have been major themes in history and social science. The traditional approaches or 'explanations' of social organisation and change fall essentially into two categories: functionalist, which sees society as an organic organisational entity; and Marxist, based on notions of conflicting material interests between different classes or social groupings. Functionalism, particularly with the American sociologist Talcott Parsons, emphasises a social harmony and efficiency arising from divisions of labour based upon different individual effort and natural endowment. This in turn gives rise to unequal rewards. Obviously, functionalism has conservative and static implications and it is difficult to believe that the egregious inequalities of Edwardian Britain could have provided an acceptable long-run social harmony, quite apart from any question of efficiency. As noted in the previous chapter, in the world's greatest and richest country some 10 per cent of the population lived in absolute or primary poverty without enough to keep body and soul together. It is not easy to accept that this was efficient or necessary, especially at a time when there was rapid accumulation and gross extravagance at the other end of the social scale (Marwick 1967).

Crude Marxism is a particular view of history based upon economic determinism and the notion of class struggle. Like functionalism, in the opinion of most historians, it fails to provide an adequate framework for analysing British economic and social development since 1900. In recent years several social historians have made use of the notion of social 'hegemony' put forward by the Italian neo-Marxist philosopher, Gramsci. This rather more subtle approach suggests that a capitalist elite may establish and keep control, not through direct economic power or force, but through the establishment of a 'dominant ideology': in other words, through the use and manipulation of ideas, values and culture. There is no shortage of historical evidence to support such notions. Stevenson (1977: 48), for example, refers to the 'cohesive and solidaristic aspects of British society'. By this he means the rich and highly variegated network of institutions, societies and organisations at national, regional and local levels which did so much to cement the fabric of British social life by inculcating an acceptance of the established order. In more fundamental terms, British society was highly efficient in socialising and integrating most individuals and identification with particular institutions, such as firms, localities, streets, was powerful. The First World War also had an integrating influence which built upon decades of popular imperialism. Far from being alienated, many felt an enhanced sense of belonging which was often heightened by military service and fuller and more remunerative integration into the workforce. By the interwar years the legitimacy of British institutions, including the monarchy, the empire and the Westminster system of Parliamentary democracy, was accepted with unquestioning enthusiasm by the vast majority. Further reinforcements came from new media creations in the interwar years including a national press, BBC radio, and the institutionalisation of sport and leisure (Jones 1986).

In recent years many social historians have attempted to analyse such popular institutions as instruments of 'social control'. Approaching social history through notions of hegemony provides interesting insights but it can be argued that the concept of 'dominant ideology' is essentially tautological and incapable of disproof by anything other than social collapse. In Britain the working-class majority did not passively accept the handing down of ruling-class ideas and institutions. Indeed, there are many counter-examples involving either rejection or adaptation. The legendary British fondness for alcoholic drink, for example, survived determined attempts to suppress, regulate and restrict sales and the probably inevitable fall in consumption was less than might have been anticipated. Similarly, the professionalisation of sports such as boxing, cricket and association football persisted against disapproval from social superiors and gambling remained an established working-class habit. The truth appears to be that, just as economic history is much too complicated to be explained by economic theory, social theory offers insights rather than explanations of social history.

## GENDER AND SOCIETY

One of the most fertile areas of academic enquiry in recent years has resulted from the rise of intellectual feminism. Apart from producing new streams of literature in most areas of social and historical enquiry, the feminist renaissance has made us much more aware that large areas of economic and social activity are governed not by rational motivation but by culturally engendered and often irrational sexist attitudes. The employment and remuneration of women, for example, can be understood only in these terms. It has been claimed that women have been 'hidden from history' (Rowbotham 1977), and that most history has been written by men and about men and in terms of male considerations and values: literally HIS-story. These rather dramatic accusations are not without validity although they apply less to social and economic history than to political and diplomatic. Women have not been ignored in social history but they have been treated in ways which many feminists consider inappropriate. These deficiencies are now beginning to be rectified and it has been suggested that the gender approach to history may be potentially as productive and stimulating as the notions of class conflict first put forward by Marx. It is perhaps unfortunate that the idea of conflict has carried over and some feminist writers have indulged themselves in the 'women as victim' approach. Of course, sexual stereotyping affects both men and women and both may suffer in the process. If Victorian women were confined by the drudgery of domestic management and child-rearing, most men were subject to lifelong regimes of hard physical labour, awesome by modern standards. Also, we should remember that there is much which cannot be explained in terms of gender. As the previous section made clear, there were vertical as well as horizontal divisions in society, and social class may have been more important than gender.

Before the Industrial Revolution most productive activity in agriculture, industry and commerce was carried out in or near the home with women playing, very often, an active and integral part. With industrialisation and the advent of the factory system a separation became common if not universal and the male role as 'breadwinner' became more clearly established and circumscribed (Pinchbeck 1981). During the nineteenth century it became the middle-class norm that wives did not seek paid employment and that they employed servants in the home. Middle-class values seem to have been gradually accepted by most of the population and where married women worked outside the home this was normally seen as a matter of necessity and something to be avoided where possible. During the late nineteenth century female participation tended to decline slightly (Baines 1981) and this can be interpreted as a response to higher living standards. Marriage was seen in respectable Victorian society as a gender-specific contract under which women gained the right to be maintained financially in return for services in the home. Because of low and interrupted wages many men were unable to fulfil their part of the bargain and wives had to seek employment. For women there were strong economic incentives to marry in that female employment was not only limited in supply and restricted in scope but also relatively poorly paid. Single, separated and widowed women were often condemned to poverty. For men there were few economic incentives to marry since marriage for many carried the near certainty of poverty at least after the arrival of children. It is clear, therefore, that there were powerful social, psychological and emotional or romantic

pressures which built upon the natural instinct to bond in pairs. However, not all individuals were susceptible to these pressures and strict
sexual controls in society were necessary. Sex outside marriage, or
fornication, was strongly discouraged and attempts were made to suppress prostitution. Bastardy was subjected to social stigma and legal
disadvantage. As living standards rose in the interwar years marriage
became more popular and people married earlier.

During the early part of this century women made significant if
limited social and political advances extending over a wide area. In
1918 women over thirty gained the right to vote and this was extended
to women over twenty-one in 1928. There were some minor legal
advances in female status in relation to property, divorce and rights
over children, but, in general, women still tended to be viewed and
treated as second class citizens. It was still assumed, with marriage,
that paternal control and responsibility passed to the husband, so that
most women were assumed to be under some form of male authority. Of
course, these formalistic assumptions did not always square with reality.
At all levels in society women were able to assert themselves by force of
personality and emotional controls. In describing the Salford 'slum' on
the eve of the First World War, for example, Robert Roberts (1971) refers
with a mixture of awe and admiration to the matriarchy of grand-
mothers who controlled social opinion. Indeed, there can be little doubt
that women in their various roles as wives, mothers, teachers, nurses
and home-makers played a crucial part in the complex process of
socialisation underpinning social order and stability. It is perhaps inevitable that most were more concerned with their own integration into the
existing structure than with female advancement in its own right.

There can be little doubt that the most important change affecting
females was the reduction in family size. The typical working-class
wife during the late Victorian period experienced, on average, ten
pregnancies (Titmuss 1958: 91). This meant a period of about 14 years
of being either pregnant or looking after a child of less than 12 months
old, or both. By the end of the interwar period declining fertility had cut
this formidable experience by two-thirds. Largely as a result, female
mortality improved at a faster rate than male and it seems clear that
there were consequent qualitative improvements in living standards for
men and women, especially in the domestic environment and increasing
home orientation especially for men. It is very probable that women
played the dominant part in setting these trends.

It has already been pointed out that female participation in paid
employment was largely dictated by cultural, social and biological
rather than simply economic factors. The Victorian work ethic was
seen by men as essentially a male concern and female employment
was, in general, considered to be a necessity rather than a virtue. These

attitudes probably explain why female participation in paid employ-ment appears to have declined during the late nineteenth century and remained below the 1871 level until the 1950s (Lewis 1984: 146). How-ever, the employment statistics have to be viewed with a good deal of caution. There is no doubt that female employment is under-recorded, quite apart from the non-recording of domestic employment from 1881.

Female participation during the first half of the twentieth century appears, on the surface, to be remarkably constant with women supply-ing about 30 per cent of the work-force (see Table 3.3). This changed briefly but dramatically during the First World War when 1.4 million women entered paid employment and many all-male employment areas were entered by women for the first time. However, at the end of the war participation reverted to prewar levels and, by 1921, was lower than in 1911.

The apparent constancy in female participation is to some extent misleading as there were important variations in participation region-ally and between different categories. In mining areas, for example, participation was usually low, reflecting traditionally good pay for men, larger families and few opportunities for women. Textile regions often had high participation rates for women and relatively lower male–female earnings differentials. In general, it may be said that female participation diminished sharply with age and with marriage. Younger and single women were the most likely to be in employment. Between 1900 and the 1940s, about three-quarters of the women in employment were single and the participation rate for single women tended to increase over time. The majority of young women worked in paid employment before marriage and, in terms of age, participation peaked in the early twenties (Ferguson 1975). Participation rates for married women did not increase significantly before the 1940s and rates for

Table 3.3 Female participation, 1901–51

| | Percentage of work-force female | Participation rates[a] | | | |
|---|---|---|---|---|---|
| | | All women | Single | Married | Widowed |
| 1901 | 29.1 | 345 | – | 301 | – |
| 1911 | 29.7 | 356 | 677 | 103 | 261 |
| 1921 | 29.5 | 337 | 683 | 91 | 261 |
| 1931 | 29.7 | 342 | 791 | 104 | 216 |
| 1951 | 30.8 | 349 | 730 | 225 | 212 |

Note: [a]Female participation equals number per 1,000 in each category in the labour force. Figures take account of variations in school-leaving age. See source for details.
Source: Lewis 1984: 147–50.

widows were declining, partly, no doubt, as a result of better pension provisions. The apparent constancy in female participation, therefore, conceals an increasing tendency for young single women to be in paid employment while participation for married and widowed women was static or declining.

In the late nineteenth century the occupational distribution of female employment was very restricted and three-quarters were in personal service, textiles and clothing in 1901. During the first half of the twentieth century the most notable areas of expansion in female employment were in teaching, retailing and clerical work. In 1931, a quarter of women in work were still in domestic service and 11 per cent were in other forms of personal service. Textiles and clothing still absorbed 20 per cent so the traditional areas of employment had well over half the female workforce (James 1962). However, over 20 per cent were involved in clerical (including typing) and commercial and financial occupations. The rise in clerical occupations reflects the advent of the typewriter and other office machines and the gradual replacement of the male clerk by the female secretary. In the interwar period women were making modest inroads into less well-paid, less prestigious and mainly private-sector office work. The major breakthrough into office work, including government and public offices, did not come until the 1940s.

While much has been made of the dependence of the new industries on female labour, this should not be exaggerated. Some of the new 'light' industries, especially rayon and electrical goods, did employ considerable numbers of women and the numbers covered by national insurance increased, but this may have been offset by declining female employment in other areas, especially textiles. In the interwar period there are some modest signs of a changing pattern in female employment but, again, dramatic change only comes after 1940.

Male–female differentials in pay and occupational status appear to have been maintained and in industry average female earnings were 40–50 per cent of average male earnings. In part, this reflected differences in age, productivity and hours worked but equal pay for equal work was virtually unknown. Even in weaving, where women came nearest to the ideal of equal pay, there was discrimination in favour of male earners. Women schoolteachers had to settle for 80 per cent of male earnings, and this was a relatively high female–male earnings ratio. Equal pay was a matter for debate during the interwar period and women in professional occupations, such as teaching and the civil service, campaigned for parity of status and remuneration.

It is clear that prior to the Second World War female employment opportunities remained restricted and women were relatively badly paid. Of course, simple economic theory tells us that better pay might have meant even more restricted employment. In the interwar years better living standards for many families probably reinforced the traditional tendency for married women to leave paid employment, unless necessity dictated otherwise. At the same time more acceptable female employment in clerical, retailing and professional (teaching and nursing) work was becoming available and in many instances this proved attractive, especially to single women. Of course, unemployment in the interwar years had major consequences for women and made female earnings much more important in some families. Women probably carried a heavy burden in terms of deprivation resulting from unemployment and the mother stinting herself to feed husband and children has become a classic figure in accounts of the poverty of unemployment. Also, the rise in domestic service, despite its low pay and unpopularity, may in part reflect increasing female desperation in the labour market. The impact of unemployment on women is largely uncharted and unknown since many did not register, but the dramatic changes in female participation after 1940 imply a great, unused potential. Of course, we are dealing with a mixture of countervailing forces, some traditional and some new. It was still assumed that married women, ideally, should not work and they were often laid off first. The Anomalies Act of 1931 assumed, in effect, that married women who lost employment had left the work-force, so they could be deprived of benefits. At the same time, economic change was producing new opportunities for women in certain areas of employment – especially shops and offices – and there were changes in the pattern of employment. In general, it can be said that the reduction in family size was not fully reflected in increased female participation and the main changes in aggregate came after 1940. The pattern and timing of change is closely related to the nature and level of demand for female labour and we should look here for explanations rather than to changing mores or gender attitudes. The sharp rise in female participation after 1940 was the result of 'full employment' and, perhaps more important, of the emergence of *acceptable* forms of employment for married women. Social and gender attitudes appear to have taken account of and adjusted to economic circumstances.

## POLITICAL DEVELOPMENT

The interwar years are of particular interest to social scientists because they saw the establishment of modern systems of politics and public administration. Although it does some violence to the complexities of political reality, the interwar period can be seen as a long period of Conservative government broken only by two relatively brief minority governments in 1924 and 1929–31. It may also be said, again as a considerable simplification, that the period was politically an age of transition from one two-party system to another. That is, from the late nineteenth-century pattern of Liberal versus Conservative to the post-World War Two party pattern of Conservative versus Labour. In effect, there was a three-party system in the 1920s and 1930s but there was a clear tendency towards Conservative dominance with the opposition being split between Labour and Liberal. It is clear that during the first half of the twentieth century there is a good deal of political realignment as modern democratic circumstances emerged. In 1918 all men over 21, and women over 30 became entitled to vote and this trebled the size of the electorate; women obtained the same rights as men in 1928. Thus it was not until the interwar period that voting in national elections became a habit and a right for the adult majority.

During the early nineteenth century the Conservative or Tory Party had represented the rural, landowning interests and the Liberal Party emerged after the 1832 Reform Bill as the party of the newly enfranchised and burgeoning urban middle classes. The pattern of British politics is complex, rich in detail, and all generalisations are likely to oversimplify reality. However, in the later decades of the nineteenth century the Liberals were clearly established as the party which stood for free trade, tight control over public spending, individualism and laissez-faire. It is clear that the 'Victorian values' which were stressed in the 1980s by Margaret Thatcher and others are essentially Liberal in the nineteenth-century sense, and liberal in the more general sense.

By the late nineteenth century the Conservative Party had adjusted with remarkable success to the widened franchise of 1867 and 1884 and broadened its base from the traditional rural interests. The Conservatives captured a substantial middle-class vote from new suburban areas and also began to attract working-class support, mainly from the poorest sections of the population. From the 1880s the issue of protection arose in British politics and sections of the business community began to move towards the Conservatives. By the 1920s the Conservatives were supported by most of the British business and financial communities.

The Liberals faced two problems. Despite the efforts of Lloyd George and other 'reformers' the party remained essentially non-interventionist at a time when the drift of events and opinion was towards state intervention. Social inequalities and economic issues demanded attention; there was growing concern about 'national efficiency'; British industry was beginning to face severe overseas competition and some producers could see the advantages of protection and government assistance. Second, the party was split from 1916 when Lloyd George led his faction into coalition with the Conservatives leaving Asquith to head the non-interventionists. During the interwar period the Liberals continued to attract considerable electoral support but division continued and they never became the principal party of government again.

Gradually they were replaced by Labour as the main opposition party. The Liberals sought to claim the middle ground but this became increasingly difficult as political attitudes hardened on social class lines.

The Labour Party began to emerge at the end of the nineteenth century out of an uneasy alliance between certain trade unions and socialist societies. The Labour Party dates officially from 1906 but, in the early years, the intention was to work with and through the Liberal Party and Lib-Labism remained a force until the First World War (Pelling 1991). Labour emerged strengthened from the First World War and supported by a much larger and more confident trade union movement. In 1918 the new constitution committed the party to public ownership and therefore to something which could definitely be called socialism. MacDonald, the undisputed leader until 1931, led the party with considerable authority and skill aiming, in the 1920s, to establish Labour as a credible alternative party of government and to attract the many better-off working-class voters who remained loyal to the Liberal Party (Booth 1987b). In the mind of the Labour leaders radical policies conflicted with these aims. In the 1920s the Parliamentary Labour Party distanced itself from radical and socialist policies and from the pragmatic demands of trade union leaders (Lyman 1957; Skidelsky 1967; Wrigley 1976). In doing so they successfully established Labour as a governing party which did not fundamentally threaten the political and economic system. Labour combined constitutionalism with an ultimate but essentially vague commitment to socialism. This uneasy combination provided an endless source of internal conflict. Since the Party had emerged at a relatively early stage in modern British history and pre-empted the radical working-class vote, British socialists, in general, saw no real electoral alternative to Labour. Communists and others attempted to work through the Labour Party and this gave rise to internal friction and endless talk of expulsions of individuals and groups. Labour's opponents adopted the tactic of branding the Party with extremism, particularly after the Russian Revolution in 1917. In the 1924 election a Red Scare in the form of the Zinoviev letter was used effectively against Labour and relations with the Soviet Union became a constantly debated issue in interwar politics (Williams 1992).

The uneasy mix of constitutionalism and a vague commitment to socialism also handicapped Labour during its brief periods of government. Skidelsky has concluded that the 1929–31 government believed that only socialism was a total cure for poverty and unemployment but that it lacked a theory of the transition to socialism; it had little alternative but to govern without conviction a system it did not believe in but saw no real prospect of changing. It struggled to defend the working class as long as it knew how, and when it could defend them no longer, it resigned (Skidelsky 1967: 394–5). But alternative policies were available:

they were advocated by Keynes, Mosley and others, including some within the Party (Booth and Pack 1985). Alternatives were rejected by the Labour leadership, not because of a blinding vision of utopian socialism, but for sound pragmatic reasons. Even the most radical Labour leaders were aware that, in the event of economic collapse, their own followers would probably suffer first and most. For the British working class violent and destructive confrontation of the capitalist system could only have been, in the short run at least, self-defeating. Such methods could only be employed *in extremis* when more acceptable alternatives had failed. Revolutions occurred in Russia and other European countries during and shortly after the First World War and the British authorities were extremely apprehensive, especially in 1919 (Gilbert 1970: 67), but the revolutionary potential of the British working class should not be exaggerated. Demonstration and riot were more or less acceptable ways of expressing grievance and were regularly resorted to where it was felt that the regular channels had failed. Revolution was quite another matter and it should be emphasised that changes in modern industrial democracies are rarely effected by such crude devices. Of course, the dominant groups in British society were prepared to concede and to make limited adjustments within the constitutional framework and to defend, if necessary with force, against threats which could be labelled unconstitutional. The general strike, discussed in Chapter 5, illustrates these points.

At the same time, the mere existence of the Labour Party did have an important influence in promoting political and economic compromise and we should beware of underestimating the party's impact. In direct terms, Labour helped to improve housing, education and social services as well as welfare benefits. More important, the existence of Labour as an alternative compelled other parties towards consensus politics and helped to prevent a full-scale assault on trade unions and the wage earner. Throughout the interwar period Baldwin and other non-Labour leaders were well aware that an overt general attack on wages, or attempts to deal harshly with the unemployed, would almost certainly be translated into a surge of support for Labour. It is clear, therefore, that Labour simply by existing played a crucial role in the political and economic compromise which prevailed in British society during the interwar period.

Several writers in looking at interwar politics have emphasised consensus which is summed-up in the slogan 'safety first' (Addison 1977). This followed a decade of conflict and dramatic change between 1911 and 1921. There had been a strong trade union offensive before the First World War and this continued in the postwar boom until 1920. By the time the boom ended Labour was in a much stronger position and was prepared to defend the gains which had been made. Changes in financial and business organisation and the rise of employers' associations threatened a situation of corporate and class confrontation. This was prevented, or largely avoided as a result of the influence of unemployment and the emergence of political compromise. Unemployment placed the trade unions on the defensive and the downturn of 1920–1 coincided with strong demands for wage cuts and policies of economic orthodoxy. This was repeated in 1930–2. It is interesting to note that it was the Conservative Party which benefited from this despite the Liberal association with Gladstonian finance. By the early 1920s Lloyd George was no longer trusted by the electorate or by his Parliamentary colleagues and he never regained office after 1922 in spite of many attempts. Baldwin emerged as Conservative Chancellor and then leader in 1922; this deceptive and enigmatic figure played a dominant role in interwar politics (Middlemas and Barnes 1969) and in the creation of modern Conservatism. At the end of the 1920s he successfully presented the Conservatives as the party of 'safety first' – capturing the middle ground of British politics and persuading a substantial part of the electorate that the other parties were less trustworthy. While following economic and financial orthodoxy and refusing to tackle unemployment in effective ways, Baldwin managed to convey a 'one nation' image promising social unity, cohesion and concern. As the patrician head of a family business he personified new directions in Tory leadership and his gentlemanly air concealed great political shrewdness and skill. The approach was essentially pragmatic orthodoxy, pursued in a flexible manner. Where it seemed appropriate, for example, the long established policy of free trade could be breached. Issues such as tariff policy and rationalisation were cleverly presented, both as a means of preserving party unity and, at the same time, convincing the electorate that the Conservatives had policies to deal with the nation's problems (Booth 1987b: 45–6). Tory success in the interwar period owed much to these skills but the electoral system and the weakness of the other parties were perhaps more important.

Politically, then, interwar Britain opted for 'safety first' rather than radical alternatives and this was at a time when there was a good deal of experimentation elsewhere. The rise of fascism and socialism in Europe and the New Deal in America were observed with interest rather than enthusiasm. The British reaction to economic adversity was cautious orthodoxy which received strong electoral support. Of course, Britain's problems were less severe than elsewhere and conditions, at least for the majority, tended to improve. These circumstances were repeated in the 1980s and, once again, there was electoral support for harsh economic measures. In the longer run there obviously was a political reaction to the miseries and waste of the 1920s and 1930s and this was reflected in the election of a radical Labour government with a large majority in

1945. By that time, however, policies and perceptions had changed. The Second World War brought 'full employment' and a postwar continuation seemed both desirable and possible. Also, new social policies were being suggested and enthusiastically supported.

# Chapter 4

# Industrial development

## THE PATTERN OF INDUSTRIAL CHANGE

Industry is frequently divided into primary, secondary and tertiary sectors. The primary sector is concerned with growing or extracting natural products and includes agriculture, forestry, fishing and (usually) mining. The secondary or manufacturing sector includes industries which process and change physical goods so that they acquire an added value. All other industries fall into the tertiary or service sector and are concerned with supplying some form of service. These distinctions are useful, although boundaries between sectors are not always clear and the classification of particular industries (such as mining) may be arbitrary. It is well established that, as economies develop and industrialise, the primary sector tends to become relatively less important in employment and output terms, even though its output may continue to increase absolutely. Since the Industrial Revolution British expansion has been centred on manufacturing. However, by the early twentieth century the proportion of the work-force in manufacturing reached its peak. In the interwar period manufacturing ceased to expand as an employer of labour (not in terms of output) and employment in the primary sector continued its sharp decline. Over half the work-force and the main growth area of employment was in the tertiary sector. These changes took place because of income and productivity effects. As incomes increased more of the increase was spent on services than on goods (for a fuller discussion, see Chapter 12). Also, while it proved possible to make substantial improvements in productivity in the primary and secondary sectors, in the tertiary sector productivity actually declined. In modern industrial economies the essential dynamic, but not the bulk of employment, is to be found in manufacturing industry, not least because it is usually assumed that the tertiary sector 'services' and derives demand from primary and secondary activities. The fortunes of the British economy during the interwar period were closely connected to developments in manufacturing.

Table 4.1 Growth of output, 1920–38 (1913 = 100)

|            | 1920 | 1938  | Percentage change |
|------------|------|-------|-------------------|
| Primary    | 71.5 | 85.0  | 19                |
| Secondary  | 97.9 | 158.7 | 62                |
| Tertiary   | 93.8 | 101.1 | 17                |
| Transport  | 95.1 | 137.6 | 44                |
| GDP        | 93.7 | 127.1 | 35                |

Source: Feinstein 1976: Table 8.

Table 4.1 indicates that output grew most rapidly in manufacturing industry and that the service (excluding transport) and primary sectors grew more slowly than total output. However, the pattern of employment growth was very different (Table 4.2).

In the primary sector there was continued and sharp work-force decline and output failed to regain the 1913 level. In manufacturing total employment declined slightly, but output grew more than 50 per cent between 1920 and 1938. The main growth in employment was in the tertiary sector with building and distribution playing a major role. There are serious conceptual and practical problems in attempting to measure output in the tertiary sector but the available data suggests only moderate growth of output outside building, public utilities (gas, water, electricity) and transport. By the interwar period the tertiary sector was responsible for over half of total output and claimed two-thirds of fixed assets, but its contribution to growth in output and productivity was modest. In most service industries productivity declined. This

Table 4.2 Employment by industry, 1920–38 (thousands)

|                             | 1920   | 1938   | Percentage change |
|-----------------------------|--------|--------|-------------------|
| Agriculture and forestry    | 1,661  | 1,221  | −27               |
| Fishing                     | 80     | 51     | −37               |
| Mining and quarrying        | 1,325  | 904    | −37               |
| Manufacturing               | 7,208  | 6,970  | −4                |
| Building and contracting    | 927    | 1,226  | 32                |
| Gas, electricity, water     | 185    | 291    | 57                |
| Transport and communications| 1,641  | 1,692  | 0                 |
| Distribution                | 2,452  | 3,090  | 31                |
| Insurance and finance       | 369    | 475    | 28                |
| Civil service               | 257    | 245    | −5                |
| Armed forces                | 760    | 432    | −44               |
| Local government            | 380    | 556    | 46                |
| Professional services       | 845    | 1,115  | 31                |
| Other services              | 2,307  | 3,110  | 34                |
| TOTAL                       | 20,297 | 21,418 | 5                 |

Source: Feinstein 1972b: Table 59, T129.

record is quite consistent with a period of rapid improvement in housing, transport and general infrastructure.

It follows that manufacturing industry had a crucial role to play in the
process of economic growth but performance in the sector was very
varied; there were clear signs of, on the one hand, strong industrial
growth and, on the other, chronic industrial decline and depression. In
analysing interwar manufacturing attempts have been made to define
distinct industrial types, and in particular a distinction has been drawn
between a group of long-established industries, often called the 'old
staples', which experienced severe problems and other, often newer
industries, which grew rapidly. Unfortunately, the old–new industry
approach is too simplistic and it has been heavily criticised (Dowie
1968). This approach ignores important influences. There was, for example, a regional dimension to the interwar economy and there is evidence
that in some of the depressed regions *all* types of industry did worse
than the national average (Champernowne 1937–8). Also, different
industries exhibited very different experience over the trade cycle,
with producer goods industries generally fluctuating more wildly than
those selling directly to consumers. There was also divergence within
industrial types. All old staples had prosperous sectors while in the
growth industries there were failures and disappointments. The basic
problem then is one of attempting to make meaningful generalisations
against a background of complex and sometimes conflicting evidence.

During the interwar period the total output of manufacturing industry
in Britain grew more rapidly than before and by 1938 output was more
than 50 per cent higher than in 1913 (see Table 4.1). Overall, British
industrial output grew at an average rate of 2 per cent per annum
compared with an average of 1.6 per cent for other industrial countries. However, this conceals major fluctuations from year to year. Since
it is often claimed that growth was much faster during the 1930s than the
1920s it is worth examining the detailed record of industrial output
(Figure 4.1).

It is clear that there were major troughs in 1921 and 1931–2, with
peaks in 1929 and 1937. Measuring from trough to trough, the growth
of output was actually greater during the 1920s (1921–9) than during the
1930s (1932–7). Dowie and others have taken three years of similar
employment levels and measured changes between them. On this
basis, measuring 1924–29 and 1929–37, the later period emerges as one
of faster growth and this is emphasised if allowance is made for the
rather lower capacity utilisation in 1924 than in 1929 and 1937 (Buxton
and Aldcroft 1979). Growth assessments depend very much on the
choice of terminal years and the precise periods to be compared. The
1920s and 1930s represent broadly comparable periods of economic

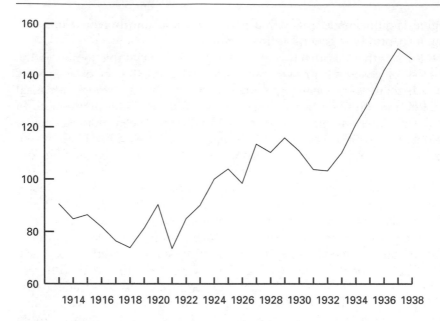

*Figure 4.1* Index of industrial output, UK, 1913–38 (1924 = 100)
*Source*: Lomax 1964.

growth and it may be wrong to make too much of the differences between them.

Productivity also grew faster in the interwar period after relative stagnation between 1900 and 1913, as will be seen below. It has often been observed that the British economy faced severe structural problems during the interwar period. These may be traced back to the Industrial Revolution, carried by a small group of spectacularly successful industries which continued to dominate the economy and, in particular, Britain's exports right up to the interwar years. These industries, known as the 'old staples', consisted of coal, cotton, iron and steel, heavy engineering and shipbuilding. Britain's structural problem during the interwar period emanated from the problems of these industries and the failure to replace them fully with alternatives.

Mature industrial economies are sufficiently diversified so that failure in one industry will be offset by expansion in others, although individual people, firms and localities may suffer. Richardson (1965) has, however, argued that British economic development in the nineteenth century became unbalanced by 'overcommitment', relying too heavily on the 'old staples' both for employment and export earnings while, at the same time, neglecting to diversify and to exploit more fully a range of new inventions and technologies which included the internal combustion engine, radio, electricity and new chemical processes. Industrial leadership moved to Germany and the United States and Britain entered a long process of relative decline. The reasons for this have been much debated and debate will certainly continue (McCloskey 1970 and 1981; Kennedy 1987; Kirby 1981; Levine 1967; Wiener 1981).

Whatever the outcome of these debates in relation to the Victorian economy, it will be clear from Chapter 2 that deceleration was a lengthy process which may have been shaped in part by international trends (Floud 1981). In fact, it was not until after 1920 that clear and unambiguous evidence of Britain's industrial weakness began to emerge in terms of balance of payments and unemployment problems. This weakness was essentially on external account. In the interwar period, as we have seen, British industry, as a whole, grew quite rapidly by supplying an expanding home market. The analysis of the industrial difficulties of interwar Britain suggests two essential problems: first, the failure of the traditional industries or 'old staples' as exporters and employers of labour and, second, the failure to replace them, as exporters and employers, with new industries. Lack of industrial growth as such was not the problem. There was substantial growth during the interwar period but Britain was left with a weak balance of payments and heavy unemployment.

Britain's share of world trade was about the same in 1938 as in 1913 but there is evidence that manufactured exports were becoming less competitive. Britain's share of world trade in manufactures fell from 14 per cent in 1913 to less than 10 per cent in the late 1930s. Exports continued to be dominated by the old staples which were showing features of terminal decline, but Britain's loss of world trade share was, according to Tyszynsky (1951), due to competitive failure across more or less the whole range of exports rather than the result of structural factors. Nevertheless, Britain remained the world's leading exporter of manufactures although challenged by Germany in the late 1930s. Exports in the interwar period were lower in volume terms than in 1914, but this was to a large extent offset by the favourable shifts in the terms of trade already noted in Chapter 2.

In 1913 Britain's exports were dominated by textiles, coal, iron and steel and machinery. These industries between them supplied about two-thirds of total exports. Cotton alone supplied 24 per cent and wool 6 per cent. Throughout the interwar period these same industries continued to dominate British exports and in 1929, for example, supplied about one-half of total exports. By 1938 the share had fallen still further, to just under half of total exports, in large part because of the fall of cotton to a mere 10 per cent of total exports, compared with 24 per cent in 1913. Machinery increased in importance and by 1938 the new industries, notably electrical goods, vehicles and aircraft, were beginning to make a significant contribution to exports. The picture which emerges is one of continuing dependence for both export earnings and manufacturing employment, and to a lesser extent for output, on the old staple industries. This in turn helps to explain why Britain had a weak balance of payments and a continuing unemployment problem during the interwar period.

## DECLINING INDUSTRIES

It is common to speak of declining industries in this period but in fact only shipbuilding and drink (mainly beer, which was taxed more heavily and subjected to restricted pub-opening hours) experienced an actual overall decline in output between 1920 and 1939. In the former industry output per worker grew at a respectable rate and only in the latter did productivity actually decline. When we refer to industrial decline we

*Table 4.3* Rate of growth of output and productivity in British industry, 1920–38 (average annual rates)

| Old Industries | | | New Industries | | |
|---|---|---|---|---|---|
| | *Output* | *Output per worker* | | *Output* | *Output per worker* |
| Building and contracting | 5.4 | 3.6 | Vehicles | 6.6 | 3.6 |
| Timber and furniture | 5.2 | 5.0 | Electricity, gas, water | 5.0 | 2.3 |
| Non-ferrous metals | 4.8 | 3.6 | Electrical engineering | 4.7 | 1.1 |
| Building materials | 3.7 | 1.6 | Precision instruments | 2.7 | 1.0 |
| Food | 3.6 | 2.1 | Chemicals | 1.9 | 1.5 |
| Clothing | 2.7 | 2.9 | | | |
| Paper and printing | 2.6 | 1.3 | | | |
| Metal goods not elsewhere stated | 2.5 | 2.1 | | | |
| Tobacco | 2.2 | 1.7 | | | |
| Leather | 2.1 | 2.3 | | | |
| Mechanical engineering | 1.7 | 3.7 | | | |
| Iron and steel | 1.1 | 3.5 | | | |
| Textiles | 0.2 | 1.6 | | | |
| Mining and quarrying | 0.2 | 2.5 | | | |
| Drink | −0.2 | −1.0 | | | |
| Shipbuilding | −2.7 | 1.9 | ALL INDUSTRY | 2.8 | 2.9 |

*Source*: Aldcroft 1970: 121.

Table 4.4 Index of industrial production, 1913–37 (1913 = 100)

|  | 1913 | 1937 |
|---|---|---|
| Manufacturing | 100 | 162 |
| Chemicals | 100 | 164 |
| Metal manufacture | 100 | 150 |
| Ferrous metals | 100 | 139 |
| Shipbuilding | 100 | 75 |
| Mechanical engineering | 100 | 124 |
| Electrical engineering | 100 | 339 |
| Vehicles | 100 | 504 |
| Textiles | 100 | 101 |
| Clothing | 100 | 108 |
| Food | 100 | 198 |
| Drink | 100 | 79 |
| Paper and printing | 100 | 188 |
| Building and contracting | 100 | 274 |
| Gas, water, electricity | 100 | 291 |

Source: Feinstein 1972b: Tables 51 and 52, T111–115 (rounded).

really mean a decline in employment and perhaps also in export earnings (Aldcroft and Fearon 1969: ch.1).

The most dramatic sectoral decline took place in Britain's leading export industry, cotton textiles. Cotton had pioneered the Industrial Revolution and before 1914 Britain had supplied two-thirds of world cotton exports. As much as 80 per cent of British cotton manufacture was exported at certain times and in 1913 cotton provided a quarter of total British exports (Allen 1959: 217). From the late nineteenth century the cotton industry had tended to lag behind best practice techniques abroad although this may have been justified in the short run by supply factors including the abundance of cheap skilled or semi-skilled labour (Sandberg 1974). During the First World War the industry was adversely affected by manpower and shipping shortages but there was a rapid expansion during the postwar boom when prices rose sharply. For a brief period profitability was high and there was high company turnover with firms changing hands at inflated prices. In the postwar speculative boom 42 per cent of spinning capacity changed hands at up to seven times prewar values and capacity increased. This lent a particular vulnerability in the ensuing sharp decline which resulted from loss of overseas markets. By 1922 exports had fallen to half the 1913 level. The modest increase in domestic demand failed to compensate for export loss and price decline resulting from new capacity, competition and protected markets overseas. Between 1912 and 1938 British cotton output was halved. Yarn exports fell from 244 to 123 million lbs and export of piece goods from 6.9 billion (6,900 million) to 1.5 billion (1,500 million) square yards. Also, there were sharp reductions in the number of looms and spindles in use and the total work-force in spinning, doubling and weaving fell from 621,500 in 1912 to 393,000 in 1938.

There were heavy losses in most overseas markets except Africa where import replacement, tariff protection and competition from rival producers was much less pronounced. Japan emerged as a major and highly competitive rival, especially in Far Eastern markets. The most damaging losses were in India which had absorbed a third of British cotton piece goods exports before 1914. By 1938 Indian production in cotton piece goods had quadrupled over 1913 and British exports to India had fallen to only one-tenth of the pre-1913 level. India approached self-sufficiency in cotton production and Japan captured most of the export market which remained there.

Beset by market loss, falling prices and profits and heavily in debt, cotton manufacturers shed labour and worked outdated machinery and plant more intensively. Nationally a good deal of capacity was eliminated and productivity improved, but only massive investment in new equipment and radical reorganisation could have saved the cotton industry from dramatic decline. Lancashire in general seems to have accepted decline as inevitable and there was despair about the prospects of competing with cheap foreign labour.

However, the quality end of the industry and more efficient firms continued to prosper and the domestic market remained buoyant and was protected in the 1930s. This indicated that the precipitate decline of

*Table 4.5* Total employment in British manufacturing, 1920–38 (thousands)

|  | 1920 | 1921 | 1929 | 1932 | 1938 |
|---|---|---|---|---|---|
| Food, drink, tobacco | 619 | 590 | 664 | 662 | 767 |
| Chemicals and allied trades | 253 | 220 | 240 | 219 | 274 |
| Iron and steel | 541 | 279 | 358 | 247 | 357 |
| Electrical goods | 188 | 186 | 210 | 220 | 337 |
| Mechanical engineering and shipbuilding | 1,313 | 861 | 738 | 49 | 882 |
| Vehicles | 353 | 301 | 479 | 439 | 623 |
| Other metal industries | 515 | 364 | 468 | 402 | 532 |
| Textiles | 1,331 | 1,053 | 1,304 | 1,094 | 1,007 |
| Clothing | 896 | 764 | 811 | 779 | 814 |
| Bricks, pottery, glass, cement, etc. | 209 | 170 | 256 | 227 | 298 |
| Timber, furniture, etc. | 323 | 287 | 301 | 277 | 322 |
| Paper, printing, publishing | 393 | 355 | 440 | 444 | 492 |
| Leather and other manufactures | 274 | 235 | 253 | 235 | 265 |
| TOTAL | 7,208 | 5,665 | 6,522 | 5,744 | 6,970 |

*Source*: Feinstein 1972: Table 59.

Table 4.6 Main British exports, 1913–38

|  | Current values (£m) | | Percentage of total | |
|---|---|---|---|---|
|  | 1913 | 1938 | 1913 | 1938 |
| Cotton yarn and piece goods | 127.2 | 49.7 | 24.2 | 10.5 |
| Woollens | 31.8 | 23.6 | 6.1 | 5.0 |
| Linen | 9.5 | 6.3 | 1.8 | 1.5 |
| Hats, haberdashery, apparel, etc. | 13.3 | 7.7 | 2.5 | 1.6 |
| Coal | 53.7 | 40.7 | 10.2 | 8.6 |
| Iron and steel | 55.4 | 42.9 | 10.5 | 9.1 |
| Non-ferrous metal manufactures | 12.0 | 12.3 | 2.3 | 2.6 |
| Machinery | 37.0 | 60.7 | 7.0 | 12.9 |
| Ships and boats (new) | 11.0 | 8.5 | 2.1 | 1.5 |
| Road vehicles and aircraft | 5.4 | 24.7 | 1.0 | 5.5 |
| Electrical goods | 5.4 | 13.4 | 1.0 | 2.0 |
| Chemicals | 22.0 | 22.1 | 4.2 | 4.7 |

Source: Mitchell and Deane 1962: 305–6.

the cotton industry was the result of outmoded technology, organisation and structure in the face of changing world supply and technology. From the early 1920s attention turned to the need to reduce excess capacity but this proved to be a difficult process in an industry with low levels of integration and many small, independent producers. There were a number of voluntary rationalisation schemes from 1927 in a vain attempt to reduce capacity and hold up prices. In the early 1930s industrial relations in the industry degenerated into something approaching anarchy and this prompted government intervention. The Bank of England had already become involved in 1929–30 through the creation of the Lancashire Cotton Corporation – a body which attempted to promote rationalisation but which was principally designed to rescue banks which had over extended their lending to cotton companies (Alford 1981: 325).

Under the Cotton Industry (Reorganisation) Act of 1936 a compulsory levy was imposed on cotton machinery and the proceeds used to scrap surplus spindles. By 1938 the Spindles Board had scrapped 5 million spindles. Between 1930 and 1938 spindles were reduced from 63 to 42 million and looms from 700,000 to 495,000. In 1939 provision was made for cartelisation of the industry under government sponsorship. These measures reduced but failed to solve the problems of the industry; excess capacity and inefficiency remained and decline continued.

The coal industry has received a good deal of attention from historians and this reflects its outstanding importance in this period (Supple 1987 and 1988). The problems of the coal industry resulted from stagnating demand in home markets, heavy losses in overseas markets, intense competition and bitter industrial relations. Coal was being used more efficiently and there was growing competition from alternative power sources and rival coal producers: 'Before 1914 the consumption of coal had been rising by about 4 per cent annually; subsequently, however, its annual growth rate was a mere 0.7 per cent in 1913–29, and 0.3 per cent in 1913–37' (Supple 1988: 567). By the late 1930s British average annual output was approximately 40 million tons less than the average annual output of 268 million tons between 1907 and 1914. Because of improved productivity the decline in the work-force was more precipitate from a peak of 1.3 million in 1920 to 702,000 in 1938 (Court 1945).

The severity of the industry's problems were masked by wartime government control which lasted until 1921 and disruptions to US and German supply in the early 1920s. However, in 1925 there was a serious loss of overseas markets with sharp decline in output, profits and prices. Labour formed a high proportion of total costs (75 per cent in 1924) and, inevitably, the coal owners sought a solution in terms of reduced wages and longer hours of work. In 1925 a temporary government subsidy delayed the eventual showdown which came with the General Strike of 1926 (Chapter 5).

Even after the crushing defeat of the miners and wage reductions in 1926–7 sections of the industry continued to make losses and there was growing appreciation of the need to reduce both competition and capacity. In coal mining competition failed to eliminate the least efficient mines (Supple 1988: 579). Marginal companies continued to operate in the hope of a trade revival. Also, the problem of excess capacity was aggravated by the multiplicity and fragmentation of ownership. In 1924 some 75 per cent of miners were employed by 1,385 mines owned by 467 colliery firms (Supple 1987: tables 9.1, 9.4) and this pattern made any kind of amalgamation, rationalisation or price maintenance difficult. It was this 'excessive competition' (Supple 1988: 579) together with the high profile and egregious problems of the industry which prompted government intervention.

The British Coal Mines Act of 1930 was designed to raise the price of coal and improve profitability so that hours of work could be reduced without corresponding cuts in pay. It established compulsory cartelisation on a district basis so that each colliery was given a production quota. Also under the Act the Coal Mines Reorganisation Commission was established to promote amalgamation and rationalisation. The 1930 Act enabled the industry to deter further falls in prices and profit rates, but in the 1930s profits remained at half the prewar level and markets continued to stagnate. Excess capacity remained and the Commission's efforts were largely in vain because of inadequate powers, government doubts and the opposition of colliery owners to rationalisation. During the late 1930s the industry enjoyed a more stable period.

The most severe industrial contraction of the interwar years occurred in British shipbuilding. During 1909–1913 the industry had launched an annual average of 1.5 million gross tons (Pollard and Robertson 1979). During the First World War Britain lost some two-thirds of its merchant fleet and a depleted work-force struggled to meet naval and commercial replacement demand. As a result of the war and postwar boom in 1919–20 world shipbuilding capacity was more than doubled and came to outpace demand. British output rose to a peak of 2 million tons in 1920 but this level was never regained and output fluctuated between 0.6 and 1.5 million tons to 1929. During the world depression the industry came close to total shutdown with an output of only 0.13 million tons in 1933. Recovery from this low point was very limited but by 1938 output had climbed to 1.1 million tons (Allen 1951).

There was a world surplus of shipping after 1920 and a large part of shipbuilding capacity remained idle. While there were sharp reductions in overseas orders the most serious damage to the industry resulted from the decline in demand for British merchant ships, in part because of the decline in trade but also because British buyers turned to cheaper foreign suppliers and naval demands remained low until the end of the re-armament phase of the late 1930s. Foreign competition was enhanced by overseas government subsidies and the overvaluation of sterling during the 1920s. While productivity improved and there was a good deal of innovation, the industry was less efficient than many of its overseas competitors (Sturmey 1962; Jones 1957).

Shipbuilding suffered high unemployment and the work-force in the industry fell by a quarter between 1924 and 1937. Drastic reorganisation was embarked on to reduce excess capacity and to improve efficiency. This was organised on a voluntary basis within the industry. In 1930 National Shipbuilders Security Ltd. was established with support from most major shipbuilders and from the Banker's Industrial Development Corporation. By 1937 rationalisation had removed over 1 million tons of capacity and many firms had gone into liquidation, with others such as Harland & Wolff, Palmers, Hawthorne-Leslie and Vickers-Armstrong surviving only through merger. Even so, gross excess capacity persisted and the industry remained relatively high cost and inefficient and was slow to develop new types of ships and building techniques.

The iron and steel industry had many features of decline although it fared rather better than the industries mentioned so far. The main decline was in pig iron production which fell more or less continuously through-out the period but this reflected in part a shift from iron to steel as well as increasing use of recycled scrap iron. By 1924 steel output had risen above the 1913 level and the 1918 level of 9.6 million tons, which reflected war demand, had been exceeded by 1929. In the downturn of 1929–33 steel output was cut in half but there was recovery to the 1929 level by 1935. A peak interwar output of 13 million tons was reached in 1937 (Carr and Taplin 1962). The iron and steel industry lost heavily in export markets and failed to regain the 1913 level. However, the home market was buoyant, and in the 1930s, there was protection from overseas competition (Burnham and Hoskins 1943). In return for tariff protection government insisted that the industry should be reorganised but rationalisation was very limited. Expansion in the 1930s rested on a protected home market, aided by the growth of the motor industry and the rearmament boom. While iron exports declined sharply steel exports grew and the industry expanded. The main technical changes involved a continued shift from acid to basic processes in steel and in iron a shift from Bessemer to open hearth processes. Geographically there was a shift to East Midlands ore deposits and new plants developed at Corby and Scunthorpe. Steel manufacture tended to remain too dispersed and scale economies were unrealised despite some amalgamation and the industry remained inefficient compared with overseas producers (Tolliday 1987).

This brief look at industries in decline suggests that there was a broadly similar pattern. In stereotype the typical declining old staple industry was long established, highly localised, labour intensive and heavily geared to export markets. Decline resulted primarily from a loss of export markets caused by intensified overseas competition, import substitution and trade barriers. Also, the war had caused disruption and distortion, with over expansion followed by severe contraction. The latter resulted in gross excess capacity and heavy indebtedness. In circumstances of sharp fluctuations and decline it proved difficult to introduce new technology and this was not always justified in terms of product markets, costs and short-run profitability criteria. Export competitiveness may have been further weakened by the rise in wages, shorter hours and increased unit costs which resulted from developments during the postwar boom. In the 1920s an overvalued exchange rate and high real rates of interest imposed added burdens and industrial relations became bitter with drastic shedding of labour and attempted reorganisation. In the 1930s cartels were formed and attempts were made, behind protective barriers, to control prices in the home market. Government connived at this in return for rationalisation and improved efficiency but these had only very limited success. Improved productivity resulted mainly from labour shakeout rather than new investment and technical improvement. At the end of the interwar period these industries remained vulnerable and inefficient by international standards.

# EXPANDING INDUSTRIES

While there is no doubt that the major industries in decline during the interwar years were old industries it is not the case that all the expanding industries were new. Any list of expanding industries would probably include transport and communications, building, electricity generation and supply, electrical and radio equipment, rayon (or artificial silk), aluminium, rubber, synthetic dyestuffs, plastics, chemicals, precision instruments, aircraft, motor vehicles and possibly also food canning and processing, the extraction of oil from coal, beet sugar and films. None of these were, strictly speaking, new industries, since all predated 1914 and many went back to the nineteenth century. Some were offshoots of old staple industries and some, such as rayon, represented product or process diversification in old areas. Some industries such as engineering or chemicals were hybrids with sectors of rapid expansion and others with sharp decline (Musson 1978). Many growth industries were exploiting a cluster of scientific discoveries and new processes which dated from the late nineteenth century but the largest growth industry of all, building, was traditional. Building grew more rapidly than any other industry except motor vehicles and far exceeded any other in terms of aggregate importance. The fortunes of the industry are examined later in this chapter.

The motor vehicle industry in Britain lagged badly behind that of the United States and only limited progress had been made before 1914 (Richardson and O'Gallagher 1977). Nevertheless, there was rapid growth based on the home market during the interwar period and Britain outpaced Western Europe, if not the USA, as a car-producer. From 1915 the home market was protected (the McKenna Duties) and by the late 1930s Britain was beginning to emerge as a major car exporter, albeit mainly to sheltered Dominion markets. Rapid expansion had to await technical improvements, protection, rising incomes and sharp reduction in vehicle prices which could only be achieved by mass production methods (Church 1979), but mass production methods in turn were limited by the relatively small size of the British market, and the pattern of labour relations and managerial limitations (Zeitlin and Tolliday 1986).

The breakthrough came in the 1920s with 100 firms in 1922 being reduced to 33 by 1939. Three large producers emerged in the 1920s, Morris, Austin and Singer. Ford also commenced production in Manchester and the giant Dagenham plant opened in 1932, but this remained too large until the 1950s and the company was, at first, relatively unsuccessful in Britain. Morris and Austin, in particular, were more pragmatic and better geared to the more segmented British market, competing on models as well as price (Overy 1976). Their production methods were less capital intensive and rigid and perhaps better suited than Fordism to British market circumstances. By the end of the 1930s Singer had declined and American subsidiaries were more prominent; six major producers dominated the British market. The high-quality end of the market remained, with firms such as Rolls-Royce, but output was small. In the 1920s the motor cycle industry also boomed but declined with the collapse of exports in the early 1930s (Musson 1978: 346). Bicycle production also expanded strongly with 40 per cent of output being exported in 1937.

Output grew from 34,000 vehicles in 1913 to 73,000 in 1922 after a fall during the war. By 1929 output reached 240,000 vehicles of all types and 146,000 motor cycles. By 1939 Britain had an annual production of 2 million cars and 500,000 commercial vehicles. Employment in the industry rose less rapidly than output from 227,000 in 1920 to 516,000 by 1938. The average value of British cars ex-factory fell from £260 in 1924 to £130 in 1935–6 and the demand proved to be, to a degree, both income and price elastic (Plummer 1937: 87). Geographically the industry tended to concentrate in the Midlands and to a lesser extent the South East. Large plants became dominant but these were dependent on a host of smaller ancillary companies and supplies of components and materials. Despite the elimination of many small producers the industry remained highly competitive in terms of models although less so on prices. Motor vehicles remained a middle-class luxury and this was reflected to some extent in the organisation of the industry. Greater concentration might have enabled the industry to make greater realisation of scale, technical and managerial economies, but the experience of Fords at Dagenham places a question mark against this conclusion (Lewchuk 1986). The aircraft industry which was closely related to the quality end of the motor trades, slumped after the First World War and remained small until the rearmament phase of the late 1930s (Fearon 1974).

Rayon, which was an artificial fibre based on wood pulp and cotton lintels, unlike other textiles, grew rapidly during the interwar period (Coleman 1969). Rayon was really a hybrid industry combining chemicals and textiles. Output rose from 6 million lb. of yarn in 1920 to 58 million in 1930 and 173 million in 1939, based on rapid technological advances, changes in taste, in clothing, and product price reductions with improvements in quality. The main use for rayon was as 'artificial silk', widely used for female garments including stockings. However, it also became complementary to other fibres as well as a substitute for them. The rayon industry was dominated by Courtaulds, which produced two-thirds of total output by 1939, and, to a much lesser extent, British Celanese, but in the late 1920s these were challenged by a number of small firms after the industry was given tariff protection in 1925. The two leaders continued to dominate through pricing policy and advantages of size, superior techniques and organisation. Nevertheless the UK lost its early lead in this industry and by the 1930s was failing to compete effectively in overseas markets.

Electricity made a major breakthrough in the interwar period and, while making many new industries, production processes and new locations possible, became a major industry in its own right. Developments in electricity and the electrical industry are examined in a later section of this chapter.

Many of the growth industries had some important features in common. They were usually producers of consumer rather than producer goods and were geared to the domestic rather than foreign markets. As time went on some of the new-growth industries developed limited export markets but these were rarely as important as in the old staple industries and they tended to focus on the 'soft' markets of the Dominions. Exports usually made up less than 10 per cent of total output although they reached a higher level in the motor industry. Not only were most growth industries dependent on home markets, many of them also relied on protection. In general, they commenced from small beginnings and took time to gain the economies of scale which were possible. As a result, most of them grew more rapidly in the 1930s than in the 1920s (Dowie 1968). Also, they tended to operate in larger units than the old industries and production was often in the hands of a few firms. In general they were less competitive, both internally and externally, than the old staples and Crafts and Thomas have suggested that Britain's comparative international advantage continued to rest with the old staples (Crafts and Thomas 1986).

## INDUSTRIAL PRODUCTIVITY

During the interwar period the British economy returned to a higher rate of productivity growth and the rate of growth in manufacturing productivity was even better: what are we to make of this? Was it simply a reversion to the pattern of late nineteenth century growth after the Edwardian hiatus when productivity improvement had virtually ceased? Or was it a breakthrough to new growth levels? We do not have definitive answers to these questions but it is generally accepted that the essential dynamic in the economy springs from the manufacturing sector. With this in mind this section will focus on productivity in British manufacturing industry.

British industrial performance had already begun to slip behind that of the USA and Germany before the First World War. By 1914 productivity in USA manufacturing was 70 per cent higher than in Britain and Germany had just overtaken Britain (Rostas 1948). In the interwar years British industrial productivity, on the basis of estimates which now appear to be widely accepted, grew more rapidly than ever before (Lomax 1959 and 1964). Between 1913 and 1938 the average rate of growth on an annual compound basis was 2.1 per cent per annum compared with 0.6 per cent per annum in 1900–13 and the improved performance is almost entirely accounted for by strong growth in manufacturing productivity.

The substantial productivity growth which occurred took place without any corresponding increase in capital stock. In other words, there is no substantial increase in industrial investment rates to explain productivity growth. In part the explanation may lie in qualitative shifts including the movement of capital into new-growth industries. Also there were technical improvements and organisational changes which required only limited investment. Replacement investment may have been a major vehicle for improvement, encompassing, for example, the shift to electrical power and motorised transport. Above all, however, labour shakeout and more intensive use of labour appears to have

*Table 4.7* Rates of change of output, employment and productivity in UK manufacturing, 1924–37 (% per annum)

|  | *Output* | *Employment* | *Output per worker* |
| --- | --- | --- | --- |
| Building materials | 4.7 | 2.4 | 2.3 |
| Chemicals | 3.1 | 1.4 | 1.8 |
| Ferrous metals | 3.0 | 0.8 | 2.2 |
| Non-ferrous metals | 4.9 | 2.4 | 2.5 |
| Shipbuilding | 1.2 | −1.4 | 2.6 |
| Mechanical engineering | 1.9 | 1.9 | 0.0 |
| Electrical engineering | 6.3 | 5.6 | 0.7 |
| Vehicles | 6.2 | 2.9 | 3.3 |
| Precision instruments | 3.5 | 0.3 | 3.2 |
| Textiles | 1.6 | −0.8 | 2.4 |
| Leather | 1.8 | 0.6 | 1.2 |
| Clothing | 2.1 | 0.5 | 1.7 |
| Food | 3.9 | 1.8 | 2.1 |
| Drink | 0.7 | 0.8 | −0.2 |
| Tobacco | 3.5 | 0.6 | 2.9 |
| Paper and printing | 2.7 | 1.8 | 1.0 |
| Total manufacturing | 3.5 | 1.2 | 2.1 |

*Source*: Dowie 1968.

*Table 4.8* Annual growth rates in manufacturing, Britain, 1920–38

| *Output* | *Output/worker* | *Employment* | *Capital* | *TFI* | *TFP* |
| --- | --- | --- | --- | --- | --- |
| 2.6 | 2.7 | −0.1 | 0.7 | 0.1 | 2.5 |

*Source*: Aldcroft 1970: 121.

played a crucial role in productivity improvements and this provides the key to why productivity growth was spread across industry, occurring in old and declining industries as well as in new-growth sectors. Shipbuilding, for example, had a higher than average rate of growth in productivity. There appear to have been three main influences in promoting productivity growth, these were, changing technology, organisational improvements and labour shakeout. The precise influence of each cannot be disentangled. Moreover, it is clear that the improvement in manufacturing output resulted, overwhelmingly, from productivity improvements rather than increased factor inputs. Employment actually declined and there was only a very modest increase in investment.

By 1913 there was a backlog of new methods and technologies waiting to be exploited. Several new developments were stimulated by war, notably petrol, chemicals, artificial fibres and plastics, automatic welding, fuel economy techniques, precision control, alloy metallurgy and steel. The war may also have stimulated some improvements in research and industrial organisation, not least in the machine tool industry which had lagged notoriously in Britain. In the 1920s there was rapid technical progress. Sayers (1950) lists as the most influential inventions the internal combustion engine, ball-bearings, alloy metallurgy, welding, new chemical processes and precision control.

Unfortunately, the picture of rapid progress presented so far has to be severely qualified. The new developments, albeit impressive by previous standards, failed to break the structural impasse. The improvements in productivity performance failed to restore British industrial competitive-

*Table 4.9* Index of US and German relative output per operative in manufacturing (UK = 100)

|  | UK 1935 | Germany 1936 | USA 1937 |
| --- | --- | --- | --- |
| Iron and steel | 100 | 122 | 249 |
| Engineering, vehicles, shipbuilding | 100 | 126 | 254 |
| Non-ferrous metals | 100 | 142 | 227 |
| Chemicals | 100 | 106 | 186 |
| Textiles | 100 | 129 | 200 |
| Clothing | 100 | 130 | 212 |
| Leather | 100 | 114 | 176 |
| Rubber | 100 | 109 | 184 |
| Clay and stone | 100 | 82 | 247 |
| Timber | 100 | 89 | 172 |
| Paper and printing | 100 | 78 | 261 |
| Food, drink, tobacco | 100 | 86 | 156 |
| Miscellaneous | 100 | 95 | 213 |
| Total factory trade | 100 | 111 | 225 |

*Source*: Rostas 1948: 28.

ness. The new-growth industries failed to develop substantial export markets and productivity performance did not match the best else-where (Table 4.9): the USA achieved manufacturing productivity levels twice as high as in the UK and Germany also overtook Britain in 1935 (Rostas 1948).

There are more recent productivity comparisons between Britain, Germany and the USA in the interwar period and these suggest a rather more complex situation than in the Rostas data (Broadberry and Fremdling 1990; Broadberry and Crafts 1992). Broadberry and Fremdling indicate that the German productivity advantage was mainly in heavy industry and that in a number of light industries Britain retained a substantial lead. They suggest that UK performance was particularly poor, relatively, in metals and engineering, where plant size was rela-tively small. However, Broadberry and Crafts conclude that 'British plant sizes were generally larger than those in America' (1990: 397). More recently, the same authors have argued that scale economies and capital per worker were less important in determining productivity differences than 'lower British human capital' and 'the competitive environment' (1992: 554). Recent discussions of international manufac-turing productivity have not changed the broad relativities suggested by Rostas, but they serve to highlight the underlying complexities which comparisons involve and underline the difficulties of explanation and understanding.

Crafts and Thomas (1986: 643) have shown that during the interwar period Britain's competitive strength continued to reside in the old staple industries where productivity levels were comparatively low and the human capital (see the discussion of labour management below) in the work-force was inadequately developed. Their views are controversial but they provide a powerful corrective against over opti-mistic assessments of the interwar period, without, of course, explaining the undoubted improvements in productivity performance. The basic point appears to be that Britain did do better than before but failed to solve its fundamental weaknesses relative to other economies.

The structural problem was an historical legacy which defied a short-run solution. Any departure from the overcommitment to the old staple industries depended, initially at least, on domestic demand. In the 1920s Britain was drawn into a vicious circle of international economic stagna-tion which culminated in the virtual collapse of international trade after 1929. During the interwar period the export sector lagged badly and this was exacerbated by Britain's declining competitiveness (Svennilson 1954). Expanding industries were geared to the domestic product mar-ket which was constrained by the level and structure of consumer demand. During the late Victorian and Edwardian periods the more buoyant industrial sectors had produced cheap consumer goods such as biscuits, soap, cigarettes and bicycles. However, in the development of more expensive consumer durables Britain lagged badly behind the USA. For example, Britain did not reach the 1938 level of motor vehicle ownership in the USA until the late 1960s. In interwar Britain demand for new industrial output lacked social depth, as previous comments on the motor car industry have made clear.

## INDUSTRIAL POLICY AND ORGANISATION

By the end of the 1930s British industry had assumed patterns and policies which contrasted sharply with the late nineteenth century position. The major changes involved an increasing degree of government intervention in industrial affairs; a reduction in competition; a change in industrial attitudes; and a tendency for both firms and the scale of operations to increase in size.

Small, privately owned and often family firms continued to predominate, but the average size of industrial plants increased and an increasing share of total production was produced by large firms. The share of the 100 largest firms rose from 17 per cent in 1919 to 26 per cent in 1930 before falling back to 23 per cent in the later 1930s (Hannah 1983: 216). There was strong merger activity in the 1920s (a merger is defined as the acquisition by one company of more than 50 per cent of the voting power of another) and in the later 1930s. Industrial concentration involving both horizontal and vertical integration became fashionable and to some extent was viewed with favour by government. Instead of taking company organisation for granted and concentrating on product markets, managers came increasingly to realise that they had to create companies and mergers were seen as a route to company growth. This happened in many of the new industries and also became a feature of some of the old industries with the 'rationalisation' movement. Merger activity was largely voluntary and hostile take-over was rare. Thus the merger wave did not represent market elimination of inefficient or excess capacity. Concentration was urged by a series of public enquiries including the Royal Commission on the Coal Industry (Cmd 1926: XXII), the (Balfour) Committee on Industry and Trade (Cmd 3282 1929), the Liberal Industrial Inquiry (1928) and encouraged by the Bank of England through the Bankers' Industrial Development Company and the Securities Management Trust. In 1935 tax concessions were made to larger companies. Government pressure was important in rationalising and concentrating the old staple industries, as noted above.

The economic pressures promoting increases in size included the desire to take advantage of economies of scale and this was often promoted through the introduction of new technology and new products. However, the most important factor promoting concentration was the desire to control wages, output and prices. Production in many industries became oligopolistic, with only a small number of firms being responsible for the bulk of output, and there was an increasing tendency towards collusion between producers as well as national wage bargaining. These developments may have had important implications for industrial efficiency in that the reduction in competition meant that the least efficient firms were less likely to be eliminated and new producers may have experienced entry problems. While the economics textbooks continued to highlight the virtues of competition British businessmen and, to some extent also, policy-makers, made moves in the direction of market control. Also in the interwar years there was an accelerated influx of foreign multinationals including Ford, General Motors (Vauxhall) and Procter and Gamble, while bringing new organisation and technology this also appears to have intensified the march of oligopoly. The nineteenth century faith in competition gave way to a pursuit of production and market control and this may have inhibited structural change. By the end of the interwar period free competition in industry was possibly the exception rather than the rule (Compton and Bott 1940: 252). The deliberate removal or reduction of price competition was arranged through a variety of means ranging from, at one extreme, near monopoly in the public utilities, soap and cement, to unwritten 'gentlemen's agreements' at the other. Between these extremes lay cartels, amalgamations and business association controls. Usually the aim was to maintain or raise prices through collusive action, or to restrict output so that market prices would rise. At the same time it should not be denied that association and concentration may have had some socially beneficial effects through the promotion of better organisation, improving technology and better management. Increases in size required managerial and other innovations in order to overcome diseconomies. ICI, for example, developed a multi-divisional structure on both a regional and a product basis (Reader 1975). Attempts at market control were frequently unsuccessful. Price agreements often failed, especially where there were many producers.

The First World War appears to have marked a turning point in government attitudes and intervention. Before 1914 the governmental role had been limited and mainly confined to general legislation designed to promote efficiency, to improve safety and to protect the consumer from the abuse of monopoly power. In the interwar period these aims gave way to government desires to support industry in adverse circumstances, improve profitability and preserve employment with much less emphasis on consumer protection and industrial efficiency (Robson 1937).

During the First World War government had moved towards a command economy but opinion during the postwar boom favoured a return to prewar 'normality' and, from 1920, this was underwritten with the decision to restore the gold standard. While there were concerns about British industrial efficiency and international competitiveness, articulated especially by the Balfour Committee, it was not proposed to solve these through government intervention but by policies which placed a downward pressure on wages. While cuts in public spending, high real interest rates and the eventual return to gold at an overvalued exchange rate may have been seriously damaging to industry, it was generally believed that the restoration of 'sound finance' was the only route to industrial revival and the restoration of Britain's prewar position in world trade (Kirby 1987: 128–9).

During the course of the 1920s it became clear that this policy was a failure. From 1921 there was growing concern about persistent and heavy unemployment and the plight of the old staple industries. The General Strike in 1926 revealed the economic social and political costs of an attack on wages and there was a search for alternatives. Perhaps the most important of these was the rationalisation movement. While events and circumstances appeared to dictate a need for more direct government intervention there was a continuing reluctance in both interwar decades to embark decisively in this direction and vacillation continued over both ends and means in industrial policy (Garside 1990: 223; Kirby 1987: 125).

Rationalisation became an increasingly popular panacea after 1926. Strictly defined the term 'rationalisation' meant the elimination of inefficient and excess capacity, concentration of output and more efficient organisation and management. In practice, however, rationalisation became a label for amalgamations of almost any kind and sometimes a cover for the restraint of competition. Some people saw rationalisation as an alternative to nationalisation and tariff protection or as a cure for unemployment problems in declining industries. However, insofar as it reduced capacity, rationalisation was more likely to create unemployment than to reduce it, although, in the long run it was hoped that increased efficiency and competitiveness in export markets would create higher employment. Governments were unwilling to enforce rationalisation, though ministers and civil servants were active behind the scenes in trying to persuade industrialists in the old staples to rationalise (Roberts 1984). The general effect of government policy and pressure on industry was to reduce competition and, in some cases, to promote cartelisation and monopoly which may have delayed structural change and the elimination of excess and inefficient capacity. However, it is not clear that industrial diplomacy went very far beyond what might have happened anyway. State intervention was piecemeal and indirect and lacked a coherent strategy. Government moved from free trade to protection; compulsorily amalgamated the railways in 1921; established centralised control over electricity supply with the creation of the Central Electricity Board in 1926; created the BBC in the 1920s; and, in the 1930s, attempted cartelisation in agriculture, coal, cotton and iron and steel. But this activity stopped well short of the sort of planning adopted elsewhere in Europe in the 1930s (Compton and Bott 1940: 16). But clearly policy was no longer driven by the *laissez faire* model of anti interventionism (Turner 1984). Middlemas (1979) has argued that a 'corporate economy' had begun to emerge in Britain by the interwar period in the continuing contacts between government and industry, laying the foundations for business and trade unions to become, effectively, part of the governing structure in society after 1940. In fact, the evidence for corporate development before 1939 is limited. The trades unions had little impact on policy and business failed to put forward consistent views or to act in unison. There were major differences, for example, in relation to tariff policy. Informal contacts between government and industry made officials aware that circumstances and attitudes differed widely and may have been a factor in the failure to develop a coherent industrial strategy. Nevertheless, slowly, but surely, the state was being drawn into the affairs of the boardroom just as industrialists were becoming accustomed to and dependent upon state direction and support (Kirby 1987: 139). The belief that radical intervention was needed, except in the case of a few severely troubled staple industries, was not widespread. New industries were emerging and industrial performance, particularly during the upswing of the 1930s, was impressive. But in a longer-term perspective Britain's industrial problem was much more serious and complex than had been imagined. The structural problem was far from being solved at the end of the 1930s. There was also a barely perceived problem of Britain's poor industrial competitiveness. Even where new industries developed they appeared to encounter difficulties in export markets and, to some extent, inefficient organisation may have been translated from old industries into new.

Above all it is important to stress the gradual and patchy nature of industrial change. Some firms such as ICI did emerge on modernised lines with elaborate managerial hierarchies and multi-divisional structures. But all too often the larger conglomerates were little more than holding companies which aimed at market control while leaving production processes largely unchanged in constituent units which continued to be managed along largely traditional lines. The smaller and medium size family firms which continued to predominate operated against exceptional fluctuations in demand while seeking product differentiation, limited production runs and catering to highly individual consumer requirements. In these circumstances a switch to modern mass production methods, or 'Fordism', was problematic. Most firms were unable or unwilling to risk the heavy overheads and investment which large scale modernisation and reorganisation demanded. These problems were compounded by managerial and organisational limitations and conditions of labour supply and management (Gospel 1992: 60).

## LABOUR ORGANISATION AND MANAGEMENT

Gospel has charted the slow and incomplete transition from market-based to internalised strategies in British labour management. During the nineteenth century British industry paid little attention to training and had relied on the external market for labour, recruiting and laying off workers as demand fluctuated, by filling vacancies with external as well as internal candidates as they arose, and fixing wages largely on the basis of external market signals. The process of internalisation commenced when mass markets and production began to permit high volume throughput in production and marketing. Growth strategies developed around increasing scale and small, single-product, single-plant units were gradually transformed into large, multi-unit, multi-product enterprises. According to Chandler and others this process was the crucial factor in American industrial success and Britain's relative failure to develop larger internalised business corporations explains its comparative industrial failure (Chandler 1970; 1980; 1990; Elbaum and Lazonick 1986). The slowness to move in this direction was not confined to labour management, but it is in this area where some of the factors inhibiting change are most readily apparent.

From the late nineteenth century an embryonic system of industrial relations began to develop in Britain on the basis of increasing union recognition through employer associations. Gradually there was a move from regional towards national bargaining, mainly as a result of employer initiatives, but this appears to have been welcomed by national union organisers. This system was greatly enhanced by the First World War, with strong union growth and increasing recognition in a tight labour market. Meanwhile, paternalism tended to decline as unions extended their influence and state welfare systems developed. In the 1920s employers sought to continue this system of labour relations despite heavy unemployment which placed them in a stronger position. Clearly these arrangements were symptomatic of an ongoing desire to externalise industrial relations from the shop floor and to extend market control to wages as well as prices. National collective bargaining may have served to maintain industrial peace because disputes were likely to be extremely costly. The system reduced wage competition, thus enhancing market control, and may have preserved internal managerial prerogatives to some extent. In practice, national bargaining provided only a skeletal framework which at best was only loose (Clegg 1970: 133). The system may have limited the downward path of wages during depressed periods although it failed to prevent wage drift (Gospel 1992: 61).

Thus the employers recognised unions while trying to exclude union activity from the workplace. During the early 1920s there were wage reductions, in line with prices, often as a result of cost of living agreements but these declined in importance and employers failed to carry out a successful assault on money wages. In part this may have been because of an implicit emphasis upon efficiency wages, although the main emphasis appears to have been on money wages (Austin and Lloyd 1926). While time payment continued to be the system for most workers there was growing emphasis on piecework and payment by results, especially in engineering (Yates 1937: ch. 7). Also, employers relied upon work intensification to improve productivity rather than seeking managerial and organisational changes of production processes. In some cases these efforts were backed by attempts at 'scientific management' including Bedaux systems (see Chapter 5). Industry tended to become locked into outmoded production systems as a result of the inflexibilities ensuing from market and labour supply conditions and continued reliance on externalised market systems. Even larger firms lacked the strategy and co-ordination to push through changes in production. In addition, the labour supply situation encouraged the maintenance of unskilled-labour and craft-intensive methods of production rather than more physical and human capital intensive methods (Gospel 1992: 60).

Craft workers continued to be in plentiful supply and, in conditions of heavy unemployment, training incentives were diminished. Apprenticeship was the principal formal method of training and, in some ways, a further example of externalisation since it was organised by craftsmen and involved the inculcation of transferable skills. To some extent apprenticeship gave ground to the rising importance of semi-skilled workers trained through special programmes. In addition there was growth in external training through night schools and technical colleges for such qualifications as City and Guilds and Ordinary and Higher National Certificates. But employers consistently opposed the raising of the school leaving age and showed general indifference to new training initiatives. Their preference for intensification of work rather than the development of human capital was short-sighted (Gospel 1992: 66; Wrigley 1987).

With craft workers dominating workshop production processes there was less need for the extension of managerial functions and the elaboration of management hierarchies. Nevertheless, there was a significant increase in white-collar staff and some extension in functional specialisation at more senior levels. The proportion of administrative, technical and clerical staff grew and more sophisticated management began to emerge, especially in larger firms and particularly in the personnel area. However, management training was rare and the 'gentleman amateur' remained a common type in higher-level management, while at the middle and lower levels the 'practical man', who possessed little in the way of formal qualifications, remained dominant (Gospel 1992: 49).

## CHANGES IN INDUSTRIAL LOCATION AND REGIONAL PROBLEMS

During the nineteenth century the industrial centres of South Wales, Lancashire, West Yorkshire, Tyneside and Central Scotland, together with lesser concentrations in the Midlands and Belfast had been relatively prosperous with higher average wages and a greater degree of urbanisation than elsewhere. From the late nineteenth century the southern parts of Britain, hitherto dominated by low-wage agriculture, began to become more industrial and also more prosperous relative to other regions. Meanwhile, the old industrial areas began to encounter severe problems of industrial decline, heavy unemployment and poverty. The reasons for these changes are complex and inadequately researched. However, the basic explanation is in terms of the decline of the old staple industries and the tendency for new and growing industries to develop most rapidly and extensively outside the old industrial areas.

In deciding where to locate the old industries had been constrained by the need to be near water and coal supplies and to have canal and rail links. New industries after 1914 had new sources of power in the form of oil and electricity and new means of transport with the arrival of motor vehicles. This gave them greater freedom in their choice of location and there was a substantial shift in British industrial distribution from the coalfield areas towards the Midlands and the South East. This, together with the decline of the old staple industries gave rise to regional imbalance and the emergence of depressed areas. In 1924 the 'old industrial areas', as officially defined, were producing 50 per cent of net industrial output. By 1935 this had fallen to 38 per cent. The 'new industrial' areas (mainly London and the West Midlands) were producing 29 per cent in 1924 and this rose to 37 per cent by 1937 (Von Tunzelmann 1981: 247).

By the late 1930s there was an approximate balance between the 'old' and the 'new' industrial areas in terms of net industrial output. It was not that London and the Midlands had attracted more new industries or that industry had moved bodily from north to south. In the 'old' areas new industrial development did take place but was inhibited by general decline and swamped in aggregate terms by the adverse fortunes of the old staples. In the 'new' industrial areas circumstances were more buoyant and new industries were more successful. The London area became an increasingly attractive location as the major population concentration and the largest consumer market in Britain. Industries locating near London may have gained significant economies in distribution through cheaper and more flexible deliveries and better after sales service. In the Midlands there was a traditional interest in metal manufacturing which was an advantage in the expansion of metal-working consumer goods in the twentieth century (Allen 1959: 10).

While the balance of industry had shifted, people had tended to remain immobile. Over the course of the interwar period about 4 per cent of the UK population moved from north to south (Cmd. 1948 7695). In 1923 some 46.8 per cent of the insured population lived in Inner Britain; by 1929 the figure had risen to 49.1, and by 1938 to 52.3 per cent (Dennison 1939). The North West, Wales and the North East provided most of these emigrants and the main destination was London and the Home Counties. Between 1923 and 1937 British employment increased by 22 per cent but only London and the Home Counties and the Midlands exceeded the national average – growing by 43 and 28 per cent respectively. In Glamorgan and Monmouth employment actually declined in this period by 4 per cent and other areas grew much less than the national average (Pollard 1983: 78). Nevertheless, this did not prevent the appearance of major differentials in employment levels and chronic unemployment in the old industrial areas (P.E.P. 1939).

By the late 1920s the authorities began to accept the long term nature of Britain's regional problems (Garside 1990: 242). In 1928 the government established the Industrial Transference Board to encourage movement from the depressed areas to other areas, both in the UK and overseas. This initiative which focused on mining areas, was inadequate and doomed to failure in the face of circumstances. With the renewed downturn after 1929 and acute unemployment in all areas transference was clearly inappropriate and attention shifted to the possibility of promoting industrial development in the depressed (or 'special') areas. Government activity was however less than half-hearted and designed to mollify political critics rather than 'solve' the problem of regional economic and social imbalance (Booth 1978: 139–57). Nevertheless, it marks the beginning of regional policy in Britain in the face of an intractable problem.

## AGRICULTURE

By 1919 Britain was unique among the major industrial powers in having a very small agricultural sector. In 1919 agriculture still accounted for 15 per cent of American GDP and employed 25 per cent of the work-force. In 1938 French agriculture produced 22 per cent of GDP and employed 33 per cent of the work-force. In interwar Britain agriculture accounted for only about 6 per cent of GDP and a similar proportion of the work-force (Solomou 1988). In the circumstances this was undoubtedly an advantage for Britain, especially in the 1930s when agriculture on a world basis was severely depressed. Britain's relatively successful recovery in the 1930s owed something to a lack of dependence on agriculture and to cheaper imports of primary produce (Thompson 1963: 332–3).

Since the seventeenth century much of British agriculture had been gradually assuming a pyramidic structure involving large landowners, tenant farmers and wage labourers. In the twentieth century agriculture became increasingly the preserve of farmers who owned their land in freehold and rentier landowners and wage labourers became much less important in the system. By the First World War land values had probably become too high in relation to the income from land and the positional premium in terms of social status and influence had declined (Offer 1991: 15). There was a rush of land sales and speculation in land from 1917 to 1921, prompted by war deaths, rising taxation and, in particular, death duties. However, the major influence was probably the increased ability of tenants to purchase land. Controls during the First World War prevented rent increases although food prices soared. Also, the war was followed by legislation which improved the rights and security of tenure. Thus for a variety of reasons landowners became both willing and able to sell large quantities of land. Most of the purchasers were tenant farmers and owner occupancy increased from 11 per cent in 1914 to 36 per cent by 1927. In all, probably one-quarter of English farmland changed hands in the period (Thompson 1963: 332–3).

The later years of the First World War had brought government subsidies, price guarantees and market and wage controls which continued until 1921. The war also brought an enhanced sense of the national and strategic importance of agriculture and precedents for government intervention were created. However, controls were rapidly dismantled in 1921–2 after agricultural prices had fallen sharply and slower decline tended to continue through the 1920s. There was a further sharp fall of 34 per cent between 1929 and 1932 followed by slow recovery from 1933, although the 1929 level was not regained during the 1930s. Production costs tended to fall less than prices and profits were squeezed or eliminated. Tenants who had purchased during the 1917–22 period were frequently left with debts which tended to grow in real terms. Rents and wages also tended to remain stable while prices fell (Brown 1987).

British agriculture has always been a mixed production system with much diversity, both regional and local, in land organisation, ownership and use, which makes generalisations hazardous. A number of changes are, however, evident. Production was becoming increasingly specialised and concentrated in commodities which were least affected by overseas competition, where price reductions were least and where production was less labour-intensive. Grain became much less important relatively and livestock continued to increase in importance. By the 1920s the major part of farm income was derived from milk, meat, poultry, eggs and potatoes and the most prosperous parts of agriculture were involved in providing fresh food supplies to domestic consumers. The most depressed areas of agriculture included the grain farmers of the eastern counties and hill farmers who were unable to find a feasible alternative to sheep. Between 1919 and 1939 net agricultural output does not appear to have increased although there were improvements in technology and labour productivity (Ojala 1952).

During the depression of the 1930s there was a dramatic reversal in British government attitudes and policies towards agriculture. Since the repeal of the corn laws in 1846 British agriculture had been left unprotected. The dangers of dependence on imported cheap food were exposed during the First World War but it was not until 1932 that serious moves were made to make fundamental policy changes. The motives were in part strategic and in part reflected the continuing social and political significance of the rural community despite its dwindling numbers (Armstrong 1988). There was a national desire to preserve the countryside and rural life and to prevent further decline. Increased support for agriculture merely paralleled industrial protection noted above. From 1932 assistance took the form principally of maintenance of farm income by regulation of food imports, and marketing, with subsidies and price guarantees for farmers. Small steps had already been taken in the 1920s by removing the burden of rates from farm property, reducing tithes, promoting voluntary co-operation and self-help and subsidies to sugar-beet growing.

Gradually during the 1930s protection was spread over a wide range of farm products. By 1939 there were 17 marketing boards although only those dealing with milk, potatoes and hops had much success during the 1930s but others provided a useful basis for the reorganisation and control of agriculture during the Second World War.

The Import Duties Act of 1932 and the Ottawa Agreements Act restricted food imports to provide home and empire producers with a larger share of the home market. By 1935 food imports had fallen 12 per cent. Imports from the empire increased 42 per cent while foreign supplies fell 32 per cent. This represented a considerable trade diversion in the supply of the world's biggest food importer, but did little to raise farm incomes in Britain since, by the 1930s, not much import-competing agriculture remained. British farm production was relatively high-cost compared with overseas supplies and demand was price-elastic. British agriculture could only make major inroads into the domestic market through subsidies which were needed to support import controls.

Beet, sugar and cattle were directly subsidised and, from 1932, price deficiency payments (guaranteed prices involving variable subsidies) were extended over a range of products. By 1939 there were guaranteed prices for wheat, barley, oats, milk, pigs and sheep. Most assistance was given to wheat and beet growers in the severely depressed eastern counties. In financial terms total subsidies (which reached an interwar annual peak of £19 million in 1938–9) were small beer by postwar standards, but by the end of the 1930s Britain had embarked upon a policy of subsidising agricultural production while retaining cheap food prices for consumers. This policy remained until EEC entry (Chapters 11 and 12). Government measures in the 1930s may have placed a floor under agricultural decline but farming made little progress in terms of output or income.

## BUILDING, TRANSPORT AND SERVICES

The aggregate importance of the tertiary sector in the interwar economy has already been indicated. Services, including building, employed two-thirds of fixed assets and more than half the work-force and recorded negative productivity growth. Generalisations about the service sector tend to be meaningless because of major differences between components as well as measurement difficulties.

Building (including housing, industrial and commercial building) assumed a greatly enhanced importance in the interwar period and it may have played a crucial role in the 1930s recovery. Building and contracting grew more rapidly than any other industry, except vehicles, with an average annual growth rate of 5.4 per cent between 1920 and 1938 (Aldcroft 1970: 202). Building boomed almost throughout the interwar years and assumed an importance in the economy greater than at any other time in modern history. Since there was virtually no growth in productivity most of the extra output translated directly into increases in employment and the industry's share of total industrial employment grew from 10.4 per cent in 1920 (800,000) to 15.2 per cent in 1938 (1.3 million). Building's share of total fixed investment grew to almost half in the 1930s. It absorbed labour and capital in a period when factor supply exceeded demand and tended to have a counter-cyclical and stabilising effect (Richardson and Aldcroft 1968).

Housebuilding accounted for only about a third of activity in the industry but the boom in housing was extensive with important linkage and multiplier effects. Housing was a labour-intensive activity with limited productivity growth but important employment and final consumer demand effects. In the 1920s there was rapid growth in both output, employment and productivity. The latter rose by 3.9 per cent per annum between 1924 and 1929. However, there was no improvement in productivity after 1929 (Dowie 1968: Table 1, 108). In the building supply industry there was more even growth in productivity and large firms became dominant. This was in marked contrast to building itself where firms typically remained small.

In the area of transport and communications it is possible to find almost the entire gamut of interwar industrial experience. Railways, shipping, canals and tramways may be grouped with the declining old staple industries whose experience they tended to share. At the modern end of the economy lay road and air transport and telecommunications (Dyos and Aldcroft 1969).

Railways, which had monopolised long-distance land transport in Britain, came to the end of a long period of expansion in 1914. After government control during the First World War the different companies were compelled to create four private (but regulated) systems under the Railway Act of 1921. In the interwar years rail freight declined, profits failed to regain pre-1914 levels and passenger traffic grew less rapidly. The railway work-force fell by 18 per cent and a large part of the rail network became uneconomic (Bagwell 1988). This reflected the rise of road transport as well as the decline of industries such as coal and other old staples which had been closely connected with railways. Despite these symptoms of decline rail transport remained important and the rail system was improved. By the 1930s Britain had the largest electrified suburban rail network in the world and long-distance services, especially between London and Scotland, were streamlined. Between 1918 and 1938 the number of road vehicles in Britain multiplied by ten. By 1938 there were 2 million cars, 50,000 buses and almost half-a-million goods vehicles (Walker 1947: 128). An urgent need for new government regulation of the greatly increased volume of road traffic arose and there was a series of acts after 1930 which *inter alia* made third party insurance mandatory, imposed driving tests, regulated public transport vehicles and licensed goods vehicles. Existing bus and freight operators were protected and competition tended to be reduced (Fenelon 1935). Road vehicles and fuel became important sources of government revenue although there was a corresponding rise in public spending on roads. Substantial government spending on roads, while railways were only marginally assisted, represents one of the most proactive forms of government economic intervention during the period. In London a co-ordinated public transport system emerged (Barker and Robbins 1974).

Between 1914 and 1938 Britain's share of world merchant shipping fell from 43 to 26 per cent. While total world tonnage grew 46 per cent in the same period there was a 6 per cent decline in British tonnage. This sharp decline in Britain's role as the world's carrier reflected war losses and a shift to 'flags of convenience', but in the main it resulted from economic changes. In particular, the end of rapid growth in world trade, and migration, excess capacity and growing competition in world shipping and the decline in British exports (Isserlis 1935). Despite some government assistance British shipping was unable to withstand the challenge from cheaper carriers. In 1935 tramp shipping which had suffered most severely was given a subsidy of £2 million and a 'scrap and build' scheme was introduced at the same time. This failed to have much impact in modernising the British merchant fleet and Britain fell behind in several areas including oil tankers (Duff 1949).

As with the motor industry, electricity made a spectacular breakthrough in the interwar period. Before 1914 development had been slow, scattered, inefficient and haphazard, and Britain lagged behind the USA and European leaders in the use of electricity. American and German companies tended to dominate the early electrical industry in Britain and there was dependence on overseas imports and techniques. Rapid development of electricity in Britain had to await the production of cheap electricity on the basis of an efficient system of generation and distribution, which followed the manifest failure of the private sector to produce an efficient pattern of development (Hannah 1979). Under the Electricity (Supply) Act of 1926 the Central Electricity Board was established and given a monopoly of electricity wholesale supply to concentrate production so that large numbers of small and inefficient generating outlets could be eliminated. A 'national grid' of sub-stations linked by high-tension transmission cables was established and by 1938 electricity unit prices had been halved. There were sharp increases in electricity consumption and the number of consumers grew from 0.7 million in 1920 to 2.8 million in 1929 and 9.0 million in 1938. While there was a fourfold increase in the amount of electricity generated between 1925 and 1939, improvements in the efficiency of generation were not matched by similar improvements in distribution and British electricity remained expensive compared with overseas supplies in competitor economies. Nevertheless, there was rapid growth in electricity consumption in response to falling costs indicating that demand was price elastic. There were important gains in industrial productivity as costs fell and growing use of electrical power enabled greater flexibility in factory location and layout (Plummer 1937: ch. 2). Home consumption was also price and income elastic and the use of electric consumer durables increased. However, the main domestic use of electricity was for lighting and home use of electrical appliances remained limited until after the Second World War. While clearly there were demand-side constraints as a result of limited growth in incomes and unemployment, there were also problems on the supply side. Greater efficiencies in electricity supply and the production of durables might have generated a mass market at an earlier stage. While there was rapid growth in electrical engineering and the (insured) work-force in the industry more than doubled between 1924 and 1937 to reach 367,000, the productivity performance of this sector was disappointing. In particular, mass production techniques in the production of heavy equipment developed only slowly. While the industry was protected from 1921 it was dominated by foreign subsidiaries, albeit to a declining extent.

## CONCLUSION

Between 1914 and 1950 British industry made substantial gains in terms of growth in both output and productivity and there was a marked improvement in performance compared with the pre-1914 period. This was all the more impressive in view of the fact that there were major shocks to the system in terms of war and depression and the problem of the declining old staples was unresolved. There were also continuing difficulties in achieving internationally competitive performance in other more buoyant sectors of industry. The failure to change industrial scale and structures and, especially, management and organisation to meet best foreign practice must be explained in terms of the nature of labour and product markets and the existence of barriers to change within industry. In the face of adversity, British industry, with government connivance, sought market control rather than radical reorganisation.

# Chapter 5

# Unemployment and the labour market

Unemployment was an important feature of Britain during the interwar years and a conditioning influence on economy and society. Indeed, unemployment is a defining characteristic of the period. The aim in what follows is to examine the extent, nature and causes of the unemployment problem which Britain faced in the 1920s and 1930s.

## THE EXTENT OF UNEMPLOYMENT

All unemployment statistics rest upon arbitrary assumptions and imperfect information. It is important, therefore, to know the basis and limitations of quoted statistics (Garside 1980). Official figures before 1914 were compiled by the Board of Trade from returns made by certain trade unions which paid unemployment benefits to their members. These returns reflect a biased labour force sample of mainly skilled workers, but from industries which were prone to fluctuation. They indicate an average level of 4 to 5 per cent unemployment between 1855 and 1914, fluctuating from 2 to 10 per cent over the trade cycle. Beveridge suggested that the average rate of unemployment before 1914 was rather higher than these figures indicate (Beveridge 1960: 73) but it is impossible to know how much higher. It is clear that in the pre-1914 labour market there was a good deal of casual hiring and underemployment which is not captured in the unemployment statistics and which probably continued after 1918, providing a further reminder of the limitations of official statistics (Whiteside and Gillespie 1991). Employment and unemployment do not fall neatly into distinct categories and there may be a range of multiform circumstances between full-time work and complete unemployment.

With the advent of the NIS (National Insurance Scheme) in 1911, and its extension in 1916 and 1920 to 60 per cent of the work-force, new statistics became available and formed the basis for an official series. This was based upon spot monthly tallies (and, therefore, does *not* give accurate monthly averages) of the numbers registered at labour exchanges as being unemployed and these were published monthly in the Ministry of Labour *Gazette*. Unfortunately, the NIS figures thus derived, and widely used by historians and others, relate to only about 60 per cent of the work-force, on a national basis, and to widely varying proportions on an industrial, regional and local basis (Glynn and Booth 1983). The NIS statistics suggest an average annual level of unemployment of just over 14 per cent between 1920 and 1938; a minimum level of just under 10 per cent; and a maximum of 22 per cent in 1932.

There is an alternative source of data in the 1931 census which was the first to successfully and systematically record unemployment on a national basis. Feinstein has compiled an alternative series based on extrapolation from the (revised) 1931 census, using annual NIS figures, and allowing for the 'temporarily stopped', and the wider NIS coverage in the 1930s. Workforce figures are based on Chapman's estimates of man-years of employment (Feinstein 1972a: 221; 1972b Table 56, T128; Chapman and Knight: 1953). An assessment of this series depends upon an evaluation of the questions asked in the 1931 census as a means of eliciting information about unemployment. It is clear that the questions were less rigorous than those employed in contemporary surveys. Feinstein's alternative estimates indicate an average annual level of unemployment of 10.9 per cent (1921–38), a minimum of just under 8 per cent (in 1924) and a maximum of 17 per cent (in 1932).

After 1945 the NIS was extended to include all the work-force and the official *Labour Gazette* series continued. However, it is clear that official interwar unemployment statistics are not strictly comparable with the official series for pre-1914 and post-1945. It is possible to compare NIS statistics for most of the post-Second World War period with those for the interwar years by using a crude deflator of 8/13 on the interwar data (Metcalf *et al.* 1982). The deflator excludes the proportion of the work-force which was not covered by the NIS but we should note that this section tended to have lower percentage rates of unemployment than insured workers. On this basis the interwar annual average level of insured unemployment of 14.2 per cent converts to 8.7 per cent.

On the basis of the various statistics quoted so far it is possible to make some very approximate historical comparisons and these enable us to make an assessment of the relative magnitude and intensity of interwar unemployment. Of course, we should bear in mind that the statistics may conceal important differences in the structure, quality and duration of unemployment in each period.

This very approximate comparison indicates that, in terms of the magnitude and intensity of unemployment, the interwar period is not perhaps such an exceptional period as was previously thought. Contemporary opinion leaves little room for doubt that unemployment in the

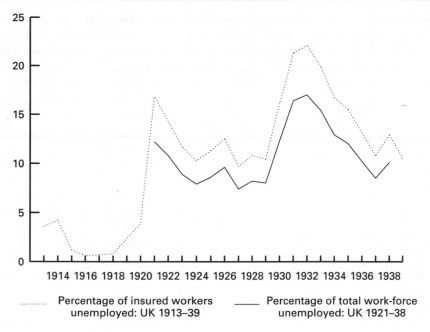

| | Percentage of insured workers unemployed: UK 1913–39 | _____ | Percentage of total work-force unemployed: UK 1921–38 |

*Figure 5.1* British unemployment, 1913–39 (%)
*Sources*: Department of Employment 1971: 306; Feinstein 1972: Table 58, T 128.

interwar years was sharply higher than it had been before 1914, but the difference was not so great as the available statistics suggest. What really stands out is the highly exceptional period between 1945 and 1968 when unemployment levels, on NIS data, rarely rose above 2 per cent. Since the early 1980s it seems that levels of unemployment have returned to

*Table 5.1* Measures of unemployment, 1920–39

| | |
|---|---|
| National Insurance Registration: Official series: | |
| Average | 14.2 |
| Minimum | 9.6 |
| Maximum | 23.1 |
| Feinstein series based on 1931 Census and NIS data: | |
| Average | 10.9 |
| Minimum | 8.0 |
| Maximum | 17.0 |
| Postwar comparison with official series 1945–81 using 8/13 deflator: | |
| Average | 8.7 |
| Minimum | 5.9 |
| Maximum | 14.2 |

*Sources*: Department of Employment, *Gazette*; Glynn and Booth 1987; Feinstein 1972; Metcalf *et al.* 1982.

heights which are clearly comparable, and arguably higher, than average levels in the interwar period (Chapter 13).

In the NIS statistics 10 per cent unemployment, which was about the minimum level between 1920 and 1939, represented about 1.2 million workers with (typically) two dependants (wife and one child). But there was a fairly rapid turnover of the unemployed so that an average annual figure at this level meant approximately 4 million periods of unemployment, affecting perhaps 12 million people. Long-term unemployment (usually defined as one year or more) was comparatively rare in the 1920s, averaging 5.8 per cent of the insured unemployed. After 1929 it rose sharply and a hard core of 25 per cent had developed by the mid-1930s. It is clear that long-term unemployment is cumulative and self-reinforcing (Crafts 1987; Layard 1986). People became trapped in long-term unemployment for several reasons and many commentators have argued that workers who experienced long-term unemployment became unemployable and incapable of work for both physical and mental reasons; in effect, outside the labour market. Such views have to be treated with considerable scepticism as most of the long-term unemployed of the 1930s returned to the active work-force in the 1940s and there is no evidence of widespread unemployability. Individuals became trapped in long term unemployment largely because of employer attitudes and reluctance to hire those who had been out of work for long periods when more recently employed workers were available.

So far we have quoted only national average annual statistics. Unemployment varied greatly on a disaggregated basis, not least according to age. For reasons which are complex and unclear, juveniles were less likely to be unemployed – the opposite of the 1980s and 1990s experience. This may be attributed to lower wages, lower benefits or non-payment of benefits and non-registration, but there was no serious juvenile unemployment problem as such in the interwar period. At the other end of the age range older men, especially, found it harder to

*Table 5.2* Participation rates: males and females: Great Britain, 1931 (%)

|  | *Males* | *Females* |
|---|---|---|
| Total population | 21,495,000 | 23,336,000 |
| Percentage aged 15–64 | 68 | 70 |
| Percentage unemployed[a] | 12 | 3 |
| Percentage employed[a] | 57 | 23 |

*Note:*
a These estimates include persons in the work-force, but outside the 15–64 age group.
*Source*: Clark 1937: 30–31 and 1931 Census.

obtain new employment once they became unemployed. As a result, unemployment increased with age.

Information on female unemployment is limited but we can be sure that it was much more extensive than the official figures suggest. It is impossible to obtain any realistic assessment of female unemployment since there is no way of knowing how many unoccupied women would have been willing to seek paid employment at prevailing wage rates had it been available (Booth and Glynn 1975: 615). The failure to apply for work because it is simply not available is known as the 'discouraged worker effect' and this, together with the fact that married women and others were not usually entitled to benefits, explains the inadequate statistical record of female unemployment. The 'discouraged worker effect' will obviously affect the female participation rate, which was discussed in Chapter 3 (see Table 3.3). But there were also strong regional variations: in 1931 female participation in paid employment varied from 14.5 per cent in South Wales to 32.2 per cent in Greater London (Booth and Glynn 1975: 616).

Although in certain industries and areas there were social pressures and conventions that women, and married women in particular, should be the first to lose their jobs, this was not always the case. Women earned about half as much as men, on average, and the absence of equal pay for equal work may have protected female employment. Many industries dominated by female labour, especially in services, suffered rather less from unemployment than male-dominated heavy manufacturing. In some families, therefore, women became the main earners as a result of unemployment.

It is clear that there was a pronounced social and skill dimension to

*Table 5.3* Male unemployment by occupation, 1931

| | |
|---|---|
| Unskilled manual workers | 30.5 |
| Skilled and semi-skilled manual workers | 14.4 |
| Agricultural workers | 7.6 |
| Forces | 0.0 |
| Personal service workers | 9.9 |
| Salesmen and shop assistants | 7.9 |
| Clerks and typists | 5.5 |
| Higher office workers | 5.1 |
| Professions | 5.5[a] |
| Retail traders | 2.3 |
| Farmers | 0.5 |
| Other proprietors and managers | 1.3 |

*Note:*
a Swollen by unemployed musicians. Average for other professions was about half this level.
*Source*: Clark 1951: 470.

*Table 5.4* Percentage of insured workers unemployed: selected industries, 1924–37

|  | 1924 | 1929 | 1932 | 1937 |
|---|---|---|---|---|
| Coalmining | 5.8 | 19.0 | 34.5 | 16.1 |
| Chemicals | 9.9 | 6.5 | 17.3 | 6.8 |
| Pig Iron | 14.1 | 14.4 | 43.8 | 10.7 |
| Iron and steel | 22.0 | 20.1 | 47.9 | 11.4 |
| General engineering | 16.9 | 9.9 | 29.1 | 5.8 |
| Electrical engineering | 5.5 | 4.6 | 16.8 | 3.1 |
| Motor vehicles | 8.9 | 7.1 | 22.4 | 5.0 |
| Shipbuilding | 30.3 | 25.3 | 62.0 | 24.4 |
| Electrical cable, apparatus, etc. | 7.7 | 5.3 | 13.3 | 5.0 |
| Cotton textiles | 15.9 | 12.9 | 30.6 | 10.9 |
| Wool textiles | 8.4 | 15.5 | 22.4 | 8.8 |
| Building | 12.5 | 14.3 | 30.2 | 14.6 |
| Gas, water, electricity | 6.3 | 6.1 | 10.9 | 8.3 |
| Distributive trades | 6.4 | 6.2 | 12.6 | 8.9 |
| Hotel, public house, etc. | 11.3 | 8.7 | 17.5 | 13.9 |

*Source:* Department of Employment and Productivity 1971: 314–5.

interwar unemployment. Better paid and more skilled workers were less likely to be unemployed. As the following table shows, unskilled male manual workers were six times more likely to be unemployed than office workers or professional groups.

Unemployment also varied by industry and region. The former is difficult to measure accurately since there is no satisfactory definition of the work-force applying to a particular industry, other than those actually engaged in employment. Nevertheless, it is clear that a very high proportion of the unemployed had previously been engaged in the old staple industries and this applied especially to the long term unemployed. Table 5.4 shows unemployment at the three cyclical peak years of 1924, 1929 and 1937 and during the severe depression of 1932, measured on the basis of previous employment.

In the interwar period a severe problem of regional unemployment emerged in a pattern which has become familiar in modern Britain (see Table 5.5). The old industrial areas in the North, Scotland, Wales and Northern Ireland became the regions with highest unemployment, having previously been the more prosperous parts of the country for wage earners. The sharp regional variations in unemployment which were characteristic of interwar Britain can be explained in terms of adverse economic circumstances affecting the old staple industries. While new industries developed they tended to locate elsewhere and failed to compensate in terms of better employment and export earnings. Mean-

*Table 5.5* Insured unemployment by administrative region, 1923–38 (annual average percentage)

| | 1923 | 1924 | 1925 | 1926 | 1927 | 1928 | 1929 | 1930 | 1931 | 1932 | 1933 | 1934 | 1935 | 1936 | 1937 | 1938 |
|---|---|---|---|---|---|---|---|---|---|---|---|---|---|---|---|---|
| London | 10.1 | 9.0 | 7.8 | 6.9 | 5.8 | 5.6 | 5.6 | 8.1 | 12.2 | 13.5 | 11.8 | 9.2 | 8.5 | 7.2 | 6.3 | 8.0 |
| South East | 9.2 | 7.5 | 5.9 | 5.4 | 5.0 | 5.4 | 5.6 | 8.0 | 12.0 | 14.3 | 11.5 | 8.7 | 8.1 | 7.3 | 6.1 | 7.4 |
| South West | 10.6 | 9.1 | 8.5 | 8.4 | 7.2 | 8.1 | 8.1 | 10.4 | 14.5 | 17.1 | 15.7 | 13.1 | 11.6 | 9.4 | 7.3 | 7.6 |
| Midlands | 10.7 | 9.0 | 9.1 | 11.0 | 8.4 | 9.9 | 9.3 | 14.7 | 20.3 | 20.1 | 17.4 | 12.9 | 11.2 | 9.2 | 7.1 | 10.8 |
| North East | 12.2 | 10.9 | 15.0 | 17.2 | 13.7 | 15.1 | 13.7 | 20.2 | 27.4 | 28.5 | 26.0 | 22.1 | 20.7 | 16.8 | 10.7 | 13.2 |
| Northern | carved out of North East and North West based on Newcastle | | | | | | | | | | | | | | 17.0 | 18.0 |
| North West | 14.5 | 12.9 | 11.4 | 14.7 | 10.7 | 12.4 | 13.3 | 23.8 | 28.2 | 25.8 | 23.5 | 20.8 | 19.7 | 17.1 | 13.9 | 17.7 |
| Scotland | 14.3 | 12.4 | 15.2 | 16.4 | 10.6 | 11.7 | 12.1 | 18.5 | 26.6 | 27.7 | 26.1 | 23.1 | 21.3 | 18.7 | 15.3 | 15.7 |
| Wales | 6.4 | 8.6 | 16.5 | 18.0 | 19.5 | 23.0 | 19.3 | 25.9 | 32.4 | 36.5 | 34.6 | 23.3 | 31.2 | 29.4 | 21.7 | 24.1 |
| Northern Ireland | 18.2 | 16.6 | 23.9 | 23.2 | 13.2 | 17.0 | 14.8 | 23.8 | 27.8 | 27.2 | 26.5 | 23.4 | 24.8 | 22.7 | — | |

*Note:* Includes agricultural labourers after 1935.

*Source:* Gilbert 1970: 312.

while, the working population remained largely immobilised (Thomas 1937) as was seen in Chapter 4.

There was much greater variation in unemployment on the basis of area rather than region and there were phenomenal rates of unemployment in some localities where structural decline was compounded by cyclical depression. In January 1933, some 91 per cent of the insured labour force was unemployed at Saltburn, 77 per cent at Jarrow, 64 per cent at Cleator Moor, 60 per cent at Wishaw, 54 per cent at Clydebank, 82 per cent at Taffs Well, 72 per cent at Pontycymmer, 68 per cent at Merthyr and 66 per cent at Abertillery (McCrone 1969: 91). This is simply a selection of areas blighted by massive unemployment and the list could be greatly extended. The town of Jarrow has become the symbol of interwar unemployment as a result of the famous march following the closure in 1936 of Palmer's Shipyard, which was the town's main source of employment. It will be clear that there were many Jarrows and it was not the worst hit place, nor was its march the largest or the first. The Jarrow march was well organised and gained media attention, not least from journalists such as Richie Calder, and, unlike other protests, was not obstructed by heavy policing. Also the town's MP Ellen Wilkinson did much to give prominence to the unemployment problem in what she called, in her book on the subject, *The Town that was Murdered*. Jarrow's unemployment problem was precipitated by a Bank of England approved rationalisation in shipbuilding.

For the bulk of the population migration was not an option for a variety of reasons. Both 'push' and 'pull' factors were relatively weak since people were unwilling to break from highly cohesive working-class communities in the north to face the comparative isolation of living in the south. Those miners who migrated to the newly opened Kent coalfield encountered a range of difficulties in terms of working conditions and finding accommodation, and, above all, they faced the intense hostility of local Kentish people. Higher wage differentials, had they existed, might have induced more to move but transfer and housing costs were major deterrents. Also, rent controls persuaded some to remain where they were despite unemployment. In many cases a move would have involved a loss of skilled status. Skilled and semi-skilled workers in coalmining, textiles, shipbuilding and other old staple industries had little to gain in terms of job status through moving south. However, the main obstacle to mobility was the fact that unemployment was high even in the most prosperous areas and movement did not guarantee a job (Hatton 1983). As a result, 'pull' factors were crucially weak. In the absence of the 'dole' it is possible that many would have been forced to move in a desperate search for work, but most were not faced with the stark choice. Nevertheless, there was a dramatic increase in the number of vagrants and people living 'rough'.

The social consequences of unemployment were examined in numerous investigations which surveyed the income, mental and physical health, diet, attitudes and behaviour of the unemployed. The grim findings of most contrasted with official attitudes which stressed how well British unemployed workers and their families were treated in comparison with elsewhere. While the national insurance scheme and the benefit system were relatively generous and reliable there is no doubt that unemployment imposed considerable costs, both to the individual and society, which may have been underestimated by some historians. Apart from the question of Exchequer costs, there were wide-ranging discussions at the time of the effects of unemployment on increasing social dependency, on mental and physical health, crime, disability, vagrancy and political attitudes (Webster 1985). As in the 1980s, there is evidence of a 'bash the victim' syndrome whereby there was a tendency to blame the unemployed for their own predicament. In part, this reflected a qualitative judgement of the unemployed. However, there was a 'filtering down' process, in physical capacity, as with skill, with the better qualified and fitter workers tending to take over the jobs of the unskilled and less healthy, who therefore became disproportionately represented among the unemployed (Whiteside 1987: 23).

Official statistics and attitudes have been strongly criticised by Webster and others for painting an over-optimistic impression and concealing the true costs of unemployment (Webster 1982). Nor should the apparent political stability of the interwar years be taken to indicate an absence of any political reaction. This came in the longer run and, in particular, in 1945, when the electorate voted emphatically for 'full employment' and increased welfare. The interwar association with mass unemployment became a deep and abiding folk memory which sustained a determination not to return to similar conditions after the Second World War.

## THE CAUSES OF UNEMPLOYMENT

The revival of neo-classical economics since the 1960s has given rise to new views and a new and unresolved debate about the causes of unemployment. In attempting to analyse and define unemployment economists have identified different types which may be attributed to specific causes. Commonly-used categories include seasonal, frictional, technological, structural and cyclical unemployment. Seasonal unemployment is the result of variations in the weather; frictional unemployment arises from labour turnover, that is, people between jobs; technological unemployment is the result of technical change and structural unemployment arises from supply-demand mismatches which may arise for a variety of reasons. If entire industries contract as a result of technical and economic changes the resulting unemployment is defined as 'structural'. Where the economy as a whole experiences a contraction this may give rise to high levels of 'cyclical' unemployment on a temporary basis. As a simplification, it is possible to think of a hard core of structural unemployment, involving on average in the best years approximately 6 per cent of the insured work-force, which persisted throughout most of the interwar period. If we add to this the fairly persistent levels of seasonal and frictional unemployment, which may have amounted to 3 or 4 per cent of the insured work-force, this would explain the interwar minimum unemployment levels of about 10 per cent. Superimposed upon these were varying levels of cyclical unemployment which was most intense in 1921 and during the depression period 1929–33 (Glynn and Oxborrow 1976: 157).

This simplification may assist understanding but it fails to do justice to the complexities of the interwar unemployment problem which can be attributed to a number of causes. More recently unemployment has been defined as 'Keynesian', 'Classical' and 'new microeconomic' (Malinvaud 1977). Again, it can be argued that all types are present and also that there are problems in distinguishing between them.

The classical view of unemployment predominated during the interwar years among professional economists as well as in government and the City of London. Based upon Say's Law, or the idea that supply created its own demand, so that a general deficiency of demand in a free market was essentially a short-run abnormality. Thus the economy tended towards full employment and the existence of involuntary unemployment was attributed to market imperfections. Full employment was normal and coincided with (Walrasian) equilibrium. As a rule the classical view tended to attribute unemployment to 'wage rigidity' – wages were too high (Winch 1969: 50). The persistence of unemployment throughout the interwar years tended to make the classical view untenable, at least as a real world practicality. Most economists recognised the political and social problems which stood in the way of wage reductions and many were in favour of public works to alleviate the problem.

Although the Keynesian view was advanced in the interwar years it failed to win general support until the 1940s (Glynn and Booth 1987). The turning point appears to have come from 1936 when Keynes, after years of frustration on the fringes of politics, set out to convince academic opinion with the publication of the *General Theory of Employment Interest and Money*. The essential feature of the Keynesian explanation of unemployment is in terms of deficient demand and the recognition that the economy could stabilise below full employment level. In a situation of 'Keynesian' unemployment, producers are unable to sell output which it would be profitable to produce at existing wage and price levels. Thus there is a quantity constraint which is imposed by a deficiency of market demand. Reducing wages will not help this situation and may indeed make matters worse by further depressing demand.

The 'new micro-economic' theory was developed more recently by Friedman and other, mainly American, economists. In essence it represents a further development and refinement of the classical view. Friedman's notion of a 'natural rate' of unemployment assumes that there is a given level of unemployment in any economy which is consistent with price stability (or non-accelerating-inflation) (see Chapter 13). The persistence of unemployment is explained in terms of 'search theory' which holds that individuals indulge in voluntary unemployment while endeavouring to maximise future wage income through investing in information seeking and job search. Thus unemployment, in this view, tends to be seen as largely a supply-side and voluntary phenomenon (Bleaney 1976).

The 'Keynesian' view that interwar unemployment was largely the result of deficient demand was widely held for many years after the Second World War. In fact, Keynes himself may have held this view only up to a point. In 1937, for example, he called for restraint, in the belief that the economy was becoming overheated, at a time when unemployment was running at about 10 per cent (Hutchison 1977: 13–14). But in the confident years of the 'Keynesian era' many British economists believed that a permanent cure for mass unemployment had been found (Stewart 1967: 151–70).

However, Booth and Glynn (1975) questioned the simple Keynesian explanation of interwar unemployment arguing that the problem was too complex to yield to a monocausal explanation. In particular they stressed the structural and regional elements emanating from the difficulties of the old staple industries and their slow and inadequate replacement by new industries. Also, they drew attention to the limitations which might have been set against a possible simple 'Keynesian solution' in terms of budgetary and balance of payments constraints. Glynn and Howells sought to highlight and further explore these constraints by attempting an empirical investigation of the feasibility of Keynesian policies during the early 1930s when unemployment was at a peak. They concluded that, because of a range of probable limitations, including low national and regional multiplier effects, that 'the Keynesian solution', even if it had been accepted, could not have solved Britain's unemployment problem in the interwar period. The Keynesian approach was essentially macro-economic and counter-cyclical. The problem was multiple and complex, but essentially structural/regional, rather than cyclical (Glynn and Howells 1980: 44). These and similar views were disputed, in particular by Garside and Hatton who have reasserted Keynesian views (Garside and Hatton 1985: 83–8).

With the revival in neo-classical economics in the 1970s there were a number of new approaches to the interwar unemployment problem. These tended to lay stress on the supply side and the role of real wages. Fundamentally, they are built upon the premiss that since Keynesian policies in the post-1945 period have not only failed to live up to their promise but have proved to be the direct precursor of the deep-rooted economic malaise of stagflation in the 1970s and after, then 'Keynesian-type' programmes urged upon the uninitiated between the wars must at least have been misguided and, at worst, positively harmful (Garside 1990: 367). Thus Benjamin and Kochin have applied search theory to the interwar economy and argued that the major part of unemployment was 'voluntary' and induced by generous unemployment benefits relative to wages (Benjamin and Kochin 1979: 441–78). Few historians accept this view, which contrasts sharply with the historical evidence, and economists also have been critical both of the authors' findings and methodology (*Journal of Political Economy* 1982).

Several other writers have reasserted classical views by stressing the importance of high real wages in creating unemployment. The essential argument is that when prices fell (usually as a result of demand-side changes) this caused real wages to rise and gave rise to heavy unemployment. Broadberry attaches particular importance to the reduction of hours (with wages maintained) in 1919–20 (Broadberry 1990). Beenstock and colleagues have estimated employer demand for labour in manufacturing by constructing an employers' own product real wage series (nominal wages deflated against the price of manufactures) (Beenstock *et al.* 1984; Beenstock 1986). They conclude that the major part of job losses during 1929–32 was due to real wage growth and that much of the growth in employment after 1932 was due to real wages falling back. Capie (1987) has shown that real wages may have had an important influence on the size of the work-force, so that growth in real wages induced more people to seek employment. These views have been criticised by Dimsdale and others but the view persists that wage levels and rigidities were important contributing factors in interwar unemployment. The fact remains that lower wages and costs would not have solved the problems of the old staple industries since there were several other influences including trade barriers and obsolescence. Also, lower real wages would have reduced the level of aggregate consumer demand and thus would have had an adverse influence, not least on the new industries (Dimsdale 1984: 94–103). The essential question appears to be, did employers shed labour because costs were too high or because demand was too low?

In summary, it is possible to see the interwar unemployment problem as resulting from a multiplicity of overlapping causes rather than a monocausal influence in the economy. A basic cause lies in the problems considered in the previous chapter: the difficulties of the old staple industries resulting from loss of markets, particularly overseas, as a consequence of declining competitiveness, trade barriers and changes in technology; the increasing tendency to resort to new technology and the substitution of capital for labour, resulting in fewer workers being required to produce a given output; the failure of the new-growth industries to compensate for the contraction of the old staples as employers of labour and exporters. Thus, the interwar acceleration in growth rates failed to sustain the level of employment. Indeed, manufacturing employment remained below the 1920 level in 1938 and total employment did not exceed the 1920 level of 19.01 million until 1936, although the work-force increased as a result of demographic changes. The economy was also subjected to short periods of severe cyclical unemployment, particularly during 1921 and 1929–33. Certain government policies such as the decision to return to gold may have contributed to unemployment, while others such as rearmament helped to ease the problem. Above all, the government failed to develop both an effective domestic policy and international economic co-operation to deal with unemployment (Glynn 1991). These issues are examined in Chapter 7.

## THE LABOUR MARKET

All markets are social creations and this is especially true where the main item of exchange is human labour. In the early twentieth century the British labour market was conditioned by institutions and traditions which had developed gradually, in some cases over several centuries, and these governed wage levels and differentials, work practices and relationships and employment contracts. Institutional arrangements interacted with short-term economic influences which varied considerably throughout the period. In the interwar years full employment and labour scarcity between 1914 and 1920 was followed by two decades during which chronic unemployment persisted.

It is not surprising that British labour history has been dominated by institutional and social class approaches. The Webbs saw British workers defending their class interests through the institutional development of trade unions and the Labour Party (Webb 1920). The institutional approach has been followed by many other writers and complemented by the 'Oxford School' of Clegg, Fox, Thompson and others who have analysed industrial relations institutions as a system (Clegg *et al.* 1985). More recently labour history has been broadened into working class history, informed quite often by Marxist concepts. Zeitlin has suggested that labour history should involve the study of relationships between workers, trade unions, employers and the state (Zeitlin 1986). In other words, there needs to be more systematic analysis of labour market functions and dynamics as well as comparative studies.

The period 1910–20 is one of remarkable trade union advance and labour militancy. Trade union membership took off from 2.5 million in 1910 rising to a peak of 8.3 million in 1920. Between 1900 and 1910 the industrial labour movement appeared to languish with the trade unions on the rearguard after the employer offensive of the 1890s with the defeat of the engineers in 1897–8, the Taff Vale decision of 1901 and the Osborne Judgment of 1908. Between 1910 and 1914 there was a growth in labour unrest which seems to have been associated with a threat to living standards as the rate of growth in real wages slackened and productivity faltered (Feinstein 1990). Workers turned to trade unions to solve these problems and membership was increasing strongly when war commenced.

The First World War was a major turning point for labour in more ways than one (Wrigley 1987: ch. 1). As a result of the war the British working class gained a new sense of its own importance. The spread of collective bargaining and, in particular, national negotiations accelerated and both union and employer organisation was extended. The Federation of British Industries was established in 1916 and the National Confederation of Employers' Organisations in 1919. Trade unions gained status, membership and potential power, although the latter was not fully exploited. In return for greater recognition, including the entry of unionists to the cabinet, the trade union leaders supported the war effort and renounced the strike weapon. Rank and file discontent continued, reflecting several issues including the dilution of skill, as unskilled and semi-skilled workers replaced skilled; falling real wages and longer working hours; forced changes in work practices; concern over housing conditions and wartime profiteering by employers. Strikes did occur and a strong shop stewards' movement emerged. The war also led to the establishment of joint industrial councils ('Whitley Councils') after the report of the Whitley Committee of the Ministry of Reconstruction. These did not extend as widely as had been hoped but at their peak in 1920 the Whitley Councils covered nearly 4 million workers. After 1921 they declined rapidly and survived in only a few areas. The Whitley Committee also gave rise to the Industrial Court which was established in 1919 and provided an industrial arbitration service.

The war was followed by a frenetic period of union and working class militancy against a background of full employment and rising real wages. In this period, as Wrigley has shown, government rather than employers was often in the forefront of industrial disputes and intervention was frequent (Wrigley 1987: 74–7). In 1919–20 unions achieved sharp reductions in the basic working week while wages were more or less maintained (Dowie 1975). In this period of postwar militancy workers demanded higher wages, greater control at the workplace, the nationalisation of coal and other industries, and a host of social reforms connected with housing, health and employment and, in addition, they exhibited a frightening taste for 'direct action', a distrust of the Parliamentary political process and a marked independence from any formal leadership (Cronin 1984: 20–1). Many men had been radicalised and disillusioned during war service and, as a result of wartime pledges and victory, some were inclined to think in terms of a 'peace dividend'. These feelings appear to have been spontaneous and were not fully orchestrated by trade unions or the Labour Party. With the onset of mass unemployment after 1920 the mood soon evaporated.

During most of the interwar years the British labour market was characterised by excess supply and the trade unions struggled to retain what they had gained during the 1910–20 period. In the two decades after 1920 prices tended to fall, so if money wages could be held, real incomes rose. As a general description, that is what tended to happen, although the fortunes of individual groups differed widely. Trade union methods and policies reflected the changing pattern of economic circumstances, tempered by institutional arrangements. On each side of industry the strongest weapons were used when bargaining power was at its greatest. Disputes in 1919–20 were usually initiated by trade unions, which were mainly successful. With the economic downturn of 1920 the advantage swung to the employers. Most disputes during 1921–2 resulted from employer action and were mainly decided in their favour. The general strike appears to run counter to this trend but it can, of course, be seen as a lock-out of the miners.

Within the union movement the level of economic activity had an important influence on the relationship and distribution of power between national leaders and local rank-and-file influences. The latter tended to weaken during periods of heavy unemployment. With the

*Table 5.6* Union membership and industrial disputes, 1900–38

| | Total membership of trade unions (millions) | Working days lost due to strikes (millions) | Percentage of total days lost which were in coal-mining |
|---|---|---|---|
| 1900–10 | 2.2 | 4.1 | 39 |
| 1912 | 3.4 | 40.9 | 77 |
| 1920 | 8.3 | 26.6 | 66 |
| 1921 | 6.6 | 85.9 | 85 |
| 1922–5 | 5.5 | 11.7 | 16 |
| 1926 | 5.2 | 162.2 | 90 |
| 1927–30 | 4.9 | 3.8 | 16 |
| 1931–8 | 5.0 | 3.6 | 29 |

Where a period is shown in the first column the figures are given for the average of inclusive years.
*Source*: Department of Employment and Productivity 1971: Tables 196, 197.

onset of heavy unemployment after 1920 the militant shop stewards' movement which had emerged during the First World War was gradually eliminated or absorbed into official union structure.

From 1920 the strike was being used less frequently as a union method, surviving as a last resort and being to some degree replaced by national negotiation and arbitration. Between 1910 and 1920 the national strike had been a prominent feature of British industrial relations (Lovell 1977). After 1920 national disputes were almost entirely confined to coal and textiles and strikes became less frequent and increasingly local and unofficial. Collective bargaining had gradually shifted from the local to the national level but there was some reversion after 1920. Both unions and employers appear to have favoured a drift towards nationally negotiated wage and work agreements. From the employers' point of view this had made sense during the militant phase between 1910 and 1920 but it is less clear why they often appear to have favoured a continuation of such policies during the interwar period when this clearly assisted a weakened trade union movement struggling on the defensive during economic adversity. However, by the early 1920s nationally organised employers' associations had been established on a broad front and a national industrial relations system had begun to emerge. National collective bargaining placed more power in the hands of full-time union officials who were generally less militant and more cautious than local leaders (Gospel 1992: ch. 5).

Trade union structure evolved in order to meet a complex range of industrial circumstances and changing economic conditions. There were three types of union: craft, industrial and general. From the late nineteenth century the exclusive craft unions which had dominated the trade union movement gradually gave ground to industrial and general unions which organised the unskilled, but craft unions remained an important influence. As skilled status was threatened by changing technology craft unions opened their ranks to the less skilled. In some industries, notably coal, railways, iron and steel, industrial unions became dominant but the more typical pattern by the 1920s was for organised workers in particular industries to be divided between craft and general unions.

Under the Trade Union (Amalgamation) Act of 1917 it became easier for trade unions to amalgamate. National bargaining and organisation also promoted amalgamation. Between 1917 and 1924 two large amalgamations emerged: the Transport and General Workers Union, Britain's largest trade union, with its main strength in road transport and the docks, and the National Union of General and Municipal Workers which organised public sector and public utility workers. During the early 1920s the Parliamentary Committee of the Trades Union Congress, which had acted as TUC Executive since 1871, was replaced with a

General Council of 30 members which was to act as a co-ordinating and representative body for the trade union movement (Roberts 1958; Lovell and Roberts 1968). However, individual unions retained complete autonomy and there was no attempt or intention to establish central power or direction. The new General Council was given the power to co-ordinate industrial action, to promote common action and to mediate and settle disputes between member unions, but in the final analysis its power and influence depended upon the co-operation of individual member unions. The TUC disappointed left wing hopes for strong leadership and radical action, proving to be a force for moderation and stability in industrial relations. In part this may have been due to the fact that by the time the General Council was established in 1921 the postwar boom was over and the movement had been forced into a defensive position. The political aims of the postwar period had included full employment, public works, minimum wage legislation, nationalisation of coal and other industries and an extension of Whitley Councils. None was realised as the TUC lacked the power and organisation to press its objectives effectively. After 1921, with the continuation of mass unemployment, successive governments found it possible to ignore the attitudes and opinions of trade unions to a much greater extent. In the interwar period trade union militancy and influence was controlled by economic circumstances and the moulding of public opinion rather than by legislation or repression. With the decline of employment in the old heavy industries some of the main areas of union strength were threatened. Meanwhile, the unions had difficulties in organising new groups of workers in the new and expanding industries which were frequently located in areas where trade unionism was less well established. On a gradual basis through the interwar period the General Council asserted itself as the rule-maker and arbitrator of the movement.

## LABOUR ISSUES OF THE 1920s

After the First World War British government had to face rising social class tension when there was serious dissatisfaction, verging on mutiny, in the army, the navy and the police force. After the demobilisation crisis during which there were mutinies and defiance of orders, there was a serious shortage of military manpower to deal with commitments in Ireland, Russia, Germany and the Empire. There were police strikes in August, 1918, and May, 1919, and there was little confidence at cabinet level that workers could be confronted on a general basis on wages and other issues. British intervention against the Russian Bolsheviks gave rise to the *Jolly George* affair in which trade unionists took a political stand in refusing to load supplies destined for Poland. When the Red Army threatened Warsaw in August, 1920, the labour movement threatened a general strike to prevent British intervention. The Russian revolution of 1917 had created ripples throughout Europe. In Britain there was hostility to Bolshevism at government level and working class sympathy from the beginning. During the interwar years Communist Russia was an inspiration to some and a monstrous threat to others. These views divided the labour movement on right-left lines but also enabled its opponents to level accusations of national disloyalty. In 1924 the first Labour Government was smeared with the, probably forged, 'Zinoviev letter' and the right-wing British press invented its longest running feature – the 'Red threat' (Wrigley 1987: 81–82).

By making concessions in 1919, the cabinet exacerbated inflation and the tight labour market but by late 1920 the postwar boom had run its course. The first signs of rising unemployment coincided with new resolve on the part of government and employers. The former had accepted the recommendations of the Cunliffe Committee and resolved on a restoration of the gold standard as soon as possible. In essence, this meant a restoration of Anglo-American price relativities at the prewar level. British prices had to fall relative to American. In turn, this meant resisting wage increases and attempting to drive wages down, which involved supporting employers as far as possible (see Chapter 6).

By 1921 the employers were gaining successes in most negotiations. The employer offensive was aimed at longer working hours, lower money wages and, in some cases, local rather than national bargaining. In 1920–1 as prices fell sharply, money wages were also reduced, often as a result of sliding-scale agreements. Real wages thereafter tended to increase though the increments were on average, very modest, and applied, of course, only to those in employment. With the end of the postwar boom at least 10 per cent of the insured work-force was to be unemployed at any time over the next two decades. Also, overtime was reduced and many workers were forced onto short-time with a consequent loss of earnings. The offensive against wages failed and money wages in general fell less than prices, working hours also tended to remain shorter than before 1918 and national bargaining remained the general rule throughout most of industry. In the 1920s employers failed to take full advantage of the industrial situation. Even where victories were won they were not followed up. In 1921 the engineering companies turned a dispute over the Amalgamated Engineering Union's embargo on overtime into a major confrontation over the 'right to manage' which the unions in the industry were compelled to accept (Wigham 1973). In fact, the engineering employers continued to be divided and, in practice, skilled workers often retained workshop consultation over overtime and other issues (Price 1986: 167). Nevertheless, the interwar years were a time of retreat for skilled workers in many industries as unemployment strengthened the hand of employers and forced dilution and deskilling through the introduction of new technology. As a result of the work of Braverman deskilling has become a major and debatable issue in labour history (Braverman 1974). The suggestion that employers used technology in order to de-skill labour and weaken worker bargaining power has been disputed but interwar Britain may provide more supporting evidence for the hypothesis than any other period. In engineering, for example, the proportion of skilled workers fell from 64 to 43 per cent between 1916 and 1935 (Price 1986: 178).

The 1920s also saw the beginning of new styles of management in Britain, as noted in Chapter 4. Scientific management or 'Taylorism' had become influential in the USA before 1914 and it was inevitable that American success would induce emulation. The search for greater efficiency meant attempts to displace and defeat trade unions and a more rational and speeded-up organisation of production. The scope for new managerial control over work processes depended to a large extent upon a diminution of craft status and larger units of operation in industry. The Bedaux system which was a derivative of Taylorism became available in Britain from 1926. This promised increases in productivity of up to 30 per cent through 'time and motion' studies. By 1929, some 250 companies had taken advantage of the Bedaux company's services giving rise to worker resentment and apprehension and, in some cases, strikes. In essence the Bedaux system, behind its pseudo-scientific jargon, was a simple attempt to speed up work processes and extend managerial influence and control (Price 1986: 181). In fact, Britain failed to establish a distinctive, self-conscious managerial hierarchy on American lines and 'scientific management' made few inroads. In general, craft workers retained an important place in control over work processes, firms remained small and general depression failed to shift the industrial balance of power irrevocably in favour of management. British industrial management remained 'gentlemanly', reliant upon partnership, consultation and persuasion.

## THE GENERAL STRIKE

In 1921 the coal mines, which had been taken into state control during the First World War, were returned to private hands at a critical time when the economic tide had turned. The mine owners faced with higher costs and falling prices immediately demanded drastically lower wages and longer working hours. The miners responded by attempting to revive the Triple Alliance, an agreement dating back to 1914 under which the miners, the railwaymen and transport workers were pledged to assist each other in industrial disputes. In 1919 the threat of a national coal strike, supported by the Triple Alliance, had been sufficient to

produce a victory on pay and hours for the miners and the appointment
of the Coal Industry (Sankey) Commission. This had eventually, on the
chairman's casting vote, come down in favour of coal nationalisation. In
1921 the government felt strong enough to ignore both the miners'
wishes and the Sankey verdict.

On 15 April 1921, (subsequently known as 'Black Friday') the Triple
Alliance failed when other unions withdrew their support from the
miners. The eventual result was a bitter three-month coal strike and a
defeat for the miners on pay and a partial return to local, as opposed to
national, pay agreements. The reasons for the failure of the Triple
Alliance are obscure but owed something to the fear of unemployment
and a threat of state intervention. There was a lack of commitment to the
main issues on the part of other unions and J.H. Thomas, leader of the
railwaymen, had an important role. Above all, there appears to have
been a failure of communication about negotiations, if not an actual
betrayal of the miners. This feeling of betrayal on the part of miners is
a significant prelude to the general strike as well as a factor in the reform
of the TUC General Council. In 1925–6, in the run-up to the General
Strike, sympathy for the miners and a belief that they had been sold out
on 'Black Friday' were important influences (Morris 1976).

During the 1920s the coal industry became the cockpit of British
industrial relations with a high proportion of disputes and total working days lost through disputes. The struggle for control in the coal
industry became symbolic of the clash between labour and capital,
supported by government, and coal was seen by employers and workers in other industries as a test case, especially over wages. Coal was a
major industry and employer with a total work-force of 1.3 million in
1920. Output, despite declining productivity, had continued to expand
up to 1920 when the industry peaked. In the early 1920s falling prices,
competition and loss of markets, especially overseas, produced a changed situation. The miners were well organised and militant with a long
tradition of direct action. Many coal owners also had traditionally
resorted to locking workers out in order to force wage cuts in adverse
times. Miner militancy resulted in part from the nature of their living
and working conditions, although traditions varied from area to area,
and the relative decline of wages during the First World War. By the mid-
1920s the miners were the only substantial work group faced with the
threat that wages would revert to pre-1914 standards. Above all they
demanded nationalisation as a means of securing fairer rewards and
better working conditions. Meanwhile, government had to give particular attention to the coal industry because of its size and strategic importance as well as the peculiar nature of its problems (Renshaw 1975).

In 1924 there was an upturn in the fortunes of British coal largely as a
result of the French occupation of the Ruhr and American coal strikes.

The miners succeeded in changing the 1921 agreement and securing better hours and wage conditions. In 1925 foreign competition revived and the coal companies once again faced a cost–price squeeze. The miners responded to company demands for a return to the 1921 conditions by calling on the TUC for support. There is some dispute as to whether the subsequent industrial action in the industry was a strike or a lock-out.

When the request for support came the TUC General Council may have been, as a result of membership changes, more left-wing than usual. In any event, the miners had a powerful reserve of sympathy dating from 'Black Friday'. With TUC support there was a threat to the movement of coal and government responded on 'Red Friday' (31 July 1925) by offering a temporary nine-month subsidy to the coal industry so that existing wage rates could be maintained. At the same time it announced yet another official enquiry under Sir Herbert Samuel. This was the fourth official enquiry in six years. In the event, like its predecessors, it was destined to be largely ignored by government. When the Samuel Commission reported it favoured eventual nationalisation and made useful suggestions for the reform of the industry. While it argued in favour of wage reductions, these were less drastic than the coal companies had demanded and many shades of opinion, including some trade unionists, saw the Samuel proposals as a possible compromise. In fact, by recommending pay cuts the Samuel enquiry made it easier for government to take a hard line. The miners, meanwhile, stood firm on the slogan of their leader A.J. Cook: 'Not a penny off the pay, not a second on the day'.

The temporary subsidy granted on 'Red Friday' gave government nine months to prepare for the conflict which had been threatened since the early 1920s. While careful and deliberate preparations were made there is no direct evidence that government intended confrontation. Indeed the Prime Minister, Stanley Baldwin, had consistently sought to defuse class conflict. Nevertheless, preparations were in hand and government was well prepared by May, 1926. In September 1920, a miners' strike and the threat of Triple Alliance involvement had induced government to introduce the Emergency Powers Act. Under this Act, the government was empowered to govern by decree if vital supplies were threatened. These powers had been used during the coal dispute of 1921 and were used again during the general strike. Emergency stocks had been accumulated and emergency organisation prepared. The Emergency Committee for Supply and Transport was established and ten Civil Commissioners with wide emergency powers were appointed. With government approval the Organisation for the Maintenance of Supplies had been established to recruit and organise volunteers who were willing to work during a national strike.

Meanwhile the TUC hoped to avoid a General Strike and made no special preparations. At the 1925 Congress right-wing leadership was reasserted and the new General Council was lukewarm in its support for the miners. The pledge to support the miners remained but the TUC hoped they would compromise, perhaps on the basis of the Samuel proposals. At the end of April 1926, the temporary subsidy expired and wage cuts were imposed in the mines. In effect the miners were locked out and the TUC was obliged to honour its pledge of support. On 3 May 1926, it called a sympathy strike which began the following day. Workers in printing, transport, iron and steel, gas, building and electricity were asked to strike and on 11 May workers in engineering and shipbuilding were also called upon. Strictly speaking this was not a general strike, although it involved a million miners and between one and two million others. Despite the weak leadership of the TUC local strike organisation was highly effective and the response to the strike call was high. Local organising committees showed great initiative and enthusiasm, despite the lack of liaison, co-ordination and direction from above.

As a result of the action a large part of normal life and industrial activity was brought to a standstill. However, government measures, on the whole, ensured that essential supplies reached their destinations. There was little actual use of force by government, but the threat of force, especially in breaking the blockade of the London docks, was a factor. It seems possible that the TUC was mistaken in calling out printers and preventing normal newspaper publication although the press was almost entirely hostile. In the propaganda battle the *British Gazette*, a temporary government newspaper run by Winston Churchill, was more successful than the TUC's *British Worker* and the BBC was compelled to bow to government influence. Basically, however, the strike as a threat to essential supplies was broken and the TUC declined to prolong the conflict despite the effectiveness of labour organisation. Had the strike lasted longer than nine days the outcome might have been different. Stocks played a vital role and these would have been exhausted by longer action (Phillips 1976).

During the general strike it appears that the more militant element of the cabinet, who desired a showdown with the trade unions, were able to gain the ascendancy. The TUC found itself in an invidious position: the strike could not be won by normal industrial methods if government refused to negotiate and intervene in the coal industry. Although the unions were repeatedly accused of acting unconstitutionally and challenging a democratically elected government, they had no wish to move beyond an industrial dispute. Rather than seeking to extend the strike the TUC was anxious to contain it and bring matters to a conclusion as soon as possible. After nine days the General Council terminated the strike, without any consultation with the miners, on the basis of a compromise formula put forward on a private initiative by Sir Herbert Samuel. At first it was widely assumed that assurances had been given by government and the Samuel compromise accepted by both sides. Soon it became clear that no assurances had been given and the miners had been left on their own. It was inevitable that there would be accusations of betrayal, not simply from the miners. Most miners continued to strike until the winter of 1926 when they were forced to admit defeat and return to work on the basis of local agreements.

The general strike was a costly defeat and a blow to the morale of the trade unions. Beneath this apparent failure was a victory. The organised working class had shown its solidarity, despite weak leadership, and its determination to fight wage cuts. While the miners and certain other work groups did experience wage cuts and there was victimisation, wages in general appear to have held (Glynn and Shaw 1981). It is wrong to see the general strike as a major turning point in trade union history since most important trends were already underway by 1926 (Clegg 1954). The real turning point appears to be 1920–1 when membership and the number of industrial disputes began to decline. After 1926 the decline continued, perhaps rather more rapidly for a time, and cautious leadership continued to prevail. In 1927 the government sealed its victory by introducing the anti-trade union Trade Disputes and Trade Unions Act which made general sympathy strikes illegal and attacked the legal position of unions in other ways. It also attacked the Labour Party by making it necessary for union members to 'contract-in' to the political levy. Apart from its symbolic importance the Act had little real impact. It is more important to note the new spirit of compromise after the general strike. All the major parties, employers, TUC and government feared a repetition. The TUC had been made aware of the blind alley into which industrial action could lead while government and employers had seen the awesome power of organised labour determined and united. The alternatives to compromise threatened the status quo and were too awful to contemplate.

This new spirit of compromise was epitomised by the symbolism of the Mond-Turner talks of 1928–9. These were named after Ben Turner, President of the TUC, and Sir Alfred Mond, a prominent industrialist, and were talks between the TUC General Council and a group of leading businessmen. The talks followed an employers' invitation, in December 1927, for joint discussions on broad-ranging issues in industrial relations (McDonald and Gospel 1973). They ended in March, 1933, and there were four joint reports on the Gold Standard, union recognition, victimisation and recommendations for the establishment of a joint industrial council, along Whitley lines, on a national basis. Most employers were hostile to the talks and the official employers' associations were not prepared to accept the recommendations. While they came to nothing the Mond–Turner talks indicated that, on both sides of industry, there were some who believed in not only a need to compromise but also to find common interests. Perhaps also they were evidence of the fact that some of the larger employers, at least, were developing an interest in raising productivity and not simply aiming at reducing costs. Between 1929 and 1932 the TUC also held talks which were moderately successful with the FBI and both unions and industry were able to find some common ground in the hearings of the Macmillan Committee.

## LABOUR ISSUES IN THE 1930s

In the severe world downturn of 1929–32 the unions reached their lowest point in terms of bargaining strength and membership and were forced, once again, onto the defensive. In 1931 the second minority Labour Government disintegrated and, in the ensuing general election, the Party suffered a humiliating defeat. Membership reached its nadir in 1933 and then began to recover. Between 1933 and 1939 membership grew by 43 per cent and from the mid-1930s unions, assisted by the rearmament programme, began to secure better pay and working conditions. There were reductions in hours of work and an increasing number of workers secured paid holidays (Bienefeld 1972).

Unlike some of its equivalents elsewhere, the British trade union movement was able to survive the depression more or less intact and, despite an employer offensive, the basic structure of industrial relations, hours and payments systems endured. The TUC consolidated its representative and leadership role. The 1930s witnessed less industrial action and militancy than the 1920s with an annual average of less than 3 million working days lost in strikes. This reflected general depression and unemployment as well as a new spirit of moderation on both sides of industry. Price stability also ensured that there was less need to make wage adjustments. The fall in import prices made real wage increases possible without eroding profits. By the 1930s national collective bargaining had become well established in most industries and national strikes virtually ceased. Both unions and employers came to regard national industrial action as a very cumbersome as well as highly expensive procedure which should be avoided as far as possible. This placed a premium on negotiated settlements. Most strikes which occurred during the 1930s were local and unofficial. With the improvement in economic activity and employment during the second half of the decade there was some increase in strike activity although this was mainly the result of unofficial militancy.

During the 1930s the textile industry which was in severe decline replaced coal as the leading arena for industrial disputes. Employers attempted to respond to the dramatic decline in export markets by cutting wages and increasing hours of work. There were massive lay-offs and forced changes in work practices which caused resentment and disputes which were often promoted by rank and file rather than official trade union action. Employer attempts to force weavers to operate more looms were resisted, more or less successfully and a national employer lockout in 1931 collapsed (Wrigley, 1987: 106). However, this led to a virtual cessation of collective bargaining and the weaving industry moved into an anarchic situation which forced government intervention after a national strike in 1932. This was the last national strike of the interwar period. In 1934 the government introduced the Cotton Manu-facturing (Temporary Provisions) Act which legalised national agree-ments and forced some discipline on the employer side.

During the 1930s the 'responsible moderation' epitomised by Walter Citrine and Ernest Bevin, who became the TUC's most influential fig-ures, came to dominate British trade union attitudes at official levels. The perceived threat from the communist Minority Movement was finally destroyed in 1932 and left-wing elements suffered defeat and were expelled from most sections of the official labour movement. Moderate leadership did not believe in the imminent demise of capitalism and therefore favoured its accommodation. Indeed, they realised that any influence which undermined the existing system would hit workers first and hardest. The way forward lay through negotiation and co-operation at the industrial level while seeking control through increased govern-ment intervention under a democratic regime. Increasingly the TUC sought to be consulted by government on issues affecting members of its affiliated unions. No such right was clearly established but there were frequent consultations by government during the 1930s (Wrigley 1987: 120) and this represented a move towards the post-1945 situation when the TUC did have its say on issues affecting the economy and industrial relations. It could be said that the TUC made a much more successful attempt than the Labour Party to come to terms with economic reality during the 1930s.

The unions also faced continuing problems of attempting to organise in new and growing industries while coping with decline in traditional areas of strength. The changing location of industry meant that new worker groups and working class communities were established. These were often more dispersed and less homogenous than the traditional working-class areas, which had established round the old staple indus-tries. In many areas of the Midlands and the South class consciousness and solidarity were less pronounced and new groups of relatively affluent workers began to emerge. In some new industries there was a relatively high proportion of female, juvenile and unskilled workers, often from a rural and service background, and such groups were notoriously difficult to organise. Above all, the new industries developed in a general context of heavy unemployment and employer hostility to trade unions. The official union leadership failed to launch any concerted effort to organise the new industries and the main effort was left to local and individual initiative. From the later 1930s, however, there was growing success in organising the new industries although the main strength of unions continued to be in the old industrial areas (Charles 1973).

The unions also had to cope with major changes in technology and the pattern of work. In many ways conditions improved as employers gave more attention to welfare issues, fringe benefits and personnel problems. Larger and more progressive employers began to view their workers as human capital and to develop internal labour markets. Specialist personnel management was developed on a widespread basis and represents the most important managerial change of the period. There were improvements in factory hygiene and in canteen and social facilities, especially in larger firms. Also a range of fringe benefits and welfare policies began to emerge with occupational pensions being one of the most significant areas of initiative. On the other hand, increasing mechanisation and speed-up of processes placed workers under more strain. During the 1930s the number of work accidents tended to increase rapidly and this reflected the changing pattern of work as well as better reporting.

These new patterns did not, on the whole, reflect fundamental changes in managerial systems. As noted in Chapter 4, in 1939 British industry was left with an outmoded industrial structure on the one hand with, on the other, a greatly augmented and well established trade union movement. In the meantime the bitter struggles of the period together with the scourge of mass unemployment had left scarred memories. The main hope for stability lay in the firm establishment of a moderate and responsible trade union movement which was determined to work within the system. The main danger was that the system had become, in international terms, inefficient and inadequate to meet the needs and aspirations of its participants.

# Chapter 6

# Britain and the international economy

## THE INTERNATIONAL SYSTEM BEFORE 1914

Britain had been a major trading nation and an important exporter of manufactured goods long before the Industrial Revolution. Industrialisation built upon early success in trade and shipping and by 1870 Britain dominated world manufactured trade to an extent not seen before or since. By the late nineteenth century 25–30 per cent of British national income was traded in the form of imports and exports; foreign trade played an important role in the economy. There was an increasing dependence on imported food and raw materials and a corresponding need to pay for a growing volume of imports through the export of goods and services.

In these circumstances Britain had an apparent vested interest in removing barriers to trade and in ensuring an efficient and smoothly functioning system of international financial settlements. Free trade and the international gold standard were the methods chosen to promote these interests. During the nineteenth century world trade grew very rapidly, expanding faster than 25 per cent in every decade after 1830 (Kuznets 1966: 306). Expansion was facilitated by a comparative absence of barriers to the free movement of goods, capital and people. In retrospect, the decades before 1914 have come to be viewed as a remarkable period of economic freedom. Factors of production, labour and capital flowed to where they were most productive and countries specialised in producing those goods and services that they were most efficient in producing, in line with the theory of comparative advantage. In theory the system promoted efficiency and optimised world income. In practice things were less simple. Markets were not perfect and economic liberalism produced winners and losers. Countries and governments became less willing to accept the pattern of economic life which international market circumstances dictated. Governments increasingly sought to protect and promote development through tariffs and other barriers to trade and there was less willingness to accept the painful adjustments

which the international system occasionally demanded. These impedi-
ments to the free flow of goods and factors of production increased and
the liberal system was finally shattered by the First World War
(Kenwood and Lougheed 1971).

The gold standard became broadly established on an international
basis during the late nineteenth century. In theory, at least, it provided
an automatic mechanism for international adjustments free from government control. In practice its adoption implied the acceptance of certain
rules and its operations involved intervention by central banks. In effect,
adherence to the gold standard denied to policy-makers many forms of
intervention which have become commonplace since 1914. Also, it
implied that international and external economic considerations took
precedence over domestic concerns (Foreman-Peck 1983: ch. 6).

There were two basic rules of the gold standard. First, currencies were
fixed at official values in terms of a given quantity of gold. Second,
countries agreed to allow the free movement of gold in unlimited
quantities. The level of world gold reserves was, of course, determined
randomly by the market for gold, the geological occurrence and discovery of gold and mining technology. The almost universal acceptance of
gold meant that it could become the basis of the world monetary system.
In individual countries gold reserves were determined in part by historical accident but increasingly through trade performance. In theory,
central banks linked interest rates, and thus the level of economic
activity, to gold reserves, raising rates when reserves fell and vice versa
(Eichengreen 1985: chs 3–8).

Adherence to these rules meant that economies made, in theory, more
or less automatic adjustments without a need for government intervention. For example, a nation experiencing a persistent balance-of-
payments deficit on current account would find that its actual exchange
rate would fall below official values as demand for its currency fell. As a
result, individuals would find it worthwhile to sell its currency for gold
at the official rate of exchange. Thus a speculator could make a profit by
purchasing the currency at the market rate, exchanging this for gold at
the official rate, and then converting back to his original currency. The
result would be an outflow of gold and this would have deflationary
effects on the national economy, not least because the central bank
would react to falling reserves by raising interest rates. The resulting
fall in prices would reduce imports (as their relative price increased for
domestic consumers) and increase exports (as foreigners found them
cheaper). The eventual result of these changes would be to eliminate
the current account deficit, thus providing automatic adjustment, not
just for the exchange rate but also for the balance of payments. A country
experiencing a persistent balance-of-payments surplus would find that
gold flowed in and that this had a reflationary effect. As prices rose

exports would fall and imports would rise so that the payments surplus would eventually be eliminated. This, in very simple theory, is how the gold standard is supposed to have operated. In practice, things were much less simple and automatic than the theory implies. There were many complicating factors including, for example, capital flows, the activities of central banks and governments. In practice also, the adjustments could be painful where, for example, they took the form of widespread unemployment and bankruptcies. The eventual failure of the gold standard resulted from an unwillingness on the part of individual member countries to make and accept adjustments. The operation of the gold standard has attracted considerable and continuing scholarly interest which has been 'additive and revisionist' (Drummond 1987). Research and discussion seems set to continue and serves to create a growing impression that the system was less simple, both in theory and practice, than previously supposed.

Before 1914 the gold standard was accepted, largely without question. Although the system appears to have worked quite well for Britain, other countries had to make painful adjustments. This applied especially to small primary-producing economies on the periphery of the system (Ford 1962). It should also be said that the apparent success of the gold standard system depended very much on the special position which Britain had assumed in the international economy (Eichengreen 1985: 141). In particular, the system depended upon the special circumstances relating to Britain's balance of payments.

The balance of payments is a formal statement, in simple accounting terms, of a country's overseas transactions in so far as they involve payments of foreign currencies or gold. Like any balance sheet there is a credit and debit side. The balance of payments is normally divided into three parts:

1 **The balance of trade** – which relates to 'visible' imports and exports. In other words, actual goods exported and goods imported.
2 **The balance of payments on current account** – this includes the balance of trade, that is imports and exports of goods, plus 'invisible' trade (the import and export of services), plus interest and dividends on overseas investment.
3 **The basic balance of payments** – this includes the sum of (1) and (2) above plus capital movements and balancing items so that the figure on the debit side is always equal to the figure on the credit side. This item includes the total acquisition and disposal of foreign currencies plus gold, with official reserves or liabilities as a balancing item.

Between the mid-nineteenth century and 1914 Britain's annual balance of trade was almost always in deficit. In other words, the value of goods exported failed to match the value of goods imported. This reflected

Britain's growing dependence on imported food and raw materials and the sacrifice of British agriculture in favour of free trade. The persistent deficit in visible trade was overcome by a healthy surplus on invisibles, mainly on shipping, financial services such as insurance, and interest and dividends on overseas investment. As a result, Britain had a very strong balance of payments on current account. Since one country's surplus must imply another's deficit, Britain's immensely strong balance of payments might have created serious international adjustment problems. But Britain recycled its current surplus in heavy overseas investment (a deficit on capital account), which rose strongly to a peak in 1914. Between 1870 and 1914 a third of British savings were invested abroad, mainly in the regions of recent European settlement. In this period, overseas investment averaged 5.2 per cent of GNP per annum and between 1907 and 1914 Britain made more new investment abroad than at home (Kennedy 1973–4). Thus international liquidity was maintained by Britain's free trade policy, which enabled overseas producers, particularily of primary products, to earn sterling, and heavy overseas lending which offset the current account surplus (Edelstein 1982).

The current account surplus made sterling a very strong currency and other countries often held their reserves in sterling which was regarded as being 'as good as gold'. Monetary management by the Bank of England was a comparatively simple matter. If sterling came under temporary pressure the underlying strength of the current account could easily be mobilised through higher interest rates, which had the effect of reducing overseas investment. When the crisis passed interest rates could be lowered and overseas lending resumed. This, in turn, reduced liquidity problems elsewhere. It may be said, therefore, that the late nineteenth-century gold standard system was really a 'sterling standard' which depended for its apparent stability and success on the special features and strengths of Britain's balance of payments and British financial leadership (Cottrell 1975). As we shall see, after 1914, in changed circumstances, the system failed to operate in the old way.

## BRITAIN'S INTERNATIONAL POSITION AFTER THE FIRST WORLD WAR

The First World War brought about a profound change in Britain's international position. In part this was because some adverse long-run changes, already underway, were accelerated and the war itself brought new problems. The net result of these changes was a weakening of the balance of payments so that Britain could no longer continue the kind of world financial and economic leadership which it had asserted before 1914.

About 10 per cent of overseas investment was sold during the war and

Britain became heavily indebted to the USA. On paper this was offset by new British lending to wartime allies, but the American debt was seen as a serious problem during the interwar period. After the war British visible exports in volume terms were reduced by about 10 per cent of the prewar level and imports were approximately 10 per cent higher. This reflected a decline in British competitiveness and an all-round weakening in the balance of payments (Cairncross and Eichengreen 1983). Wartime disruption had promoted import replacement and the erection of trade barriers in traditional markets as well as the advance of some competing exporters, notably the USA and Japan. Heavy industrial output had tended to expand in all the belligerent economies to levels which could not be justified by peacetime demands adversely affecting some of the old staple industries. As a result of the war the USA emerged as the world's leading economic and financial power and the leading creditor. However, America failed to assume Britain's pivotal pre-1914 role and the world monetary system faltered during the 1920s and finally broke down during the crisis of 1929–33. The strong growth in world trade which had been evident in the decades before 1914 came to an end. Between 1920 and 1929 trade grew only by eight per cent before falling steeply after 1929. By 1939 it had barely recovered to the 1929 level. Thus the interwar period can be seen as a time of relative stagnation in world trade and a period of payments crisis and instability (Kindleberger 1973).

On the surface at least the available statistics do not suggest that Britain's balance of payments weakness during the interwar years was chronic. However, the available figures are not very accurate; there is a margin of error of 10 per cent for mechandise trade and 15 per cent for the other main items (shipping, government services and transfers, property income) (Feinstein 1972a: 114). Annual imports of merchandise in these years ranged from £600 million to £1.2 billion and 10 per cent of these figures is a substantial amount. Balance-of-payments estimates include substantial 'balancing items' which are included to cover errors and omissions in the estimates. During 1930–8 the cumulative 'balancing item' totals £784 million, which is twice the estimated cumulative current account deficit for that period (Aldcroft 1970: 216).

On the basis of the available statistics the current account remained in surplus throughout the 1920s and averaged £114 million. This was lower, in real terms, than the average annual pre-1914 current account surplus: also, there was a declining trend in the later 1920s. Nevertheless, these statistics do not suggest dramatic balance of payments deterioration. In the 1930s the current account did run into deficits which averaged £40 million during 1930–8. There were deficits in all years during the 1930s apart from 1930 and 1935. Apart from 1931 these were small deficits well within the margins of error mentioned above. In the 1920s Britain re-emerged as a major overseas lender, although not on the pre-1914 scale, with average net annual capital exports of £116 million. In the 1930s there was a small net capital inflow. On the basis of these figures it cannot be said that Britain had a chronic balance-of-payments weakness, yet concern over the external account became a major influence on economic policy and Britain clearly lost its predominant position in the international economy. There were also questions of confidence and concerns relating to short term capital movements.

During the First World War Britain had ceased to be a net lender of short-term capital (Morgan 1953: 343). In the 1920s the authorities became concerned about a dangerous build-up of short-term debts in London. Although it is not precisely clear how these arose there was a belief that by resuming heavy overseas lending in the 1920s Britain had, in effect, created long-term credits through the creation of short-term liabilities. In fact, the lending of the 1920s should have been more or less covered by current account surpluses. There is no doubt that heavy short-term liabilities were created and these were underestimated by the Macmillan Committee of 1931 (Williams 1963). When confidence in Britain's ability to maintain the fixed rate of exchange for sterling against gold was undermined in 1931 the withdrawal of these funds was the central feature of the financial crisis.

The Cunliffe Committee, which mainly reflected financial interests, was appointed to consider postwar financial policy and, in its interim report in August 1918, recommended a return to the gold standard as soon as possible after the war (Cd.9182: 1918). This recommendation was adopted by the Cabinet and became official policy in 1919. The decision provided the basis for British economic policy during the 1920s and there is a full discussion of this policy, and its implications for domestic affairs in Chapter 7. In simple terms, the aim was to restore the pre-1914 world financial and economic order. In Pollard's view, 'It was essentially a bankers' policy, not directly concerned with industry at all, but as it happened it required constant and sustained restriction and deflation from its inception, and therefore did grave harm to industrial capital, output and employment' (Pollard 1970: 2). While there were some minor impositions of protection during and after the war, Britain also continued its policy of free trade.

Although, on the available evidence, Britain did not have a chronic balance of payment weakness in the interwar years, there was also severe unemployment and in a fully employed economy the balance of payments situation might have been quite different. It could be said that in the 1920s the unemployed paid the price of Britain's ability to re-emerge as a major overseas lender as part of the attempt to restore the pre-1914 system.

It has been argued that sterling was overvalued during the period of currency management between 1920 and the return to gold in 1925, at least against the US dollar (Morgan 1953; Broadberry 1990: 271–82). However, this appears not to have had much impact and the latter currency was, in any event, undervalued. After 1925, when Britain returned to the gold standard, there is general agreement that there was serious overvaluation and Keynes's original estimate of a 10 per cent overvaluation against the US dollar has been supported by more recent research. Redmond (1984: 530) has estimated that the pound may have been overvalued by as much as 25 per cent.

During the 1920s international problems arose from the complex network of inter-allied war debts and the attempt by the victorious allies to extract large sums as reparations from the defeated powers and, in particular, Germany. Debt and reparations problems were a destabilising influence on the international economy during the 1920s and a contributor to the breakdown of 1929. In the event, most of the debts and reparations were never paid and there was widespread repudiation during the early 1930s (Aldcroft 1978: ch. 4).

The sums involved were enormous. Inter-allied war debts totalled $26.5 billion, mainly owing to the USA and Britain, and the initial claim for reparations against Germany amounted to $33.0 billion. These were scaled down during the endless negotiations of the 1920s. The pressures on Germany together with action by the German authorities gave rise to hyperinflation and financial collapse in 1922–3 and in January 1923, France and Belgium occupied the Ruhr. These developments gave rise to a new approach to reparations in the form of the Dawes Plan of 1924. Annual payments were reduced and a more stable Germany was able to import capital which was used in part to pay reparations. However, when US lending to Germany ceased in 1929 this marked the beginning of the world financial crisis. Reparations were ended in 1931 under the Lausanne Agreement (Sayers 1976).

Inter-allied war debts had arisen in dealing with a common enemy in a war in which the major creditor, the USA, had become a combatant at a very late stage. The European allies took the view that war debts should be cancelled but the USA insisted on payment. Britain owed the USA $4.7 billion but had loaned $11.1 billion to other countries and, on paper at least, had emerged from the war a net creditor. Most of these debts were not repaid. There was a long series of negotiations during the 1920s when it became clear that the Europeans, with the exception of Britain, could not meet their obligations. The USA was obliged to make some concessions but the problem lingered on, solved only in part by a payments triangle involving American lending to Germany, German payment of reparations to former allies of the USA and repayment by them, in turn, of war debt to the USA. This system worked for a few years during the late 1920s but collapsed in 1929 (Field 1984). Debt and reparations problems in the 1920s were a diversionary and divisive influence which damaged the international payments system and prevented more fundamental international issues from gaining attention and being tackled in a co-operative manner.

## BRITAIN AND THE WORLD CRISIS 1929–33

The world financial and economic crisis commencing in 1929 is a major turning point in world economic history. Despite this there is no generally accepted explanation of the causes of the downturn. Cyclical downturns were not new in the British economy but the crisis of 1929–33 was on a world scale and it has never been equalled in terms of severity. During the crisis the value of world trade fell by 65 per cent and recovery was hardly complete by the end of the 1930s (Kindleberger 1973).

The downturn of 1929 appears to have been precipitated by a cessation of American overseas lending in 1928 following the sharp rise in stock prices on Wall Street. This caused problems for debtor nations and many were forced to cut imports and to adopt deflationary policies. In October 1929, the American stock market crashed, the US economy turned sharply downwards, and further pressures were placed on debtor nations. Primary product prices, which had been weakening since the mid-1920s, fell sharply, and this compounded the crisis. Primary producers faced massive reductions in export earnings and crippling debt repayment charges. This led to abandonment of the gold standard and currency devaluations. In 1930 there were some modest signs of possible recovery in the US economy but American economic policy had the effect of turning crisis into disaster (Eichengreen and Portes 1989: 599–640). The US Treasury insisted that loans should be repaid. In June 1930, President Hoover accepted the Hawley–Smoot Tariff which imposed sharp increases in duties despite the US trade surplus. Widespread retaliation followed and there was a sharp contraction in international trade. Worst affected were the primary producers in Latin America, southern and eastern Europe and Australasia. In turn, falling demand for exports produced massive unemployment in the industrial countries. Widespread defaults on debt followed (Lewis 1949).

In Europe the crisis helped to bring the Nazis to power in Germany in 1933 and there was widespread financial crisis. In May, 1931, the Credit Anstalt in Austria collapsed and this was followed by financial panic throughout Eastern Europe. This appears to have precipitated the British financial crisis of 1931.

In attempting to explain the 'great' depression of the 1930s economists and historians have put forward different views. Samuelson and others have seen the crisis as an unfortunate coincidence of adverse circumstances: the financial and industrial crises in America, the international debt problem and the slowing down in world demand for primary products. Keynesian economists such as Galbraith (1961) have emphasised the failure of demand in the US economy while leading monetarists have blamed the American authorities for failing to expand money supply, placing the main burden of adjustment on other countries (Friedman and Schwartz 1963: 361). Others have drawn attention to the collapse in the terms of trade for and overproduction of primary products (Svennilson 1954). According to Lewis the crisis might have been short-lived had it not been for the problems faced by primary producers (Lewis 1949). The other factor which has been highlighted is the failure of international economic co-operation (Kindleberger 1973: ch. 14). In effect, the US had replaced Britain as the world's leading financial and commercial power. However, the US failed to fulfil the role previously played by Britain; the suspension of US overseas lending, the accumulation of gold in the US reserves and the Hawley–Smoot tariff all exacerbated the international crisis. In 1933 the world economic conference in London was effectively sabotaged by President Roosevelt who refused to stabilise the $US and adopted devaluation and isolationist economic policies.

Britain also made its contribution to the world crisis when sterling began to come under serious pressure in 1931. The current account of the balance of payments peaked at £124 million in 1928, deteriorating to a deficit of over £100 million in 1931 (Tomlinson 1990: 74). This balance-of-payments weakness exposed London's reliance on short-term funds and the inadequacy of Bank of England reserves in the face of a possible run on sterling. The Macmillan Committee which reported in 1931 denied that Britain had financed its long-term overseas lending by borrowing on a short-term basis (Cmd.3897: 1930–1). However, by the time the Committee reported a major sterling crisis was underway.

The 1931 financial crisis, which became a political crisis, arose when short-term funds held in London began to be withdrawn on a substantial basis. Many primary producing countries had already been forced off the gold standard and the financial crisis in Austria and central Europe (Williams 1963) further reduced confidence and tied up some British assets. The minority Labour government had encountered a budgetary deficit as revenues fell and the costs of unemployment relief mounted. Expert opinion held that financial confidence must be restored by balancing the budget, not by raising taxes but through cuts in expenditure. There were alternative strategies including devaluation, but this does not appear to have been seriously considered or properly understood. Keynes had advocated a 'revenue tariff' but this was not accepted and only served to annoy fellow economists (Peden 1991: 90). He later proposed a devaluation of at least 25 per cent. (Howson and Winch 1977: 88–91).

The crisis became political because the parliamentary opposition demanded cuts in public expenditure and did everything possible to undermine the government. Snowden the Labour Chancellor, who was known for his orthodox approach to economic policy, was unable to secure cabinet agreement for the cuts he proposed. During the crisis the May Committee published its report. This had the effect of undermining confidence still further. The May Committee recommended that unemployment benefit should be reduced by 20 per cent, that public-sector pay should be cut, and painted a gloomy picture of public-sector finance (Peden 1991: 91). During the crisis the Bank of England struggled to keep Britain on the gold standard by borrowing from banks in Paris and New York and by raising interest rates. Foreign bankers insisted that the recommendations of the May Committee should be implemented. A majority of the Cabinet as well as the TUC were opposed to cuts in unemployment benefit at a time when rentier incomes were increasing in real terms. MacDonald, the Labour prime minister, resigned on 24 August 1931, and then proceeded to form a 'national' government which excluded the Labour party (Skidelsky 1967). Despite further loans and cuts imposed by the National government, Britain was forced to leave the gold standard less than one month later. The many gloomy predictions which had been made about a departure from gold proved to be wrong. The effects of the departure from gold were immediately beneficial. Devaluation helped to improve the balance of payments and the pressure was removed from interest rates. Funds once again flowed back into London and the economy turned the corner of recovery (Pollard 1970).

In retrospect it seems possible that the crisis might have been avoided by adopting alternative policies and it was probably not justified by Britain's underlying balance-of-payments situation. The loans which were raised were rapidly repaid and the economy moved into a strong economic recovery. However, the departure from gold by Britain was far from being costless. In leaving gold Britain made its contribution to the general breakdown in international trade and finance which followed in the 1930s. The costs of this on a world basis were enormous (Drummond 1981; Howson 1980b: 2). Britain's recovery in the 1930s was based largely on the domestic economy while the export sector diminished and continued to languish (Arndt 1944).

## BRITAIN'S INTERNATIONAL POSITION DURING THE 1930s

The 1930s is an exceptional period in modern British history in the sense that British economic policy came to be dominated by internal rather than external considerations. The National government which succeeded Labour in 1931 combined orthodoxy with innovation and there were important changes in Britain's external economic relationships.

After departing from the gold standard in 1931 sterling became a floating currency and remained so until the Second World War when it was again pegged at $4.03 to the pound sterling. The float during the 1930s was not a free float. In 1932 the Exchange Equalisation Account (EEA) was established and this marks the transfer of control over the exchange rate from the Bank of England to the Treasury (Howson 1980a). The aim of the EEA was to control and prevent excessive fluctuations in the value of sterling by buying or selling sterling as the need arose. At certain times also there were attempts to push or keep sterling below its market level in order to assist the export industries. It is not clear how successful these attempts were since the effects of the EEA cannot be clearly distinguished from market influences. There have been various attempts to measure 'real exchange rates' (Redmond 1980; Broadberry 1980; Dimsdale 1981) and, while these differ in both methods and results, it is agreed that the real exchange rate fell sharply in 1931–2 after the departure from gold, and remained below the 1929 level throughout the 1930s. It was hoped that this would assist export industries by making exports cheaper. The authorities may also have hoped to stimulate a rise in prices in the domestic economy as a means of enhancing profits (Booth 1987a; 1989: 28). In the 1920s interest rates were kept high in order to meet an exchange rate target. After 1931 this policy was reversed. The primary aim was to maintain 'cheap money' internally and the exchange rate was managed with this in mind. During much of the 1930s capital flowed into London and the authorities sold sterling and accumulated reserves in attempting to hold sterling below market levels (Howson 1980b).

The departure from gold led to the emergence of what became known as the 'sterling area'. This was a group of countries who maintained a substantial part of their reserves in sterling, either because they were British colonies or had important links with Britain. This included most of the empire and Scandinavia as well as Japan and Argentina. The sterling area was seen by Britain as a means to international stability and an enhancement for sterling (Drummond 1987b). The arrangement worked well in the 1930s but the 'sterling balances' provided an excuse for monetary and fiscal conservatism and in the long-run there were serious problems for Britain. Despite the sterling area Britain was no longer able to dominate and lead the international monetary system. Meanwhile the USA focused its attention on domestic problems and failed to assume Britain's former role (Kindleberger 1973).

In 1931 Britain also made a fundamental change in trade policy by ending free trade and turning to protection and empire preferences. The return to protection had important internal as well as external aspects. In the discussion which follows we focus on the latter and the domestic aspects of protection are examined in Chapter 7. Free trade had been a basic item of British policy since the middle of the nineteenth century and Britain continued to adhere to free trade long after most other nations had adopted protection. Towards the end of the nineteenth century much of the Conservative Party had been converted to protection but in seeking a mandate for tariffs they had been rejected by the electorate in 1906 and again in 1923. Many people feared that protection would mean a higher cost of living and, in particular, higher food prices. The Liberal Party remained firmly devoted to free trade and this stance was also adopted by the Labour Party (Capie 1980).

While some new tariffs were introduced during the First World War and more in the early 1920s to protect new industries, Britain remained overwhelmingly free trade until 1931 with over 80 per cent of imports free of duty. The National government in its election manifesto in 1931 stated that it would 'give attention' to the question of tariffs, commercial treaties and mutual economic arrangements with the Dominions. This did not represent a clear mandate for protection, but the government did nothing to dispel the belief in the business community that protection was on the way. Business in general was now heavily in favour of protection (Garside 1990: ch. 6). The election was followed by a flood of imports as traders sought to beat the tariff. Thus the belief became a self-fulfilling one. The government seized the opportunity to introduce tariffs to prevent the flood of imports. The Abnormal Importations and the Horticultural Products Acts were rushed through Parliament and emergency duties were imposed on non-empire produce. The Import Duties Act of 1932 followed. It imposed a 10 per cent *ad valorem* tariff on most goods apart from food, raw materials and certain Empire products (Capie 1983: ch. 3). Trade with the British Dominions (the self-governing parts of the Empire including Australia, New Zealand, Canada, South Africa and Eire) was to be dealt with at the Ottawa Conference in July, 1932. It was also made clear that negotiations with other countries would follow (Drummond 1972: 92).

It is possible also that some members of the government saw protection as a means of preventing further depreciation of the exchange rate and stabilising prices (Eichengreen 1981). During the 1930s many countries turned to bilateral bargaining. As a major importer Britain had considerable bargaining potential which could only be utilised if free trade came to an end.

The aim of the so-called Imperial visionaries of the 1920s to create a self-sufficient empire on a free trade basis failed to be realised in the 1930s (Drummond 1972; 1974). Different parts of the empire were at widely differing stages of development and most empire countries, including Britain, had important non-imperial markets. Also, Britain wished to assist and protect its agriculture while the Dominions had embarked upon policies designed to promote the development of their manufacturing industries. As a result the Ottawa Conference was not a great success. The Dominions were unwilling to allow unrestricted access to British manufacturers and Britain was unwilling to grant Dominion primary products unrestricted and privileged access into the home market at the expense of cheaper foreign suppliers and British farmers. Ottawa took the form of a series of bi-lateral agreements between Britain and particular Dominions with specific agreements on specific items. In general, preferences were established by imposing new and higher duties or quotas on non-empire products, rather than through tariff reductions. Thus the effect of Ottawa was to increase world levels of protection and the agreement has to be seen as an important escalation of protectionism which non-empire countries, in particular the USA, bitterly resented. The effects on British industry and agriculture are considered in Chapter 4.

During the 1930s there was also a series of bilateral agreements with non-empire producers in which Britain attempted to make use of the enhanced bargaining power which had resulted from protection. Between 1932 and 1935 there were fifteen commercial agreements between Britain and other non-empire countries. These were mainly with small, primary producers such as Denmark and the scope and impact of the resulting treaties was limited (Rooth 1984; 1986).

The economic effects of protection are difficult to assess, not least because it is difficult to disentangle tariff effects from other influences such as the level of the exchange rate and extent of retaliation by other countries. We simply do not know what the pattern of trade would have been in the absence of protection. If the tariff did help to improve Britain's trade position this may have been at least partially offset by higher exchange rates for sterling resulting from protection (Broadberry 1986: 136).

## CONCLUSIONS

During the interwar period the liberal international economic order which had flourished before the First World War came to an end. The expansion in world trade which had been characteristic of previous decades gave way to a sharp contraction and trade became a source of stagnation rather than growth. Barriers to trade and interventions in the international order increased and became endemic with the onset of international crisis from 1929. Britain participated in this process with the return to protection and the departure from the gold standard in 1931. Britain as the former pivot of the international system and a highly open and trade-orientated economy had much to lose from these developments. In the event, there was compensation from a resilient domestic economy which, to some extent, provided a counter to adverse influences on external account.

# Chapter 7

# Economic policy

## THE DEVELOPMENT OF POLICY

Economic policy can be defined as the ability and willingness of government to influence the economy and the motivations and intentions in so doing. During the later nineteenth century a policy, usually known as *laissez-faire*, evolved in Britain. Government largely confined itself to basic functions including defence and the maintenance of law and order. The economy was left very largely to its own devices and operated through market mechanisms within an established legal and institutional framework which included the gold standard, rules of conduct for the financial sector and the regulation of monopolies. The interwar period can be seen as a transition period for economic policy during which there was a movement away from *laissez-faire* towards increased levels and more detailed government interventions (Tomlinson 1990: ch. 2). These moves were promoted by the emergence of hitherto neglected interest groups, greater demands on government and growing complexities in both internal and external economic relationships. By the mid-twentieth century government sought to influence not only the level of economic activity but also the structure and development of the economy. This escalation of intervention was not smooth. In the 1920s there was an attempt to revert to the pre-1914 system. Major events including wars and severe depression were important influences, as were changes in economic theory, but the creation of universal suffrage and the emergence of modern democratic politics were more fundamental in placing new demands on government. As a result of social and political changes, governments were obliged to find new ways of attempting to cope with rising expectations. In the 1970s with the emergence of inflation and related problems a reaction against government intervention gathered momentum and in the 1980s Margaret Thatcher presided over an attempt to establish free market policies which, in theory at least, had something in common with nineteenth-century *laissez-faire* (Skidelsky 1988). Thus in the 1980s some commentators were able to suggest that

British economic policy had come full circle over a hundred-year period. As we will see, the reality was rather more complex than these observations suggested.

The two institutions which became largely responsible for the imposition of economic policy were the Treasury and the Bank of England. Before 1914 the Treasury had been mainly concerned with running the civil service and supervising the public accounts. The Bank remained a private institution but over a long period it had assumed responsibility for the control of government debt as well as regulation of the banking system and the gold standard. During the 1920s under the governorship of the eccentric Montagu Norman the Bank was particularly influential, in part because of concern with debt and exchange rate problems (Sayers 1976). In the 1930s the Treasury became relatively more important (Strange 1971). Of course, policy was not the sole monopoly of the Bank and the Treasury. Other ministries and pressure groups, including employers' associations and the TUC, had some influence, although this appears to have been very limited at least in relation to macro-economic policy, as is evident in the comparative failure of the Economic Advisory Council, created by Ramsay MacDonald in 1930 as a counterweight to the Treasury. The Council comprised representatives from industry, the trade unions and academic economists but the inevitable disagreement between such a wide range of interests weakened its impact (Howson and Winch 1977). Nominally, at least, politicians and civil servants were in charge of the policy regime but their main function appears to have been in eliminating radical alternatives.

## ECONOMIC POLICY AND THE FIRST WORLD WAR

The war undoubtedly brought a fundamental change in the government's relationship with the economy. Before 1914 there had been a trend towards more intervention and new assumptions of responsibility, but on a very limited scale (Tomlinson 1990: ch. 3; Winch 1969: chs 1–3). The Liberal government entered the war while denying a management role. But it proved impossible to fight a large-scale, continental war on the basis of 'business as usual'. The sudden mobilisation and deployment of a million men by the end of 1914 caused severe dislocation and attempts to secure many wartime supplies on the open market gave rise to severe shortages, price increases, and discontent. After the 'great shell scandal' of early 1915 a Ministry of Munitions was created under David Lloyd George whose determination to pursue the war with vigour helped to make him Prime Minister in 1916 (Peden 1991: 36). In the early years of the war markets were 'cleared' by rising prices and, in the face of widespread scarcities of supply, government found an alternative in the extension of controls over a wide area of the economy. By 1918 government had direct or indirect control over all industries of significance as well as shipping, agriculture, water and railways. There were controls over the production, transportation and distribution of food and other essential supplies. Imports were also controlled. By 1918 most aspects of production were subject to important government influence and controls and the state had become a major producer and employer in its own right. However, the economy was controlled rather than managed in the modern sense and, in retrospect, there were severe shortcomings in wartime policy. There were weaknesses in labour controls and monetary policy allowed inflation and created a postwar legacy of massive public indebtedness. Both of these were important factors in British economic weakness during the interwar period.

Although there were sharp increases in taxation much of the cost of the war was met through increased borrowing. Externally there was a dramatic growth in borrowing from the USA. While this was technically more than offset by new lending to allies, international war debts were a continuing problem during the 1920s (see Chapter 6). Internally, the government relied upon printing paper money and borrowing through the banking system rather than from the general public. Under the so-called 'McKenna rule' taxation was intended to cover only the usual peacetime government outgoings plus the extra demands arising from the need to service war debts. Both the prewar revenue base and the savings of the general public were inadequate to finance wartime expenditure. The resulting increase in the money supply in a situation of general scarcity was inevitably inflationary (Peden 1991: 40–1). In 1917–18 there was increased reliance on short-term Treasury Bills and medium-term bonds which were absorbed, again, by the banks. When these matured after the war there was renewed inflation. By 1920 prices were 150 per cent above 1914 levels. This was phenomenal inflation by pre-1914 standards and there was general agreement, in official circles, that this, together with the associated debt legacy, had been extremely damaging to Britain's international standing. The determination to avoid further inflation was an important feature of economic policy during the 1920s (Morgan 1953).

As noted in Chapter 5, labour established a new-found importance during the First World War. Wartime shortages of manpower in the armed forces and industry and conditions of full employment gave labour much enhanced bargaining power. While this was not fully utilised during wartime, real hourly wage rates, if not weekly earnings, actually fell, the institutional and political impact was undeniable. Trade unions and the Labour party achieved new power and recognition. Despite the privations of those in the factories and trenches, morale was more or less maintained through a combination of promises and propaganda. Since Germany probably lost the war on the home front rather than in the trenches, morale may have been the most crucial factor in the war effort. In any event, the impression was created that things would have to be better after the war and this implied increased government intervention. Lloyd George, in particular, issued promises of social reform and better housing. Thus the war almost certainly marked an important turning point in the importance of public opinion and socio-economic circumstances in the framing of economic policy.

There was concern about postwar reconstruction at an early stage during the war. In 1916 the Balfour Committee (on Commercial and Industrial Policy after the War) was established to consider the best means of restoring British financial and commercial hegemony (Cmd. 1929 3282). Also, in 1916, a Reconstruction Committee was established and, in the following year, this became the Ministry of Reconstruction. In particular, the Ministry was concerned with labour market and housing problems and the looming issue of mass demobilisation. Inevitably, there were concerns about enhanced aspirations and the need for social improvements as well as about economic efficiency. Under Lloyd George reconstruction acquired far-reaching, if vague, promise which helped to limit war-weariness, cynicism and declining morale in the trenches and munitions factories (Burke 1982). In postwar political circumstances the Ministry's efforts proved to be inconclusive and doomed to failure but important precedents had been created (Johnson 1968). By 1921, de-control and depression in a general atmosphere of class conflict made most of the wartime promises seem, in retrospect, an empty mockery (Abrams 1963). While many wartime promises and aspirations faded away in the harsh reality of postwar circumstances the genie was out of the bottle and to some degree government was compelled to assume a new role. To an extent also, mass disappointments were reflected in a legacy of class bitterness. Increasingly the labour movement looked to the state to solve problems of social organisation and human need.

## ECONOMIC POLICY DURING THE 1920s

Clearly the First World War had a dramatic influence on the role of government in British society. Although these changes were largely forced by events there were influences of longer standing. Lloyd George had been closely associated with prewar reforms and war had given him an opportunity to extend these as well as causing him to seek a new political base independent from traditional Liberal Party support (Wrigley 1976). Also, by 1918 the Labour Party had come to view the state less as an instrument of class oppression and more as a means of working class advancement (Booth and Pack 1985). After the war, there-fore, there were forces in British society which were strongly committed to new departures in economic and social policy. In the aftermath of war there was a struggle between these tendencies and those who favoured a restoration of market forces and a withdrawal of government to restore the prewar situation. The government's decision to continue wartime inflation to ease postwar adjustment and perhaps, also, to prevent social and political unrest has already been noted in Chapters 5 and 6, as has the wider significance of the cabinet's decision in December 1919 to accept the recommendation of the interim report of the Cunliffe Com-mittee (Cd.9182 1918) to end government borrowing and impose tighter control over interest rates and currency issue with a view towards restoring the gold standard as soon as possible at the prewar parity with the US dollar. By the end of 1920 a combination of political, institutional and personal influences had generated a general abandon-ment of controls and policy was determined by a commitment to restore the pre-1914 situation as far as possible.

The Balfour Committee also placed a premium on the restoration of industrial efficiency through rapid de-control and the restoration of market influences. This was supported by the Treasury and the Bank of England as concern about inflation and debt continued. During the brief postwar boom between 1918 and 1920 it was clear that inflation needed to be controlled. Unfortunately, the determined assault on infla-tion and the thrust of de-control coincided with the end of the boom (Howson 1975: 20). Fiscal tightening combined with high interest rates helped to precipitate and intensify a sharp cyclical downturn and the onset of mass unemployment which was to persist throughout the interwar period. It had been clear all along that decontrol and govern-ment disengagement meant deflation and there was concern about the social and political consequences, not least because wage cuts were clearly implied. In the event, the main thrust of policy coincided with circumstances to produce a chronically underemployed economy throughout the 1920s.

Policy decisions taken after the war meant that Britain had a clear and coherent economic policy during the 1920s. The aim was to restore Britain, as far as possible, to its prewar pre-eminence in financial and economic terms. This was to be achieved through the operation of market forces and the cornerstone of policy was to return Britain to the gold standard. The second goal of 1920s economic policy was to reduce the debt burden as a means of solving budgetary problems, reducing taxes and raising levels of investment. Only the gold stan-dard, it was believed, could ensure financial freedom and the removal of damaging political intervention in the economic system (Tomlinson 1990: ch. 3). The approach was based upon a fundamental belief that the free market had made Britain strong in the past and could do so again. Government intervention had been inflationary and high wages had priced British goods out of overseas markets. Returning to the gold standard (at prewar parity with the US dollar) meant reducing the level of prices and this, in turn, had clear implications for wages (Glynn and Shaw 1981). Treasury officials saw the gold standard as a means of controlling politicians who were tempted by political pressures into excessive spending. Thus in the early 1920s the authorities were attempting to control credit creation and public expenditure as a means of restoring financial stability.

With the exception of unemployment, no single issue of interwar economic policy has received more attention than the gold standard (Drummond 1987). International aspects of the gold standard are discussed in chapter 6 and here we focus on the domestic implications. Apart from J.M. Keynes there was virtually no opposition to the view of the Cunliffe Committee that Britain should return to gold at the prewar parity as soon as circumstances made this possible. The possibility of returning at a lower parity than $4.86 = £1 was never seriously considered by the authorities (Moggridge 1969; 1972). In effect, this meant a policy of returning when the British price level, distorted by war and postwar inflation, regained its prewar relativity with American prices, which had not risen to the same extent. The Bank of England had to regain control over the British money market and the British relative price level had to fall, either as a result of deflation in Britain, or inflation abroad, or both. The gold standard was formally renounced in April, 1919, and sterling continued as a 'managed' currency, but the long-run aim of returning to gold remained clearly established, conditioning the whole approach to economic policy.

By early 1923 the Bank had regained its control of money markets and the fall in the general price level had gone sufficiently far to bring a return to gold within the bounds of short-run possibility. In the meantime, the price of deflation in terms of unemployment, falling money wages and labour market tensions was apparent and industry was also feeling the effects of a constrained home market and high real interest rates. Clearly the policy was much less attractive to labour and industry than to the financial interests of the City of London (Pollard 1970). However, the main weight of informed opinion remained in favour of official policy and there was little general support for Keynes's *Tract on Monetary Reform* (1923) which argued against a return because of the costs of deflation and unemployment.

The actual decision to return to gold, taken by the Chancellor of the Exchequer, Winston Churchill, in April 1925, has usually been seen, in retrospect, as a mistake. However, at the time it was a rational political decision which was more or less inevitable in the circumstances.

Churchill was certainly not ignorant of the costs and dangers involved in official policy and he pressed his advisors to justify their advice. Alternative views such as that of Keynes had little support from politically significant pressure groups or expert opinion (Moggeridge 1969). At the practical level, the policy was well established by 1925 and it was believed that the additional costs of return would not be unduly high given the anticipated rise in American prices. When this failed to occur, sterling was overvalued, as noted in Chapter 6, with obvious implications for domestic costs and industrial relations, as Keynes pointed out in his polemical pamphlet *The Economic Consequences of Mr. Churchill* (1925).

During the late 1920s Britain tended to lag behind a generally buoyant American economy and unemployment remained high. The restored gold standard was not a success either for the economy in general, or the financial interests who had advocated it. By 1927 even Montagu Norman conceded that the policy had been a mistake (Tomlinson 1991: 73). Sterling failed to regain its prewar strength and it proved impossible to operate the gold standard in the old way. Britain remained on gold by virtue of financial manipulation and expedients and the restored system was far from being automatic. Full restoration could only have been achieved by severe deflation involving reductions in money wages and was politically out of the question after the general strike of 1926. In the late 1920s Britain's weakened balance of payments situation could not support a restoration of the old order, as noted in Chapter 6.

Gold standard policies during the 1920s involved a decade of varying levels of deflation, including cuts in public spending and high interest rates. While these policies strained the system they failed to produce the required adjustment. This being said, it would be wrong to attribute all Britain's economic problems to gold standard policy. In Chapter 2 we noted that growth in the 1920s was quite good in terms of historical comparison. This appears to reflect a buoyant home market and the main impact of gold standard policy may have fallen on the traditional export industries. However, these industries were already in difficulty long before 1925 because of declining competitiveness and increasing protection in overseas markets. While the authorities hoped that the restoration of pre-1914 liberalism in economic affairs, both internally and externally, would resolve these problems, they were disappointed.

Pollard's account of the return to gold is a biting indictment of the narrow and selfish interests of the City of London, represented by the Bank of England:

> Thus in just over ten years of this rake's progress, London had been reduced from the most powerful European financial centre by far, disputing the lead with New York, to a weak, dependent and

insecure money market, a symbol of failure and default. Even the City in the end had lost out by having its narrow interests protected too selfishly. Yet the poor, tortured, and mentally unstable Governor . . . was not dismissed but stayed on for another thirteen years. . . . It is hardly conceivable that a political leader could have got away so easily with such a massive failure, and the fact that Norman did does not increase one's trust in the Central Banks as against the politicians.

(Pollard 1970: 21)

It became increasingly difficult for the Treasury to produce an annually balanced budget, including a surplus for the redemption of national debt. Unfortunately, the decision to return to gold made reduction of the national debt all the more difficult to achieve as it raised interest rates and unemployment. The increase in public spending after the First World War made budgets larger and more difficult to manage. Along with the need to repay or service the swollen national debt, there was much higher spending on social items including housing, education, health insurance and services, old age, war and widow's pensions, public works and a range of other items. Social spending, especially on unemployment benefits, tended to move inversely with revenue and this posed serious problems. Despite the many 'Geddes Axe' cuts of the early 1920s, social spending remained well above prewar levels. Outgoings on the National Debt in the form of interest and other charges tended to increase in real terms during the 1920s as interest rates remained high and prices fell. Debt repayment and servicing absorbed about 40 per cent of the annual budget and was a matter of grave concern for the Treasury throughout (Middleton 1985; 1987).

The war had seen substantial increases in both direct and indirect taxation and there were pressures through the 1920s for tax reductions. Changes in the tax system in 1917 and especially the 1920 budget limited the progressive implications of wartime tax increases. The wartime duty on excess profits was removed in 1921 and income tax, which fell largely on the middle classes, was reduced in 1922–3 and again in 1925. Income tax had been almost a voluntary form of taxation before 1914 but was now more rigorously organised and progressive (Field et al. 1977). From 1925 the standard rate of income tax remained at 20 per cent. While war had made the taxation system more progressive, so that a greater burden fell on higher incomes, there was still a relatively heavy reliance on indirect taxes which were mainly paid by the poorer section of the population, in particular, through the consumption of alcohol and tobacco. Indirect taxes increased further in 1932 with the return to protection which eased Treasury reliance on other forms of tax. During the interwar years budgets were more or less balanced according to circumstances and the approach of individual Chancellors. Balanced budgets became an important factor in creating the climate of business and financial opinion. Favourable market opinion, or lack of it, may have been more important than the actual impact of the budget on the economy (Aldcroft 1986: 26–7). The scope for 'creative accounting', or disguised departures from balance, was limited although often used (Middleton 1985). Unbalanced budgets might have threatened overseas confidence in sterling at a time when the first aim of policy was to restore and maintain prewar parity which was seen in the 1920s as the key to economic recovery. Thus the Treasury took a firm stand against public works expenditure both by central and local government (Peden 1984; 1988).

In the early 1920s unemployment problems had given rise to wide-spread local authority public works as a means of job creation (Garside 1990: ch. 11). These were often supported by central funds provided through the Unemployment Grants Committee which had been estab-lished in 1920. This was based upon ideas of counter-cyclical public works developed during the Edwardian period and recommended in the Minority Report of the Royal Commission on the Poor Laws (Cmd. 4499 1909: vol. III). However, by the mid-1920s it was clear that the core of unemployment was structural rather than cyclical and the Treasury had become increasingly aware that job creation was an extremely costly process. Progressively restrictive criteria for local authority public works were introduced. The most cost-effective way of alleviating unemploy-ment was to provide unemployment benefits on an insurance basis, as modestly as public opinion would allow. Providing employment through public works was estimated to cost £250 per annum per job in the late 1920s (Glynn and Howells 1980: 32). This was approximately double the average wage and about five times the level of unemploy-ment benefit for a family of five. Of course, the estimate made no allowance for multiplier and other effects although these were probably quite modest.

In 1929 the Liberal Party under Lloyd George put forward an election manifesto which proposed to solve the unemployment problem through a large scale public works programme. In reply to the Liberal party (1929) manifesto, *We can conquer unemployment*, the Treasury produced a White Paper (Cmd. 3331 1929) which set out its objections to the proposals. This document represents the central statement of the infa-mous 'Treasury view' on the unemployment problem. Apart from its obvious desire to defend orthodox notions of finance and the need to maintain commercial confidence, at the heart of the Treasury view was the notion of 'crowding out' (Middleton 1987: 114). The funds employed for government spending on public works could only come from taxa-tion or borrowing – either of which would detract from private sector

activity. According to the Treasury view substantial reductions in unemployment could only come about as a result of wage flexibility which
meant lower money wages, greater efficiency and structural changes in
industry. Direct government intervention in the form of heavy investment in public works schemes was rejected on the ground that since
there was only a fixed amount of savings available for investment in the
economy, public works investment would simply divert capital from
'normal' or private channels without increasing the aggregate level of
investment or employment. Public works would push up interest rates
in the private sector by diverting capital into wasteful and inefficient
channels, creating at the same time considerable administrative and
budgetary difficulties. Thus it was believed that the appropriate scope
for independent action by government was very limited and that any
drastic action was likely to damage the long-run prospects for industry
and the economy, especially in export markets (Middleton 1985: ch. 8).
Apart from these financial objections to public works there were others,
for example in terms of administrative difficulties and problems of
political control. By the late 1920s a 'Whitehall view' involving ministers, political parties and administrators had emerged. This held that
public works were not the answer to unemployment (Garside 1990: 327–
47). The main hope for a solution to unemployment lay in a revival of the
international economy through a restoration of pre-1914 liberalism.

This rationalisation of inactivity dominated government thinking in
relation to unemployment throughout the 1920s. In his *General Theory*
(1936) Keynes rejected the argument that full employment would result
naturally from market forces, given factor price flexibility. In the Keynesian view, the level of total output, and employment, was determined
by aggregate demand (consumption plus investment plus government
spending) which might be less than was necessary to ensure full employment. In such a situation, wage cuts were likely to increase, rather than
reduce unemployment by reducing aggregate demand. The solution lay
through government intervention to encourage private investment by
reducing interest rates, raising consumption through budget deficits and
increasing public investment through public works and other schemes.

The Treasury view prevailed during the interwar years because it
appeared to be firmly based in orthodox economic theory which was
not successfully challenged by Keynes until 1936. More crucially, it
appeared to support the immediate interests of employers and other
pressure groups and because it placed full employment behind other
priorities including price stability, the free trade system and the gold
standard (Peden 1988). In the light of more recent developments in
economic theory it is now possible to defend the Treasury attitudes of
the 1920s in theoretical terms. Indeed, clear comparisons can be made

between the 1920s and the 1980s when Nigel Lawson, as Chancellor, echoed the Treasury views of former years (Glynn 1991).

## ECONOMIC POLICY IN THE 1930s

There were major changes in British economic policy during the 1930s although it is debatable how much these resulted from changing attitudes rather than circumstances. The world financial and economic crisis of 1929–33, and the British crisis of 1931, forced changes in reality to which economic reasoning struggled to adjust.

The financial crisis of 1931 forced Britain to depart from the gold standard and the basic policy thrust of the 1920s was abandoned. Sterling was allowed to depreciate and became a managed, and manipulated, currency. Cheap money in the form of low interest rates became possible since sterling no longer had to be defended in the old way. The 1930s depression also brought about the abandonment of free trade and tariffs and empire preferences were introduced. Along with these changes more flexible attitudes towards budgets also began to develop, although a belief in long-term balance remained. These were enhanced by the need to finance rearmament in the later 1930s. Thus there were some major relaxations and changes in policy attitudes during the 1930s (Tomlinson 1990: ch. 5; Peden 1985: ch. 5).

The Labour government which came into office under Ramsay MacDonald in 1929 felt it had to continue the economic policies of its predecessors (Skidelsky 1967). As the international crisis intensified the maintenance of overseas confidence in sterling through budget 'soundness' came to assume a central importance. The Labour Chancellor, Phillip Snowden, accepted the prevailing economic orthodoxy with peculiar vigour and used his strong position in the Cabinet and the Party to enforce unpopular policies. Public works were not seen as a solution to the unemployment problem although the trade unions and the labour movement in general continued to demand them (Glynn and Shaw 1981). Snowden struggled to maintain a balanced budget against intensifying depression and rising unemployment. Higher taxes in 1930 were followed by the economy campaign of 1931, but this failed to satisfy financial opinion at home and overseas. By mid-1931, a major crisis of confidence had developed (Chapter 6). The Labour government disintegrated after a cabinet split generated by proposals to cut spending, including unemployment benefits and, in December 1931, the new 'National' Government was forced to take Britain off the gold standard.

The enforced departure from gold was followed by a period in which sterling fell and found its market level. From 1932 after recovering to higher levels, it was managed through the Exchange Equalisation Account (Howson 1980a) and, as noted in Chapter 6, it was hoped

that keeping sterling undervalued would help exports while also per-
mitting low interest rates to be maintained in the domestic economy.
Exchange rate policy in the 1930s had a domestic focus in contrast with
the 1920s. The successful establishment of a managed currency released
domestic monetary policy from the external constraints which had
applied during the 1920s. The Treasury favoured lower interest rates
as a means of easing the public debt problem and sought to take
advantage of an influx of overseas funds into London from the first
half of 1932 as confidence returned. In June 1932, Bank rate was reduced
to 2 per cent and it remained at this level until 1939. This helped to
promote a general easing of interest rates and a nominal reduction in
rentier incomes. Debt conversion on a massive scale commenced in 1932.
This involved, in effect, paying off government debt at existing rates and
raising new loans at lower rates. Thus, in 1932, some £2.085 billion of
war loan, or about one-quarter of the national debt, was converted from
5 per cent to 3 1/2 per cent (Howson 1975).

However, cheap money was soon being hailed as a recovery measure.
In theory, at least, lower interest rates should stimulate investment and
we can safely conclude that cheap money did not deter recovery. On the
other hand there is no clear and indisputable evidence that lower interest
rates played a very important part in the strong recovery of the 1930s.
Even if we could be sure what the real influences on recovery were, it is
impossible to isolate and measure the effect of one factor (Alford 1972).
In assessing the impact of cheap money attention has focussed on its
impact on investment in industrial and housing development. In fact,
bank lending contracted sharply during the early 1930s and failed to
grow very strongly after that (Worswick 1984).

Between the demise of liberalism in the slump of 1929–32 and the
emergence of the Keynesian consensus in the 1940s, economic policy
went through a period when precise aims were less clearly perceived. As
a result there has been a great deal of debate among historians about the
conceptions of policy during the 1930s (Tomlinson 1990: ch. 5). Keynes
and the Keynesians have seen Treasury policy in the 1930s as a continuation of outmoded and theoretically flawed classical orthodoxy
(Winch 1969). This view was accepted by historians at least until the
1970s and the Treasury was blamed for exacerbating rather than
attempting to solve the unemployment problem; in particular, for continued adherence to the balanced budget dogma and for opposition to
public works (Stewart 1967). However, with the opening of the state
papers to public access in the 1970s new attitudes began to emerge as it
became clear that senior Treasury officials were less rigid and hidebound
by classical theory than had been supposed (Howson 1975: Middleton
1985). Some historians have detected Keynesian influences in the 1930s
Treasury although there is continued debate about the precise nature

and timing of the emergence of Keynesian orthodoxy. In any event, the Treasury accepted protection, cheap money, exchange rate manipulation and other departures from *laissez-faire* as well as developing more flexible attitudes towards the budget. Since the 1970s significant changes in economic attitudes and theory have also gone some way towards exonerating the Treasury from some of the traditional Keynesian assertions. In criticism it may be claimed that this revisionism is, to a large extent, simply claiming that Treasury mandarins were more sophisticated in their private opinions, but assumed it was necessary to defer to the prejudices of financial opinion in the City and elsewhere. This is a controversial subject with disagreements among historians reflecting both contemporary economic debate and ongoing historical research. Booth (1987) has suggested that there was, in effect, an important role for prices in Treasury thinking during the 1930s. This involved an aim to restore profitability through a controlled rise in prices. Since wage cuts on any substantial scale were believed to be politically impossible, it was hoped that prices could rise without a corresponding increase in wages. An undervalued pound, cheap money and industrial policy were means to this end. At the same time the essential limits of budgetary orthodoxy were retained in order to sustain business confidence (Middleton 1987). In effect, therefore, the Treasury may have been using both unorthodox and orthodox measures with the aim of restoring the British capitalist system, perhaps with a long-run aim of returning to pre-1929 liberalism.

Questions relating to the emergence of Keynesianism are more complex. Booth (1989) has questioned the tendency to define Keynesianism simply in terms of a departure from balanced budgets and has suggested that the central feature of Keynesian economic theory as expounded by Keynes was interest rate manipulation. In the 1920s the policy stance had ensured high real interest rates and this had a retarding effect on growth and employment. However, from 1932 there was a policy of cheap money and Britain experienced very rapid growth in the recovery phase, although unemployment remained stubbornly high. The unemployment problem could have been solved only through an even more rapid rate of growth or special employment measures (although it could be argued that more effective policies at an earlier stage might have diminished the severity of the downturn). Thus, it appears that the essential argument between Keynes and the Treasury, and more recent disputes between Keynesians and others, relate to the question of special employment measures in the form of public works.

As already indicated, Treasury opposition to public works was based in part upon considerations of cost and administrative complexity and, more fundamentally, in a belief that public works were an ineffective means of employment creation. Recent research suggests that the impact of public works schemes in the early 1930s would have been constrained by limited multiplier effects, not least in the depressed areas (Glynn and Howells 1980; Thomas 1981: 337). Thomas has concluded that the Lloyd George programme of 1929 would probably have failed and Glynn and Howells have indicated the enormity of the unemployment problem in the early 1930s and raise serious doubts about the feasibility of a simply Keynesian solution through public works. These views are disputed by Garside and Hatton who argue that a simple Keynesian remedy could have worked (Garside and Hatton 1985). It seems unlikely that these differences will be resolved in the near future and historians and others will continue to debate the issues.

One of the most remarkable features of British economic policy during the 1930s is that purely domestic considerations appear to have taken precedence over international concerns. Before 1929 the need to maintain Britain's international role had been paramount. Agriculture, for example, had been sacrificed to free trade and, in the 1920s, industrial decline and unemployment had been tolerated in the interests of liberalism. After the Second World War balance of payments considerations became a dominant issue in economic policy and, again, domestic interests were subordinated. Thus, the 1930s is unusual, if not unique, in peacetime circumstances. It is perhaps not surprising, therefore, that the 1930s brought Britain's return to protection which was examined in terms of external policy considerations in the previous chapter. Protection also had important domestic aspects.

In Britain the war brought the first protectionist measures since the first half of the nineteenth century. The McKenna Duties of 1915 involved the introduction of a 33 1/3 per cent tariff on certain 'luxury' items plus an increase in specific duties. A wartime system of import licensing was also introduced covering a wide range of commodities. The general aim was to assist wartime economic planning as well as saving both foreign exchange and shipping space. However, some of these measures were continued after the war and the McKenna Duties were renewed on an annual basis. In 1926 they were extended to cover commercial vehicles and parts. The McKenna Duties were not the only exception to Britain's free trade stance. The Dyestuffs (Import Regulation) Act of 1920 was a prelude to the Safeguarding of Industries Act of 1921. Tariff protection was granted to a range of industries including dye stuffs, chemicals, glass and scientific instruments. In 1925 the Act was broadened to cover cutlery, pottery, lace and other items. Also, in 1927, the British film industry was given protection against American competition (Capie 1983).

These steps towards both protection and imperial preference were significant, but very limited in extent. However, in an increasingly protectionist world Britain was out of step as well as being inhibited in terms of commercial and imperial diplomacy. As a major trading nation and a large-scale importer Britain had enormous bargaining power but this could not be utilised while free trade prevailed. Protection offered alternative revenue sources and a means of easing budget constraints. More fundamentally, protection was an obvious palliative in relation to balance of payments and industrial and employment problems. However, such was the strength of established opinion in favour of free trade that national debate on the issue of protection was more or less impossible (McGuire 1939).

Ironically, while Britain's departure from the gold standard and the depreciation of sterling solved the problems of external constraint it was followed by a return to protection made possible by the 1931 crisis. The National Government was overwhelmingly Conservative and protectionist and its advent gave rise to a flood of imports which provided an opportunity to introduce protection without a mandate. Under the Abnormal Importations (Customs Duties) Act and the Horticultural Products (Emergency Duties) Act duties of up to 50 per cent were imposed on a wide range of items. Under the shelter of this emergency legislation tariffs were imposed under Treasury order and new tariff machinery was rapidly established. In February, 1932, these measures were replaced by the Import Duties Act which established a general tariff of 20 per cent. Empire products and certain foods and raw materials were exempted. The Import Duties Advisory Committee was established to make recommendations on tariff policy (Capie 1983).

There has been some debate about the precise impact of tariffs. While some industries may have benefited, protection was probably not a major influence in the recovery of the 1930s. The return to protection may be more important in political rather than economic terms, although some saw protection as part of a move towards more general government intervention. Protection did create possible scope for expansionist and interventionist policies, but these were not forthcoming. The Conservative governments of the 1930s saw tariffs as being part of micro- rather than macro-economic policy. They were intended to protect particular industries against cheap foreign labour rather than to give more scope for macro-economic intervention.

Capie has examined the impact of tariffs using the concept of 'effective protection' which measures protection on the domestic added value rather than nominal rates of duty (Capie 1983). For most industries, where raw materials were imported free of duty, effective protection was much higher than nominal rates. However, in the case of shipbuilding, there was a negative rate of protection because steel, the major input, was protected, while ships were not. A similar situation applied to housing and also iron and steel. Foreman-Peck (1981) has criticised Capie's estimates and provided alternatives which suggest quite different conclusions in relation to some industries, notably iron and steel.

Thus there are considerable complexities and differences of opinion in attempting to assess the impact of protection at the micro- and macro-economic levels. There can be little doubt that some industries benefited from the imposition of tariffs, both directly and in terms of business confidence. Tariffs were a useful device in promoting rationalisation and in generating a new approach towards the domestic market in some industries, notably iron and steel. The macro-economic effects are more difficult to evaluate since it is impossible to isolate the effects of protec-tion from other influences such as exchange depreciation in 1931 and appreciation from 1932. Kitson and Solomou (1989) argue that tariffs probably did have a positive impact in the circumstances of the 1930s but Broadberry (1986) has suggested that the effect of the tariff was to appreciate the exchange rate from 1932 and that, therefore, it did not serve to increase output or employment. Most commentators have taken the view that the aggregate impact of protection was probably not very great. Nevertheless, the departure from free trade in the early 1930s has considerable symbolic importance in that it marks a major departure from economic liberalism and a more domestic orientation in economic policy.

The rearmament programme which commenced in 1935 provides an interesting illustration of the possible scope for effective government intervention in reducing unemployment. Thomas (1983) estimates that, by 1938, the programme had created a million jobs, mainly in the iron and steel, coal and engineering industries. This estimate may be on the high side since Thomas neglects the possible diversions into exports. Nevertheless, there is no doubt that rearmament stimulated some ailing industries in areas which had experienced heavy unemployment, and muted the economic downturn of 1937. It is interesting to note that the Labour party, which had favoured public works over many years, was opposed to rearmament while the Treasury, which had taken an opposite line, accepted the programme without much opposition. Indeed the Treasury also accepted the need for large-scale borrowing and a more flexible attitude towards budgets, aiming to achieve balance over the cycle rather than in individual years. In the placement of rearmament contracts some attention was given to regional and industrial problems including unemployment. Indeed, it could be said that the rearmament programme was the nearest government came during the 1930s to eco-nomic planning and reflationary policy. However, the main impact came after 1937 and rearmament probably has to be seen as a general exception to basic policy stances. Quite clearly the rearmament programme has implications for the general debate about what governments could have done to reduce unemployment in the interwar period. If rearmament did lead to a sharp reduction in unemployment then this implies that more could have been done in earlier years.

## CONCLUSION

There has been a good deal of debate about economic policy during the 1930s and this seems likely to continue in future. While it is clear that there were some important changes in policy, particularly the abandonment of gold, cheap money, protection and rearmament, these appear to have been prompted by events rather than representing a fundamental change in economic thinking. The 'Keynesian revolution' in economic policy which became established by the 1950s probably owed more to the influence of the Second World War and to changes in economic theory than to developments during the 1930s. At the same time, these new attitudes owed much to the belief that the 1930s had been a time of wasted opportunities when more could and should have been done to tackle Britain's economic problems. In particular, the problem of unemployment had not been solved.

# Chapter 8

# Britain at war

In the present century, nations have mobilised *en masse* to wage total war. It is tempting to think that disruption on this scale should have had lasting effects on economic and social life. Historians and social scientists have developed ambitious theories in which war is the critical force in long-run economic social change, but these views are highly controversial. To measure the effects of war we must estimate how economy and society would have evolved in its absence and measure this counter-factual development path against what actually happened. This is a very demanding test which ambitious theories have not always passed (Milward 1970).

## WARTIME ECONOMIC PLANNING

Learning the lessons of 1914–18, the government was well prepared in September 1939 with plans for control of key sectors (railways, shipping and agriculture) and the allocation of important resources (raw materials and labour) (Hancock and Gowing 1949: 3–100). Its grand strategy was based upon time, naval strength and financial power: British plans depended on holding a German *blitzkrieg* in northern France. The strength of the Royal Navy was needed to guarantee British and restrict German essential imports and Britain's overseas financial assets could be liquidated to pay for imported food, raw materials and armaments. Britain and its allies needed time to rearm in depth. At the outbreak of war Britain's annual output of steel was barely 60 per cent of that of Germany and machine tool production was a meagre 20 per cent. The grand strategy thus implied steady progress to a full war economy, with the first priority an enormous expansion of munitions-making capacity and then rearmament in depth financed by a phased reduction of foreign currency reserves (Robinson 1951: 35–7).

Everything changed in the early summer of 1940 when Germany conquered most of western Europe. Much of the equipment of the

British army was left on the beaches of Dunkirk. With German forces only twenty miles from the coast the government's meticulous plans had to be shredded. Imported munitions and materials were needed no matter what the cost in foreign currency. At home, all production plans were sacrificed to the need for air defence. In the short term, the new mood of urgency was successful. Enough Spitfires and Hurricanes were produced and repaired to win the Battle of Britain and make invasion less likely. However, these methods were ill-suited to longer-term needs. In aircraft production, for example, giving priority in resource allocation to fighter production slowed bomber production, which was equally important to the war effort (Robertson 1982). Tighter central control of the allocation of resources was needed once the immediate danger of invasion and defeat had begun to recede.

In 1941–2 Britain developed what is usually called a 'planned economy', but the term is misleading as planning usually implies concern with the medium as well as the short term. British wartime policymakers had little interest in anything but short-run 'programming' of resources to ensure that the maximum output was achieved. The main strategic questions (such as the size of the army or the balance between munitions production and the output of civilian consumption goods) were decided at cabinet level and turned into economic plans by a network of Cabinet committees, dominated from 1941 onwards by the Lord President's committee (Chester 1951a: 9–13). This system attempted to reconcile the demands of politicians and military commanders with the supplies of available resources and is most successful when it allocates resources in scarcest supply. During 1939–41, reserves of gold and foreign currency, munitions capacity, specific raw materials, the volume of imports and supplies of labour were all constraints on production and had to be considered by economic planners. After 1941, the *labour famine* emerged as the single most serious constraint on production and the 'macro-economics of war' were dominated by the allocation of labour (Robinson 1951: 47–54).

Labour policy had been stalled by the mutual suspicion between Chamberlain's government and unions opposed to government attempts to regulate labour (Middlemas 1979: 256; Gowing 1972: 149–50). When Churchill came to power he made the inspired choice of Ernest Bevin, head of the Transport and General Workers Union, as Minister of Labour with powers to help organise wartime production. The Churchill government imposed far-reaching controls over the labour market, notably with the Essential Works Order of 1941 which made it impossible for essential workers to be dismissed or leave without the minister's consent. As the EWOs were not popular with workers, Bevin used them as sparingly as possible and ensured that workers affected received adequate wages, working conditions and welfare (Bullock 1967: 36–63). He

gave the labour movement confidence and, in sharp contrast to the First
World War, wartime production proceeded without major disruption
from industrial unrest, except in the coal industry (Harris 1984: 60–70).

Wartime labour supply was an immense problem. Men and women
had to be withdrawn from the civilian labour force into fighting services
but at the same time the output of munitions had to rise to equip those
forces. There were limits to the extent that the civilian economy could be
drained of labour. The war cabinet knew only too well that the maintenance of civilian morale depended on the ability of the government to
provide adequate supplies of food, clothing and shelter to all its citizens.
The optimum mobilisation had each soldier matched by roughly one
worker in the defence industries and two more in the civilian economy
to produce necessities for war workers and soldiers (Harrison 1988: 188).
The impact on the distribution of national income can be seen in Table
8.1, in the massive rise in the share taken by the government for war
purposes. The impact on the labour market is evident from Table 8.2; the
huge rises in employment in the war sector were matched by contraction
elsewhere, especially in building and industries producing consumer
goods. A more dramatic picture emerges from production statistics;
the output of munitions increased very rapidly, especially from 1939 to
1942 as new munitions-building capacity was created (Table 8.3). Normal civilian consumption had to contract to free resources for the war
effort; consumers' expenditure as a proportion of total expenditure fell
consistently from 1938 to 1943 (Table 8.1). Despite the scale of this
disruption to the fabric of the British economy, aggregate output
increased steadily to 1943, after which it tailed off (Aldcroft 1986: 170).
The peak of production was 27 per cent above 1938. New supplies of
labour, especially married women, were found to replace conscripts into
the services. In March 1941 the government introduced the compulsory

Table 8.1 Approximate percentage shares of net national product, 1938–45

|  | Government expenditure | | Consumers' expenditure | Net non-war capital formation |
|---|---|---|---|---|
|  | War | Civil |  |  |
| 1938 | 7 | 10 | 78 | 5 |
| 1939 | 15 | 9.5 | 73.5 | 2 |
| 1940 | 44 | 8 | 64 | −16 |
| 1941 | 54 | 7 | 56 | −17 |
| 1942 | 52 | 8 | 52 | −12 |
| 1943 | 56 | 7 | 49 | −12 |
| 1944 | 54 | 7 | 51 | −12 |
| 1945 | 49 | 7 | 54 | −10 |

Source: Pollard 1983: 214.

Table 8.2 Distribution of total employment in Great Britain, 1938–43
(thousands)

| | June 1938 | June 1943 | Percentage change |
|---|---|---|---|
| Allied forces and auxiliary services | 385 | 4,761 | 1,136.6 |
| Total in civil employment | 17,378 | 17,444 | 0.4 |
| Metals, engineering, vehicles, shipbuilding | 2,590 | 4,659 | 79.9 |
| Chemicals, explosives, paints, oils | 276 | 574 | 108.0 |
| National and local govt. incl. civil defence | 1,386 | 2,109 | 52.2 |
| Agriculture and fishing | 949 | 1,047 | 10.3 |
| Mining and quarrying | 849 | 818 | −3.7 |
| Textiles | 861 | 669 | −22.3 |
| Clothing, boots, shoes | 717 | 493 | −31.2 |
| Food, drink, tobacco | 640 | 519 | −18.9 |
| Cement, bricks, pottery, glass, etc. | 271 | 170 | −37.3 |
| Leather, wood, paper, etc. | 844 | 539 | −36.1 |
| Other manufactures | 164 | 123 | −25.0 |
| Building, civil engineering | 1,264 | 726 | −42.6 |
| Gas, water, electricity | 240 | 200 | −16.7 |
| Transport, shipping | 1,225 | 1,176 | −4.0 |
| Distributive trades | 2,882 | 2,009 | −30.3 |
| Commerce, banking, insurance, finance | 414 | 282 | −31.9 |
| Miscellaneous services | 1,806 | 1,331 | −26.3 |
| Registered insured unemployed | 1,710 | 60 | – |
| Total working population | 19,473 | 22,285[a] | 14.4 |

Note:
a Includes 20,000 ex-members of the armed forces in employment.
Source: Aldcroft 1986: 167.

registration of females for employment, the first of a series of measures to steer women into the munitions factories (Summerfield 1984: 34–6). Bevin also improved workplace welfare to enable married women to enter factory work. The policy was enormously successful, with a significant rise in the number of women employed and substantial changes in the age profile, marital status and occupational structure of the female work-force, as Table 8.4 illustrates.

In some consumer goods industries production was 'concentrated' into the most efficient factories to maximise the release of labour (Allen 1951). In furniture and clothing new 'utility' standards were adopted to produce plain, simple designs which minimised the use of materials and labour time. These measures, together with the reduction of unemployment to negligible levels and more intensive working, helped to alleviate the **national** labour famine. However, there were very severe local shortages, particularly in the Midlands and South East, and government

Table 8.3 Output of selected products, Great Britain, 1938–44

| | 1938 | 1939 | 1940 | 1941 | 1942 | 1943 | 1944 |
|---|---|---|---|---|---|---|---|
| Aircraft (no.) | 2,828 | 7,940 | 15,049 | 20,094 | 23,672 | 26,263 | 26,461 |
| Aircraft bombs (short tons) | — | — | 51,093 | 147,848 | 211,048 | 233,807 | 309,366 |
| Tanks and self-propelled guns (no.) | 419 | 969 | 1,399 | 4,841 | 8,611 | 7,476 | — |
| Aircraft engines (no.) | 5,431 | 12,499 | 24,074 | 36,551 | 53,916 | 57,985 | 56,931 |
| Wireless sets (no.) | 3,567[a] | — | 19,616 | 26,015 | 101,145 | 193,096 | 144,161 |
| Coal (million tons) | — | 231 | 224 | 206 | 205 | 199 | 183 |
| Steel (thousand tons) | 10,398 | 13,221 | 12,975 | 12,312 | 12,942 | 13,031 | 12,142 |
| Iron ore (thousand tons) | 11,859 | 14,486 | 17,702 | 18,974 | 19,906 | 18,494 | 15,472 |
| Electricity (million kilowatt hours) | — | 27,733 | 29,976 | 33,577 | 36,903 | 38,217 | 39,649 |
| Cotton yarn (million lbs) | 1,234[b] | 1,092 | 1,191 | 821 | 733 | 712 | 665 |
| Tractors (number) | 10,679 | 15,733 | 19,316 | 24,401 | 27,056 | 25,059 | 23,022 |
| Ploughs (number) | 12,580 | 16,665 | 23,172 | 24,657 | 21,414 | 19,246 | 23,701 |

Notes:
a Average April 1936–August 1939
b 1937
Source: Aldcroft 1986: 172.

*Table 8.4* Aspects of the wartime female labour market

8.4(a) Changes in the distribution of female workers, 1923–43 (percentage of female workers in the total insured work-force of selected industries)

|  | 1923 | 1939 | 1943 |
|---|---|---|---|
| Clothing | 65 | 70 | — |
| Textiles | 60 | 60 | — |
| Pottery, earthenware | 51 | 56 | — |
| Leather | 30 | 38 | — |
| Food, drink, tobacco | 40 | 42 | — |
| Distribution | 40 | 40 | — |
| Miscellaneous manufacturing | 31 | 39 | — |
| Miscellaneous metal industries | 30 | 32 | 46 |
| Chemicals | 25 | 27 | 52 |
| Commerce | 35 | 35 | — |
| National and local government | 9 | 17 | 46 |
| Engineering | 6 | 10 | 34 |
| Vehicles | 9 | 9 | 34 |
| Metal manufacture | 5 | 6 | 22 |
| Gas, water, electricity | 4 | 5 | 17 |
| Transport | 4 | 5 | 20 |
| Shipbuilding | — | 2 | 9 |

8.4(b) Women workers by marital status, 1931–51 (%)

|  | 1931 | 1943 | 1951 |
|---|---|---|---|
| Single | 77 | 49 | 50 |
| Married | 16 | 43 | 43 |
| Widowed/divorced | 7 | 7 | 7 |
| Total | 100 | 99 | 100 |

8.4(c) Women workers by age, 1931–51 (%)

|  | 1931 | 1943 | 1951 |
|---|---|---|---|
| Under 24 years | 41 | 27 | 34 |
| 25–34 years | 27 | 31 | 21 |
| 35–44 years | 16 | 26 | 21 |
| 45–59 years | 16 | 16 | 24 |
| Total | 100 | 100 | 100 |

*Source*: Summerfield 1984: 196,199.

established increasingly sophisticated methods of directing work elsewhere. There is no doubt that the government managed the tight wartime labour market with great success. It is less clear that labour was utilised effectively in the production process.

## INDUSTRY IN THE WAR YEARS

Our perspective on the war economy has been challenged in a recent and controversial book by Correlli Barnett (1986). Using wartime government records, he has argued forcefully that poor management, lack of technical expertise, failure to utilise labour effectively and confrontational industrial relations were the rule rather than the exception in the wartime economy. Such weaknesses were deeply entrenched in the older, 'staple' industries but Barnett also identifies similar failures in the modern growth industries. Clearly, the enormous efforts to manage the wartime labour market are much less impressive if labour productivity stagnated on the shopfloor. As there is insufficient space to consider the full range of Barnett's evidence, we shall concentrate on three industries: shipbuilding, coal and aircraft manufacture.

Shipbuilding output almost doubled between 1938 and its wartime peak, but losses of merchant shipping, especially during the Battle of the Atlantic, were considerable and shortage of ships was a threat to the war effort (Hancock and Gowing 1949: 255, 417). British shipbuilding remained craft-intensive but shipyard workers, scarred by their interwar experiences, opposed dilution and interchangeability of craft work (Inman 1957: 132–54). They did not want to make concessions during wartime which might undermine their peacetime work prospects. The effects of the interwar slump were also seen in the poor quality of shipyard management, where levels of technical and managerial training were low, in the failure to modernise yards which were ill-sited, cramped and ill-equipped and in the fragmentation of the industry (Barnett 1986: 109–23). During the war the employers had little incentive to sort out these problems as they had negotiated a system of contracts which brought satisfactory profits to all shipbuilders (Ashworth 1953: 106–17). It was left to an increasingly frustrated government to press for more urgency. In 1942–4, the government fostered the most ambitious programme of capital investment in the industry for at least half a century, but fundamental problems remained and ministers warned in 1944 that there was a real danger of 'the fossilisation of inefficiency' in the industry (Barnett 1986: 119–23).

There were many similarities in coal mining. Interwar depression had left its mark in low investment, an ageing work-force and confrontational industrial relations. The output of deep-mined coal fell throughout the war and the industry was in crisis after 1941. From 1939 to 1941, falling output merely reflected the drop in the number of miners, but output per manshift began a steady decline from mid-1940. The physical hardship of the work took its toll on the ageing work-force (Barnett 1986: 66; Court 1951: 273–332). The EWOs which prevented miners from leaving the industry to take up better paid, less physically demanding and less dangerous work in the munitions factories were bitterly resented. The best seams were worked out and capital equipment deteriorated during wartime; shifts were lost because of breakdowns and journeys to the coalface increased throughout the war. Thus, the number of shifts worked per worker began to fall in 1941 and accelerated in 1944–5.

Both owners and miners had an eye to the postwar organisation of the coal industry: miners were reluctant to adopt more flexible working for fear that the owners' profits would be augmented and so weaken the prospects for nationalisation (Court 1951: 313–4; Barnett 1986: 66); owners were reluctant to reorganise with the threat of nationalisation on the horizon (Barnett 1986: 84). Accordingly the government had to cope with declining output of the major energy source. It gave miners substantial pay increases, sent conscripts to the mines to augment the workforce and produced both new mining equipment and technical advice when the owners would not invest. Neither increased mechanisation nor the substantial development of open cast mining were sufficient to offset the forces of decline. Coal use was controlled, distribution was made more efficient, greater fuel economy was encouraged, and the domestic consumer was obliged to sit and shiver. By these means crisis was not so much avoided as postponed until after the war, but declining production and productivity were persistent worries.

Although aircraft production was a twentieth century growth industry it had experienced severe relative decline in the interwar years, becoming technologically backward, under-capitalised and with insufficient resources devoted to research and development (Fearon 1979: 232). Most companies were little more than design teams with facilities for building some aircraft. Their inexperience in volume production was exposed during rearmament and the Air Ministry compelled firms to strengthen their production management. The ministry hoped that the 'shadow factory' scheme (under which aircraft would be built by firms with experience of mass production, especially from motor car manufacture) would solve production problems (Barnett 1986: 146). Output rose dramatically; 2,827 aircraft were delivered in 1938 rising to 26,461 in 1944. The aircraft of 1944 were much more 'efficient', expensive and sophisticated than had been the case in the 1930s. But even in this rapidly innovated modern industry Britain's use of labour was comparatively lavish. Annual average productivity in the US was twice that in the UK and Germany recorded a figure 20 per cent higher than Britain's (Barnett 1986: 146).

The British wartime aircraft industry had three main failings. First, poor technical education led to shortages of production engineers and inefficient design; the airframe of the Spitfire Mk.VC required 13,000 man-hours to build whereas the comparable German fighter, the

Messerschmitt ME109G, needed only 4,000 (Barnett 1986: 148). Second, even in this newly created industry, British productive units were small, cramped and poorly equipped. Finally, the climate of industrial relations was poor. Strikes and go-slows were common, although illegal. Managements could not win the respect of their workers. As a result of these three weaknesses, productivity was low. A survey of Coventry aircraft firms in 1943, for example, found that there would be no need for additional labour to meet production targets if an efficient level of output could be secured from the existing labour force (Barnett 1986: 155–6).

Barnett's evidence is accurate and balanced. Large parts of British manufacturing industry had been inefficient relative to the USA and Germany in the 1930s (Broadberry and Crafts 1990; Broadberry and Fremdling 1990), so it is scarcely surprising that problems continued into wartime. The essence of wartime economic policy was to secure additional munitions output as quickly as possible from a work-force which had to be extensively retrained. In such circumstances, efficiency was bound to take rather lower priority than output which, in many cases, was needed urgently whatever the costs of production. There was, after all, a war on. In these circumstances, Barnett's evidence is rather less damning than he believes. His central point is that a 'British disease' (confrontational industrial relations, obstructive trade unions and low levels of technical and vocational training) was exposed rather than confronted during wartime to the cost of postwar economic performance. But it is not at all certain that the British system of industrial relations and structure of trade unionism are so uniquely bad. Other countries, notably in Scandinavia, have had strikes, class conscious trade unions and governments which have striven to protect the industrial power of trade unions and yet have grown faster than the UK in the postwar years (Martin 1979). Barnett is rather naive in his treatment of wartime science and technology. He has shown conclusively that many British scientific discoveries had to be exported to the USA to exploit greater American technical and engineering skills in mass production. Radio and radar, for long regarded as British wartime triumphs, were the most celebrated examples (Barnett 1986: 159–83). Britain was dependent on the USA for 51 per cent of its tanks, 19 per cent of combat aircraft and 28 per cent of military vehicles (Ranki, 1988, 337). It is, however, totally unrealistic to believe that Britain could produce all the munitions it needed, plus all the fighting forces it needed, plus all the consumer goods it needed to preserve civilian morale. If the USA had a comparative advantage in producing technologically sophisticated products, it was logical and more efficient to produce these items in bulk in the USA, no matter who made the original scientific breakthrough. Barnett has, however, fulfilled a useful role in correcting the view that the British economy performed heroically during wartime.

## MONETARY AND FISCAL POLICY AND PAYING FOR THE WAR

The impression that wartime macro-economic problems were handled better than those at the micro-economic level is confirmed by an examination of monetary and fiscal policies. Mindful of the conflicts generated by inflation in 1914–18, the Treasury had been concerned about movements in the official cost of living index since 1938. The threat of inflationary spiral during wartime loomed when rising import costs triggered a sharp increase in the cost of living and wages in September 1939. Treasury officials wanted higher taxes to mop up purchasing power and a statement from ministers cancelling the indexation of wages to the cost of living. But decisive action was impossible because of the tension and suspicion between the Chamberlain government and the TUC. Reluctantly, therefore, the Treasury tried another tack, ensuring that government-controlled food prices did not rise. Exchequer subsidies were used to hold down the cost of living; 'stabilisation' policy, with strict controls over the prices of basic goods, had begun.

This innovatory policy attracted considerable criticism, notably from the *Economist* and J.M. Keynes. Keynes calculated the value of the armaments which the British economy could produce when fully mobilised and estimated how the Treasury might raise money to finance this programme: overseas assets could be liquidated; savings could be increased, especially from industry's depreciation funds; and there were the proceeds of existing taxation (Keynes 1940 and 1972: 367–439). With some inspired statistical guesstimates, Keynes demonstrated that 'income' would not meet 'expenditure' without major increases of taxation. If taxation were not increased, consumers would hold purchasing power well in excess of the value of available civilian consumer goods and this excess demand would cause prices and then wages to rise. Keynes proposed to treat higher taxation as a forced loan or 'deferred pay'. In short, if the government did not substantially increase taxation, inflation would accelerate. The Treasury did not accept this view at once but slowly the pieces of wartime anti-inflationary policy (stabilisation of the cost of living by subsidies and price controls, Keynesian budgetary arithmetic and close co-operation with the unions) came together in the 1941 budget and helped to hold inflation as measured by the cost of living index in check after 1941. The index was, however, a very out-of-date indicator of working class expenditure patterns and other price indexes suggest a more limited (and realistic) achievement (Pollard 1983: 211). Nevertheless, the record of control over inflation was much better than in the First World War. An increase of 48 per cent in the price of essential items between 1938 and 1945 is much better than the 100 per cent increase in the five years 1913–18. With price inflation apparently controlled, wage rates rose less (50 per cent) in 1938–45 than in the First World War (79 per cent).

An important by-product of Keynes's wartime fiscal policy was greater breadth in the social basis of direct taxation. Before 1939, the payment of income tax had been a largely middle class affair. Changed wartime circumstances brought more working class taxpayers and new administrative procedures with the introduction in 1942 of PAYE. At a more general level, rates of income tax rose with the standard rate doubling from 5s. 0d. (25p) in the £ in 1937 to 10s. 0d. (50p) in 1941–2, where it remained until the end of the war. Personal allowances were reduced and surtax rates were raised dramatically (Sayers 1956: 513–14). Working-class consumers also felt the pinch of wartime changes in indirect taxation. As drink, tobacco and entertainment had a very low weighting in the cost of living index, the government could increase duties on these items without raising the official inflation rate.

The government's successful control of inflation also rested upon its ability to mobilise the nation's savings cheaply and efficiently. It quickly imposed exchange and capital issues controls, giving capital holders few alternatives other than to lend to the government. The Treasury decided that the cheap money policy of the 1930s should continue into war. Astute debt management held the long-term interest rate at 3 per cent. Given the controls over civilian investment, it is not surprising that the banking system was transformed into an agent for the absorption of funds from the public for use by the government (Pollard 1983: 216). The '3 per cent war' succeeded in containing interest payments on the national debt; although the debt stood at more than three times its level of 1919, the total interest charge was only 56 per cent higher than in 1919 (Harrod 1972: 582).

The function of wartime monetary and fiscal policies was, as noted above, to depress civilian consumption and to help find the domestic finance for the war effort. Diverting resources to the government in this way is much easier in a rapidly expanding economy (as was Britain from 1939 to 1945) than in one which is stagnant (Germany) or declining (the USSR). The British economy grew by more than a quarter between 1939 and 1943, and this growth supplied just over a half of the domestic finance required for the supply of resources for war (Harrison 1988: 185). There was also a large contribution from capital consumption (Table 8.1). Essential imports were financed to a very large extent by running down Britain's overseas assets and running up new external liabilities. Cairncross (1985: 12) has estimated that US lend-lease aid, sales of foreign assets and the increase of external liabilities (all discussed below) contributed £10 billion to the finance of Britain's war effort, equivalent to two full years' output of the entire labour force. Thus, Britain paid for the war primarily by reducing civilian consumption, increasing output and overseas borrowings of various forms.

## WAR AND FUNDAMENTAL ECONOMIC CHANGE

It should already be apparent that the Second World War had a wide-ranging impact on the British economy which both harmed the competitive position of some British industries and also helped to accelerate necessary economic change. The war certainly caused loss and destruction. An estimated 360,000 people (civilian and military) were killed (approximately half the casualties of the First World War). After the war the return of settled conditions led to a 'baby boom' which tended to lessen the impact of wartime population loss at least in the aggregate (Winter 1986b). The wartime expansion of the labour force was short-lived, with the return of many married female workers to the home and demands from war-weary workers for a shorter working week (Matthews et al. 1982: 72). The loss of capital equipment was also substantial; in 1945 the merchant fleet was approximately 70 per cent of the 1938 gross tonnage, approximately one-third of the prewar housing stock had been damaged or destroyed, to which must be added the destruction and lack of maintenance in factories, plant and machinery, schools, hospitals and other buildings (Worswick 1952: 21). Indeed, it has been estimated that one-quarter of Britain's prewar wealth was destroyed during wartime (Broadberry 1988). But in aggregate these domestic assets were replenished extraordinarily rapidly; Feinstein (1972: Table 44) has estimated that there was an increase of 6 per cent in the reproducible capital stock between 1938 and 1948. However, capital requirements had increased so that capacity had to be expanded well beyond the level of 1938 (Cairncross 1985: 13). Thus, the obvious effect of the war was to destroy factors of production, though that loss was less economically significant than must have been feared at the time.

This conclusion can be reinforced by reference to the growth accounting methods outlined in Chapter 2. Matthews and colleagues (1982) have identified a 'transwar' period considerably longer than the war itself, but which gives a good indication of the medium-term impact of war on the British economy (Table 8.5). Although there was a fall in the rates of growth of both labour and capital inputs, both remained positive for the period 1937–51. The wartime destruction of capital assets was clearly made good very rapidly and there was no major impact on labour input from either wartime loss of life or the shorter working week in the late 1940s. Of greater significance is the rapid growth of total factor productivity, faster than at any period since the mid-nineteenth century. Clearly,

*Table 8.5* Changes in output, inputs and total factor productivity, UK, 1873–1951 (% per annum)

|  | Labour[a] | Capital[b] | Total factor input | Total factor productivity | GDP |
|---|---|---|---|---|---|
| 1873–1913 | 1.7 | 1.9 | 1.8 | 0.0 | 1.8 |
| *1913–24* | *−0.4* | *0.9* | *0.1* | *−0.2* | *−0.1* |
| 1924–37 | 2.1 | 1.8 | 2.0 | 0.2 | 2.2 |
| *1937–51* | *1.1* | *1.1* | *1.1* | *0.7* | *1.8* |

*Notes*:

Figures in italics are designated 'wartime phases' in the original source.

a Adjusted for changes in 'quality' arising from changes in the 'age-sex-nationality' distribution, in the 'intensity of work' and in the 'average years of formal schooling'.

b Gross.

*Source*: Matthews *et al.* 1982: 22, 501.

these figures put Barnett's vivid descriptions of industrial relations problems into perspective. There seems to have been much less damage to the British economy from the Second World War than from the first, especially in the critical areas of output and productivity growth. It is likely that in the 1940s the positive rather than negative effects of war predominated: established attitudes were jolted helping to accelerate the rate of growth of TFP after the war; the sense of national solidarity created by war (in sharp contrast to 1914–18) helped avoid intense postwar industrial unrest; the willingness to continue controls for much longer after 1945 than 1918 smoothed the transition from the war economy (probably due to the sense of national solidarity); and there was much greater scope for increasing exports after 1945 as competitors had suffered a much more substantial setback than had been the case after 1918 (Matthews *et al.* 1982: 545–6).

The damage to competitors was of considerable significance as Britain's external position suffered badly as a result of the war. As was seen above, Britain had originally intended to deplete its reserves, which would include the proceeds of a wartime export drive, over a three-year period but was forced in 1940 to abandon 'financial prudence' in the face of emergency. By early 1941 gold and dollar reserves were almost gone (Sayers 1956: 496) and only the passage of the US Lend-Lease Act in March 1941 rescued the position. Under lend-lease the US government supplied Britain with material and equipment which was deemed necessary 'for the defense of the United States'; and payment would be made not in money but in some 'consideration' which would be negotiated (Sayers 1956: 374). But before the passage of the Lend-Lease Act, the UK reserves had been almost exhausted and British-owned assets in the USA had been sold, often at knock-down prices. During the war, sales of overseas assets amounted to £1.1 billion, or one quarter of the prewar total. Lend-lease aid and asset sales helped finance imports from the USA, but Britain also incurred other wartime costs. Imports from countries within the sterling area tended to be financed by simple debt, otherwise known as the 'sterling balances', which amounted to £3 billion by the end of the war.

Thus, the Second World War had both positive and negative effects. Wealth and capital equipment were lost, but the war also created the sense of national solidarity and administrative machinery which made it possible to continue controls after the war so that resources were freed to rebuild the capital stock. Britain never regained its relative wealth, but growth was much faster after the war and productivity rose at twice the interwar rate. There was undoubtedly much greater mobilisation of science for the war economic effort (Pollard 1983: 202–5; Marwick 1970: 284–8), but the old failings in applying science to the manufacturing process were also exposed. Under the pressures of war there was some modernisation of the capital equipment of the staple industries, but entrenched weaknesses remained. Britain's competitive position was severely weakened but new opportunities opened up in Europe. The list of effects could be extended almost indefinitely, with each negative effect balanced by a corresponding gain or opportunity. As opportunities are impossible to quantify, a concise balance sheet of the impact of the Second World War is simply beyond our understanding. But we can say with some certainty that the economic effects of the Second World War seem to have been less damaging than those of the first and that the determination to build a better future at both national and international levels after 1944 (see below) helped to repair damage and restore losses much more quickly than even optimists could have hoped.

## WAR AND FUNDAMENTAL SOCIAL CHANGE

Until the early 1960s it was widely believed that the war had profoundly reshaped British society. This analysis rested to a greater or lesser extent upon the formulation of the 'military participation ratio' (mpr) hypothesis. In its most general form, the mpr hypothesis asserts that social change is fostered by social welfare and that the extent of social welfare varies with the degree to which groups within society have to be mobilised to wage war (Andrzejewski 1954). The most sophisticated and influential version of the mpr hypothesis was put forward by Titmuss (1950) in his official history of social policy during the Second World War. He argued that public attitudes changed profoundly during the war, especially in 1940 when Dunkirk and the threat of invasion created an unprecedented sense of national and social solidarity. This new mood found expression in egalitarian measures (such as the extension of the hospital service and food policy) and proposals for social reform.

Titmuss's ideas have been revised and extended by Marwick in various studies of twentieth century social history. He too believes that the Second World War profoundly shaped British society, but denies that Dunkirk was a watershed and concentrates less on social reform than on the 'unguided' forces which have produced change in British society (Marwick 1974). He prefers to study the impact of war on society by exploring four 'dimensions' (Marwick 1981): war as 'destruction and disruption'; as a 'test' of existing social institutions; involving the 'participation' of hitherto underprivileged social classes and groups; and war as a great 'psychological experience'. The 'disruptiveness' of war forced people into new patterns of behaviour which changed their outlook. The evacuation policy, for example, led to greater social mixing, providing the basis for more constructive social policies in future while the extent of destruction produced a strong drive in favour of reconstruction. The 'test' dimension is best illustrated by the Emergency Hospital Service, planned in 1938 but made effective only when air raids revealed the uneven geographical distribution and differing standards of health care of the interwar system. The 'participation' effect is demonstrated, according to Marwick, by the gains won by the working class; universalism became the key principle in welfare legislation and workers won the right to have their needs considered in economic policy. The 'psychological experience' of war cemented national solidarity, being strongest among the articulate middle and upper classes, and fostered a desire to improve the lot of those lower down the social scale. At the same time, those lower down the scale were much more willing to make demands on their own behalf. There was a 'heightening of consciousness' on all sides. In sum, according to Marwick, the war brought about a social and economic revolution (Marwick 1970: 322–3).

Although there have long been historians who doubted this interpretation (Calder 1969; Pelling 1970), recent literature on class and the role of women has done much more to undermine the hypothesis of war as the midwife of a social revolution. Marwick's evidence for the wartime rise of the working class is difficult to measure. He argues that the working class had great power at the end of the war but it was exercised passively; the working class had asserted its impatience, indicated its desires and, reasonably satisfied, allowed the existing establishment to get on with it (Marwick 1981: 229). Of course, this sort of negative power is extremely elusive to formal academic investigation, but evidence for more tangible working class gains is distinctly difficult to find. Summerfield (1986) has surveyed changes in income and wealth in the decade after 1938 and has found little sign of any permanent narrowing of economic differentials. Following Seers's (1949) pioneering work, she notes that over the period 1938–47 the real incomes of the working class rose by 9 per cent and those of the middle class fell by 7 per cent. These movements were based upon fiscal policy changes (subsidies to the cost of living and heavy, progressive direct taxes) which were already being reversed in 1947 and were dismantled by the mid-1950s. Over the period 1935–55, there was little major narrowing of these earnings differentials (Routh 1965: 106–7). The levelling, albeit temporary, of earned income was not matched by any great redistribution of wealth. Individuals and companies were forced to relinquish overseas assets, all companies were prevented from distributing profits during the war and rents were controlled. In the short term, therefore, owners of capital suffered loss. However, dividend constraints probably increased long-run capital values and strengthened the position of rentier incomes. Corresponding increases in working-class asset-holding are difficult to find. Working-class savings increased, but were generally earmarked for the restocking of consumer durable goods after the war; pots and pans, crockery and furniture were more or less unavailable for ordinary consumers during wartime (Summerfield 1986: 183–5). Middle-class savings, on the other hand, were much more likely to be used to acquire assets which gave additional income after the war (Summerfield 1986: 201). Thus, war did little to reduce differentials between classes but had an impact on stratification within classes. The heavy demand for skilled engineering workers consolidated a group of affluent workers within the manual working class. At the same time the influx of women into administrative and clerical work depressed average salaries in this non-manual group. Thus, the war helped to increase differentials within the two main classes without disturbing the basic class structure (Summerfield 1986: 201).

Similar conclusions emerge from a study of the impact of the war on women. Marwick's position has again been difficult to tie down. On the one hand, he has concluded that the expansion of wartime work in the factories was a turning point in the emancipation of women, leading to new social and economic freedoms, as well as a marked change in political consciousness (Marwick 1974: 16). On the other, he has also noted that those women dependent on the miserable allowance paid to soldiers' wives were very poor; also the great majority of married women in wartime work wanted to return after the war to the tradi- tional roles of mother and housewife. To navigate through these contradictory waters there are helpful guides from Smith (1981; 1984; 1986a) and Summerfield (1984) which tend to support Marwick's second view that the war had little effect on women's economic and social position.

Smith (1986a: 211) has pointed out that the argument that the war was

a turning point in the emancipation of women has rested on a number of
often implicit assumptions: that most women were drawn into paid
employment for the first time during the war; that they welcomed this
opportunity of paid work; that the war undermined the gender segregation of jobs; and that war work permanently changed women's consciousness and made them dissatisfied with traditional roles in the home
and family. None of these assumptions will bear much investigation. It
had long been the custom for young women to work until marriage;
most of the additional 2,250,000 women who had joined the labour force
by 1943 would merely have been returning to employment which they
had given up on marriage. The increase of female employment came
only after great pressure had been exerted by the Ministry of Labour and
even then middle-class women showed a strong preference for the
Women's Land Army, the Auxiliary Ambulance Service and the Emergency Hospital Service as alternatives to the factories which were
regarded as boring, dirty and of low status. Not surprisingly, government efforts to steer women into factory work became increasingly
reliant upon compulsion (Summerfield 1984: 29–66). Despite the influx
of women into new areas of the labour market such as the shipyards and
munitions factories, the gender segregation of employment was little
changed. Women workers were seen by employers as being adept at
simple repetitive work but incapable of work equal to and paid at the
same rate as that of men; often a job was altered by dividing it between
two women or by introducing new machinery so as to avoid paying the
male rate (Smith 1981: 657). Women's average industrial earnings were
at best 53 per cent of those of men during the war (Summerfield 1984:
167–70). Thus, gender segregation of employment and pay was extremely resilient. Finally, there is little indication that many women who
were at work during the war had their attitudes to gender roles greatly
changed by their wartime experiences. In a major wartime survey of
employed women only 25 per cent responded unequivocally that they
wanted to continue in paid employment, with professionals and
administrators being far more enthusiastic than the unskilled (Smith
1986a: 217). Far from bringing about a revolution in the economic and
social position of women, the war seems rather to have reinforced the
traditional position of women in society (Summerfield 1984: 185).

Only one qualification needs to be considered, the position of married
women in the labour market. It had been the custom in the interwar
years for employers in many industries to impose a 'marriage bar',
forcing women to leave paid employment on marriage. After the war
employer practices changed. Whereas in 1931 only 16 per cent of the
female work-force was married, in 1943 and 1951 the figure was 43 per
cent. Marwick (1974: 160) has seen the end of the marriage bar as the
most positive result of women's wartime work but the evidence points

to a different conclusion. During the war most employers were planning to reimpose the bar but were forced to change their mind after 1945 when they were faced by strong demand for their products and a very tight labour market (Smith 1986a: 220–1). At the same time, there were fewer single women available for employment because of the effect of the war on the marriage rate. In the interwar years, approximately 20 per cent of women remained unmarried; in the postwar years only about 5 per cent did so. After the war women tended to marry much younger than in the 1930s (Winter 1986b: 159); employers who were short of labour had little alternative but to offer a warmer welcome to married women. The wartime increase in nuptiality, beginning in 1944, led to a minor wartime baby boom and was followed by a more substantial postwar baby bulge (Winter 1986b 154). After the war women were clearly opting for their traditional roles in the home and family.

## WAR AND RECONSTRUCTION

If there is scant hard evidence that 'unguided forces' unleashed by war led to substantial social change, what becomes of the argument that reconstruction after the war was driven by wartime developments? The most sophisticated account of the relationship between war and reconstruction has been suggested by Addison's *The Road to 1945* (1977). He argues that there were two main forces which propelled social and economic reconstruction. The first was the strong leftward drift in public opinion, especially after May 1940. The blame for leaving the country poorly armed and ill-prepared to resist the threat of German invasion was placed squarely on the Conservative-dominated governments of the 1930s. The 'production crisis' of 1941 led to widespread, bitter criticism of owners and managers of industry (Hinton 1980: 96–102). At the same time the politically articulate called for a better world to be created from the destruction of war. Public opinion thus became more radical and idealistic but it ran into the apparently firm opposition of sections of the coalition government. Labour ministers would have liked nothing more than to exploit these favourable currents but the Conservatives were wary of any attempts to make changes during wartime which would have implications for peacetime policies and institutions. Churchill, remembering the friction over reconstruction in Lloyd George's War Cabinet during 1917–18, tried to ensure that the wartime government would concern itself only with the prosecution of the war and leave postwar questions to a postwar general election. Into this impasse, according to Addison, stepped experts from prewar academic or professional life who lacked formal party political affiliations. Their plans for reform, often honed in the debates of the 1930s, could be presented to the left as ways of resolving some of the problems of British economic and social life and to the right as ways of outflanking the demand for more radical change. A consensus on limited change was thus established during wartime and laid the foundations of postwar economic and social policy.

Addison identifies the Beveridge Report (1942) as the key to postwar social policy. The original function of the committee on social and allied services had been to find ways of tidying up the patchwork of social services which had evolved since the turn of the century. But Beveridge quickly saw the potential for shaping postwar social policy and began to lobby for his ideas (Harris 1981: 408–60). The Beveridge Report contained both radical and more limited proposals and has been subject to a variety of interpretations. At its core, the report contained a far from revolutionary proposal to maintain the prewar system of contributory insurance schemes for health, unemployment and old age, with standard levels of contributions (from employees, employers and the state – as had been the case between the wars) and benefits, and those benefits available to all who could show the required contribution record. Rather more radical was the proposal that benefits should be at subsistence level – though Beveridge knew that the actual rates he proposed were below this level (Veit-Wilson 1992). Most radical of all was the way the proposals were framed. Beveridge identified five 'evil giants' of economic and social life – Want, Disease, Ignorance, Squalor and Idleness – and argued that no scheme of social security could be effective unless supported by family allowances, comprehensive health and rehabilitation services and the avoidance of mass unemployment. He campaigned for these proposals with great force and helped create a climate of expectation not only for a comprehensive social security scheme, but also for a radical new approach to the state's responsibilities towards its citizens after the war. The Beveridge Report created acute political tensions when it came to cabinet at the end of 1942. A number of Conservatives tried to have the report rejected but Labour ministers pressed for complete acceptance. In the end, the report and its broad assumptions about the postwar world was accepted 'in spirit' but when the coalition published its own white paper on social insurance the proposed levels of benefit drew sharp criticism from Labour's backbenches. Much remained to be decided after the war (Morgan 1984: 142–5). There are obvious implications for the nature of the wartime consensus; it was less firmly-based, less complete and less decisive than Addison implies.

The absence of firm agreement between Labour and Conservatives extends to other aspects of social reform associated with the Beveridge Report. Beveridge had argued that mass unemployment must be abolished and had assumed that postwar unemployment would, on average, be no worse than the best level recorded between 1922 and 1938 of 8.5 per cent of the insured work-force. The Economic Section of the war cabinet secretariat, a group of wartime civil servants drawn from university economics departments and including a number of prewar disciples of Keynes, believed that this target could be exceeded if the government managed peacetime demand as Keynes had proposed in the 1930s and the wartime government had followed since the 1941 budget. Treasury officials were suspicious of Keynesian postwar employment policy, especially of the assumption that deficit-financing would be needed to counter rising unemployment (Peden 1983). They already anticipated Britain's postwar balance of payments weakness and desperately wanted to avoid domestic policy commitments which might make external economic policy more difficult. In employment policy the main wartime disagreements were between two conflicting 'technocratic' views rather than between the political parties. Labour favoured 'economic planning' and the Conservatives supported a 'hands off industry' approach (Tiratsoo and Tomlinson 1993: 45–55), but these views rarely intruded into wartime discussions. The differences between the Treasury and the Economic Section appeared irreconcilable, but in 1943–4 opinion polls were showing that postwar employment and housing were causing great public concern (McLaine 1979). The government had to try to find a compromise despite the differences in Whitehall. The result was the white paper *Employment Policy* (Cmd. 6527 1944) which, although often seen as a pledge to maintain full employment in peacetime, actually committed the government to secure 'high and stable employment' after the war. When a postwar depression threatened, the government would expand aggregate demand by reducing interest rates, increasing public works expenditure and adopting measures to sustain aggregate consumption. However, the budgetary consequences were highly confused; there was certainly no explicit commitment to run a budget deficit. The white paper was so full of qualifications that it seems to have been more an exercise in deflating expectations than a blueprint for peacetime full employment (Booth 1987c).

The other measures placed on the agenda by the Beveridge Report reveal a similarly tangled interaction of interwar and prewar, radical and reactionary influences. The case for family allowances, for example, was revolutionised by the war. First the Treasury began to support family allowances for the first time in 1939–40 as a method of making heavier taxation more politically acceptable. It was also soon recognised that postwar family allowances would also have a role in the reorganisation of the social services, not least in justifying benefit levels for dependent children at below subsistence level in the social insurance scheme (Macnicol 1980: 211). The Treasury's remaining task was to control the cost of the scheme, and this was done by insisting that benefits were below the level recommended by Beveridge.

The influences which shaped wartime discussions of postwar health care can be incorporated even less easily into a simple 'war and society' model. For most of the interwar period the goal of the Ministry of Health had been to make health care much more widely available. The ministry hoped to create a regional structure which placed the hospital with its expensive diagnostic facilities at the apex of the system (Fox 1986). The problems of wartime, and in particular the fears of massive casualties from air attack, only strengthened this opinion – the emergency hospital system was based on regions each of which was designed to have sufficient hospital beds for the population at risk. There was less general agreement about how postwar health care was to be organised and real conflict emerged over such issues as the future of private practice, the methods of payment and the contractual status of doctors, and the role of the local authority services in the system; none was decided before 1945 (Morgan 1984: 152–63; Webster 1988: 24–133). In 1944–5 opinions began to polarise, with disagreements among ministers on party lines and a growing resistance to change from within the British Medical Association. Although there had been wartime agreement on the broad structure of a postwar NHS, much remained to be decided by the postwar government.

In education policy, a series of official reports during the interwar years had recommended the creation of a meritocratic system, with a split into primary and secondary stages, and the secondary stage in turn divided into various types of school to which children would be allocated on the basis of competitive examinations. The interwar Board of Education had accepted these proposals but had lacked the finance to implement change (Thom 1986: 101–8). The main responsibility for the running of the education system lay with the local authorities rather than with central government and the more progressive authorities continued to force the pace of change (as they had in the 1930s), leaving government with little option but to legislate. The 1944 Education Act was also profoundly shaped by lobbying from vested interests, determined to protect their own position (Barnett 1986: 280–5; Lowe 1993: 201–2). The net effect was that the Act maintained the *status quo* to a much greater extent than even the most lukewarm of reformers would have wished (Thom 1986: 124).

Most of the discussions of reconstruction planning imply that the 'white paper chase' was concerned exclusively with domestic questions and that British policy-makers had considerable autonomy. That impression is misleading because the issue which absorbed most cabinet time was external economic policy. From a very early stage much effort in Anglo–American relations was preoccupied with the future of trade and payments. Britain was concerned about her postwar balance of payments but so too was the USA. There had been a huge recovery of the US economy during the war and sections of US opinion feared the return of depression unless new markets could be found. The USA desired freer trade and removal of the barriers to multilateral clearing which had developed in the 1930s (Chapter 6). On the other hand Britain proposed a system of international trade and payments after the war which would permit restrictions such as imperial preference and the sterling area. The USA had the great advantage of immense economic and financial power and at the Bretton Woods conference in 1944 the US view prevailed. Two new international organisations were established, the International Monetary Fund and the International Bank for Reconstruction and Development (now known as the World Bank). Under the articles of the IMF, each member state agreed to peg its exchange rate with the dollar which was, in turn, pegged to gold. Members subscribed to a fund from which they could borrow to meet short-term difficulties in their balance of payments. After a short transitional period, all restrictions on currency convertibility (such as the sterling area arrangements) would have to be disbanded, except where the 'scarce currency clause' could be invoked against a country running a persistent balance of payments surplus. Against a longer-term balance of payments problem ('fundamental disequilibrium' as it was described in the IMF articles), countries could, with permission from the IMF, devalue. The IBRD was to supervise long-term international lending.

But why would countries with shattered industrial and agricultural sectors and starving populations dare to liberalise postwar international trade and payments? The answer lay in economic ideas and short-term political gain. According to economic theory, world incomes would be maximised by a system of free, multilateral trade and payments; many countries had come to realise that the strong domestic demand for economic growth and full employment could be achieved only if world trade would grow after the war at faster rates than in the 1930s. At the same time, the only source of the reconstruction finance which all countries needed was the USA and the US Treasury made acceptance of the IMF treaty a condition of access to US aid. From the US perspective, therefore, countries would receive help to restore their economies to health, whereupon the expansion of trade would carry recovery forward. Matters looked rather different from the receiving end. Reconstruction planners in Britain were faced by severe US pressures for liberalisation in the international economy. Some could be blocked, as was the US demand for Britain to end imperial preferences, but no-one knew for how long or how much damage to Britain's external position might be caused by the IMF. US optimism about the potential growth of international trade was regarded, probably rightly, as a sham (Kolko

1968). At the same time, the idealistic mood of the British people, especially from 1942 to 1944, meant that domestic reforms could not be denied. It is scarcely surprising that the aim of the Treasury in the latter half of the war was to pare down these demands for reform and to keep the cost to the minimum.

One method of resolving these problems might have been to ensure that fundamental problems within British industry were tackled. Indeed, Barnett (1986) has argued controversially that attention should have been devoted to industrial revival rather than to the 'new Jerusalem' of the welfare state. He implies that welfare policy handicapped industrial competitiveness, but is unconvincing (Tomlinson 1990: 168–9). However, the question of the failure to tackle the problems of British industry remains. The wartime government was aware of the depths of British industrial weakness (Tiratsoo and Tomlinson 1993: 21–63). However, almost nothing was done during wartime to promote postwar industrial competitiveness, with the exception of the Reid Report (Ministry of Fuel and Power 1945) on the coal mining industry. During wartime there was a party political dogfight on industrial policy. Coalition partners were much more concerned with ideological approaches than finding consensus. Labour calls for nationalisation, an anti-monopoly policy and planning collided with the Conservatives' desire to allow industrialists to resolve their own problems in their own way, even if this meant continuing the market-sharing and price-fixing agreements of the 1930s (Addison 1977: 256, 262–5). Even if politicians had been able to reach agreement, vested interests had gained immense negative power since 1939. Trade union leaders and industrialists had been drawn into the making and execution of production policy. This form of tripartism gave industrialists an effective veto over radical reforms of private industry and trade unionists the power to block changes in the collective bargaining system (Middlemas 1986: 83–109). The Board of Trade's enthusiasm for reform was blunted by opposition from industrialists (Tiratsoo and Tomlinson 1993: 60–3). It was vital for government to keep good relations with industrial interest groups to accelerate peacetime production and exploit Britain's head start over its continental rivals to correct the current account imbalance. Also, debates within Whitehall over postwar macro-economic policy almost certainly diverted attention from industrial problems (Booth 1989: 107–13; Glynn 1987: 172–4).

There have been several occasions during the present century when the fundamental problems of British industry might have been faced (Newton and Porter 1988). The period of reconstruction planning from 1943 to 1945 was undeniably the best opportunity, but the chance was lost. The worst features of the party system, the bureaucracy and producer politics combined to avoid a fundamental reappraisal of the future of British industry. Strategic planning with clear long-term goals and the machinery to implement them was conspicuously absent from economic policy-making (Stevenson 1986: 75). This would not be the last time that the short-term view prevailed and long-term costs were allowed to mount.

# Part II

# Postwar Britain

# Chapter 9

# Social and political development

## POPULATION SIZE AND DISTRIBUTION

Postwar demographic experience has done much to undermine the rather apocalyptic views expressed in the 1930s on the effects of a stagnant or declining population (Chapter 3). The UK population has continued to grow from census to census, but once again the picture has been more varied at regional level (Table 9.1). Both the Scottish and Welsh populations have been static since 1971, and even the total UK population has increased only slowly over the past two decades. In the second half of the 1970s, there were falls in the UK population in 1975–6, 1977–8 and 1978–9 and the total period fertility rate (the number of children that would be born per woman if prevailing age-specific ferti-lity rates persisted through her childbearing lifespan) has since 1972 been consistently below the levels needed for the natural replacement of the population (OPCS 1990). Nevertheless, apart from the later 1970s, the UK population has continued to rise, albeit at a lower rate than hitherto. There has been a positive rate of natural increase (that is, the fall in the birth rate has been matched in most years by continuing falls in the death rate) and this has been enough to offset a net loss through migration in most years (Table 9.2).

*Table 9.1* UK population, 1931–91 (thousands)

|  | England & Wales | Scotland | Northern Ireland | UK |
|---|---|---|---|---|
| 1931 | 39,952 | 4,843 | 1,243 | 46,038 |
| 1951 | 43,758 | 5,096 | 1,371 | 50,225 |
| 1961 | 46,105 | 5,179 | 1,425 | 52,704 |
| 1971 | 48,750 | 5,220 | 1,536 | 55,515 |
| 1981 | 49,155 | 5,131 | 1,533 | 55,848 |
| 1991 | 49,890 | 4,999 | 1,578 | 56,467 |

*Source: Annual Abstract of Statistics, 1993.*

Table 9.2 Components of population increase in the UK, 1931–91 (thousands)

|  | Population at beginning of period | Natural increase | Net migration | Total increase[a] |
|---|---|---|---|---|
| 1931–51 | 46,038 | 190 | +22 | 213 |
| 1951–01 | 50,290 | 246 | −7 | 252 |
| 1961–71 | 52,807 | 324 | −32 | 310 |
| 1971–81 | 55,928 | 69 | −44 | 42 |
| 1981–91 | 56,352 | 103 | +21 | 130 |

Note:
a After 1951, the authorities introduced a further category, 'Other adjustments', which was to take account of changes in the numbers of members of the armed forces within the UK, the visitor balance and other minor adjustments. Thus 'Total increase' is not simply the sum of 'Natural increase' and 'Net migration'.
Source:  Annual Abstract of Statistics, 1993.

The birth rate has gone through cycles which were initially very similar to those of the interwar years. There was a huge rise in 1947 (to 20.5 births per thousand women), occurring two years after the armistice just as had been the case after the First World War. The steep decline in the birth rate from 1947 to 1952 mirrors that in the five years after the 1920 peak. At this point, however, the patterns diverge. Interwar birth rates remained broadly flat, apart from a small fall in the slump years and minor recovery thereafter. In the postwar period, on the other hand, there was a long, unchecked rise in the birth rate from 1955 to 1964. Indeed, the number of postwar births peaked in 1964 (when it reached 18.5 per thousand women) as the baby boomers of 1947 produced their own offspring. Two factors underwrote this sustained rise in the birth rate. First, there was a definite trend to earlier marriage. Second, the full employment and rising real wages of the 'long boom' in the postwar economy provided a secure and optimistic climate that encouraged couples to have children. There were, however, also influences which pulled in the opposite direction. The full employment of the 1950s and 1960s increased the demand for female labour, bringing married women into employment in increasing numbers. The availability of work for women has traditionally been a cause of low fertility. In addition, contraceptives have become much more readily available over time. The birth rate fell to a trough of 11.2 in 1977 and has not risen above 14 since.

Family limitation was certainly not invented in 1948, as Chapter 3 has made clear, but there have been two significant changes in the postwar years. First, the use of some type of birth control has 'saturated' the population. Between the wars, just under half of unskilled working class married couples did not begin to use contraception at marriage; by the 1960s, only 7 per cent of middle-class and 11 per cent of working-class couples did not start contraception as they embarked on married life (Mitchison 1977: 32). If there were class differences in contraceptive measures in the 1960s, it was that middle-class women tended to use so-called 'appliance' techniques (the pill, IUD – intra-uterine device, the cap, sheaths, etc.) whereas 'non-appliance methods' (withdrawal and the 'rhythm method') tended to be favoured by the working class. Official figures suggest that since the 1970s appliance methods have become much more common and are extensively used by single women. Furthermore, in 1967 abortion was legalised in certain circumstances but the impact on the birth rate should not be exaggerated. Abortions were performed before 1967 and there is almost no evidence that the availability of legal abortion has influenced the birth rate significantly.

One additional factor needs attention as a potential influence on the birth rate, the rise in the status of women in society. The issues will be discussed more fully below, but since the Equal Pay Act of 1970 and the Sex Discrimination Act of 1975 career opportunities have opened for women, albeit less dramatically than the architects of the legislation intended. For an increasing number of women in the 1970s and 1980s, raising a family has had to compete with career development. Such pressures undoubtedly existed before 1939, but they have increased immeasurably since the mid-1970s.

A more detailed picture of the interaction of these various forces can be obtained from age-specific birth rates (Table 9.3). The baby boom of 1947 embraced mothers of all age groups (except teenagers) but from the 1950s into the late 1970s when the birth rate reached its postwar low, there was an increasing trend for women to produce their children relatively early in marriage. This pattern seems to be consistent with women responding to employment opportunities by restricting the span of child production and rearing in order to re-enter the labour market for relatively long spells from their late twenties or early thirties. The trend to earlier births is most obvious in the dramatic rise of the birth rate among teenage mothers from the war years to 1971. It was accompanied by a growth in the number of teenage marriages but also, and more fundamentally, by a rise in the economic, social and cultural status of young people, especially after the end of national service in 1960.

After the peak in the birth rate in 1964, there began a long decline in fertility. Optimism about the economy began to wane in the later 1960s and was seriously jolted in the 1970s. Birth control pills became readily accessible in the 1960s and freely available from the NHS from the mid-1970s and the fears about long-term side-effects had not yet lodged in women's consciousness. These two factors, together with the expansion of employment and career opportunities for women after 1970, go some

Table 9.3 Age-specific live birth rates, England and Wales, 1947–90

| | | Age-specific live birth rates per thousand women aged: | | | | | | |
|---|---|---|---|---|---|---|---|---|
| | Total live births (thousands) | >20 | 20–4 | 25–9 | 30–4 | 35–9 | 40–4 | 45< |
| 1947 | 881 | 19 | 146 | 170 | 118 | 66 | 19 | 1 |
| 1951 | 678 | 21 | 126 | 134 | 89 | 45 | 13 | 1 |
| 1956 | 700 | 27 | 147 | 151 | 88 | 45 | 12 | * |
| 1961 | 811 | 34 | 175 | 185 | 113 | 57 | 16 | * |
| 1964 | 876 | 39 | 185 | 197 | 119 | 58 | 15 | * |
| 1971 | 783 | 51 | 154 | 154 | 78 | 33 | 8 | * |
| 1977 | 569 | 30 | 105 | 119 | 59 | 18 | 4 | * |
| 1981 | 634 | 28 | 105 | 129 | 69 | 22 | 4 | * |
| 1986 | 661 | 30 | 93 | 124 | 78 | 25 | 5 | * |
| 1990 | 706 | 33 | 92 | 122 | 87 | 31 | 5 | * |

Note:
* Less than one per thousand women
Source: Annual Abstract of Statistics, various issues.

way to explaining why the birth rate might have fallen in the mid-1960s. When the birth rate picked up again in the late 1970s, it was accompanied by a shift to an older pattern of fertility. Although the peak child-bearing age remained 25–9 throughout the 1980s, fertility rates of women in their twenties declined. In contrast, fertility rates of women in their thirties have increased substantially. In 1990, the fertility of women in their early thirties was only slightly less than for those in their early twenties (OPCS 1990). There has also been a major change in the impact of social class on fertility. The lowest unskilled families and the very poor still tend to have the largest families but, in a reversal of the trend of the first half of the twentieth century, most working class families were having the smallest number of children, whereas middle- and upper-class parents have been having slightly larger families (Marwick 1982: 64). The influences which have shaped the birth rate have changed substantially, not only since the 1930s, but within the postwar period itself. In the 1970s and 1980s, women appear to have been planning their fertility according to rather different criteria than in the 1950s and 1960s. The extension of higher education and the opening up of career paths for women almost certainly tells part of the story, but so too does the steep rise in male unemployment during the 1980s by reducing family income for the poorest and encouraging more women into employment.

Changes in mortality since 1945 have been much less complex. Chapter 3 noted the importance of improved nutrition, better housing, clothing and public health advances in promoting lower mortality during the first half of the present century. After 1945, the new drugs (sulphona-mides, antibiotics), improved access to better health care and the devel-opment of immunisation programmes for all the major childhood killer diseases have helped to lower death rates still further. Frequent changes in the classification system make it difficult to chart changes in the cause of death, but at a very broad level there has been a fall in the role of infectious disease, such as TB, whooping cough and diphtheria and a rise of so-called 'degenerative diseases' such as cancer and heart disease. There has been a marked fall in deaths from bronchitis, reflecting improved environmental conditions and the decline of employment in heavy industries, such as coal mining, in which lung complaints were a notorious problem. The number of road accident deaths has not kept pace with the number of motor vehicles. Deaths from violence (which includes motor accidents) rose from the end of the war to a plateau in the 1960s and 1970s, and fell steeply in the 1980s. Despite the decline in industrial diseases and the rising affluence of the postwar years, high class differentials in mortality have remained, though governments have been less than keen on having the matter debated (Black 1980; Townsend and Davidson 1982; Le Grand *et al.* 1990: 92).

Although the fall in mortality has been experienced at all ages, it has been concentrated among the young and the old. The infant mortality rate is commonly regarded as the most sensitive indicator of the state of the national health. Apart from isolated hiccups in 1970 and 1986, there has been a strong downward trend in infant mortality throughout the period, reflecting better prenatal monitoring and care for premature babies, as well as the general factors mentioned in the previous para-graph. The rate in 1991 was less than one-tenth that of 1920 and one-quarter that of 1950–2, but Britain's record is by no means the best in Europe and lags significantly behind the Scandinavian nations. At the other end of the age scale, the decline in mortality has meant an increas-ing expectation of life (Table 9.4). Almost one in six of the total popula-tion is now in the 'retired' age group and, unless something very dramatic happens to the birth rate, this proportion will increase. Mor-tality is higher for males than for females at every age group with the result that the elderly comprise a disproportionate number of single or widowed women. This gender imbalance has important implications for social policy. Postwar governments have been increasingly keen to encourage the growth of occupational pensions as a supplement to the basic state pension (Titmuss 1958; Cutler *et al.* 1986: ch. 2; Hannah 1986: chs 4–5). But this form of job-related welfare has produced greater benefit for men than women. Female employees have gained little occupational welfare from their increased labour market participation since 1950; their periods of work tend to be broken to raise a family and female employment tends to be in low-paid, part-time jobs, which have been unattractive to suppliers of private pensions (Cutler *et al.* 1986: 60). Attempts to reform state pensions to give long-term benefit to those without occupational pensions, primarily the low-paid and women, have failed. Retired women have thus made up a large proportion of the poor in social surveys since 1945 (Atkinson 1970: ch. 3) since they have been disproportionately dependent upon the state pension which has become, especially since 1979, a base level of provision (Lowe 1993: 157–9; 313–15). The 'burden' of the old age pension in an ageing society is much more concerned with politics than demographics. In 1983 the value of employer and employee contributions to occupational schemes covering the richer half of the population was almost the same as the value of contributions to national insurance providing for the entire population (Cutler *et al.* 1986: 45). The 'nation' is manifestly capable of diverting resources from those in work to those in retirement but is apparently unable to redistribute from relatively wealthy employees to poor pensioners.

Migration patterns also reveal continuity and change. Internal migration has continued the earlier pattern of a drift from Scotland, Wales and the northern English regions to southern England. The South East and the Midlands were the main receiving areas before 1960 and East Anglia and the South West thereafter. The rural–urban drift continued into the 1950s, but was accompanied by movement away from the major conurbations into smaller towns and cities. From 1961, the rural–urban drift

*Table 9.4* Expectation of life, by age and sex, UK, 1901–91

|  |  | Year of birth | | | | |
| --- | --- | --- | --- | --- | --- | --- |
|  |  | *1901* | *1931* | *1961* | *1981* | *1991* |
| Further number of years which a person might expect to live: | | | | | | |
| Males | | | | | | |
| at birth |  | 45.5 | 58.4 | 67.9 | 70.8 | 73.2 |
| at age: | 1 year | 53.6 | 62.1 | 68.6 | 70.7 | 72.8 |
|  | 10 years | 50.4 | 55.6 | 60.0 | 62.0 | 64.0 |
|  | 20 years | 41.7 | 46.7 | 50.4 | 52.3 | 54.2 |
|  | 40 years | 26.1 | 29.5 | 31.5 | 33.2 | 35.1 |
|  | 60 years | 13.3 | 14.4 | 15.0 | 16.3 | 17.6 |
|  | 80 years | 4.9 | 4.9 | 5.2 | 5.7 | 6.3 |
| Females | | | | | | |
| at birth |  | 49.0 | 62.4 | 73.8 | 76.8 | 78.8 |
| at age: | 1 year | 55.8 | 65.1 | 74.2 | 76.6 | 78.3 |
|  | 10 years | 52.7 | 58.6 | 65.5 | 67.8 | 69.5 |
|  | 20 years | 44.1 | 49.6 | 55.7 | 57.9 | 59.6 |
|  | 40 years | 28.3 | 32.4 | 36.5 | 38.5 | 40.0 |
|  | 60 years | 14.6 | 16.4 | 19.0 | 20.8 | 21.9 |
|  | 80 years | 5.3 | 5.4 | 6.3 | 7.5 | 8.3 |

*Source: Social Trends*, 1992: 123.

was reversed, though this had much less to do with the expansion of employment in the countryside than with the growing ease of commuting by car from the countryside to urban employment.

The aspect of migration which has attracted most attention is however international movement. From Table 9.2 it is evident that 'net migration' has had only marginal impact on population change since 1945. Immigration exceeded emigration before 1951 and in the 1980s. For the period 1951–81, on balance Britain supplied the rest of the world with a small flow of 'economic migrants'. In most postwar years the UK has absorbed approximately 200,000 immigrants, and up to half have been returning British citizens. There were also substantial outflows of population from the UK throughout the period, initially to countries of the old Commonwealth and South Africa and latterly (since 1973) a growing tide to EU countries and the Middle East (especially in the early 1980s). The USA has also continued to be a popular destination for British emigrants.

The focus of controversy has been immigration from the countries of the new Commonwealth and Pakistan (NCWP). Although blacks and Asians had lived in Britain for many years before 1939, numbers were small and geographically concentrated (Holmes 1991). As the British economy began to run into labour shortages in the late 1940s migrant workers were attracted from the Caribbean and the Indian subcontinent in increasing numbers. There were also substantial inflows of Irish throughout the period, Poles in the late 1940s and Italians in the 1950s and 1960s, but comparatively little attention has been paid to them. Immigrants from the West Indies and India however met racist attitudes, especially in parts of London and the West Midlands. Immigration of blacks and Asians was running at approximately 14,000 per annum in the 1950s, but in 1961 there was a large rise and the Macmillan government introduced its Commonwealth Immigrants Act of 1962 which for the first time placed restrictions upon the entry of Commonwealth citizens. Successive governments have tightened further what might be termed 'primary' immigration (those with a definite right of entry under the Immigration Act of 1971) so that by 1973 a tight network of controls limited numbers from NCWP to less than 4,000 per annum in the 1970s. But in addition to these primary immigrants, there were considerable numbers of dependants so that the total inflow from NCWP amounted to between 30,000 and 50,000 per annum. Further legislation in the 1980s (when it had become much easier for EU nationals to enter) was designed to curb non-European immigration still further as 'an increasingly pronounced fortress policy on immigration' was established (Holmes 1991: 222).

It is difficult to see any real basis for the fears exploited by Enoch Powell and others that Britain would be swamped by a tide of black and Asian immigration. The largest 'ethnic minority' in Britain is probably still the Irish, and data from the mid-1980s suggest that those of Indian ethnic origin (many of whom will have been born in the UK and will never have seen India) amount to approximately 1.5 per cent of the total UK population, West Indians approximately 1 per cent, and Bangladeshis and Pakistanis together a further 1 per cent (*Social Trends* 1990: 25). It is certainly true that these groups have higher than the national average fertility rate, but there has been substantial convergence with that national average so that by the late 1980s the total period fertility rate (see above) of the longest established group, those of Caribbean origin, was identical to that of the UK as a whole (*Social Trends* 1990: 29).

## SOCIAL ORDER AND STRUCTURE

Since 1945 two main changes have taken place in the British occupational and class structures described in Chapter 3. The occupational pyramid has become still longer and more sophisticated but there have also been major shifts in the composition of the work-force, especially since 1970, which have led many to question the relevance of occupational strata in shaping people's lives.

There were three critical features of discussions of social structure before 1939. The most important was the use of the occupation of the male head of household in the classification system. Second, there was an implicit presumption of shared experiences, beliefs and identity among members of these broad occupational categories, and that these occupational cleavages were of greater significance in understanding social position than other divisions potentially unrelated to occupation, such as ethnic origin, gender or family connections. Finally, it was assumed that position in the social hierarchy was determined more by factors relating to production (occupation) than to consumption. These three propositions were undoubtedly pertinent in 1914 and also in 1939, though there were already signs of the break-up of traditional working class communities in which such factors as housing, consumption patterns, leisure activities, social life and much else were profoundly shaped by occupation. The archetypal 'Jarrows', mining communities and dockwork settlements still existed at the outbreak of the Second World War, and some may have survived into the 1950s (Willmott and Young 1960: 10), but so, too, did the more diverse, affluent manual worker settlements around Slough, Coventry, Luton and Bristol.

As a result of frequent changes in occupational classifications, postwar official statistics cannot provide consistent data on occupational change since 1945. The best estimates are given in Table 9.5 which illustrates the enormous expansion of managerial and technical work and the parallel contraction of manual labour, particularly that done by skilled workers

*Table 9.5* Distribution of the economically active population by occupational category, Great Britain, 1951–81 (percentage in each category)

|  | 1951 | 1961 | 1971 | 1981 |
|---|---|---|---|---|
| Employers and own account | 6.7 | 6.4 | 6.5 | 6.4 |
| Managers and administrators | 5.4 | 5.3 | 8.0 | 10.1 |
| Professionals and technicians | 6.6 | 9.0 | 11.1 | 14.7 |
| Clerical and sales | 16.3 | 18.6 | 19.5 | 19.3 |
| Supervisors and foremen | 2.6 | 2.9 | 3.9 | 4.2 |
| Skilled manual | 23.8 | 24.1 | 20.2 | 16.0 |
| Semi-skilled manual | 26.6 | 25.1 | 19.3 | 19.0 |
| Unskilled manual | 11.9 | 8.5 | 11.6 | 10.4 |
| Total | 99.9 | 99.9 | 100.1 | 100.1 |
| Total (millions) | 22.5 | 23.6 | 25.0 | 25.4 |

*Source*: Heath and MacDonald 1987: 365.

(though by the end of the 1980s the proportion of the work-force performing unskilled manual work had halved since 1981).

But this occupational classification is not that used by researchers investigating social mobility and social class and so has limited value for study of the dynamics of the postwar class structure. For a more detailed examination of the processes of change it is necessary to turn to the work of John Goldthorpe (1980), the leading interpreter of the British class structure. Concentrating only on adult males, Goldthorpe has divided the occupational structure into seven categories and has grouped these seven categories into three main classes as is shown in Table 9.6. In the postwar period there has been a 'managerial revolution' in Britain; an enormous expansion of the service class (males employed in administrative, professional and managerial occupations). Positions in the service class have expanded at a faster rate than could be filled by

*Table 9.6* Goldthorpe's class schema

| | | |
|---|---|---|
| I | Higher } | { Professional, administrative |
| II | Lower } | { and managerial |
| III | Routine non-manual | |
| IV | Small proprietors and self-employed | |
| V | Lower technical and supervisory | |
| VI | Skilled manual | |
| VII | Semi- and un-skilled manual | |

| | |
|---|---|
| I–II | Service class |
| III–V | Intermediate class |
| VI–VII | Working class |

*Source*: Goldthorpe 1980: 39–41.

sons of service class fathers. Thus, there has been substantial mobility into service class employment from both the intermediate and the working classes. Social mobility has taken the form of both intra-generational mobility (men have worked up the occupational ladder into service class positions during their own working life) and inter-generational mobility (sons achieving higher occupational status than their fathers, usually by the acquisition of higher educational qualifications). The amount of relative social mobility (that is, the chance of a working class father reaching a service class position compared with that of his son, or relative downward mobility from the service class) has not changed either within the period or, as far as can be seen from less reliable data, from earlier periods. Furthermore, service class employment seems to be relatively stable; the overwhelming majority of those who began their working lives in the service class remained there and have been able to guide their sons into similar service class positions.

These findings are echoed in an authoritative study of social class and educational attainment which plotted the impact of the expansion of higher education on social mobility (Halsey *et al.* 1980). The principal conclusion is that the fastest rates of growth of 'take up' of post-compulsory education since 1945 has been experienced by the working class, but the biggest absolute increases in education after sixteen were gained by the upper middle (or service) class. Students in higher education have been drawn mainly from service-class families but the expansion of places has allowed more working-class children to gain higher qualifications. Coverage of the Halsey study ends in the 1970s, but more recent work suggests that further expansion of higher education in the 1960s created places which have been taken up disproportionately by those from the working class (Glennerster and Low 1991: 71–2).

At the other end of the ladder, the working class has contracted markedly over the postwar period and has become the most homogeneous of the British occupational classes (in other words, it contained the largest ratio of those who were born into the class). Moreover, the British working class is, and has long been, overwhelmingly an industrial working class, more so than in any other developed nation because the agricultural sector contracted much earlier in Britain than elsewhere. Between these two relatively stable, self-recruiting classes, is the intermediate class which is much more difficult to define and understand. Positions in Goldthorpe's occupational classes III, IV and V frequently do not represent final destinations in men's working lives. This is an intermediate class in all senses of the word.

However, problems arise with Goldthorpe's analysis at either end of the occupational hierarchy. The service class has been drawn with sufficient width to contain both the managerial elite and relatively poorly-paid public sector workers such as those in universities. The designation of a large and growing service class should not be seen as an argument that the 'upper', 'governing' or 'ruling' class has disappeared. A study of the history of the coal-owning, industrial and banking families of the North East has shown how the leaders have become integrated into a nation-wide upper class in the present century (Benwell C.D.P. 1979). Intermarriage within the group has created powerful dynasties, the members of which still sit on local authorities, planning bodies, the boards of finance corporations and multinational companies. They held substantial family seats in Northumberland, were members of exclusive London clubs and, in one case, sat at the cabinet table in the Thatcher government. More generally, members of established wealthy, propertied families still own a massive proportion of private disposable capital. In 1970, 8 per cent of all shareholders (amounting to 0.5 per cent of the entire adult population) controlled nearly 70 per cent of all corporate capital in private hands. From this elite are drawn the strategic managers of British industry, those directors who sit on the board of more than one company (Westergaard and Resler 1976: 159–65). This inner circle will meet socially and send their children to the best public schools and on to the ancient universities; they will be related by birth or marriage to other members of the charmed circle (Scott and Griff 1984: 181). The governing class has remained open to new blood, but the combination of great wealth, kinship ties and excellent social contacts have given the children of upper-class families a disproportionately better chance of gaining elite positions in their turn (Stanworth and Giddens 1974). The 'managerial revolution' may have swelled the relative size of the service class, but this is not incompatible with the continuation of a privileged elite.

At the other end of the social hierarchy, the 1980s have witnessed changes which have led some to doubt whether a working class still exists. As Goldthorpe's study was published, changes which called into question the occupational approach to class were becoming all too evident. The severe decline of male, full-time employment accelerated, particularly in the highly unionised sectors of industry. At the same time, female employment, often in part-time work, was much less affected by the slump of the early 1980s and continued to grow strongly later in the decade. The relevance of the male-dominated occupational hierarchy seemed questionable. The cleavages of race also deepened as the slump of the early 1980s hit young blacks more severely than any other group and racial tensions mounted. Moreover, the collapse of public consumption (publicly owned housing, public transport, public services) under the Conservative government in the 1980s has made individual ownership, particularly of housing, more important in shaping social identities, with a profound impact on voting patterns and social values more generally (Dunleavy 1980). Prompting much of this reappraisal of traditional approaches to class has been the palpable rejection of the Labour Party by large sections of the British working class in the 1970s and 1980s (Hobsbawm 1978; 1983; 1987). Extravagant theories have been built upon these changes (see Marshall *et al.* 1988) but common to all is an assessment that the working class has become increasingly sectionalised (between manual workers in the public and private sectors, between male and female workers, black and white, wage-workers and welfare claimants, those in 'outer Britain' and those in southern England), with each group pursuing its own economic interest irrespective of the rest. Class-based, or 'solidaristic' forms of social and political consciousness have given way to the values of individualism and the search for private and personal satisfactions. In its more extreme form, this 'privatisation' of manual (and routine non-manual, such as clerical and distributive) workers is related to the standardisation of tasks, closer supervision and regulation of the majority of blue and routine white-collar jobs. Lack of fulfilment at work has to be counterbalanced by a search for individual autonomy and personal satisfaction at home, in family life or in leisure (Gorz 1982). The force of international competition which has 'alienated' workers from their work has also produced disillusion with the politics of reform and intervention. Thus, class in the sense of shared identity, beliefs and perspective has little meaning.

In short, the British class structure has become much more fluid at the end of the twentieth century. It is clear that male manual workers no longer form the majority of the labour force. It is equally certain that the position of the elite has not undergone fundamental change. There has been a substantial enlargement of the 'middle classes', but within this group there are real divisions. In addition to the horizontal distinction between service-class occupations and those in more routine clerical, distributive and technical work there are vertical cleavages between those employed in the corporate, the state and the self-employed sectors. The same sort of picture is evident in the working class. In addition to the traditional distinctions between skilled, semi-skilled and unskilled workers, there are new divisions based not only on factors mentioned above (sector of employment, race and consumption patterns) but also on labour market segmentation (to be discussed in Chapter 13) between core, peripheral and the long-term unemployed workers (Hamnett *et al.* 1989: 116–9). Class has not so much disappeared as fragmented in response to a pattern of economic growth which will be described in subsequent chapters.

## GENDER AND SOCIETY

As noted in Chapter 3, interwar women had to fulfil their biological roles of childbirth and child rearing, but also carried out the vast bulk of domestic labour and were also expected to engage in the market for paid labour. They tended to manage this dual role by judicious timing of their involvement in paid employment. Middle-class women tended to enter the labour market between education and marriage and then the over-whelming majority withdrew from waged employment for good. This pattern was reinforced by a formal requirement in many so-called 'white blouse' careers that women give up their posts on marriage. Working class women would also work until marriage and most did not work thereafter. But some working class mothers took low-paid jobs, often in menial private service work, when deemed a financial necessity (Thane 1991: 195). Most often, this occurred when the children were very young but these mothers would tend to withdraw from the labour force when children became old enough to contribute to household income. As a result, the vast majority of women in the paid labour force were under the age of 35 (almost 70 per cent of working women in 1931). More women wanted to work but acceptable employment was not available. Since 1945, the pressures of the dual role have intensified. More has been expected of women in the home; the ideal of the nuclear family with mother at home caring for the children (and other aged or infirm members of the extended family) has been a powerful ideological tool at various moments since 1945. At the same time, employment oppor-tunities for women have grown. A significant proportion of these jobs have tended to be low-paid, with poor prospects and inferior status (Chapter 13), just as they were for women between the wars (Chapter 3).

The pressures on women, especially after marriage, to conceive their primary role as supplying domestic labour and caring services has been broadly based since 1945. In planning the postwar social welfare system, Beveridge assumed that women would continue to withdraw from the labour market on marriage. Key parts of the social security system were designed accordingly, restricting women's contributions and rights to social welfare benefits (Cutler *et al.* 1986: ch. 3). Indeed, there was a reassertion of traditional gender roles in 1945 when women returned to the home from wartime work (Chapter 8). The failure of successive postwar governments to provide a national system of free nursery education, as had been recommended in 1943, both reflected prevailing assumptions about where the priorities of married women should lie and at the same time reinforced the problems for women with young children in taking paid employment. The absence of state child care had not prevented some interwar mothers from taking paid work if family circumstances demanded, but the climate of ideas in the late 1940s and early 1950s had changed. There was now growing concern with the effect of maternal deprivation in early childhood on adults' psychologi-cal health. These ideas probably had very little relevance to 'ordinary' families but they created a pervasive belief that well-adjusted people

needed to spend most of their first five years in the company of their
natural mothers (Crofts 1986). These attitudes were challenged by the
feminist movement in the late 1960s and 1970s but they re-emerged in a
new, more powerful form in the 1980s in the rhetoric of the new right.
The Conservative party has been ideologically determined to blame a
range of social problems on the collapse of 'traditional' family values
which had followed increasing state intervention. In 1978, Margaret
Thatcher set out the beliefs which would drive so much legislation in
the 1980s and place increasing burdens on the caring role of women:

'We know the immense sacrifices which people will make for the care
of their own near and dear – for elderly relatives, disabled children
and so on, and the immense part which voluntary effort even outside
the confines of the family has played in these fields. Once you give
people the idea that all this can be done by the state ... then you will
begin to deprive human beings of one of the essential ingredients of
humanity – personal moral responsibility.'

(quoted in Croft 1986).

With the shift from institutional to 'community' care in many areas
and the dismantling of other structures of state-provided social support,
the home responsibilities of women have grown in the 1980s and 1990s.

The demographic forces which have been discussed in the first section
of this chapter have, however, given women greater opportunity and
incentive to participate in the market for waged work outside the home.
In 1900, a British woman aged twenty could expect that approximately
one-third of her remaining life span would be devoted to bearing and
caring for children. With falling family sizes and increasing life expectancy throughout the century, the burden of children has lessened,
particularly between 1945 and 1975 when women were having their
first baby earlier than ever before and concentrating child birth into a
shorter period. A woman aged twenty in 1975 could expect to devote
only 7 per cent of the rest of her life to her children (Halsey 1978: 101).
Married women have been able to return to work when their children
have reached school age. Since the late 1940s, both middle and working
class women have established a two-phase work pattern, with participation in the labour market interrupted by child care. The tendency in the
1980s for a growing proportion of women to produce their first child
after they have passed thirty suggests that many women have chosen to
combine career and family responsibilities. Recent social surveys have
indicated that mothers with children under five years of age form a
growing proportion of those in paid employment.

For other women, the need to combine paid employment with the
raising of young children has been more urgent. The growth of divorce

since the liberalisation of the laws beginning in the mid-1960s has recreated the disruption to early and middle family life which in previous generations resulted from early death. The speed and extent of the transformation can be seen in the ratio of married women to divorcees; in 1974 it was 30 to 1 but in 1986 only 10 to 1 (*Social Trends* 1990: ch. 2). Although legal settlements almost invariably impose maintenance payments on separated and divorced fathers for their children, non-payment has been common leaving mothers to choose between state benefits and combining paid child-care with employment. To redress some of these burdens (on both mothers and the state), the Child Support Agency was established in 1993 to ensure that fathers continued to meet their financial obligations to their children even after separation or divorce. Divorce and separation are the most common causes of the single (female) parent household; non-marriage as well as the death of the husband are also responsible. The proportion of families headed by a lone woman is as high in the late twentieth century as it was in 1890.

Economic change since 1945 has created powerful incentives on women to enter the labour market. A more detailed discussion of female employment must await Chapter 13, but the main factors are readily understood. For three decades after the war, Britain enjoyed not only full employment but an excess of vacancies over unemployed workers. The shortfall was met by the economic mobilisation of married women, particularly in part-time work. Between 1950 and 1980 the total UK work-force grew by nearly three million, which was almost exactly the increase of part-time female employment over the same period. The proportion of female employees in manufacturing remained roughly stable, despite the continuing contraction of traditionally large female employers such as textiles and clothing, but the real growth of jobs for women was in services, in both public and private sectors. The divergent trends of employment in manufacturing and services, especially after 1970 (Chapters 12, 13), sharpened the contrast between strong demand for female workers and much weaker demand for men.

Finally, the feminist movement has long been concerned with prejudice and discrimination not only in the market for waged work (discussed in Chapter 13) but also in the performance of household labour. With increasing numbers of women seeking paid employment there has been pressure for men to engage in housework and child care. The matter is sufficiently contentious for government to collect data on who does what in the home (*Social Trends* 1990: Table 2.9). Although a large majority of the adult population believes that most household tasks should be shared equally, women actually undertake most of the washing, cleaning, ironing, cooking, shopping, tending for and disciplining children; men appear to be very busy repairing household equipment. We have no firm ideas about how this compares with earlier generations. But there is little doubt that, as the twentieth century draws to a close, women still do most of the work in the home as well as increasing amounts of paid employment.

## POLITICAL DEVELOPMENT

The main theme of interest is the extent to which there has been a broad consensus between the main parties on the goals and means of policy-making in the period from the 1940s until the advent of 'Thatcherism'. 'Consensus' is a notoriously difficult word to define in an operational sense, especially when applied to the British system of adversarial politics which encourages parties to emphasise their differences in 'ritualised party conflict' (Gamble and Walkland 1984: 177). But many interpreters of the British system have argued that the political agenda changed in the 1940s. Beer identified in the mid-1960s a 'collectivist politics' which embraced the welfare state, the mixed economy and economic management; both main parties had similar policy goals and the differences between their positions were 'marginal, statistical, quantitative', despite the vigorous partisan rhetoric (Beer 1965: 242). The parties were forced together by electoral competition (Kavanagh 1992: 181), by what the civil service believed to be administratively practicable, economically affordable and politically acceptable (Kavanagh and Morris 1989: 18) and by the incorporation of producer interest groups (the employers' associations and the TUC) into policy-making (Middlemas 1979). There were equally powerful forces, notably the growing antagonism between the USA and the USSR after 1946, to ensure that foreign policy was conducted along similar, predictable lines despite changes of government. There was, however, scope for disagreement between the parties; defence and foreign policy caused major disputes (over the Suez episode or the pace of withdrawal from the world role) and in certain areas (notably relations with Europe and industrial relations policy) both main parties appear to have acted opportunistically at times when in government, giving the impression of fluidity in the policy agenda. The notion of consensus is not without its critics (Pimlott 1989), but the prevailing view points to the extent of agreement between party leaders and the continuity of policy in the period from the 1940s to the late 1970s.

Addison (1977) argued strongly that this consensus was forged during wartime but his hypothesis has come under increasing criticism as evidence has accumulated of substantial differences on party and ideological grounds within the wartime coalition (Jeffreys 1987; Chapter 8 above). The 1945 general election resulted in a landslide victory for Labour which was uniquely identified with the change of mood during the war years and the new domestic priorities which had emerged

(Morgan 1984: 44). The Conservatives quickly adapted during their period of opposition (Gamble 1974). Under Churchill's leadership the Conservatives entered the 1951 election campaign promising to conserve most of the new fabric of policy but manage it in a less intrusive, overbearing manner. Significantly even under Winston Churchill, whose anti-union sentiments had a very long pedigree, the new Conservative government preserved most, though not all, of the expanded public sector, the commitment to a broad system of state benefits and full employment, but also maintained the easy channels of communication between the TUC (and employers) and the government. The consensus had apparently come of age.

In 1951, the new government's main task had been to confound Labour's prediction that a Tory administration would create mass unemployment, abandon the welfare state and antagonise the trade unions. But Conservatives quickly seized the opportunity to claim the credit for the prosperity which flowed from the fastest rate of economic growth in Britain's industrial history. Without diminishing the interventionist, supportive role of the postwar state, the Conservatives under Macmillan began to emphasise the 'opportunity' state, in which the state encouraged individual responsibility (Lowe 1993: 82–3). After 1960, however, there was growing disquiet about foreign competition and relative decline as unemployment levels began to rise. The British party political system received some of the blame for disappointing economic performance. Political scientists claimed to have identified a 'political business cycle' in which governments boosted the economy for short-run electoral gain but had to reverse tack when the election had been won (Nordhaus 1975; MacRae 1977). Others pointed to the malign influence of 'adversary politics' (Rose 1980: chs 2–5; Finer 1975: Part 2) in which party leaders have to balance what they deem electorally 'popular' with what is 'popular' in their party. As the opinions of party activists tend to be more committed and ideologically driven than those of either the mass of voters or the party leaders exposed to the consensus-strengthening forces noted above, it is likely that, when in opposition, parties will acquire programmes which satisfy activists and emphasise partisan differences. If the party subsequently wins an election, it will implement this ideological, partisan policy before national and international economic and political 'realities' push the government back to more consensual, less extreme measures (Stewart 1977). Detailed studies have however found little of value in either the political business cycle (Mosley 1984; Chrystal and Alt 1983) or the adversary politics hypothesis (Gamble and Walkland 1984) but voters have become inclined to believe that politicians are part of the problem rather than the solution to Britain's relative economic decline.

Growing awareness of Britain's relative decline and mounting criticism of the conduct of economic policy produced unmistakable signs in the 1970s that the framework of postwar policy was under threat. Criticism of consensus politics mounted in both main parties. The Conservatives had been dominated during the 1950s and 1960s by what Anthony Seldon (1991: 249–56) has termed the 'progressive tendency', which had given strong support to the policy programme established in the 1940s. Its main exponents were Butler, Macmillan, Boyle and MacLeod. To the mid-1960s, the main opposition to this group had come from the neo-imperialist, or 'old', right which was a spent force, campaigning for one lost cause after another (anti-decolonisation, anti-immigration, anti-Europe, pro-white-Rhodesian separatists, pro-Ulster unionists). But in the mid-1960s the right was rejuvenated by a 'new' agenda of support for 'sound money', free market economics and strong Anglo–American links. The right continued to make ground in the 1970s as support for the party leader, Edward Heath collapsed in the mid-1970s. Heath's aloof, unapproachable character gave him few personal friends in the party and his general election record (played four, won one, lost three) brought mounting criticism (Campbell 1993). But it was his betrayal of the party's 1970 election programme in the U-turn of policy in 1972 (see Chapter 14) which made many in the party determined to get rid of Heath at all costs. The new right was still a minority force in the party, but in the persons of Margaret Thatcher and Keith Joseph, it led the criticism of the leadership. Having defeated Heath in 1975, Mrs Thatcher began to champion 'non-consensus conservatism' and took the party with her (Seldon 1991: 246).

Faction fighting in the Labour party in the 1970s was even more robust. Labour's feuds were broader, longer lasting and coloured by personal animosity (Pimlott 1992). The Heath government's confrontation policies of 1970–2 radicalised the Labour left, particularly in the constituencies and the unions (Ceadel 1991: 274), leading to a rejection of much of the framework of consensus. The left championed a revival of class politics with emphasis on redistribution and more extensive control over private industry. Europe also bitterly divided Labour's left and right (Pimlott 1992: 510–696). When Labour did come to power in 1974, it took office a very disunited party; the atmosphere was poisonous and antagonisms were vented in public. The government's own problems over industrial, wages and financial policies only served to deepen the gulf between left and right in the cabinet and between the bulk of MPs and the more radical constituencies and unions. These antagonisms eventually burst the party and in April 1981 the bulk of Labour's right decamped to form the Social Democratic Party.

Labour's schism could not have been better timed to aid the Conservative government. Under Margaret Thatcher's leadership, the Conservatives had been able not only to exploit dissatisfaction with the Labour government's conduct of office in the late 1970s (and especially its relations with the trade unions in the 'winter of discontent' when successive groups of public-sector workers went on strike over pay) but also to tap into more general disenchantment with the conduct of postwar politics and the failure to arrest relative economic decline. The Thatcher government's central policy was its anti-inflationary medium-term financial strategy, which went hopelessly wrong and deepened the downturn of the early 1980s (Chapter 14). The Conservatives were highly unpopular as economic conditions deteriorated. However, the government's position was restored by the triumphal campaign to regain the Falkland Islands from Argentine forces. The vigour with which the prime minister prosecuted this campaign, the first signs of recovery from the slump of 1980–2, the ability to use rising oil revenues to cut income tax, and above all the fissures in the opposition allowed the government to rebuild its popularity in unpropitious circumstances. The Conservatives duly won the 1983 general election and Margaret Thatcher's personal stature was massively increased. In its first term, the Conservative government had launched a failed experiment with monetarist policies and had laid the foundations of anti-union policy (Chapters 14 and 13) but it was in the second and third terms that 'Thatcherism' was defined and consolidated. As Gamble (1988: ch. 4) has argued, Thatcherism combines a free economy and strong state. Central government has assumed extraordinary new powers – over the unions, local government, the civil service, education – while at the same time expounding the need for personal responsibility and decentralised decision-taking within a market framework. The government was permitted to press this inconsistent mixture for so long because of the unique appeal of the prime minister (Ramsden 1991). From the late-1980s, Labour began a very painful process of coming to terms with the new agenda established by Thatcherism in the 1980s with a protracted review of all aspects of its policy programme. The 'modernising tendency' in the party has been strongly in the ascendant and Labour has become a European-style social democratic party in the 1990s. In the process, a new policy consensus appears to be emerging, with emphasis on creating an efficient competitive industrial structure, tight control over public expenditure, notably on welfare, and the promotion of labour market flexibility. Most of the principles which guided policy before the mid-1970s have been cast aside.

# Chapter 10

# Growth and welfare

The main outlines of postwar economic performance will already be clear from Chapter 2; since 1951, the British economy has grown on average more rapidly than at any time in its industrial history but other developed economies have done even better. Between 1950 and 1990, British living standards have fallen from among the highest in western Europe to among the lowest (Maddison 1991: 6–7). Until the late 1950s, British opinion took it for granted that domestic living standards were well ahead of those on the Continent. Since the early 1960s, however, concern has mounted. Economists became highly perplexed about the trajectory of British economic development, and began to portray Britain as a case study of 'de-industrialisation' (Bacon and Eltis 1976; Singh 1977; Blackaby 1978a). The economy plunged into recession in 1974 and 1979, but the upswing of the 1980s was long and strong, and soon provoked Conservative ministers to claim that the long-awaited 'economic miracle' had at last arrived (Lawson 1992). Sympathetic economists trumpeted a British economic renaissance (Walters 1986; Maynard 1988). Unfortunately, this very rosy view of economic prospects soon collapsed. A third recession unfolded from mid-1990 and, though not as deep as the downturn of 1979–82, was more long-lasting and tenacious than anything since 'the slump' of 1929–32. Opinions about British postwar economic performance have been more volatile than the economy itself. Despite the growing evidence of cyclical instability since the early 1970s, actual rates of growth of output and output per head have fluctuated within relatively narrow limits. There is a pervasive view that the British economy should have grown faster than it has, but economists have also become aware that the processes of economic development are much more complicated than was formerly believed (Crafts 1993: ch. 2; Ormerod 1992). The key to faster growth has been elusive both for economists and governments since the early 1960s.

## THE INTERNATIONAL CONTEXT

Every developed country has experienced fast growth during the long boom of 1950–73, and slower, more disturbed performance since but which, none the less, compares very well with that before 1950. The basic data are given in Table 10.1, which show rates of growth of living standards (GDP per head of population). The USA and Britain were the slowest growers, but the USA was the world's most efficient economy, at the 'technological frontier'. Britain, on the other hand, was well within that technological frontier and had much to gain from adopting or adapting US methods. This point can be considered more clearly by comparing levels of productivity, or efficiency, at various points since 1938. For this type of comparison it is appropriate to look at measures of productivity, GDP per worker or, preferably, GDP per hour worked (which takes into account international differences in productivity arising from one country having a longer normal working week or shorter annual holidays than another).

This is, however, no simple task. International estimates of hours worked are of variable quality (Prais 1981: 278, 321) and further problems occur whenever comparisons are made between *levels* rather than *rates of growth* of output. Part of this exercise involves transforming the value of output in one country into the currency of another. This can be done quickly using prevailing exchange rates. Since the 1970s, however, economists have employed 'purchasing power parities', comparing directly the cost of a selected, representative basket of goods and services for more reliable comparisons (Kravis 1976: 21–2). The figures in Table 10.2 show GDP per hour worked relative to US levels using purchasing power parities. On average, levels of productivity deteriorated markedly relative to the USA between 1870 and 1938 and remained very wide until 1950. The trend was reversed, though at

*Table 10.1* Growth rates of real GDP per head, 1870–1989 (percentage annual average compound rates)

|  | *1870–1913* | *1913–50* | *1950–73* | *1973–89* |
|---|---|---|---|---|
| France | 1.3 | 1.1 | 4.0 | 1.8 |
| Germany | 1.6 | 0.7 | 4.9 | 2.1 |
| Japan | 1.4 | 0.9 | 8.0 | 3.1 |
| UK | 1.0 | 0.8 | 2.5 | 1.8 |
| USA | 1.8 | 1.6 | 2.2 | 1.6 |
| Average of 16 OECD countries[a] | 1.4 | 1.2 | 3.8 | 2.1 |

*Note:*
a Australia, Austria, Belgium, Canada, Denmark, Finland, Italy, Netherlands, Norway, Sweden and Switzerland plus the countries listed.
*Source*: Maddison 1991: 49.

*Table 10.2* Comparative levels of productivity, 1870–1989 (US GDP per man hour = 100)

|  | 1870 | 1913 | 1938 | 1950 | 1973 | 1987 | 1989 |
|---|---|---|---|---|---|---|---|
| France | 60 | 54 | 54 | 44 | 76 | 94 | n.a. |
| Germany | 61 | 57 | 46 | 33 | 71 | 80 | 82 |
| Japan | 24 | 22 | 23 | 14 | 46 | 61 | 64 |
| UK | 114 | 81 | 63 | 56 | 64 | 80 | 78 |
| USA | 100 | 100 | 100 | 100 | 100 | 100 | 100 |
| Average of 15 OECD nations[a] | 77 | 61 | 45 | 46 | 69 | 79 | n.a. |

*Note*:
a France, Germany, Japan, the UK and the 11 countries listed in the footnote to Table 10.1.
*Source*: Maddison 1991: 53, 274–5.

uneven rates, during the long boom as the rest of the world began to 'catch up' with US levels. The process was much slower for the UK than elsewhere. Since 1973, the pattern has become rather more confused but 'catch up' appears to have continued.

From this rather messy picture of relative productivity levels has emerged a sophisticated, but easily misunderstood, hypothesis of 'economic convergence' sketched in Chapter 1. Both Abramovitz (1986) and Baumol (1986) have argued that in the long run the productivity levels of the industrial countries have tended to converge (that is, the countries with the lowest initial productivity levels have also tended to be those with the fastest rates of productivity growth) but that there is nothing automatic about the process. Each 'follower' must acquire the 'social capability' to adapt the technology of the leader to its specific circumstances if it is to grow rapidly. Social capability includes the facility to diffuse knowledge; the ability to speed structural change; and the creation of macro-economic and monetary conditions to encourage investment (Abramovitz 1986: 390). For a variety of reasons the conditions for successful catch-up were limited before 1939 but between 1950 and 1973, the elements required for rapid growth by catch up came together – a large technological gap, increased social capability in Europe and Japan, and the weakening of conservative forces as a result of war (Abramovitz 1986: 395). Convergence was therefore a driving force in the faster growth after 1950. The convergence hypothesis is however not without its problems, even for the 'long boom' between 1951 and 1973 (Crafts 1993: 29–33; Gordon 1992: 420–1; Broadberry 1993). Despite the problems it remains intuitively attractive to believe that the rapid growth in the long boom was propelled by the diffusion of technical knowledge from the USA to the rest of the world.

Accounts of slower growth since 1973 have taken two forms. On the one hand, there are those like Maddison who lay the blame on the emergence of unrelated problems in the 1970s: the potential gains from 'catch-up' had been exhausted; the liberal international order managed by the IMF and GATT (see Chapter 8) came under strain; governments became much more concerned about inflation and prepared to sacrifice growth especially after the huge rises in oil prices in 1973 (OPEC 1) which also had a strong effect on demand (Maddison 1982: 126–47). Although there is considerable scope for disagreement about the relative weight of these various parts of the jigsaw, these broad outlines have been widely accepted (Feinstein and Matthews 1990: 88–9). The alternative hypothesis begins by noting that the problems of the 1970s came almost fifty years after the slump of 1929–32, which had followed almost half a century after the great depression of the 1880s. Interest reawakened in the idea of a long cycle in world economic activity. This 'long wave' is most closely associated with the Soviet economist, Nikolai Kondratiev (1926; 1935). The recurrence of economic problems in the 1970s led to new efforts to find empirical and theoretical bases for the long wave. Empirical evidence remains patchy. The strongest signs of the long wave can be found in price series, especially when prices are put on a common gold base over the whole span from the 1780s to the 1980s (Hobbs 1985: 723). It is much more difficult to find evidence for long waves in measures of physical output which have underlying upward growth trends masking any cyclical movement (Cleary and Hobbs 1983: 166–80).

Empirical studies can neither prove nor disprove the existence of long waves. Theoretical accounts of the long wave are, however, much stronger and tend to emphasise the role of discontinuities in technical change and the associated innovations. Joseph Schumpeter (1939) argued that major (strategic) innovations appeared at regular intervals and provided entrepreneurs with new markets and new forms of industrial organisation. More recently, Mensch (1979) has argued that during depressions societies find themselves in a technological stalemate which can be ended only by the adoption of strategic innovations to create new leading sectors. Freeman et al. (1982) have distinguished between employment-creating product innovations and employment-displacing process innovations, which occur when these new product innovations are applied throughout the economy. Thus, product innovation in micro-electronics initially created jobs in computer and microchip manufacture. However, the diffusion of micro-electronics to other industries (process innovation) in control, monitoring, regulation and automation techniques led to labour-saving technologies, displacement of labour from the production process, slower growth of demand and the eventual end to the upswing. Others have explored the effects of the upswing on the capital goods sector (Mandel 1972; Forrester 1976) and on the primary producing nations (Rostow 1975; Rostow 1978: 103–362). These are still very controversial ideas but the significance of technical change and international diffusion of innovations in both convergence and many long wave hypotheses is suggestive. No firm conclusions about the causes of the changing rhythms of postwar growth are possible, but changes in the pace of diffusion of methods from the leader to the followers have clearly been significant.

## THE BRITISH GROWTH RECORD

As was noted in Chapter 2, the most reliable estimates of the growth rate are taken from peak years of the trade cycle which have reasonably comparable levels of economic activity and exclude periods in which special, temporary difficulties prevail. After 1945 readjustment to peace-time conditions took rather longer than after 1918 because the world-wide scale of physical destruction was more severe. The peak of the first postwar cycle did not occur until 1951, and 1951 is usually taken as the start of 'normal' peacetime conditions. Thereafter, there have been seven complete cycles: 1951–5, 1955–60, 1960–4, 1964–8, 1968–73, 1973–9 and 1979–90. The first five cyclical peaks occurred in years of full employ-ment and the period 1951–73 is often treated as a single unit. The complications begin after 1973. First, the peak of 1979 appears to have been weaker than that of 1973 or 1990 (Feinstein and Matthews 1990: 79). Second, there is the problem of the exploitation of North Sea oil and gas which accounted for 0.01 per cent of GDP in 1975, 3.3 per cent in 1979 and 7 per cent in 1984 (Johnson 1991: 268). There are no clear rules about the treatment of such windfall gains and it is common to give GDP estimates both with and without North Sea output. Third, the discre-pancies between the three alternative measures of national income (from the sides of output, income and expenditure) have been unusually large in the 1980s and have cast doubt on the accuracy of official figures. Finally, the depth of the slump of 1979–82 has made it extremely difficult to produce reliable estimates of the capital stock in the 1970s and 1980s, making estimates of productivity growth extremely uncertain (Muellbauer 1986: ix).

Estimates of British growth rates since 1951 are given in Table 10.3 with and without adjustments for both the 'low peak' of 1979 and North Sea output. Growth was faster during the long boom (1951–73) than since 1973, but there has been an improvement since 1979 which is unaffected by the exclusion of North Sea output from the figures. Using the distinction between factor inputs (the inputs of labour and capital needed to produce economic output) and total factor productivity (the efficiency with which these inputs are employed) discussed in Chapter 2,

*Table 10.3* Growth of United Kingdom GDP[a], 1951–88 (annual percentage growth rates)

|  | Unadjusted peak years | Adjusted peak years[b] |
|---|---|---|
| 1951–5 | 3.0 | 2.9 |
| 1955–60 | 2.5 | 2.3 |
| 1960–4 | 3.4 | 3.4 |
| 1964–8 | 2.8 | 3.0 |
| 1968–73 | 3.2 | 3.0 |
| 1973–9 | 1.4 (0.9)[c] | 1.8 (1.3)[c] |
| 1979–88 | 2.2 (2.2)[c] | 2.1 (2.0)[c] |

*Notes:*
a Using the CSO's average measure of GDP.
b Calculated using the average of the peak and the preceding year.
c Excluding extraction of mineral oil and natural gas.
*Source:* Feinstein and Matthews 1990: 79.

it is evident from Table 10.4 that the main sources of growth during the long boom were higher investment and faster TFP growth. Labour input has contracted slightly over the postwar period as a whole. The number of workers has risen since 1945 (Chapter 13), but hours of work have fallen as a result of a reduction in the length of the normal working week and an increase in official holiday entitlements (Matthews *et al.* 1982: 77). After 1973, the British economy suffered the severest setback to output relative to the previous trend rate of growth of any peacetime period

*Table 10.4* Growth of GDP[a], factor inputs and total factor productivity (TFP), 1924–88 (% per annum)

|  | GDP[a] | Labour input[b] | Capital input[c] | TFP |
|---|---|---|---|---|
| 1924–37 | 2.2 | 1.5 | 1.5 | 0.7 |
| 1951–5 | 2.8 | 0.5 | 2.3 | 1.8 |
| 1955–60 | 2.5 | −0.4 | 2.6 | 2.1 |
| 1960–4 | 3.4 | −0.2 | 3.4 | 2.5 |
| 1964–9 | 2.6 | −1.5 | 4.1 | 2.5 |
| 1968–73 | 2.6 | −0.9 | 3.7 | 2.2 |
| 1951–73 | 2.8 | −0.5 | 3.2 | 2.3 |
| 1973–9[d] | 1.3 | −0.8 | 0.1 | 0.7 |
| 1979–88[d] | 2.0 | −0.6 | 2.0 | n.a. |

*Notes:*
a Excluding extraction of mineral oil and natural gas
b Labour is measured in terms of worker/hours. Improvements in labour quality appear in TFP.
c Capital is measured gross.
d Figures for 1979 are adjusted for the low peak of the cycle. See Table 10.3 for explanation.
*Sources:* Matthews *et al.* 1982: 208, 548; Feinstein and Matthews 1990: 79, 84, 86.

since 1850 (Matthews *et al*. 1982: 548). As a result, there was much slower growth of both capital input and TFP between 1973 and 1979 with only partial recovery after 1979.

The foundations for faster growth were laid during the reconstruction period. Controls were maintained for much longer and the sense of national purpose and unity was much stronger in the 1940s than after 1918, reflected in much lower levels of social and industrial conflict after the Second than the First World War (Cairncross 1985: 3–46). Government policy of giving priority to exporters and producers of investment goods speeded recovery. Having negotiated the 'transition' successfully, the British economy shared, in its own limited way, in the forces which made for faster world growth. On the supply side, there was an investment backlog to make up after the low rates of interwar and wartime capital formation (Matthews 1968: 560–1). Higher rates of capital accumulation should have accelerated the pace of technical progress, since new technologies tend to be 'embodied' in capital equipment, but the pace of technical change has quickened on a world scale since 1940 (Matthews *et al*. 1982: 546). On the demand side, the liberalisation of world trade under the auspices of the IMF and GATT helped world demand to grow rapidly as did the widespread belief that governments could promote fast growth and full employment (Maddison 1982: 99–101). Investment was the key to faster growth in Britain as elsewhere:

> Capital accumulation was a reinforcing element in growth, encouraged both by the rapid growth of output (permitting a correspondingly rapid growth of savings and helping to keep up the marginal efficiency of investment) and by the high level of output. The process was a circular one in that the fast rate of growth of output, permitted by supply, was a contributing cause of the historically high rate of investment, which itself was a principal source of high demand.
>
> (Matthews *et al*. 1982: 546)

However, during the long boom there were indications that the engine of growth, the manufacturing sector, was running less smoothly than in other developed countries. As in the interwar period, there was no obvious 'leading sector' in British economic development and growth of output was very broadly based (Table 10.5). The growth of manufacturing output was no faster than in the interwar years, despite much higher rates of growth of investment in the sector (Tables 2.5 and 10.6). TFP growth in manufacturing was rather disappointing (Matthews *et al*. 1982: 238–43). In most industrial countries, output of industry (manufacturing plus construction) grew much faster than output of other sectors (Maddison 1982: 117). In Britain the contribution of manufacturing to total productivity growth was below that of its main European rivals both before and after 1973 (Crafts 1993: 16).

Table 10.5 Growth of output by sector, 1951–88 (% per annum)

| | GDP | Agriculture | Energy & Water | Manu-facturing | Const-ruction | Total services |
|---|---|---|---|---|---|---|
| 1950/1–72/3 | 2.7 | 2.5 | 1.8 | 2.9 | 2.8 | 2.5 |
| 1972/3–78/9 | 1.5 | 0.8 | 9.3 | 0.0 | −1.7 | 1.9 |
| 1978/9–87/8 | 2.1 | 2.7 | 1.9 | 0.4 | 2.2 | 2.7 |

Source: Feinstein and Matthews 1990: 81.

After 1973, it is clear from Table 10.4 that the 'virtuous circle' of high levels of demand, leading to high rates of capital formation, leading back into high levels of demand, was broken. The pressure of demand in 1979 was below that of previous trade cycle peaks in part because investment had stagnated since 1973. The growth of TFP, which had been low by international standards (Crafts 1993: 15) slowed still further. Manufacturing was badly hit, with no net growth of output over the cycle 1973–9. Slow growth of manufacturing output had serious repercussions for the service sector; distribution and transport grew much less rapidly than during the long boom. Manufacturing productivity stagnated in 1973–9, whether measured by TFP (Matthews *et al.* 1982: 548) or by output per worker-hour (Feinstein and Matthews 1990: 84–5). The only bright spot was the very rapid growth of North Sea oil and gas output.

In late 1979, the economy entered a slump which did not lift until the end of 1982 (Feinstein and Matthews 1990: 80). The worst effects were felt in manufacturing, with output falling by 17 per cent in 21 months (Wells 1989: 29). Manufacturing capacity was lost during the slump and was not replaced as investment in the sector virtually collapsed in the first half of the 1980s (Nolan 1989: 108). The loss of manufacturing employment was substantial: 2 million manufacturing jobs were lost during the 1980s, of which three-quarters disappeared in 1980–2 (Cairncross 1992: 231). However, manufacturing output began to rise slowly in 1983 as the economy began a long, sustained recovery. Slow growth of output and falls in employment brought faster rates of labour

Table 10.6 Growth of labour productivity, 1951–88 (% per annum)

| | GDP | | | Manufacturing | | |
|---|---|---|---|---|---|---|
| | Output | Person-hours | Labour productivity | Output | Person-hours | Labour productivity |
| 1951–73 | 3.0 | −0.6 | 3.6 | 3.1 | −0.6 | 3.7 |
| 1973–79 | 1.4 | −0.8 | 2.2 | −0.7 | −1.7 | 1.1 |
| 1979–88 | 2.2 | −0.6 | 2.8 | 0.8 | −3.2 | 4.2 |

Source: Feinstein and Matthews 1990: 84.

productivity growth in manufacturing during the 1980s. TFP growth in manufacturing was also comparable with the best rates achieved during the long boom, but the figures must be treated with caution; measurement problems are especially difficult after 1979 (Nolan 1989: 106–10). Nevertheless, productivity growth in this key sector has improved dramatically in the 1980s relative to both the rates achieved after 1973 and, more importantly, to those recorded by other developed economies in the 1980s (Gordon 1992: 418). Before we break open the champagne, it is worth pointing out that manufacturing productivity growth in the 1980s was *not* exceptional (Chapter 13) and was accompanied by a severe deterioration in the balance of trade in manufactured goods (Chapter 11). Shortage of the physical capacity to produce manufactures became a very severe problem by the end of the 1980s. Despite more than 1.6 million registered unemployed (see Chapter 13) in 1990, the signs that the economy had been overheating for some time were unmistakable: the visible trade deficit deteriorated and inflation rose.

Moreover Table 10.6 suggests (as far as the measurement problems noted above will allow) that productivity performance for the whole economy in the 1980s was less remarkable than for manufacturing; the growth rate of aggregate labour productivity was at roughly the same rate as other European OECD countries (Crafts 1993: 40). Faster productivity growth in manufacturing, energy and agriculture during the 1980s was counterbalanced by deterioration in parts of the service sector. In the interwar years, rising unemployment had contributed to expansion of low productivity work in commerce (Chapter 2). Similar forces have been at work in the 1980s, but in 'miscellaneous services' (cleaning and sanitary services, research and development, welfare and community service, sport and recreation, laundries and domestic service) where there is much low productivity work (Feinstein and Matthews 1990: 81,84–5). Thus the record of the 1980s is mixed. Despite the Conservative government's claim to have engineered ('serviced' would be more accurate) an economic miracle in the 1980s, the long, increasingly inflationary upswing of 1982–90 collapsed into a deep, protracted slump from which recovery has emerged only slowly.

## CAUSES AND CURES

It is impossible to summarise the enormous literature on Britain's relative decline in the space available (good starting points are Alford 1988; Allsopp 1985; Crafts 1991a; Matthews *et al.* 1982). The earliest accounts were framed within the Keynesian tradition which placed particular importance on Britain's relatively slow growth of investment (Hill 1964). The causes of Britain's comparatively slow growth of investment were also framed in Keynesian terms. Paish (1962: ch. 17), among others, held that the pressure of demand had been too high. Governments should run the economy with a higher margin of unemployment which would promote greater competition, and so raise investment and the underlying growth rate. The case for higher average levels of demand was equally strong. If output could be held for a sustained period at a level much closer to full capacity, firms would be forced to invest to overcome the recurrent shortages of skilled workers. The 'Maudling dash for growth' of 1963–4 and the 'Barber boom' of 1972–4 were based on such reasoning (Blackaby 1978b: 24–8, 62–7). Both relied upon a vigorous expansion of domestic demand, but Kaldor (1971) argued that the key to faster growth lay in the demand for exports which, in turn, was crucially influenced by competitiveness. By selecting a competitive exchange rate, governments could reap the favourable balance of payments consequences of export led growth; with a persistent surplus in the current account, there would be no stop–go cycle (see Chapter 14). Industrialists' expectations of future growth would be met, inducing them to invest, accelerating the rate of productivity growth, lowering unit costs and stimulating exports further (Beckerman 1965). However, this view that high rates of investment caused rapid growth is based upon an oversimplified view of the causal links between output and investment. Capital accumulation can be an independent variable operating from the supply side of the economy. But it is also affected by demand (and expectations of growth) and is also a component of expenditure. In turn it has major effects on productivity and the supply side (Allsopp 1985: 656).

The importance of the stop–go cycle has also probably been exaggerated, even in its impact on key industries, such as motor cars and electrical goods (Radcliffe 1959: 166). British industry ought to have been able to adjust to volatile demand growth. Japanese demand was as unstable as that of the UK and German car makers were more highly exposed to unpredictable export markets than British firms without unfavourable effects on investment or output growth (Panic 1976: 12). Stop–go may not have affected Japanese industrialists or German carmakers but both these economies (with Italy and Austria) had suffered a much more substantial check to output during the 1940s than the UK and were experiencing extremely rapid 'reconstruction growth' (Dumke 1990: 885–7). Stop–go possibly had more deleterious effects on investment and growth in a slowly growing economy than in those with a very different underlying dynamic. On the other hand, German and Japanese cycles were caused by occasional failures of demand, leaving periodic oversupply whereas British cycles were characteristically failures to meet demand and were accompanied by a rush of imports and balance of payments crises. It is most likely, therefore, that stop–go was a symptom rather than a cause of British problems.

Keynesian demand-side explanations of slow growth of investment were weakened as attention began to focus on the supply-side; whether capital went to the right projects, was adequately managed or its effects on productivity were neutered by restrictive practices. During the period 1950–73, the rate of investment growth was roughly similar in Britain and France but the French rate of GDP growth was more than one-and-a-half times the British rate (Crafts 1993: 15). In Britain, the growth of capital per worker in manufacturing accelerated from the mid-1950s but British firms, unlike their continental rivals, did not gain the anticipated productivity improvements (Boltho 1982: 47–8). The level of industrial investment in relation to the achieved rate of growth was three times higher in Britain than in Germany in the late 1960s and the early 1970s (Cairncross *et al.* 1983: 75). In other words, one of the reasons why capital accumulation was so slow was the disappointingly low rate of return on the investment actually made. Important supply side weaknesses existed and interacted with the demand for investment to produce a slow rate of growth of total output (see Chapters 12 and 13 for a fuller discussion).

An equally complex picture emerges from investigation of the impact of the balance of payments on growth. Under both fixed and floating exchange rates, the Treasury periodically needed to cut the pressure of domestic demand to protect the exchange rate (see Chapter 11). The argument that the growth rate was held back by a persistent external weakness rests on the difference between, on the one hand, the amount of additional British exports which will flow from a given rise in world incomes and, on the other, the rise of imports into Britain from a given

*Table 10.7* Income elasticities of demand for imports and exports since 1951, selected countries

|  | Import elasticity | Export elasticity |
|---|---|---|
| 1951–66 using the Houthakker and Magee method: | | |
| France | 1.66 | 1.53 |
| Germany | 1.80 | 2.08 |
| Japan | 1.23 | 3.55 |
| USA | 1.51 | 0.99 |
| UK | 1.66 | 0.86 |
| 1953–71, using the Balassa method: | | |
| France | | 2.04 |
| Germany | | 2.27 |
| Japan | | 2.00 |
| USA | | 2.02 |
| UK | | 2.20 |

*Sources:* Houthakker and Magee 1969: 113; Balassa 1979: 606.

rise in British incomes. It is easy to maintain pegged exchange rates if these **income elasticities of demand** are similar.

Initial calculations (Houthakker and Magee 1969) indicated that Britain's import elasticity was comparable to that of other countries, but export elasticity was extremely low (Table 10.7, upper part). If these figures had been correct, the British growth rate could have been only half that of other OECD countries to ensure that imports grew at roughly the same pace of exports. This is the essence of the argument that the root of Britain's relatively poor postwar performance lay in slow growth of world demand for British exports (Thirlwall 1986: ch. 12; Beckerman 1965: ch. 2). These ratios are, however, highly controversial because no account was taken of product quality, which will have an obvious impact on demand (Balassa 1979). By including these effects, Britain's exceptionally low export elasticity disappears (Table 10.7, lower part). Elasticities are not God-given; they reflect decisions about what is produced and how it is made. Had Britain been able to produce motor cars, for example, as cheaply and as well as the Germans and Japanese, it would have found foreign markets just as elastic as did German and Japanese producers (Pollard 1983: 356). Unfavourable elasticities ought to be rectified by devaluation, but the devaluations of 1949 and 1967 brought only transient gains for British producers (Foreman-Peck 1991: 146–7). British manufacturers lacked price competitiveness in the 1960s before devaluation (Batchelor *et al.* 1980: 56–67) and the problem reappeared in the 1970s (Cairncross *et al.* 1983: 89). There were also serious problems of non-price competitiveness in areas such as delivery dates, reliability, design and quality (Stout 1976: 12–18). These problems are more properly the subject of Chapter 12, but it must be evident that if markets were lost because of the inability of firms to produce at the price and quality which markets demanded, weakness in British industrial organisation caused balance of payments problems rather than vice versa (Crafts 1991a: 269–79; Alford 1988: 42–8).

These arguments do not, however, completely invalidate the case for a balance of payments constraint. Before the mid-1960s, British governments aspired to play a 'world role', incurring overseas expenditure which was far greater than could be borne by an economy with low reserves, large debts and heavy commitment in the early postwar years to traditional but slowly growing export markets. In the 1950s, stop phases of the policy cycle were imposed to restore confidence rather than correct underlying deficits. In this context, balance of payments weakness may have been very damaging to British performance in the 1950s (Lundberg 1968: 153).

A third approach which combines supply and demand side influences is the structural argument which draws attention to difficulties faced by the manufacturing sector in securing resources for growth. The earliest version was conceived by the Keynesian economist Nicholas Kaldor (1966). He argued that rapid growth of manufacturing was a critical condition for rapid growth in the aggregate economy; fast growth of manufacturing forced services such as transport and distribution to process an increasing flow of manufactured goods with a static or shrinking work-force, raising productivity. Kaldor also reaffirmed Verdoorn's Law that the faster the growth of manufacturing output, the faster the growth of productivity in the sector (from economies of organisation and scale and learning effects). He devised a tax on employment outside manufacturing, selective employment tax (SET), to drive labour towards industry. SET was extremely controversial and its impact on the economy is uncertain except in a single aspect; it did not cause a British economic miracle after 1966. Further research discredited Verdoorn's Law (Rowthorn 1975; Chatterji and Wickens 1982).

Similar ideas quickly reappeared in very different theoretical clothing. Bacon and Eltis (1976) constructed a controversial thesis which divided the economy into two: a 'market' sector producing output which is sold, and a 'non-market' sector producing services such as education, medical care and defence which are not bought and sold on the market. The market sector, embracing industry, agriculture and private services, will tend to produce output which has a much higher value than the materials which it consumes; this 'surplus' provides the resources from which the non-market sector can be financed. As a result, the market sector has to provide all the export needs of the economy, all the investment needs and all the private consumption. Bacon and Eltis contend that between 1960 and the mid-1970s Britain saw a major expansion of the public sector, representing non-marketed output, which was too rapid to be matched by any conceivable growth in the market sector's surplus and 'crowded out' the market sector; Britain had 'too few producers'. This hypothesis was launched with maximum publicity and has been under criticism ever since. The rapid publication of a second, much revised, edition (Bacon and Eltis, 1978) has failed to shore up the argument, at least as it applies to the period 1960–74. There is no statistical evidence that market sector investment has been crowded out as Bacon and Eltis maintain (Crafts 1991a: 271). Gomulka (1979: 179–80) has pointed out that British industry was handicapped by too many underproductive producers; the use of labour by the market sector was lavish until the late 1970s. There is no simple structural explanation for Britain's slow growth.

If the 'big theories' carry little conviction, how is British retardation to be explained? The demise of Keynesian economics and the increasing sophistication of growth accounting (Shaw 1992: 612; Denison 1967) have ensured that more recent explanations have focused much more intensively on the supply side of the economy. Growth accountants have

*Table 10.8* Sources of economic growth, 1950–87 (compound growth rates, per cent per annum)

|  | Capital | Labour | TFP | GDP |
|---|---|---|---|---|
| **1950–73** |  |  |  |  |
| France | 1.8 | 0.2 | 3.0 | 5.0 |
| Germany | 2.3 | 0.2 | 3.5 | 6.0 |
| Japan | 3.0 | 1.6 | 4.7 | 9.3 |
| UK | 1.8 | 0.0 | 1.3 | 3.0 |
| USA | 1.4 | 1.2 | 1.1 | 3.7 |
| **1973–87** |  |  |  |  |
| France | 1.5 | −0.2 | 0.9 | 2.2 |
| Germany | 1.3 | −0.5 | 1.0 | 1.8 |
| Japan | 2.3 | 0.7 | 0.8 | 3.7 |
| UK | 1.1 | −0.2 | 0.8 | 1.8 |
| USA | 1.2 | 1.3 | 0.0 | 2.5 |

*Source*: Crafts 1993:15 (figures rounded).

attributed much of the faster growth of the developed countries during the long boom to faster TFP growth. Britain seems to have performed less well than average in the miscellaneous forces which influence TFP (Table 10.8).

Crafts has interpreted the cause of Britain's relatively poor TFP growth as a series of supply-side weaknesses, of which the most significant are: the low qualifications and poor quality of British management, resulting in inadequate exploitation of scale economies in both production and organisation; an adverse climate of labour relations leading to over-manning; insufficient attention to research and development; poor training; inadequate monitoring of company performance by the stock exchange and the banking system especially before the 1960s, allowing poor managers to continue in post; the absence of a strongly competitive environment, particularly when governments were committed to the maintenance of full employment, enabling inefficient firms to remain in business (1991a: 273–9; 1991b).

The greatest attraction of this approach is its consistency with much that has gone before. These supply-side weaknesses have a direct impact on British relative 'social capability' to absorb and adapt the technological and organisational advantages developed by US industry. Supply-side weaknesses have already been invoked in the explanation of the low productivity of British investment and the unfavourable elasticities in Britain's trade. The more detailed examination of British industry in the postwar period which follows in Chapter 12 contains ample evidence of major shortcomings in British enterprise in the postwar years. Supply-side weaknesses are a significant part of the story of Britain's relatively slow growth since 1945, but how significant?

Growth accounting cannot answer this vital question. All the factors in Crafts's long list appear in growth accounting within the category 'TFP'. Maddison (1987) has attempted to make separate estimates of the impact of a number of elements which comprise TFP but without carrying great conviction. Crafts's own account is little help either. As noted in the discussion above, Britain's growth performance has improved since 1979 relative to that of other countries, especially in the manufacturing sector. Although British economic performance has improved relatively, the growth rate has fallen and, even in manufacturing, productivity growth has only regained rates achieved in 1964–73. Crafts, however, declares that fundamental causes of slow postwar growth were cast off after 1979 as the British 'performed a somewhat belated catching up exercise associated with the switch in policy regime' (1993: 50). The switch in policy regime brought a new climate of industrial relations and a government which preferred market to corporatist solutions to industrial problems. The new policy regime, however, had little impact on Britain's relative weakness in technology and in accumulating capital, both human and physical (Crafts 1993: 50–1). Unfortunately, the impact of the industrial relations system on both retardation before 1979 and acceleration thereafter is dubious (see Chapter 13). Although supply-side weaknesses were certainly apparent, no explanation of the changing rhythm of British growth since 1973 can afford to ignore demand (Feinstein and Matthews 1990: 88–9; Maddison 1991: 182–92). The most significant innovation of Thatcherism, using mass unemployment to curb wage growth (Chapter 13) has induced workers to flock into low productivity services so negating most of the benefits on aggregate productivity growth of 'the new climate of industrial relations'. Significant supply-side weaknesses have existed throughout the postwar period, but they have interacted with changes in demand to affect the aggregate rate of productivity growth.

## WELFARE

This pattern of historically high rates of growth but rapid relative decline has had a profound impact on welfare. At one level, the period since 1945 has been an undisputed 'age of affluence'. Living standards have risen throughout the period, as was seen in Table 10.1. The average Briton had more real income and more leisure time in which to enjoy it. The demographic trends examined in Chapter 9 also indicate substantial progress. Life expectancy increased and infant mortality, that key indicator of welfare, fell. Consumption patterns have also changed remarkably. Whereas only 7.2 per cent of adults owned a car in 1949, by

1966 the figure had passed 50 per cent (Halsey 1972: 551). The pattern of television ownership is similar; in 1950 only 380,000 licences were issued but by 1968 there were more than 15.5 million; more than 90 per cent of adults lived in homes which possessed a television set (Halsey 1972: 552). By 1992, some 99 per cent of all households own a television set, 89 per cent have a telephone, 88 per cent have a washing machine and 85 per cent possess a deep-freeze (*Social Trends* 1994: 85). The standards of housing space and comfort have improved greatly. The proportion of all households in England and Wales living at more than 1.5 persons per room fell from 11.5 per cent in 1931 to 5.1 per cent in 1951 and 1 per cent in 1991 (Halsey 1972: 301; *Social Trends* 1994: 113). The proportion which did not enjoy sole access to such basic amenities as hot water, a fixed bath and a WC also declined fairly rapidly from 1951 but most significant was the rise in home ownership, especially among the working class. In 1947, some 27 per cent of households were owner-occupiers, by 1990 the figure exceeded 66 per cent (Halsey 1972: 307; *Social Trends* 1994: 112). The most obvious metaphors to describe the changes taking place in the pattern of consumption have been the moving escalator noted in Chapter 2 or the column on the march: 'The last rank keeps its distance from the first and the distance between them does not lessen. But as the column advances, the last rank does eventually reach and pass the point which the first rank passed some time before' (Young and Willmott 1973: 19ff). However, this metaphor misses the point that consumption denotes social position as well as satisfies wants. Those goods and services which indicate social status are by definition in short supply and command prices which are beyond the purses of the mass of consumers. Hirsch (1977) has pointed out that in rich societies the satisfaction to be derived from ownership is determined in large part by the consumption of others. Thus, the benefits to be gained from possessing a car in the 1930s were far greater than the benefits which accrued in the 1960s and later decades, when the social cachet of car ownership has reduced. There is little to be gained from a comparison between the relatively wealthy at one point in time and of the masses several decades later; like is not being compared with like.

Hirsch's analysis introduces another perspective on 'the age of affluence'. Despite the unprecedented growth of income and the revolution in consumption, affluence has not bred contentment for the mass population. One of the most remarkable aspects of postwar economic growth has been the importance of techniques of persuasion (Alford 1988: 99). Only by stimulating wants and keeping consumers in a state of dissatisfaction has it been possible to secure the historically rapid growth of demand for the output of modern industry. Logically, disenchantment should be found in its most concentrated form at the bottom of the income distribution, among those exposed to the techniques of the

*Table 10.9* Distribution of personal income in Britain, 1949–75/6 (%)

| Per cent | 1949 | 1954 | 1964 | 1970/1 | 1975/6 |
|---|---|---|---|---|---|
| Before tax: | | | | | |
| Top 1 | 11.2 | 9.3 | 8.2 | 6.6 | 5.6 |
| Top 10 | 33.2 | 30.1 | 29.1 | 27.5 | 25.8 |
| Next 40 | 43.1 | 46.9 | 48.2 | 49.0 | 49.9 |
| Bottom 50 | 23.7 | 22.0 | 22.7 | 23.5 | 24.3 |
| Gini Co-efficient | 41.1 | 40.3 | 39.9 | 38.5 | 36.6 |
| | | | | | |
| After tax: | | | | | |
| Top 1 | 6.4 | 5.3 | 5.3 | 4.5 | 3.6 |
| Top 10 | 27.1 | 25.3 | 25.9 | 23.9 | 22.3 |
| Next 40 | 46.4 | 48.4 | 48.9 | 49.9 | 50.3 |
| Bottom 50 | 26.5 | 26.3 | 25.2 | 26.1 | 27.4 |
| Gini Co-efficient | 35.5 | 35.8 | 36.6 | 33.9 | 31.5 |

*Source*: Diamond 1979, Table A.4

advertisers and marketing experts but unable to afford an extensive range of consumer products.

## THE DISTRIBUTION OF INCOME AND WEALTH

Although there are difficulties in collecting and interpreting personal income data (Playford and Pond 1983: 36–49), the Royal Commission on the Distribution of Income and Wealth has established estimates of the distribution of personal income before 1977 (Diamond 1979: Table A7). The figures appear in Table 10.9 and show incomes before and after the payment of direct taxes.

In the postwar period a declining share went to the topmost income-earners, but the bottom half of the distribution made no relative gains, continuing the interwar pattern (Chapter 2). The Gini coefficient denotes greater equality as it declines towards zero. Thus, inequality in after-tax incomes marginally increased in the first two postwar decades. Between 1964 and 1975, however, there was substantial redistribution of income away from those at the top of the distribution towards those at the bottom through both the tax and benefit systems (Stewart 1972: 107–11). In the period 1945–75, British income distribution was more egalitarian than that of many comparable nations (Stark 1977).

Table 10.9 gives a guide to broad changes in personal income but the household is the basic unit of economic and social organisation. Household income will depend upon the number of its members in paid employment or with benefit entitlement and household needs will reflect the number and age of its members. To explore household living standards social scientists have turned to the Family Expenditure Survey

(FES). The FES has weaknesses which are well known (Goodman and Webb 1994: 6–8) but has been the basis for studies of poverty since 1953 (Piachaud 1988: 337). Expenditure data paradoxically also permit a more sophisticated definition of income. Income from employment, private pensions, investments and gifts (that is, before any government intervention) constitutes **original income**. Add cash benefits (such as state pensions, unemployment or sickness benefits) and the result is gross income. This is also the pre-tax income of Table 10.9. When direct taxes (income tax, employees' national insurance contributions, local taxes) are taken, **disposable income** (the after-tax income of Table 10.9) remains. Households also pay a variety of indirect taxes (VAT, duty on

*Table 10.10* Distribution of household income, 1977–92 (%)

| | Share of income[a] by household group | | | | Gini co-efficient |
|---|---|---|---|---|---|
| | Bottom 20% | Bottom 40% | Top 40% | Top 20% | |
| Original Income | | | | | |
| 1977 | 3.6 | 13.6 | 69 | 43 | 43 |
| 1979 | 2.4 | 12.4 | 70 | 43 | 44 |
| 1985 | 2.5 | 9.5 | 74 | 47 | 49 |
| 1992 | 2.1 | 8.1 | 76 | 50 | 52 |
| Gross Income | | | | | |
| 1977 | 8.9 | 21.9 | 61 | 37 | 29 |
| 1979 | 8.5 | 21.5 | 61 | 37 | 30 |
| 1985 | 8.3 | 20.3 | 64 | 40 | 32 |
| 1992 | 6.9 | 18.9 | 66 | 43 | 37 |
| Disposable Income | | | | | |
| 1977 | 9.7 | 23.7 | 59 | 36 | 27 |
| 1979 | 9.4 | 22.4 | 59 | 36 | 27 |
| 1985 | 9.2 | 22.2 | 61 | 38 | 29 |
| 1992 | 7.4 | 18.4 | 65 | 42 | 34 |
| Post-tax Income | | | | | |
| 1977 | 9.4 | 23.4 | 60 | 37 | 29 |
| 1979 | 9.5 | 22.5 | 60 | 37 | 29 |
| 1985 | 8.6 | 21.6 | 62 | 39 | 32 |
| 1992 | 6.5 | 17.5 | 67 | 44 | 38 |
| Final income[b] | | | | | |

*Notes:*
a All the data have been 'equivalised'; that is incomes have been adjusted to allow for household size and composition. Details can be found in CSO 1990: 84.
b The CSO does not present data on final income on a comparable basis.
*Source*: CSO 1994: 122–3.

petrol, tobacco and alcohol) which leaves **post-tax income**. Finally, households also receive benefits in kind (education, health treatment, social service help) which can be given a cash value and added to the total to give **final income**. The changes in these types of income since 1977 are given in Table 10.10. Inequality has clearly increased rapidly, especially since 1979. Significant losses have been recorded at the bottom end of the distribution and gains have been concentrated at the very top. These changes have occurred in roughly equal measure in all parts of Table 10.10.

For the richest, income derives from accumulated wealth. Wealth is even more difficult to measure than income but the figures suggest that some redistribution has taken place without reaching far down the scale of wealth-holders (Table 10.11). The figures show a persistent decline in the share of total wealth held by the exceedingly rich but must be treated with caution. Wealthy families have continued to make gifts *inter vivos*, between the living, to avoid tax at death. The increase of wealth-holding among the bottom four fifths of the population reflects the spread of home ownership and with it the expansion of private savings through pension funds, building societies and insurance companies. The value of houses and claims on pension and insurance funds are wealth, but they are also use values to be used up later in life. Among the very rich, however, ownership of shares, other securities and land (property as a source of income) is far more important. Use values constituted more than 80 per cent of the assets of those in the wealth range £10,000–£19,999 in 1974, but less than 20 per cent of those with fortunes of over £200,000 (Diamond 1976: 52–9). Thus the levelling of wealth-holding since 1949 may represent only very marginal redistribution of property as a source of income. Moreover, even in 1976, the top 1 per cent enjoyed

*Table 10.11* Shares in total wealth, England and Wales, 1923–81 (%)

|       | Top 1% | Top 5% | Top 10% | Top 20% | Bottom 80% |
|-------|--------|--------|---------|---------|------------|
| 1923  | 60.9   | 82.0   | 89.1    | 94.2    | 5.8        |
| 1938  | 55.0   | 76.9   | 85.0    | 91.2    | 8.8        |
| 1950[a] | 47.2 | 74.3   | —       | —       | —          |
| 1955[a] | 44.5 | 71.1   | —       | —       | —          |
| 1964  | 34.5   | 58.6   | 71.4    | 84.3    | 15.7       |
| 1973  | 27.3   | 50.8   | 66.8    | 84.9    | 15.1       |
| 1979  | 21.5   | 45.2   | 61.2    | 80.3    | 19.7       |
| 1981  | 22.7   | 45.9   | 62.6    | 82.3    | 17.7       |

Note:
a For these years the data do not permit estimates of the shares of the top 10 and
  20 per cent

Source: Atkinson and Harrison 1978: 159; Atkinson *et al.* 1989: 318.

respectively 5.5 times and 25 times the average for personal income and wealth (Phelps Brown 1988: 350).

## POVERTY

Living standards in the 'age of affluence' have risen faster than at any time in Britain's economic history but studies continue to show that poverty has continued and increased. It all depends, of course, on the definition of poverty. Poverty may be defined in absolute, fixed terms so that the 'poverty line' has the same real purchasing power at different times. The first clearly defined poverty threshold was in Rowntree's 1899 study of York, noted in Chapter 2. If the same real poverty line were applied in 1989, it would represent approximately half of prevailing supplementary benefit levels and would define a small number of families as poor (Piachaud 1988: 338). However, Rowntree's second survey of York in 1936 used a higher 'poverty line', recognising that the poverty threshold had changed with the general standard of living; poverty was a relative concept. The Diamond Commission endorsed this view wholeheartedly (Diamond 1978: 3). This merely poses a further question: how should relative poverty be defined? Studies have commonly taken what is called the official poverty line, based on the benefits paid by the National Assistance Board (NAB) and its successors, the Supplementary Benefits Commission (SBC) and the Social Fund (Barr 1981). Throughout the postwar period everyone has been eligible for these benefits when all other sources of income have failed. It is the minimum standard at which the state aims to keep its population. There are however real problems with this measure. It is arbitrary, having been chosen for political convenience rather than to measure actual living standards (Barr and Coulter 1990: 303–4). More importantly, if the value of benefits rises relative to wages, the number of poor people will increase; income-earners who had previously been marginally above the poverty line will fall marginally below it after the change. Social scientists have searched for alternatives since the mid-1970s but no completely satisfactory measure of poverty exists (Piachaud 1987).

Piachaud (1988) has defined a **constant relative poverty line** by reworking figures from existing studies so that the poverty threshold remains a constant proportion of prevailing living standards. He has produced results for two periods, 1899–1953 and 1953–83, reproduced in Table 10.12. The results suggest that the extent of poverty fell dramatically between 1899 and 1953 and the main proximate cause changed from low pay to old age. Relative poverty reached its lowest level ever in Britain in the early 1950s (Wilkinson 1989: 329). The increase in poverty since 1953 is, however, exaggerated by Table 10.12. The poverty line for

Table 10.12 The extent of poverty, 1899–1983

10.12(a) Changes in Poverty, 1899–1953

|  | 1899 | 1936 | 1953 |
|---|---|---|---|
| Lovol for man, woman, 1 child as percentage of personal disposable income per capita | 78 | 79 | 79 |
| Proportion of persons below level (%) | 9.9 | 8.1 | 1.2 |
| Proportion of households below level due to (%): |  |  |  |
| death of husband | 28 | 10 | 43 |
| old age | — | 24 | 28 |
| illness | 10 | 5 | 4 |
| unemployment | 3 | 35 | 3 |
| other (low wages, irregular work, large family) | 59 | 26 | 22 |

10.12(b) The Extent of Poverty, 1953–83 (proportion of each type of family/household in poverty – %).

|  | At constant relative poverty levels | | | Unadjusted |
|---|---|---|---|---|
|  | Over pension age | Under pension age | All | On SB or under 110% of SB |
| 1953[a] | 28.8 | 0.5 | 6.2 | 4.0 |
| 1960[a] | — | — | 13.3 | 9.4 |
| 1973[b] | 59.3 | 6.7 | 19.4 | 17.1 |
| 1975[b] | 36.3 | 5.4 | 14.2 | 16.4 |
| 1979[b] | 52.1 | 9.9 | 20.3 | 18.0 |
| 1983[b] | 43.0 | 17.2 | 23.3 | 23.6 |

Notes:
a Households
b Families
Source: Piachaud 1988: 341–2.

1899–1953 is more severe than that for the later period and the figures for both 1953 and 1960 relate to households whereas those for 1973–83 are for families. Piachaud (1988: 342) advises that the figures for 1953 and 1960 should be 'roughly doubled' to make them approximately comparable with 1973–83. The data since 1973 are reliable enough to show that the main causes of the increase in poverty have been rising unemployment and stagnant real incomes of the poorest in employment. The extent of poverty among pensioner families has fallen on average since 1973, but there have been substantial fluctuations over the period. Thus, roughly one quarter of all families was in poverty in the mid-1980s and included within that total are two-fifths of all pensioner families.

The Council of Europe's constant relative poverty line (those living on below half average income) fluctuates rather more violently over the period for which data are available (1961–91). In 1961 there were 5 million families in poverty so defined, falling to its lowest level of 3 million in 1977. By 1991, however, this measure of the poor numbered 11 million. Pensioners comprised 40 per cent of the poor in 1961, but only 20 per cent of the much larger number in 1991 (Goodman and Webb 1994). Between 1967 and 1991, average real incomes have risen by approximately 50 per cent whereas those for the poorest 10 per cent have remained static. However the poverty line is defined, the redistribution of income towards the rich since the later 1970s has been accompanied by a substantial increase in poverty.

One of the most unfortunate aspects of this form of redistribution has been to compound the difficulties of those whose quality of life was already impoverished. There has been substantial evidence of 'multiple deprivation' (van Slooten and Coverdale 1977: Adkin 1994). The poorest were also those in the highest danger of unemployment, in the worst housing conditions, with the least formal schooling, the highest likelihood of divorce or suicide (Townsend 1979: 369–431). An authoritative study found that the poorest had substantially worse health than the better off at all stages of life (Black 1980; Townsend and Davidson 1982). The Registrar General's figures also show that class differentials in mortality have widened since 1951 after having narrowed for three decades (Wilkinson 1989: 307–9). The black community has fared even worse than working class whites. Black Britons have tended to be found in the lowest status and least desirable occupations, are more at risk of unemployment than the indigenous white population especially for those under the age of 25, live in poor quality housing, show lower attainment at school (particularly those of West Indian origin) and are subjected to overt racial prejudice in many aspects of their daily lives (Rutter and Madge 1976: 270–301).

Postwar policy against poverty was guided by the policies and philosophy set out in the Beveridge Report (see Chapter 8). Although the Attlee government's social security policy remedied some of the shortcomings of Beveridge (especially paying full pensions from the start) many aspects were less favourable than originally proposed (Page 1991: 485). Universal insurance benefits (paid to all with the necessary contribution records regardless of income or savings) and family allowances fell below subsistence, partly because the government did not take account of wartime inflation, partly because Beveridge's definition of subsistence was deliberately confusing (Lowe 1993: 125–35; Veit-Wilson 1992). The most critical decision was, however, to set the level of insurance benefits below that of the supposedly inferior NAB scheme. In 1948 the insurance benefit for a married couple was £2.2s. (£2.10p), but the NAB benefit (paid to those who could prove need and subject to a means test) which came into effect that year was £2 plus housing expenditure. A couple with no other income and average rent would need means-tested NAB benefit plus their insurance entitlements to reach the government's own definition of subsistence (Atkinson 1969: 24). Throughout the postwar years there have been persistent difficulties in persuading people to claim means-tested benefits. This problem of 'incomplete take-up' has been explained by 'ignorance', 'inconvenience' and 'stigma' (Barr and Coulter 1990: 300-2). Claimants have been ignorant of the workings of the benefit system because of its increasing complexity. The inconvenience of means-tested benefits arises from the need to complete forms and answer potentially embarrassing questions about income and family circumstances. The stigma of NAB/SBC benefits arises because claimants believe that they might be labelled as belonging to a socially rejected group, such as the 'poor'. Stigma was especially powerful before the mid-1960s because the NAB was directly descended from hated interwar means-tested schemes. In addition, there have been problems on the side of the providers. Governments have persistently tried to curb the cost of social security, which amounted to 30–40 per cent of the state's 'social' expenditure and grew consistently faster than GDP in the period 1950–74 (Gould and Roweth 1980: 349–50). Governments have also been driven by more ideological concerns, such as equality, efficiency and the need to maintain social cohesion.

Little heed was paid to the working of the social security system before the mid-1950s because governments were confident that full employment, the welfare state and rising numbers of married women in employment had banished poverty. However, academic studies began to show that poverty was, on the contrary, increasing (Townsend 1957; Lambert 1964; Abel-Smith and Townsend 1965). The figures identified the old as a particular problem and it was in this area that reform began. In 1958, the Macmillan government introduced earnings-related contributions and a limited graduated supplement to the basic pension. In the following year, contributors were allowed to 'contract out' of the state scheme and into a private, tax-subsidised occupational pension. The Labour governments of 1964–70 enhanced earnings-related pensions and extended the principle to unemployment, sickness, industrial injury and widows' benefits in 1966 (Lowe 1993: 143). Labour also tried to reduce the stigma of means-tested benefits by terminating National Assistance, rechristening it as the Supplementary Benefits scheme, simplifying procedures and improving its image (Atkinson 1969: 61–77). The most common response of governments of the 1950s and 1960s to new demands for assistance was, however, to increase the number of means-tested benefits. The case was made for increasing the value of existing universal benefits (Atkinson 1969) but there were persistent fears of the cost of such a strategy and a counter-argument that a large proportion of state expenditure on universal benefits was 'wasted' on the relatively affluent (Dilnot *et al*. 1984).

The reforms of the late 1950s and 1960s did not have the desired impact. Earnings-related and occupational pensions favour those who remain in the same occupation throughout their working lives (the notion of a 'portable' pension which can be taken from job to job is a recent development) and are least helpful to those with fragmented work experience because of long-term illness or family commitments. Occupational pensions have been of little help to women, who form the majority of pensioners because they have a higher life expectancy than men. The old were not 'floated out' of dependence on SBC benefits before the mid-1970s. A second major cause of poverty was the re-emergence of the problem of low wages or, more precisely, of low take-home pay. During the long boom, the tax system became increasingly regressive, as thresholds (the point at which earners begin to pay tax) fell relative to benefits, leaving the poor to pay income taxes on earnings which were lower than their NAB/SBC benefit entitlements. Employee contributions to the national insurance scheme were for much of this period a flat-rate stoppage out of income and also extremely regressive. As a result, benefits rose faster than take-home pay. A contributory factor was the way that the state organised child benefit until 1975. Beveridge had hoped that male manual earnings would be sufficient under conditions of full employment to provide for a family of three. For families with more than one child, Beveridge had proposed family allowances. A cash benefit for the second and subsequent children was introduced in 1946 but at well below the subsistence level; its value was raised slightly on four subsequent occasions but it did not keep pace with inflation. The bulk of state support to families was delivered through the tax system by enabling a father to claim an allowance against tax for each child (including the first). By 1968 this form of welfare cost the Exchequer almost four times as much as family allowances (Townsend 1979: 151). The poorest families were unable to claim all their tax allowances because their earnings were so low. SBC entitlements for dependent children also increased much faster than family allowances, so large families continued to be a major cause of poverty. The state compounded the problem by operating a 'wage stop', which ensured that a person who normally earned less than the Supplementary Benefit scale would receive benefits equivalent to earnings rather than to full benefit entitlement. Approximately one-quarter of adult male claimants of sickness or unemployment benefit were caught in this trap in 1966 (Atkinson 1969: 93). In an attempt to tackle the problem of the low-paid poor, the Heath government introduced in 1971 the Family Income Supplement (FIS), now known as Family Credit. FIS provided benefits on a tapering scale to those in work but on low incomes. Despite heavy government publicity only approximately half of those eligible actually applied for this means-tested benefit. FIS was, and Family Credit remains, important because claimants automatically become eligible for a range of other central and local government benefits. A claimant with a pay rise resulting in the loss of entitlement to FIS would also lose the other benefits; an effective marginal tax rate higher than 100 per cent. The final problem which emerged during the long boom was the single-parent family. Throughout the postwar period approximately one-tenth of all families with dependent children had only one parent because of death, divorce, separation, or illegitimacy but the problem was first recognised only in the late 1960s when concern mounted at the rising divorce rate (Townsend 1979: 753–83). With poverty concentrated among pensioners, the low-paid and single-parent families, it is hardly surprising that women are at far greater risk of poverty than men. At any given stage in their lives, women are far more likely than men to be poor and their experience of poverty is likely to be far more acute (Millar and Glendinning 1989: 363).

Social security policy developed incrementally before the mid-1970s. Despite the spread of earnings-related contributions and supplements and the massive increase in the number of means-tested benefits, the core of the Beveridge scheme remained intact (Barr and Coulter 1990: 278). Since the election of the 1974 Wilson government, however, new philosophies have animated policy and the system has been subject to periodic and fundamental review. The first was undertaken by the new Labour government and produced two important policy innovations. Pensioners had been particularly susceptible to poverty as a result of the low basic pension (even after the introduction of earnings-related graduated additions) and the comparative reluctance of pensioners to apply for means-tested benefits. The new government tackled the problem in two ways. It introduced a substantial real increase in the levels of existing pensions (Gillie 1991: 230) and introduced a new scheme which was designed to give particular help to females who, as noted above, formed the majority of pensioners but were most unlikely to have secured ample occupational pensions. A new state earnings-related pension scheme (SERPS) was superimposed above the basic, flat-rate scheme and was designed to protect those with broken work patterns. Pensions were also formally indexed to changes in earnings or prices, whichever was the larger, thus protecting the real value of benefits. The Child Benefit Act, 1975, replaced family allowances and child tax allowances with a weekly, flat-rate, tax-free cash payment for each child in the family, together with an additional payment to single parents. This scheme finally ensured that poor families would receive the full amount of benefit for children and would not be penalised by having insufficient income to claim their full tax allowances. Both Table 10.12 and the Goodman and Webb (1994) study using the Council of Europe's constant relative poverty line indicate a substantial fall in 'poverty' from 1972/3 to 1977, partly as a result of these measures. Labour's changes in the value of both pensions and SBC benefits were sufficient to lift couples claiming these benefits above the Council of Europe constant relative poverty line, for example (Playford and Pond 1983: 55). The Labour government identified female pensioners, single parent families and those, with children, in low-paid employment and directed assistance to them through universal benefits. There was, however, a significant cost of this type of redistribution. Social security spending rose at just under 6 per cent per annum – about three times faster than total public expenditure and significant rises in taxation were needed on all levels of income to finance that part of total public expenditure which was not covered by borrowing (Gillie 1991: 233, 239). The most rapid growth occurred in expenditure on the elderly at a time when the pensioner population was rising. The tax system as a whole was made more progressive (that is, those with highest incomes paid a higher proportion in tax) but even the lowest income-earners were compelled to pay higher income tax. Although Labour imposed the biggest real cuts in public expenditure since the crises of the late 1940s (Jackson 1991: 73–4), it was not difficult for the Conservatives to make political capital from claims that public expenditure was out of control (Holmes 1985b: 15–16).

The Thatcher government came to power determined to cut both public expenditure and income tax but without increasing borrowing. In attempting to reconcile these various goals, Conservative governments have dramatically increased inequality and poverty since 1979, as Table 10.10 has demonstrated. The Thatcher governments introduced significant cuts in income tax, especially on the higher rates, subsidised share ownership by selling most privatisation issues at well below expected market rates (a subsidy which averaged 33 per cent) and encouraged increases in executive pay (Johnson 1991: 130, 170). The Conservatives had argued that incentives to work harder would be restored if income tax were reduced, especially on the 'wealth creators'. The gains by the very rich have been more than sufficient to offset any losses which they may have experienced between 1964 and 1979. At the other end of the income distribution, incentives would be restored only if 'dependency' could be reduced by cuts in real benefit levels and tighter administration (Johnson 1991: 238; Maynard 1988: 125). Thus, earnings-related supplements for sickness and unemployment benefits were abolished and indexation of benefits was suspended for three years from 1980 (Atkinson and Micklewright 1989). The SBC system was abolished and replaced by what has become Income Support and all the 'additional' payments, by which benefit had been adjusted to suit the needs of individuals or groups of claimants, were replaced by payments from a cash-limited Social Fund, 70 per cent of which had to be repaid by claimants (Lowe 1993: 315). In the process state support for the housing costs of claimants has been administered much more stringently (Hills and Mullings 1990: 191–4). In sharp contrast to the previous Labour government, the Conservatives reduced the scope of universal benefits and steered claimants towards means-tested benefits to try to ensure that funds were concentrated where they were most needed. In 1985, the Conservative government's review of social security resulted in further changes which have led to a deterioration in the condition of the poorest. Ministers looked with great concern at the long-term implications for public expenditure of the projections of an increasing number of elderly people dependent on a relatively diminishing working population (Chapter 9). They concluded that dependency would increase and the cost of SERPS would be insupportable by the relatively diminishing band of national insurance contributors (DHSS 1984). Accordingly, the Social Security Act of 1986 reduced the scope of SERPS, making it much less generous than originally intended. This paring down of what had been a major contribution to the alleviation of poverty among the elderly has almost certainly been based upon unsophisticated assessments of dependency (Falkingham 1989) but Conservative commitments to reducing the economic role of the state and expanding private provision of welfare prevailed. The most obvious illustration was the withdrawal in 1988 of Treasury contributions to social insurance (which had been intended by Beveridge to match employer and employee contributions) but there have been many piecemeal changes to cut all categories of social welfare expenditure (Lowe 1993: 315). Important as these administrative changes have been in reducing the income of the poorest, the main cause of the increase in poverty since the later 1970s has been the rise of unemployment. Despite the reduction in the real value of benefits to individual claimants, public expenditure on social security has risen in real terms since 1979 (Barr and Coulter 1990: 285). There has been a vast increase in the number of claimants as a result of the huge rises in unemployment in the early 1980s and 1990s (see Chapter 14). The combination of rapidly increasing need and continuous changes in administration of social security schemes to control costs has many echoes of the situation described in Chapter 2. Once again, it has been convenient for government to evoke the image of 'the scrounger' as it has tightened eligibility for benefit; during the 1980s and 1990s government has campaigned vigorously against social security 'fraud'. Once again, the corollary of mass unemployment appears to be a benefit regime which is unable to raise the victims of economic contingency (loss of earnings as a result of old age, unemployment or ill-health) out of poverty as the mass of the population would define it. Indeed, there is considerable evidence that the constant relative poverty lines considered above are significantly more stringent than poverty as defined by the mass population (Veit-Wilson 1987; Mack and Lansley 1985; Piachaud 1987: 149–52). The figures in Table 10.10 give rather low estimates of the increase in poverty since the late 1970s.

What appears to have no parallel in the interwar years is the substantial increase in inequality as mass unemployment has developed. Since 1979, the living standards of the poorest have been eroded at the same time as those at the top of the income distribution have been treated generously in terms of taxation, share ownership and salaries, as noted above. This benevolence towards the well-off has come at the end of a long period in which postwar governments of both major parties have been distributing what Titmuss (1958: 44–50) called 'fiscal welfare' to those at the top of the income distribution. In particular, there have been substantial tax benefits necessarily of greatest benefit to the wealthy for house purchase (through tax relief on mortgage interest payments) and saving (by the favourable tax treatment of occupational pension contributions and, until very recently, for life insurance contributions). In 1968, the cost to the Treasury of mortgage tax relief amounted to one and-a-third times the total cost of family allowances; by 1983 the Exchequer subvention to private pensions was almost twice as large as the total Exchequer contribution to the National Insurance Fund (Cutler *et al.* 1986: 48). In a similar vein, postwar governments have also encouraged the growth of 'occupational welfare' – such as pensions, health services, travel expenses, meal vouchers, motor cars, holiday accommodation, medical insurance, and so on (Titmuss 1958: 50–5). In some cases, such as the growth of occupational pensions, the growth of private provision has been explicitly fostered by government policy (Hannah 1986: 57) but in others employers have simply seen 'fringe benefits' of this type as a tax-efficient method of rewarding employees (Playford and Pond 1983: 42–4). Occupational welfare has expanded enormously since the late 1950s and has made the salary and wage figures increasingly unreliable as a guide to income distribution. There can be little doubt that since the early 1950s Britain has become a much less egalitarian society.

# Chapter 11

# Britain in the world economy

## INTERNATIONAL FINANCIAL RECONSTRUCTION AND THE DOLLAR SHORTAGE

Early in the Second World War the Treasury recognised that the postwar balance of payments would be difficult, but just how difficult emerged in memoranda during 1944 and 1945 (Pressnell 1986; Cairncross 1985: chs 1, 4–5). There was a huge current account deficit, with exports in 1945 at only 30 per cent of the 1938 level and imports 60 per cent; the export industries and Britain's traditional invisible earning capacity had been disrupted by war (Chapter 8). In 1945 the Treasury expected a transitional period of between three and five years before the export industries recovered fully, during which the current account would have gone £1.25 billion further into the red. On capital account, the position was even worse. More than a quarter of Britain's prewar foreign investments had been sold and very large debts had been incurred. In 1938, the sterling balances (debts to sterling area countries) had been roughly equivalent to the gold and dollar reserves at £500 million. In 1945, the sterling balances stood at approximately £3.5 billion but the reserves were just over £600 million (Cairncross 1992: 47). Keynes (1979: 410) described the position as a 'financial Dunkirk'.

The drastic balance of payments position left the postwar government with few real choices (Tomlinson 1991). It had to retain controls over imports and dealings in foreign exchange and needed measures to boost exports. Britain would have to borrow to cover the deficit on current account during the transitional period. The only country with funds available was the USA, and the Attlee government sent a team led by Keynes and Lord Halifax to Washington in autumn 1945 to seek financial assistance. The British delegation hoped for a grant (rather than an interest-bearing loan) to cover the entire £1.25 billion ($5 billion at 1945 exchange rates) projected current account deficit for the transition period (Bullen and Pelly 1986; Pressnell 1986).

The US government wanted to treat its former wartime ally fairly but many US manufacturers and farmers wanted to exploit Britain's temporary weakness and dismantle Imperial preference and the sterling area (Kolko and Kolko 1972). The US Treasury had administered the wartime mutual aid policy with these options in mind (Dobson 1986). After lengthy and often acrimonious talks, the US government gave Britain generous assistance, but less than was requested and with strings which would keep the British external position weak and open to further US pressure. Britain was finally offered $3.75 billion at a low interest rate (better terms than were offered to any other country at the time), but sterling had to be made freely convertible within twelve months of the loan coming into force. Britain also received a credit from Canada under similar terms to take the total to the figure originally requested. The convertibility clause was menacing. Under the Bretton Woods agreement, Britain had been given five years before sterling needed to be freely convertible into other currencies. The US loan agreement of 1946 effectively cut this reconstruction period dramatically. To say the least, ministers were far from enthusiastic but accepted despite their doubts about meeting the US conditions (Jay 1985: 120; Dalton 1962: 82).

In some respects, Britain's balance of payments recovered more quickly than had been anticipated in 1945. Table 11.1 suggests that the current account was probably in the black by 1948, even though the figures available at the time did not show the full extent of recovery.

Visible exports grew at a remarkable pace throughout the reconstruction period and the expansion of imports was much less strong until rearmament for the Korean War. Invisibles returned to surplus as world trade began to recover. Unfortunately, it became clear that the balance of

Table 11.1 British trade and payments, 1946–52 (£ millions)

|  |  | 1946 | 1947 | 1948 | 1949 | 1950 | 1951 | 1952 |
|---|---|---|---|---|---|---|---|---|
| Exports and re-exports | (a) | 960 | 1,180 | 1,639 | 1,863 | 2,261 | 2,735 | 2,769 |
|  | (b) | 900 | 1,125 | 1,550 | 1,790 | 2,221 | 2,708 | 2,836 |
| Imports | (a) | 1,063 | 1,541 | 1,790 | 2,000 | 2,312 | 3,424 | 3,048 |
|  | (b) | 1,100 | 1,574 | 1,768 | 1,970 | 2,374 | 3,497 | 2,927 |
| Visible balance | (a) | −103 | −361 | −151 | −137 | −51 | −689 | −279 |
|  | (b) | −200 | −449 | −218 | −180 | −153 | −789 | −91 |
| Invisible balance | (a) | −127 | −20 | +177 | +136 | +358 | +320 | +442 |
|  | (b) | −250 | −226 | +98 | +110 | +382 | +268 | +261 |
| Current balance | (a) | −230 | −381 | +26 | −1 | +307 | −369 | +163 |
|  | (b) | −450 | −675 | −120 | −70 | −229 | −521 | +170 |

Notes:
(a) as estimated in 1980
(b) as estimated at the time
Source: Cairncross 1985: 201.

trade with the dollar area was far more important than the current account as a whole. The war had strengthened the US economy. In 1945, the USA controlled 70 per cent of the world's gold and foreign exchange reserves and accounted for more than 40 per cent of world industrial output. Until the war-disrupted economies of Europe and the Far East could be restored, the USA was the obvious source of supply for manufactures and primary products but was a hard market for foreign suppliers to penetrate. The US balance of payments surplus amounted to $19.5 billion in 1946 and 1947 (Brett 1985: 106). In the late 1940s, Whitehall regarded the balance of trade with the dollar area as the main yardstick of policy (Clarke 1982: 191) and, as Table 11.2 suggests, performance was less satisfactory than in the aggregate current account. The dollar deficit was substantial, especially in 1947. In the same year the deficit of the whole sterling area was huge, equivalent to 84 per cent of the entire US loan (Cairncross 1985: 202, 150). The dollars borrowed in 1946 were disappearing far too rapidly. The pace of British recovery led to imports of machinery and metals from the dollar area (Milward 1984: 34). Other European economies faced similar import surges and shortages of dollars and, from July 1947, the convertibility clause in the US loan agreement obliged the Bank of England to make dollars available in Britain. The loss of dollars accelerated and Britain suspended convertibility after only five weeks, but not before the US loan had virtually gone. Britain needed more dollars and policies to ensure that they were expended in ways which maximised economic recovery.

Immediately after the convertibility crisis, dollars were conserved. New sources of supply became available and Britain began to discriminate much more heavily against dollar imports. Sterling area countries were requested to adopt similar policies (Sargent 1952). These discriminatory arrangements were in direct contrast to the US blueprints for liberalisation of trade and payments but new attitudes were emerging in Washington in 1947. Political friction between the USA and the USSR and a strong (but unfounded) conviction in the State Department that western Europe was about to fall under communist sway led to a new

Table 11.2 British trade with the dollar area, 1946–52 (£ millions)

|  | 1946 | 1947 | 1948 | 1949 | 1950 | 1951 | 1952 |
|---|---|---|---|---|---|---|---|
| Exports and re-exports | 100 | 130 | 196 | 195 | 324 | 393 | 410 |
| Imports | 390 | 567 | 406 | 442 | 439 | 742 | 606 |
| Visible balance | −290 | −437 | −210 | −247 | −115 | −349 | −196 |
| Invisible balance | −11 | −73 | −42 | −49 | +27 | −87 | +23 |
| Current balance | −301 | −510 | −252 | −296 | −88 | −436 | −173 |

Source: Cairncross 1985: 201.

plan for Europe, Marshall aid (Milward 1984: ch. 1; Hogan 1987: ch. 1). Marshall aid had four main aims:

1  to increase European production;
2  to increase foreign trade;
3  to restore financial stability within Europe, and
4  to encourage political and economic co-operation within western Europe (Tomlinson 1990: 191).

Dollar aid was the main instrument to achieve these goals but European countries were also granted better access to US technology and production methods (Carew 1987).

To the British government, this plan came as both a relief and a threat. Marshall aid began to flow in 1948 when the dollar reserves were almost exhausted. But the pressure for European economic and political integration was unwelcome. Ernest Bevin, the Foreign Secretary, saw Britain's political future outside Europe as a 'great power', heading a worldwide empire (Bullock 1983), even though great power status involved enormous military and political spending overseas when the current account was so weak (Tomlinson 1991; Saville 1990). But Empire and sterling area countries were sources of vital supplies and dollars (Cain and Hopkins 1993b: 279). Treasury officials believed that European countries, on the other hand, could not balance their dollar trade and would fritter away Britain's own dollar reserves (Clarke 1982: 207–10). Bevin ensured that Europe's response to Marshall's ideas were positive and that dollar aid came to Europe. Thus Britain led the way with proposals to remove quotas on intra-European trade. The Treasury was more reluctant to see Britain join the European Payments Union (EPU), a scheme to cut restrictions on the exchange of European currencies (Cairncross 1985: 287–93; Milward 1984: ch. 8). Its fingers had been burnt by the convertibility crisis and suspicion persisted that European governments would use sterling as a means of acquiring dollars. Britain joined the EPU reluctantly, only after an unanticipated rise in its reserves during 1950, but rejected any loss of sovereignty to supra-national bodies. The Treasury firmly quashed proposals for a customs union and Britain remained aloof from the European Coal and Steel Community (ECSC), designed to co-ordinate coal and steel production in Europe (Milward 1984: chs 7, 12).

Liberalisation of European trade and payments helped Britain to cope with the dollar shortage. The significant fall in the proportion of imports from the USA and the growth of European supply after 1947 are evident in Table 11.3, which also explains why Britain turned its back on European integration in the late 1940s. The sterling area was a much bigger market for British industry than Europe and could help to close the British dollar gap because there was demand in North America for

Table 11.3 The pattern of British trade, 1938–90

| | Percentage of total imports by value from: | | | | | Percentage of total exports by value to: | | | | |
|---|---|---|---|---|---|---|---|---|---|---|
| | North America | Western Europe | (EEC[a]) | Sterling area[b] | Rest of world | North America | Western Europe | (EEC[a]) | Sterling Area[b] | Rest of world |
| 1938 | 21.7 | 24.0 | — | 31.1 | 23.1 | 9.3 | 23.4 | — | 44.9 | 22.4 |
| 1946 | 33.1 | 14.9 | — | 32.8 | 19.2 | 7.5 | 28.3 | — | 45.3 | 19.0 |
| 1950 | 15.0 | 25.1 | (10.7) | 38.0 | 25.9 | 11.0 | 28.3 | (9.7) | 47.8 | 12.9 |
| 1960 | 20.7 | 29.2 | (14.6) | 33.2 | 16.9 | 15.3 | 29.0 | (14.6) | 40.2 | 15.6 |
| 1970 | 20.5 | 37.7 | (20.2) | 25.3 | 16.2 | 15.3 | 41.1 | (21.7) | 27.2 | 16.0 |
| 1980 | 15.0 | 55.9 | (41.3) | 11.0 | 18.0 | 11.3 | 57.6 | (43.4) | 14.4 | 16.6 |
| 1990 | 13.3 | 64.8 | (52.3) | 6.9 | 15.0 | 14.4 | 61.7 | (53.0) | 9.7 | 14.2 |

Notes:
a EEC 'six' in 1950.
b Consolidated totals for sterling area trade are available to 1970. After that date the figures have been compiled by summing the shares of trade of those countries designated within the sterling area in 1970.
Source: Annual Abstract of Statistics, various issues.

colonial commodity exports. No other major European country was remotely close to equilibrium in its dollar trade. Moreover, even in 1951 Britain's exports were greater than those of France and Germany combined and its industrial production was as great as that of France and Germany combined (Cairncross 1985: 278). For good short-term reasons, Britain saw its trading future with the sterling area. Thus Britain's strategy of coping with the dollar shortage after the convertibility crisis of 1947 had three main elements. The first was to discriminate against dollar area imports. The second was to secure Marshall aid and try to divert pressures for European political and economic integration in directions which did not compromise the third aspect, the development of trade within the sterling area (Tomlinson 1991). Capital exports to sterling area countries were encouraged; between 1947 and 1949 the flow of capital to the sterling area, mainly the white dominions, was greater than the size of the US loan (Conan 1952; Tomlinson 1991: 59). But at the same time, Britain exploited the poorer colonies both by manipulating the price at which colonial products were bought and by controlling the use of the sterling balances (Tomlinson 1991: 61–4). In the short term this strategy of developing the sterling area was successful. In 1949, sterling accounted for half all international transactions (Cain and Hopkins 1993b: 279–80). The longer-term consequences will be discussed below.

Britain's dollar imbalance was also reduced by US action. As noted above, Marshall aid was a response to US fears of economic collapse in Europe and the advent of the Cold War. However, from the US point of view, the discriminatory monetary and trading practices which Europe adopted to cope with the dollar shortage threatened the longer-term goal of freer, multilateral trade. Having promised aid to meet short-term needs, Washington wanted more use of the price mechanism and less use of government regulation in overcoming the dollar shortage. Rather than revalue the dollar, the US Treasury wanted devaluation everywhere else, and sterling was the key currency (Milward 1984: ch. 9). If the British government could be persuaded or cajoled into devaluation, others would follow suit. Whitehall had hitherto resisted changes in parity because in the prevailing sellers' market devaluation would have had a bigger impact on inflation (by raising import prices) than on exports (Cairncross and Eichengreen 1983: ch. 4). In 1948–9 a recession in the USA caused a reduction in US demand for imports and Britain's dollar balance of trade deteriorated. The US Treasury seized on this adverse movement and pressed strongly for devaluation, undermining international confidence and the government's policy of promoting sterling's re-emergence as a trading currency. A first-class political crisis ensued and prompted a substantial devaluation of sterling against the dollar, by 30 per cent, from £1 = $4.03 to $2.80. Most non-dollar countries followed suit, however, and Britain's devaluation against all currencies weighted by their share in British trade was 9 per cent. As can be seen in Table 11.2, Britain's exports to the USA responded and the gap in dollar trade narrowed but this favourable impact was swamped in 1951 by the Korean War.

Korea turned Cold War hostility into military conflict and world-wide rearmament. The supply of raw materials could not keep pace with demand and rising prices for primary products resulted in a large adverse shift in Britain's terms of trade. Britain rearmed with an economy which was already at full employment. The domestic economy boomed, import volumes rose and goods intended for export were diverted into the home market. The current account deteriorated (Tables 11.1 and 11.2) but inflationary forces quickly subsided and the balance of payments returned to equilibrium. The Korean War led the USA into more extensive overseas military and political involvements, with the result that its persistent current account surplus disappeared, helping supply the rest of the world with dollars (Spero 1982: 40–1). The dollar deficit would fade away in the 1950s and the emerging US current account imbalance slowly eroded confidence in the dollar. The changing status of the dollar is the backdrop to the long boom to which we now turn.

## TRADE AND PAYMENTS DURING THE LONG BOOM

There is no obvious point at which the 'transition' ended and 'normal peacetime conditions' began in the world economy, not least because of the recurrent crises during the early postwar years. The normality which emerged during the 1950s was moreover subtly different from that planned during wartime. Barriers to trade and multilateral clearing were cut, but the new international institutions played only a small role in the process. Exchange rates were pegged and most countries were moving to free convertibility as stated in the Bretton Woods charter. The IMF was, however, relatively uninvolved in the supply of dollars to Europe from 1947 to 1952 and the devaluations of 1949 had been negotiated with the US Treasury rather than the IMF board (Tew 1970: chs 17–19). Plans for an ambitious International Trade Organisation were drawn up at a series of postwar conferences, but the ITO convention could not be ratified. Instead, a more restricted General Agreement on Tariffs and Trade (GATT) provided a framework to negotiate the abolition of quotas and reduction of tariffs (Kock 1969: chs 1–2; Gardner 1956: chs 14–17).

Liberalisation proceeded regionally before being extended to a global scale. The important steps taken in Europe in the 1950s will be the focus of a later section but similar moves were also made in Africa and the

Americas in the late 1950s and early 1960s (Kenwood and Lougheed 1983: 291–2). Washington was concerned at this re-emergence of regionalism and rekindled its efforts to encourage the reduction of tariff barriers between these emerging blocs. Under the Dillon and Kennedy rounds of the GATT, substantial reductions of tariffs on trade in industrial goods were negotiated in the late 1950s and 1960s. The Kennedy round resulted in industrial tariff reductions of 35–40 per cent (Brett 1985: 77). The main step in financial liberalisation came at the end of 1958 when the Bank of England again made sterling freely convertible, but with much less discomfort than in 1947 (Cairncross 1992: 124–6). Most other western European countries introduced convertibility at the same time, making multilateral clearing available almost throughout the developed world (Tew 1970: 158–60, 245–6).

World trade expanded rapidly, especially between industrial nations (Foreman-Peck 1983: 293–302). Trade grew more rapidly than incomes, but incomes also rose in the industrial nations at an unprecedented rate between 1950 and 1973, producing consumer-driven, affluent societies. Liberalisation was not the only factor causing faster growth, as the previous chapter has tried to make clear, but it was a dynamic force (Maddison 1982). Two industrial countries appeared however to enjoy only a mild stimulus from trade. Britain and the USA grew much less rapidly than the OECD average. Britain seemed to have its growth constrained rather than stimulated by its balance of payments, especially after 1955. Balance of payments figures are notoriously unreliable and subject to major revision, as is evident from Table 11.1. Figures for subsequent periods (Tables 11.4 and 11.6) are also being constantly updated. The size of the 'balancing item' (the adjustment needed to make the figures balance) is often as big as the current surplus or deficit and gives considerable scope for later revision. But the figures for the 1950s (Table 11.4) are clear; the current account came back into surplus after the Korean War crisis and remained in the black for most of the decade thanks to the invisible surplus.

Nevertheless sterling was never strong in the 1950s and a crisis developed in 1957. In response to currency weakness, governments chose to cut the pressure of demand, initiating concern about the 'stop–go' pattern noted in the previous chapter. The source of the problem appeared to lie less in the current account than in weak reserves (Scott 1962: 224). During the 1950s the reserves averaged approximately $2.5 billion, equivalent to three months' imports at the start of the decade, and rather less at the end (Cairncross 1992: 118), but liquid liabilities, the sterling balances, at no stage fell much below $4 billion during the decade. Any problem in the external accounts could easily trigger speculation or reduction of the sterling balances, forcing higher interest rates or cuts in demand to convince opinion that sterling

Table 11.4 British trade and payments, 1951–73 (£ millions)

| | Visible balance | Invisible balance | Current balance | UK external assets and liabilities net[a] | Special items[b] | Balancing item |
|---|---|---|---|---|---|---|
| 1951 | −689 | 320 | −369 | 426 | 43 | −100 |
| 1952 | −279 | 442 | 163 | −229 | — | 66 |
| 1953 | −244 | 389 | 145 | −177 | — | 32 |
| 1954 | −204 | 321 | 117 | −174 | — | 57 |
| 1955 | −313 | 158 | −155 | 34 | — | 121 |
| 1956 | 53 | 155 | 208 | −250 | — | 42 |
| 1957 | −29 | 262 | 233 | −313 | — | 80 |
| 1958 | 29 | 321 | 350 | −411 | — | 61 |
| 1959 | −115 | 279 | 164 | −68 | −58 | −38 |
| 1960 | −401 | 164 | −237 | −7 | −32 | 276 |
| 1961 | −140 | 175 | 35 | 23 | — | −58 |
| 1962 | −100 | 243 | 143 | −195 | — | 52 |
| 1963 | −119 | 233 | 114 | −39 | — | −75 |
| 1964 | −543 | 171 | −372 | 383 | — | −11 |
| 1965 | −260 | 183 | −77 | 37 | — | 40 |
| 1966 | −108 | 236 | 128 | 12 | −44 | −96 |
| 1967 | −599 | 318 | −281 | 166 | −105 | 220 |
| 1968 | −712 | 448 | −264 | 653 | −251 | −138 |
| 1969 | −209 | 691 | 482 | −860 | — | 378 |
| 1970 | −11 | 835 | 821 | −888 | −133 | −66 |
| 1971 | 210 | 904 | 1,114 | −1,504 | 125 | 265 |
| 1972 | −742 | 945 | 203 | 448 | 124 | −775 |
| 1973 | −2,568 | 1,570 | −998 | 924 | — | 133 |

Notes:
a This column comprises direct and portfolio investment; overseas lending and borrowing by UK banks and the non-bank sector; changes in official reserves and other government assets and liabilities. Negative sums indicate an increase during the year of UK assets overseas, positive sums indicate a reduction of overseas assets.
b Exchange Equalisation Account losses on forward currency markets; Special Drawing Right allocations; IMF gold subscriptions; and special grants and capital transfers.
Source: Economic Trends, Annual Supplement 1993.

would be held within its Bretton Woods bands. There was broad agreement that the reserves should be increased (Radcliffe 1959: ch. 8).

Reserve weakness stemmed in part from the costs of the world role which Britain continued to play in the 1950s. As a result of the diplomatic, military and economic links which Bevin helped tie between Britain, the USA and Western Europe in the late 1940s (noted above), Britain had redefined its role as principal ally of the USA in containing Soviet power but nonetheless the head of a world-wide Empire (Cain and Hopkins 1993b: 266–7). The USA acted as ultimate financial guarantor of the sterling area, which became the essential prop of Britain's world role, but in return expected a much higher defence expenditure from the UK than could be justified by any rational assessment of Britain's economic position. Throughout the postwar period, Britain has had the highest defence expenditure in relation to GNP of any NATO country (Saville 1990: 149). A significant proportion of UK defence expenditure was incurred overseas, at its peak equivalent to 10 per cent of the value of exports, resulting in a persistent burden on an already weak external account (Cain and Hopkins 1993b: 282). The costs were slowly perceived and a process of withdrawal began from the late 1950s. Unfortunately the foreign exchange costs of each member of the armed forces stationed overseas rose even more rapidly than numbers fell; the cost of overseas defence commitments rose by two-thirds between 1957 and 1967 although the number of service personnel overseas fell by half (Brittan 1971: 438). Britain also incurred significant costs in developing the sterling area. The dollar earnings of sterling area countries were useful in stabilising the current account but capital outflows to develop these resources often coincided with weakness in sterling and aggravated the drain on gold and dollar reserves (Strange 1971: chs 5–6). Strange has criticised the failure to cancel or reduce the sterling balances, as the US Treasury had advised during the 1945–6 loan negotiations. The dangers of weak reserves, extensive use of sterling in international trade and finance and large sterling balances were starkly illustrated in 1956. The current account was in surplus, but the Suez invasion by Britain and France provoked speculation against sterling, in part by sterling balance holders in the Middle East. Britain had to borrow from the IMF and the USA and ultimately had to raise interest rates to the highest level for more than 50 years (Scott 1962: 220–3).

Problems also began to emerge in other parts of the current account. Although Britain retained a huge surplus in manufactured trade in the 1950s and beyond, Britain's share of world trade in manufactures began to decline after 1950 (Table 11.5). The share which Britain had secured in 1950 was based upon transitory factors, but the pace of decline thereafter cannot be explained solely or even mainly by the recovery of Britain's war-damaged competitors (Batchelor *et al.* 1980: 50). Nor was specialisation on the wrong products to blame. The war brought about changes which ended dependence on the 'old staple' industries and helped to create an export commodity structure similar to that of Germany (Maroof and Rajan 1976). Concentration on the sterling area was, however, mistaken. Its markets were growing more slowly than those in western Europe (though this may simply reflect the problems of the British economy which dominated the sterling area). By 1960 the problems of the sterling area were recognised (see Britain and Europe below).

In addition to the loss of export markets it became clear during the

*Table 11.5* Percentage shares of world exports of manufactures, 1937–88

|       | France | Germany | Japan | UK   | USA  |
|-------|--------|---------|-------|------|------|
| 1937  | 6.4    | 22.4    | 7.2   | 22.4 | 19.6 |
| 1950  | 9.9    | 7.3     | 3.4   | 25.5 | 27.3 |
| 1960  | 9.6    | 19.3    | 6.9   | 16.5 | 21.6 |
| 1971  | 10.5   | 20.9    | 13.7  | 9.1  | 16.0 |
| 1988  | 9.1    | 20.6    | 18.1  | 8.3  | 14.9 |

*Source*: *National Institute Economic Review*, various issues.

1950s that import penetration was growing (Alford 1988: 42–6) and that a 'ratchet effect' was operating, so that at every successive peak in the trade cycle the extent of import penetration increased (Hughes and Thirlwall 1977). Increasing import penetration is common to all industrial countries, but British import ratios were the highest of all OECD countries in the 1960s and 1970s (Hay 1985: 476). Thus, the main problem with the visible trade balance during the long boom was that British taste for foreign-produced goods appeared to be growing alarmingly at the same time as the world seemed less inclined to take British manufactures. In response, some economists argued strongly that the root of Britain's relatively poor postwar economic performance lay in slow growth of world demand for British exports (Thirlwall 1986: ch. 12; Beckerman 1965: ch. 2). But as noted in the previous chapter, calculations of income elasticities of demand are highly controversial and cannot support the burden of explanation which Thirlwall and others have placed upon them (see Table 10.7).

Rising dissatisfaction with stop–go, awareness that European countries were growing more rapidly than Britain and a belated realisation of the financial strains of the world role led to a reappraisal of policy in the late 1950s and early 1960s. The main conclusions were that the costs of the world role were no longer sustainable and that greater efficiency was needed in British industry. The Suez fiasco led to high-level reviews of the cost of world power status and a long process of cutting overseas military and diplomatic expenditure (Cain and Hopkins 1993b: 290). There was even some tightening of capital outflow to sterling area countries but the main features of sterling's world role remained intact (Strange 1971: 67). The new policies to raise efficiency in British industry either involved Europe (discussed below) or were part of the broad growth strategy considered in Chapter 14. The new policies of the early 1960s did not get to grips with Britain's deteriorating price competitiveness and the current account began to worsen in the 1960s (Table 11.4). Speculative pressures mounted during the mid-1960s and the Wilson government was forced into a series of measures to defend the exchange rate. A temporary tariff was adopted in 1964 though it infringed Britain's GATT commitments. Confidence in sterling was not strengthened until deep cuts were imposed in public expenditure. Even this failed to satisfy the foreign exchange markets for long, and in November 1967 the government was forced to recognise that it could no longer support the exchange rate established in 1949. Sterling was devalued by 14 per cent to $2.40. Contrary to expectation, devaluation had little impact on the exchange markets and sterling stabilised only in late 1969 after further deflationary measures (Cairncross 1992: 164–71). Just as export revenues began to increase after devaluation, so too did the rate of inflation, driven upwards by the rise of import prices after devaluation. Thus, the positive effects of the devaluation of 1967 were smaller and much less long-lasting than had been predicted.

After Britain's devaluation international speculative attention turned to the dollar. Since 1950, the US Treasury had been trying to ensure that the supply of world money kept pace with the growth of world trade. Strong support had been given to sterling's international role (Strange 1971: 63–72) and the US current account deficit had gone uncorrected. But the persistent US deficit had run down US reserves and had slowly exposed the dollar to severe speculative pressures (Triffin 1961). After 1961 the cumulative balance of payments deficit of the USA exceeded the value of the country's gold and dollar reserves for the first time (Brett 1985: 112). The US government did not, however, follow the British lead and implement deep cuts in public expenditure in large part because of the costs of the Vietnam War. Speculative pressure mounted relentlessly. The dollar was devalued in 1971 and again in 1973. At this point it was clear that the Bretton Woods system of pegged exchange rates (see Chapter 8) had disintegrated.

## FLOATING IN CHAOS, 1972–9

It is not surprising that Britain should be among the first to abandon Bretton Woods. British governments had persistently sacrificed domestic policy goals to support the exchange rate. When the Heath government began another 'dash for growth' in June 1972, it unpegged the exchanges as an integral part of the strategy. Once unpegged, the reserve currency role collapsed as the sterling balances were run down (Van Der Wee 1987: 491). The government hoped that it would now be possible to leave sterling's value to the currency markets while it concentrated on domestic economic objectives (Tomlinson 1990: 243). The early 1970s also saw the first synchronised boom in all the major industrial countries since the Korean War. Primary product prices rose rapidly, most spectacularly in the quadrupling of oil prices in 1973 (OPEC 1). The terms of trade moved sharply against the industrial countries and, faced by current account deficits, they elected to float their exchange rates rather than impose deflation. In turn, this led to higher inflation and further arguments for floating as pegged exchange rates are much more difficult to maintain when inflation accelerates. Floating exchange rates were also welcomed by economists as a method of continuous adjustment to competitive pressures (Green 1989: 166).

Unfortunately none of these advantages has been much in evidence in Britain's experience of floating rates. Theories of floating were constructed on the assumption that rates would be determined largely by trade in goods. A country with a trade deficit would experience a falling exchange rate, boosting exports and curbing imports and ultimately returning the exchange rate to an equilibrium level set by relative prices. But in the real world floating exchange rates also affect the price of internationally traded assets. Government bonds, equities and even currencies can be traded across national borders. Since 1973, this form of trade has mushroomed to become the major determinant of short-run exchange rates. There is no reason at all to expect the exchange rate in these circumstances to be appropriate to bring about equilibrium in trade in goods (Green 1989: 164–9). As a result, exchange rates have tended to 'overshoot' the levels which would have been justified by relative prices (Hacche and Townsend 1981) bringing great costs to governments. Too rapid a fall will raise import prices and give a powerful stimulus to inflation. If the exchange rate is driven up too rapidly, export markets will be lost and imports will become very competitively priced. Thus governments have been forced to manage floating exchange rates.

Britain was free of balance of payments problems in the early 1970s. The positive effects of the 1967 devaluation were still being felt in 1971–2 but the pressure of inflation was building up, as it was in all countries. The 'dash for growth' led to higher pressure of demand and the gentle fall in the exchange rate (9 per cent in the first six months of floating) raised import prices. The huge rises in commodity prices during 1973 exacerbated inflationary pressures. Non-oil commodity prices rose by 62 per cent during the year, the largest recorded annual increase (Foreman-Peck 1991: 169). Oil prices rose even faster. Like other OECD countries, Britain suffered a huge shift in its terms of trade and a substantial deterioration on external account. The current balance, already in deficit in 1973, reached a peak deficit of £3.2 billion in 1974 and then improved year by year until it emerged in surplus in 1977 (Table 11.6).

The exchange rate was relatively unaffected as the current deficit was more than matched by capital account improvement. There was a net import of long-term capital of about £3.7 billion, mainly for investment in North Sea oil extraction, and short term borrowing from the oil producers (Cairncross 1992: 209–10). OPEC countries found that they

Table 11.6 British trade and payments, 1971–91 (£ millions)

| | Oil balance | Manufacturing balance | Visible balance[a] | Invisible balance | Current balance | UK external assets and liabilities net[b] | Special items[c] | Balancing item |
|---|---|---|---|---|---|---|---|---|
| 1971 | n.a. | 2,333 | 210 | 904 | 1,114 | −1,504 | 125 | 265 |
| 1972 | n.a. | 1,688 | −742 | 945 | 203 | 448 | 124 | −775 |
| 1973 | −941 | 1,206 | −2,568 | 1,570 | −998 | 924 | −59 | 133 |
| 1974 | −3,357 | 2,022 | −5,229 | 2,047 | −3,184 | 3,119 | −75 | 140 |
| 1975 | −3,057 | 3,241 | −3,256 | 1,731 | −1,524 | 1,528 | — | −4 |
| 1976 | −3,947 | 3,935 | −3,961 | 3,189 | −772 | 356 | — | 416 |
| 1977 | −2,771 | 4,256 | −2,322 | 2,375 | 53 | −3,892 | — | 3,839 |
| 1978 | −1,984 | 3,745 | −1,592 | 2,715 | 1,123 | −2,871 | — | 1,748 |
| 1979 | −738 | 2,084 | −3,343 | 2,890 | −453 | −742 | 195 | 1,000 |
| 1980 | 308 | 4,093 | 1,357 | 1,487 | 2,843 | −3,940 | 180 | 917 |
| 1981 | 3,106 | 3,159 | 3,252 | 3,496 | 6,748 | −7,436 | 158 | 530 |
| 1982 | 4,638 | 1,257 | 1,910 | 2,741 | 4,649 | −2,519 | — | −2,130 |
| 1983 | 6,972 | −2,594 | −1,537 | 5,302 | 3,765 | −4,562 | — | 797 |
| 1984 | 6,933 | −3,965 | −5,336 | 7,134 | 1,798 | −8,414 | — | 6,616 |
| 1985 | 8,101 | −3,348 | −3,345 | 6,136 | 2,790 | −3,733 | — | 943 |
| 1986 | 4,070 | −5,191 | −9,559 | 9,625 | 66 | −3,134 | — | 3,068 |
| 1987 | 4,183 | −6,229 | −11,582 | 7,099 | −4,482 | 4,334 | — | 148 |
| 1988 | 2,797 | −11,162 | −21,480 | 5,302 | −16,179 | 9,396 | — | 6,783 |
| 1989 | 1,481 | −12,670 | −24,683 | 2,956 | −21,726 | 19,259 | — | 2,467 |
| 1990 | 1,260 | −13,947 | −18,809 | 1,778 | −17,029 | 11,091 | — | 5,938 |
| 1991 | 1,041 | −6,022 | −10,290 | 3,969 | −6,321 | 5,249 | — | 636 |

Notes:
a The visible balance contains items other than manufactures and oil (food, raw materials, minerals, etc.), and is not therefore simply a sum of the oil and manufacturing balances.
b See note a to Table 11.4.
c See note b to Table 11.4.
Sources: Economic Trends, Annual Supplement, 1993; United Kingdom Balance of Payments (the Pink Book), various issues.

could not spend all their newly acquired income and invested the surplus in western banks and financial institutions. 'Petro-dollars' were 're-cycled' to London. In 1974, 37 per cent of surplus oil income, or $21 billion, entered City markets (Metcalf 1984: 160). The Treasury also encouraged nationalised industries and local authorities to take medium-term loans from the Eurodollar markets, again effectively recycling OPEC surpluses. In the short-term, the basic balance of payments was stabilised and sterling's decline continued at a gentle pace. In the medium term, these OPEC balances were loaned on to third world countries which were much slower than the industrial nations to correct their current account deficits after OPEC 1. This further recycling of OPEC surpluses seemed a great achievement at the time but it unleashed a spate of ill-considered lending to poorly appraised projects in developing countries and to the debt crisis which damaged the third world growth and undermined the credit ratings of major US and European banks (Congdon 1988: 112–4).

Even limited dependence on inflows of short-term capital carries danger; 'hot money' can leave as quickly as it arrives. Some of the capital which had flowed in during 1974 clearly flowed out during 1975–6, driving the exchange rate down from £1 = $2.28 in mid-1975, to $2.02 at the end of the year and $1.55 in October 1976. Sterling's trade-weighted exchange rate followed a similar path (Tomlinson 1990: 278–9). There were no 'objective economic circumstances' to justify a fall of this magnitude. The market had lost confidence in government policy. The steepest falls occurred in the spring of 1976, after the Treasury had mismanaged an attempt to lower the exchange rate, and during the Labour Party conference (Pliatzky 1984: 143; Dell 1991: 236). The markets were concerned about Britain's high rate of inflation (24.3 per cent in 1975 and 16.6 per cent in 1976) and an impression that public expenditure was 'out of control'. Similar fears gripped domestic money markets making it very difficult for the government to fund its budget deficit (Tomlinson 1990: 285–8). To restore confidence the government introduced cuts in actual and planned public spending, including the imposition of cash limits, and tightened monetary policy. The screw was also turned in incomes policy (Jones 1987: 105–10). The whole episode of financial markets dictating public expenditure to a Labour government reawakened memories of 1931. In the circumstances of autumn 1976, the Chancellor of the Exchequer decided that the best way to restore confidence was to borrow from the IMF. The government would have to open itself to IMF scrutiny but, if it passed, confidence would return (Burk and Cairncross 1992). This rather humiliating process opened fissures within the Cabinet, the Labour Party, Whitehall and even the Treasury (Dell 1991; Crosland 1982: 374–83). In contrast to 1931, the Cabinet did not disintegrate, in part because the main cuts in public spending had already been accepted. The government got its loan of $3.9 billion, the largest loan ever made by the IMF, and had in return to make expenditure cuts of £1 billion in public expenditure plans in each of the two subsequent financial years (Burk and Cairncross 1992). Immediate cuts in current public expenditure above those agreed before the appeal to the IMF were not required. The recovery in the exchange rate which followed from the announcement of the loan meant that only half was used and the government had little difficulty in meeting expenditure and borrowing targets agreed with the IMF. In the short term, the IMF loan succeeded in restoring confidence; short-term capital again flowed into the country and the exchange rate soon began to recover. Confidence was boosted further by rising North Sea oil flows and falling dependence on imported oil. The government was almost as unhappy with a rising exchange rate as it had been with sterling's fall. Appreciation when Britain's inflation rate, though falling, remained higher than the OECD average weakened competitiveness (Metcalf 1984: 158). The government tried to 'cap' sterling to help industry but selling pounds to hold down the exchange rate only produced dangerous growth of the money supply, and the exchange rate was uncapped from September 1977.

Between 1972 and 1979, there were huge swings in the various components of the balance of payments and dramatic, often perverse, movements in the exchange rate. Every new policy for the balance of payments seemed to disintegrate within months of its introduction. Governments found that they could neither ignore nor manage sterling in the new unstable world of floating exchange rates and larger, more mobile flows of short-term capital. Domestic goals could not take priority over the exchange rate as governments found that they were very vulnerable to shifts in market sentiment. The retention of market confidence was more difficult at the start of the 1970s than at the end, when North Sea oil underpinned sterling. But many of the problems of the mid-1970s simply demonstrated that money markets have very short time horizons. The scale of the crisis after OPEC 1 was overdone. North Sea oil would come to the rescue. But since sterling had become a petrocurrency and susceptible to changes in the heavily manipulated price of oil, governments wisely decided to avoid a return to pegged exchanges. When in 1979 the EEC adopted a European Monetary System (EMS) with pegged central rates and wide bands of permitted fluctuation, Britain remained outside (Van Der Wee 1987: 504–6).

## FLOATING IN OIL AND IMPORTED MANUFACTURES SINCE 1979

North Sea oil and gas began to have a significant direct impact on the current account from 1977 (Dornbusch and Fischer 1980: 41), with the gains on visible trade more than outweighing the outflow of profits and dividends to foreign-owned oil companies (Green 1989: 154–9). But concern mounted quickly that the improvement in the current account would cause the exchange rate to rise, making the manufacturing sector increasingly uncompetitive, with lost exports and higher import penetration (Houthakker 1980: 352). In 1977, the government vainly attempted to hold down the exchange rate to shield British industry from more intense competition. The Conservative government which came to office in 1979 sought to manage sterling by removing exchange controls, hoping that capital exports would increase to balance the inflow of funds from sales of oil overseas, leaving the exchange rate stable and the competitive position of manufacturing unaltered in the short term. In the slightly longer term, the flow of funds into foreign securities might damage investment in domestic manufacturing but Britain would build up a stock of overseas assets just as had occurred between 1870 and 1914. Removing exchange controls would also aid the City of London to compete more effectively in the growing market for international financial services and ensure that, whatever happened to visible trade, trade in services (which the Treasury believed to be the best hope for the future – see Chapter 12) would strengthen and ensure Britain's place in the more integrated international economy which was emerging after 1973.

For these and more ideological reasons, all exchange controls were abolished when the new government came to power in 1979. The exchange rate did not however behave as expected. Sterling's rise continued; the sterling-dollar rate, which had been at $1.55 in 1976, peaked at $2.43 early in 1981. Since British inflation remained comparatively high, this is another example of the market overshooting. Treasury officials certainly had no explanation for sterling's rise (Tomlinson 1990: 316) but Treasury policies have subsequently been identified as the prime culprit. From 1979 the Treasury imposed tight control over monetary growth to curb inflation. In November 1979 Bank rate was raised by 3 points to 17 per cent and was held there for seven months to slow the rapid expansion of the money supply. High interest rates must take much of the blame for sterling's appreciation (Cairncross 1992: 240). But oil prices were also a factor. Oil prices doubled for the second time within five years between October 1978 and June 1979 (OPEC 2) just as Britain began to show a net surplus in its oil trade. Capital exports increased after the end of exchange controls, but not by enough to offset the impact on the exchange rate of oil and interest rates.

The results of a high exchange rate when British inflation was relatively high seem clear. The competitiveness of British producers was squeezed severely (Figure 11.1). In 1983 the balance of trade in manufactured goods went into deficit for the first time since the middle ages

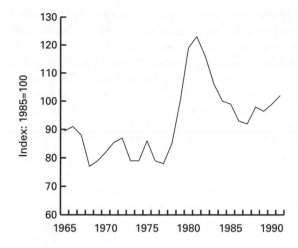

*Figure 11.1* The competitiveness of British manufacturing, 1965–91[a]
*Note:*
a Figures of normalised unit labour costs, weighted using 1985 levels of
  competitiveness as a base. This does not imply that competitiveness was at
  optimum levels in 1985, nor is any account taken of non-price factors. Upward
  movements indicate a loss of competitiveness, so the rise from 1976 to 1981
  indicates a massive handicap for producers of traded goods. For further details
  on the data and how to interpret them, see Booth 1995b: extract 2.10.
*Source: Economic Trends*, Annual Supplement, 1994, Table 1.20.

and the manufacturing sector shrank alarmingly (Chapter 12). This
deficit reached huge proportions in the late 1980s as imports were
sucked in by an increasingly inflationary boom (Table 11.6). Even
when demand pressures fell substantially in 1990–3, with the longest
recession since the 1930s, Britain's trade in manufactures did not return
to balance. But rather deeper processes were also at work. The size of the
manufacturing surplus has been declining relative to GDP since 1950
(Coutts and Godley 1992: 63), so we are looking at long- as well as short-
term processes. Some elements of short-term performance are mystify-
ing. Although competitiveness deteriorated sharply in 1979–81 the manufacturing trade balance improved in 1980 and 1981 and remained
strong in 1982 (Table 11.6). Complex changes were unfolding.

   The long-term erosion of the manufacturing trade balance has been
caused by the factors discussed in the previous section. Britain's poor
non-price competitiveness has not been reversed since 1979. There is
broad agreement that trade in manufactures has been increasingly
affected by product research and development; the poor postwar R&D
record of British firms has resulted in weak competitive performance in
key product areas (Crafts 1991a: 270). There are also indications from the
Department of Trade and Industry that despite the labour-shedding, the

new factory building and re-equipment by British industry in the 1980s (restoring cost competitiveness), British firms still have a weak and deteriorating product base resulting in poor non-price competitiveness (*Sunday Times* 1993). To this long-term weakness, the events of 1979–81 added further difficulties. Unemployment and bank lending both rose dramatically as British firms sacked workers to save costs and borrowed from the banks to maintain cash flow (Tomlinson 1990: 316). Many firms found it impossible to service this borrowing under the high interest rates of 1979–82 and went out of business. Manufacturing production fell by 17 per cent in the 18 months from March 1979. There is some evidence to suggest that the firms which survived were more committed to export markets. The export performance of British industry improved in the 1980s (Landesmann and Snell 1989) but the loss of industrial capacity in 1979–81 created structural problems. As demand for manufactures grew rapidly in the late 1980s British industry lacked the capacity to meet it and import penetration increased (Coutts and Godley 1992: 61–4). There are now fears that the loss of industrial capacity in the early 1980s will lower growth in the 1990s (Rhodes and Tyler 1993).

The Treasury was very slow to appreciate the problems. In the early 1980s, the exchange rate was regarded by leading ministers as relatively unimportant. The main Treasury goal was to reduce inflation and the high exchange rate was considered a useful secondary policy to supplement tight monetary control (Tomlinson 1990: 318). It was also Treasury dogma at this time that Britain's comparative advantage and its future prosperity lay in services rather than in industry. The place of Britain in the world supply of services is however much less rosy than the Treasury believed. Britain has maintained its share of world invisible trade (Alford 1988: 57) but the balance of invisible trade, particularly in commercial services (excluding interest, profits and dividends), has been disappointing. There has been a consistent surplus which grew as a proportion of GDP to 1977 but which has tended to decline since (Wells 1989: 44). Britain has been a very strong competitor in the market for financial services (Smith 1992) but increasingly weak in the equally rapidly growing market for international tourism. Britons have a high income elasticity of demand for foreign holidays.

With manufacturing trade in deficit and the surplus on commercial services shrinking, what kept the British balance of payments from collapse? Oil is a partial answer. The oil balance went into surplus in 1980, growing strongly to 1985 when it represented a little over 2 per cent of GDP. The balance of payments 'problem', however, reappeared in 1985–6 when the oil price slumped and wiped out the current account surplus (Table 11.6). So oil cannot be the whole answer. The surge of imports from 1987 to 1989 produced a current account deficit which mounted rapidly to 3.5 per cent of GDP in 1989. After 1987 the balance of payments was kept in equilibrium by a turnaround in the capital account (Table 11.6). The balance of portfolio investment, which had been strongly outward after the lifting of exchange controls, was reversed and there has been a strong flow of short-term capital into British financial institutions since 1987.

While these enormous changes were taking place, government policy on the exchange rate became dominated by the question of whether Britain should join the EMS. The Treasury had become somewhat disenchanted with floating exchange rates in 1984–5 when sterling's value slumped, which tended to raise import prices and threaten its anti-inflationary policy. As British inflation rose after 1987 Treasury eyes looked enviously upon the low inflation rates of those currencies within the EMS. After a period of exchange rate turbulence in the early 1980s, EMS currencies had become much more stable in the late 1980s as the member governments began to accept the need to follow Germany's tough anti-inflationary policies to preserve the exchange rate stability which was the core of the system. British business and financial opinion began to look with favour upon this re-emergence of exchange rate stability and convinced itself that all the problems of the British economy would disappear if Britain adopted fixed exchange rates; pundits began to look forward to a 'golden scenario' of low inflation, faster growth and falling unemployment if Britain pegged its exchange rate. There were many unfortunate echoes of the high hopes held in 1925 for both the British and the world economies if Britain returned to the fixed exchange rates of the gold standard (Chapter 7 and Moggridge 1972). As in 1925 the short-term costs were underplayed (very little was made of the high unemployment among EMS members) and the importance of the actual rate of exchange was almost ignored. The Prime Minister and her economic adviser, Professor Alan Walters, remained convinced of the virtues of floating. It would be possible to join a fixed exchange rate system when economic and financial conditions in all members of the system had converged but until that time the government needed floating rates to provide the independence to pursue its own monetary policy, whether anti-inflationary or expansionary; a system of pegged but adjustable rates was 'half-baked' and offered neither stability nor independence (Walters 1988).

The issue became increasingly fractious, helping to end the political careers of a Foreign Secretary (Howe), Chancellor of the Exchequer (Lawson) and Prime Minister (Thatcher). Britain joined the EMS in October 1990 at an exchange rate of DM2.95. This rate was just above that which prevailed at the time but reflected neither the competitive strength of the British and German economies nor the real purchasing powers of the two currencies (Panic 1992). Britain's monetary policy in 1990 was much tighter than that of Germany, so defence of the EMS parity depended upon Britain keeping its interest rates above those in Germany. Unfortunately, German interest rates rose. Britain's rate of inflation certainly fell, but at huge cost in terms of output and employment. The government reduced interest rates to ease the pressure on British firms and the gap between British and German rates, which had been 6 per cent during the 1980s, disappeared. The markets required rather more incentive to hold sterling and began to hedge and speculate against a sterling devaluation. But the EMS was so politically symbolic that it had to be defended to the hilt by keeping British interest rates relatively high until recession in the German economy allowed some relief (but much more pain on the employment front). The hilt was the longest recession since the 1930s, the highest level of company failures, and unemployment probably at record levels though the figures have been so manipulated that it has become impossible to uncover what has happened in the labour market.

The judgement of the currency markets could not be resisted for long. Sterling was forced from the EMS after less than two years on 'Black Wednesday', 16 September 1992 (*Guardian* 1992). The experience of the 1980s and early 1990s has left Britain with an eroded manufacturing base and structural problems in the balance of payments. Even after the intense competition in both domestic and export markets in the early 1980s and early 1990s, the DTI report of 1993 has demonstrated the long run problems of poor non-price competitiveness have not been resolved. Balance of payments weakness is a continuing problem.

## BRITAIN AND EUROPE

The main issue in postwar commercial policy has become Britain's relationship with Europe. As was seen above, at the end of the war Britain sought to rebuild its economic and financial strength within the sterling area and as a world power. The alternative of an economic and political role within Europe, simply did not appear to offer an equivalent economic or political future. This judgement was made and reinforced throughout the reconstruction period. Policy to Europe from 1947 onwards was designed to show enough enthusiasm for European co-operation to qualify for Marshall aid but enough detachment to ensure that Britain remained outside supra-national institutions such as the ECSC. When the ECSC came into force in 1953 talks were already taking place on liberalising European trade. There were two visions. The ECSC 'six' (Belgium, Netherlands, Luxembourg, France, West Germany, Italy) wanted freer internal trade in manufactures behind a common tariff wall (a customs union) but also required a protectionist, planned agricultural policy to bolster the farming interest which was powerful in each country. Britain, on the other hand, had strong links to primary producers in the Commonwealth and possessed in the early 1950s the most powerful industrial economy in Europe. It had little interest in a European agricultural policy but every incentive to push for the elimination of barriers on European industrial trade without having to compromise its global economic and political ambitions.

The 'six' produced plans for a customs union and, much to the surprise of British opinion, went on to establish the European Economic Community (now the European Union – EU) under the Treaty of Rome of 24 March 1957. In response the British proposed a broad free trade area, embracing most of western Europe, under which tariffs on intra-European trade in industrial goods would be phased out. Foodstuffs were excluded and each country would regulate its own trade with non-members according to its own needs and priorities (Treasury 1957). These proposals were rejected by the 'six', but after redrafting and the addition of an agricultural dimension, they became the blueprint for a European Free Trade Area (EFTA) of the 'seven' (Austria, Britain, Denmark, Norway, Portugal, Sweden and Switzerland) under the Stockholm Convention of 1960. EFTA was always a political rather than an economic grouping. All the members did more trade with the EU than with each other and they lacked the geographical cohesion of the 'six'. But it was thought that EFTA would have more 'clout' in negotiating with the EU than each country would possess individually (Morgan 1978: 519).

Shortly after Britain had signed the Stockholm Convention, the Prime Minister, Harold Macmillan, and some of his leading advisers concluded that in the interests of faster growth, industrial competitiveness and basic foreign policy needs, Britain would have to join the EU sooner or later (Macmillan 1973: 22). Action came very soon; only 18 months after the formation of EFTA, Britain applied for membership of the EU. A crossroads in postwar history had been reached. The sterling area had been a disappointment and was beginning to fragment. The growth areas of trade for the white dominions were increasingly in the faster growing markets of Japan, North America and Europe. Less developed Commonwealth countries were demanding independence and Britain had lost ground consistently in the Middle East, a region considered vital to postwar recovery (Cain and Hopkins 1993b: 282–7). The differentiated, fragmented markets of the sterling area had not promoted dynamism in British industry. By contrast, the 'six' had achieved fast growth, rising living standards and industrial strength by trading primarily with one another. Macmillan came to the view that British firms needed to compete in these dynamic markets if the economy was to be modernised and was prepared to make substantial concessions, not least on the rights of access of Commonwealth countries to the European market and the treatment of British agriculture, to join the Treaty of

*Table 11.7* Composition of UK imports, 1935–90 (% of total)

|  | 1935–38 average | 1948 | 1950 | 1960 | 1970 | 1980 | 1990 |
|---|---|---|---|---|---|---|---|
| Food, drink, tobacco | 43.4 | 41.2 | 39.3 | 33.8 | 22.7 | 12.4 | 9.8 |
| Basic materials | 24.4 | 29.2 | 34.9 | 23.3 | 15.1 | 7.6 | 4.5 |
| Minerals, fuels, lubricants | 4.6 | 7.5 | 7.5 | 10.6 | 10.4 | 13.8 | 6.2 |
| Manufactures | 19.8 | 17.4 | 17.6 | 31.8 | 50.6 | 62.6 | 77.9 |
| (finished manufactures) | (6.7) | n.a. | (4.2) | (11.9) | (22.9) | (35.6) | (51.9) |
| Imports as percentage of GDP | 18.6 | 19.8 | 22.4 | 20.2 | 21.0 | 25.7 | 30.0 |

*Source*: *Annual Abstract of Statistics*, various issues.

Rome. The pro-EU lobby in the British establishment had won, though divisions and doubts remained.

Changes were becoming evident in Britain's pattern of trade, but at only a slow pace. British manufacturing was still highly protected by comparison with other OECD countries (Batchelor *et al*. 1980: 8). In 1960, Britain's imports were still dominated by foodstuffs and raw materials, overwhelmingly from the sterling area (Tables 11.3 and 11.7). But imports of finished manufactures were growing rapidly and EU countries became more important in Britain's export trade after 1959 (Morgan 1978: 555).

The Macmillan government's assessment of changes in trade patterns and the need for fundamental shifts in commercial policy was prescient. Further reduction of tariffs under EFTA and the Dillon and Kennedy Rounds of GATT increased the shares of manufactures in British imports and of Western Europe in British exports (Tables 11.3 and 11.7). The reduction of tariffs was a significant cause of this changing pattern of trade but other factors such as changing consumer preferences, multinational companies and the rise of industrial efficiency in Europe relative to Britain all tended to accentuate these trends. The share of Britain's imports from EU countries, for example, grew rapidly in the mid-1960s, when tariff changes were relatively unimportant.

Britain's entry had to await the removal from the French presidency of De Gaulle, who twice vetoed British applications. Britain (with Denmark and the Irish Republic) finally joined the EU in 1973 and was given five years to complete the transition to the Treaty of Rome. Since 1973, the EU has increasingly dominated Britain's import and export trade and the structure of trade has been transformed; manufactured imports have expanded dramatically. This part of Macmillan's vision has been realised but Britain's relative manufacturing strength appears to have ebbed despite closer integration into the European economy. British firms have not responded to competition with their Continental counterparts as had been expected in 1960. At the same time, the EU has not caught the British political imagination in large part because consumers have been hit directly by higher food costs as a result of the Common Agricultural Policy (for further discussion of the CAP see Chapter 12). Compared with the hopes of 1960, the EU has been a disappointment.

To measure whether the sense of disappointment is economically justified is however an impossible undertaking. Economists who have analysed the effects of customs unions focus on trade creation and trade diversion: the elimination of tariffs between members creates trade and generates gains from the production and consumption effects of trade. But if some members of the union find that they have to pay higher prices for goods which they formerly bought from non-members, then there is trade diversion (McCormick 1988: 179–80). In practice, trade creation is particularly difficult to estimate because Britain's trade with the EU was increasing rapidly prior to entry; how much of Britain's trade would have been with Europe if the 1971 application had also been rejected? What commercial policy opportunities existed apart from the EU? Calculations of the impact of entry on British trade vary enormously, even disagreeing whether the impact on trade was positive or negative during the early period of membership (Davenport 1982: 231–2). Taking a longer view, it is clear that the lion's share of the gains of trade creation have accrued to the West German economy, which accounted for almost 40 per cent of the EU's manufacturing output between 1970 and 1985 (Cutler *et al.* 1989: 11). German producers have been more successful at penetrating the British market than British firms have been in Germany. But even so, we have no real idea of how British manufacturing would have performed outside the EU. Markets might easily have been lost to German producers if Britain had not entered in 1973.

The EU is much more than a customs union since capital transfers also take place via the budget into which member governments pay shares of both VAT revenue and the proceeds of the common external tariff. The main category of EU expenditure is agricultural support through the CAP. When Britain shouldered the full costs of membership in 1980, the government discovered that it was a substantial net contributor to the budget. Britain retains a comparatively large share of its trade outside the EU so payments to Brussels are large and the flow to Britain under the CAP is relatively small because of the smallness of the British agricultural sector (Davenport 1982). Accordingly the British government negotiated a series of *ad hoc* remissions between 1980 and 1984 until a longer term rebate was concluded at the Fontainebleau summit of 1984.

The constant bickering over budgetary contributions in the early 1980s led the British government to seek ways of presenting itself as a more enthusiastic EU member. The opportunity arose with a European

Commission White Paper of 1985, *Completing the European Market*. After twenty years of tariff-free internal trade, the Commission proposed the removal of non-tariff barriers, such as technical regulations and quality standards, border controls and restrictions on public sector contracting. This approach held many attractions for the free market wing of the Conservative government and was consistent with Britain's long standing view that the primary goal of the EU was closer integration of the economies of separate nation states which retained sovereignty over the mechanisms of domestic economic policy. The single market came into being on the last day of 1992.

The Commission had two further initiatives to capitalise on the momentum towards co-operation and integration. One was for a 'social dimension' to establish EU-wide health and safety standards and the other for monetary union, with a single European currency as a corollary of the single market. Both have raised controversy in Britain. Economic and monetary union had been one of the three goals established in the Treaty of Rome but little was achieved until the formation of the EMS in 1979. The Delors Plan of 1988 set out three steps to full monetary union. The first was for all EU currencies to be inside the EMS. Next, a European central banking system would be created to provide the institutional framework for monetary unification. Finally exchange rates between currencies would become 'irrevocably locked' together and the central bank would acquire all currency reserves and the Council of Ministers produce rules governing budgetary policy. The social dimension is a collection of modest proposals on worker participation and health and safety, including regulation of hours of work. Timetables for the completion of both the 'social chapter' and monetary integration were agreed at the Maastricht summit of December 1991. Britain managed to negotiate 'opt-outs' from both policies, and faced the prospect of continued relative decline on the fringes of a European community moving towards ever closer integration. However, the financial and economic consequences of German re-unification (which contributed in significant measure to the disruption of the EMS in September 1992) and the consequences for the CAP of the Blair House Agreement and conclusion of the Uruguay Round of GATT, have made the future direction of Europe much less certain. The external context within which Britain must tackle its fundamental domestic economic problems is once more clouded in doubt.

# Chapter 12

# Industrial development

Three conclusions about Britain's postwar economic development emerged from Chapter 10: Britain has enjoyed faster growth since 1951 than ever before; but growth was slower than recorded in most OECD countries; and commentators believed that the British economy could have grown faster. Chapter 10 also concluded that 'big theories' to explain relative decline (inappropriate demand management policies, a simple external constraint, structural problems or low social capability for catch-up) lack conviction but the argument about supply-side weaknesses deserves consideration. This chapter reviews the performance of British industry since 1945 with particular reference to the impact of management and the institutional framework. The effects of labour on industrial performance will be a principal theme of Chapter 13.

## THE PATTERN OF INDUSTRIAL CHANGE

As in most OECD countries, there has been continuing contraction of agriculture's relative contribution to output and relative decline in manufacturing from a peak in the 1960s (Table 12.1). What is distinctive about the British postwar development pattern is the early start and extent of the contraction of manufacturing's share. No other country has seen manufacturing's contribution to GDP fall by 1989 to almost half the level of 1960. Table 12.1 illustrates the composition of output; in all countries GDP was expanding throughout the period but Britain has been the only economy in which manufacturing output has scarcely grown since 1973 (Godley 1988: 9; Booth 1995b: extract 2.16). Table 12.1 merely underlines the conclusion of Chapter 10; many of Britain's postwar economic problems lie in manufacturing. It would be helpful to have consistent figures of industrial output for the entire postwar period, but frequent changes of industrial classification cause problems. Table 12.2 attempts a consistent series using pre-1973 definitions but the difficulties are enormous and the figures are only a broad indicator of change since 1973. No obvious problems are evident before 1973 but manufacturing's weaknesses are all too clear in the 1970s, as are the long-run contraction in coal-mining, and the continuing difficulties of large parts of engineering and textiles-related industries after 1973. On the other hand, agriculture, construction, the utilities and the service sector performed more strongly over the whole period, though construction experienced severe difficulties in the 1970s. The relatively strong parts of manufacturing since 1973 appear to have been food, drink and tobacco, chemicals and electrical engineering. The most dynamic sector is clearly North Sea oil and gas.

Early warning of industrial weakness came in the declining share of

*Table 12.1* Industrial structure of GDP at current prices, selected countries, 1960–89 (proportion of value added in each sector)

|  | USA | Japan | Germany | France | UK |
|---|---|---|---|---|---|
| **1960** | | | | | |
| Agriculture | 4.0 | 12.6 | 5.7 | 10.6 | 3.4 |
| Industry[a] | 38.1 | 44.5 | 53.3 | 39.0 | 42.8 |
| (Manufacturing) | (28.6) | (33.9) | (40.5) | (29.1) | (32.1) |
| Services | 57.9 | 42.9 | 41.0 | 50.4 | 53.6 |
| **1967** | | | | | |
| Agriculture | 2.9 | 9.1 | 4.1 | 7.7 | 2.7 |
| Industry[a] | 36.8 | 44.8 | 51.0 | 39.5 | 38.6 |
| (Manufacturing) | (28.0) | (33.9) | (39.3) | (28.5) | (28.1) |
| Services | 60.3 | 46.2 | 44.8 | 52.8 | 58.7 |
| **1973** | | | | | |
| Agriculture | 4.0 | 5.9 | 3.2 | 6.7 | 2.7 |
| Industry[a] | 33.8 | 46.3 | 50.8 | 38.1 | 38.4 |
| (Manufacturing) | (24.9) | (35.1) | (39.0) | (28.3) | (27.2) |
| Services | 52.2 | 47.8 | 48.0 | 55.2 | 58.9 |
| **1979** | | | | | |
| Agriculture | 3.1 | 4.3 | 2.2 | 4.8 | 1.9 |
| Industry[a] | 33.7 | 41.6 | 43.7 | 34.7 | 37.1 |
| (Manufacturing) | (23.0) | (29.3) | (33.8) | (25.6) | (24.9) |
| Services | 63.1 | 54.1 | 54.1 | 60.6 | 61.1 |
| **1989** | | | | | |
| Agriculture | 2.0[b] | 2.5 | 1.6 | 3.5 | 1.3 |
| Industry[a] | 31.2[b] | 39.1 | 39.5 | 29.1 | 29.4 |
| (Manufacturing) | (19.3)[b] | (28.9) | (31.1) | (21.3) | (18.0)[c] |
| Services | 66.8[b] | 58.4 | 58.9 | 67.4 | 69.4 |

*Notes:*
a  Defined throughout as mining and quarrying *plus* manufacturing *plus* electricity, gas and water *plus* construction.
b  1987.
c  As measured in the Blue Book for 1993 (figure not given in OECD publications).
*Sources*: OECD 1982; OECD 1991; OECD 1993; Blue Book 1993.

*Table 12.2* Rates of growth of industrial output, 1951–89 (% per annum)

|  | 1951–64 | 1964–73 | 1973–9 | 1979–89 |
|---|---|---|---|---|
| Agriculture, Forestry, Fishing | 2.6 | 2.5 | 0.7 | 2.7 |
| Mining and Quarrying | −0.7 | −3.3 | −2.6 | −2.5 |
| **Manufacturing** |  |  |  |  |
| Food, Drink, Tobacco | 2.6 | 2.7 | 0.7 | 0.7 |
| Chemicals | 5.8 | 6.2 | 2.1 | 2.6 |
| Metals[a] | 2.5 | −0.2 | −3.1 | 0.5 |
| Electrical Engineering[b] | 6.0 | 5.7 | 2.0 | 4.8 |
| Mechanical Eng. and Shipbuilding[c] | 2.4 | 3.2 | −1.3 | −0.7 |
| Vehicles[d] | 4.9 | 0.7 | −2.6 | −0.5 |
| Other Metal Industries[e] | 2.0 | 0.9 | −1.9 | —[j] |
| Textiles[f] | 0.1 | 2.9 | −3.2 | −2.6 |
| Clothing[g] | 2.2 | 1.9 | 0.7 | −0.8 |
| Bricks, Pottery, Glass, Cement[e] | 3.4 | 3.4 | −1.9 | —[j] |
| Timber and Furniture[e] | 2.2 | 3.5 | −2.5 | —[j] |
| Paper, Printing, Publishing | 4.1 | 2.7 | −0.5 | 1.4 |
| Leather and Other Manufacturing[g] | 3.2 | 4.5 | 0.8 | 1.5 |
| Total Manufacturing | 3.2 | 3.0 | −0.7 | 1.2 |
| Construction | 3.8 | 1.8 | −2.5 | 2.8 |
| Gas, Electricity, Water | 5.1 | 5.2 | 2.8 | 2.3 |
| Total Industrial Production[h] | 3.1 | 2.3 | −0.8 | 1.4 |
| Transport | 2.2 | 3.5 | 1.5 | 3.2 |
| Commerce | 3.0 | 3.0 | 1.1 | 5.0 |
| Public and Professional Services | (1.5) | (2.2) | (2.0) | (0.8) |
| GDP (output based, excludes North Sea output) | 2.8 | 2.7 | 0.5 | 2.3 |
| North Sea oil and gas | — | — | 181.0 | 1.2 |

*Notes:*
a 'Iron and Steel' up to 1979 and 'Other Metals' thereafter.
b Contains instrument engineering after 1973.
c Mechanical engineering only after 1979. 'Other Transport Equipment' is excluded from the table (1979–89).
d 'Motor Vehicles and Parts' in 1979–89.
e Included in 'Other Manufacturing' in 1979–89.
f 'Manmade Fibres' are separately identified in 1979–89 and have been included in 'Textiles'.
g The leather industry is counted in 'Clothing' before 1979 and 'Other Manufacturing' in 1979–89.
h As defined before 1973: i.e. mining and quarrying, manufacturing, construction, utilities.
j This industry is not recorded separately in the standard industrial classification in use after 1980.
*Sources:* For 1951–73 (apart from 'Total Industrial Production'): Matthews *et al.* 1982: 228–9,240–1, Gardner 1972; for 1973–89, CSO, *Blue Book,* various editions.

world manufactured trade (see Table 11.5) and signs of import penetration in the 1960s. Official estimates of the home and overseas market performance of British industry (Table 12.3), however, revealed that as import penetration increased British industries also tended to export a higher proportion of total output – admittedly from low base levels (Wells and Imber 1977). This pattern of rising import penetration and rising export sales is however consistent with the growth of international specialisation noted in Chapter 11 and appears to be common to most OECD countries (Wells and Imber 1977: 80). The figures of home and export market performance emphasise the relative strength in the 1970s of chemicals and food, drink and tobacco but cast a rather less glowing light on electrical engineering, where import penetration increased dramatically, especially in domestic appliances and audio equipment, without equivalent export growth (Hewer 1980: 99). Among the problem cases, Table 12.3 identifies the rapid growth of import penetration in the vehicles industry without compensating export gains and the steady loss of home market share by the textiles industry. Despite the adverse exchange rates of 1979–82 (Chapter 11), there was no general rush of imports, nor was there recovery of home markets in the later 1980s when exchange rates were more favourable. Export markets seem to have been somewhat more difficult in the 1980s.

Economists would begin to examine this competitive performance from prices. The most commonly used official statistics of manufacturing price competitiveness have been given in Figure 11.1. There clearly have been occasions when the decline in competitiveness has coincided with poor market performance by British industry, most obviously in 1979–82. However, many British manufacturers had managed to retain both home and export markets despite severe deterioration in competitiveness between 1968 and 1972 (Wells and Imber 1977: 88–9), but home market share was lost during the next five years when import competitiveness changed very little. Moreover, the dynamics of market performance varied widely between individual industries, as is evident from even a cursory glance at Table 12.3. Price seems to explain comparatively little of the lost market share and attention in the 1970s began to turn to non-price factors – product quality, design and reliability, ability of producers to meet delivery dates, quality of marketing and sales effort and after-sales service (Posner and Steer 1978: 159; Stout 1977: 12–18). If non-price factors are significant, the spotlight returns to potential supply-side weaknesses in business organisation, management practices, R&D activity and relations between business, finance and the state, mentioned in Chapter 10. In the remainder of this chapter, attention is directed to the performance since 1945 of important British industries to establish a firmer empirical basis for generalisations on performance and

Table 12.3 Import penetration and export–sales ratios for selected British manufacturing industries, 1968–89 (%)

| | Imports as a proportion of home demand | | | | | Proportion of total sales exported | | | | |
|---|---|---|---|---|---|---|---|---|---|---|
| | 1968 | 1973 | 1979 | 1982 | 1989[a] | 1968 | 1973 | 1979 | 1982 | 1989[a] |
| Metal manufacture | 18 | 21 | 32 | 33 | 31 | 15 | 16 | 23 | 23 | 26 |
| Chemicals and allied industries | 18 | 22 | 30 | 34 | 42 | 24 | 28 | 36 | 41 | 47 |
| Mechanical engineering | 20 | 26 | 29 | 32 | 40 | 32 | 37 | 42 | 45 | 39 |
| Electrical engineering | 14 | 27 | 31 | 39 | 52 | 20 | 24 | 33 | 38 | 46 |
| Motor Vehicles | 14 | 23 | 41 | 47 | 51 | 34 | 37 | 36 | 38 | 33 |
| Food, drink, tobacco | 21 | 20 | 18 | 16 | 18 | 4 | 6 | 10 | 11 | 12 |
| Textiles | 16 | 21 | 33 | 39 | 48 | 18 | 23 | 27 | 29 | 32 |

Note:
a First two quarters only. The series ceased publication in 1990.
Sources: Wells and Imber 1977; CSO, Business Monitor, MQ12, various issues.

practice. Discussion thereafter turns to supply-side failures, industrial policy and some final general comments on 'de-industrialisation'.

## THE PRIMARY SECTOR

Agriculture has experienced a major revival since the war; after three-quarters of a century of depression it has become profitable and expansive. Wartime subsidies brought increases in both acreage under cultivation and yield per acre (Murray 1955: 249–77) and continued in the late 1940s amid a world food shortage and domestic food rationing. From the mid-1950s, conditions changed with over-production in Western Europe and North America. Deficiency payments to farmers continued, however, covering the gap between low world prices to consumers and farmers' costs of production. Subsidies were expensive but under control, falling from £382 million in 1950 to £250–300 millions in the late 1960s and early 1970s (Pollard 1983: 277). Agricultural output rose by approximately 2.5 per cent per annum between 1951 and 1973, with a static agricultural acreage and a declining labour force (Matthews *et al.* 1982: 228–9). Labour productivity growth was impressive (5 per cent per annum from 1951 to 1964 and more than 7 per cent from 1964 to 1973). Capital stock grew comparatively slowly (1.5 per cent per annum between 1951 and 1964 and 3.3 per cent per annum between 1964 and 1973). Improved yields owed much to new techniques; intensive breeding, better pest control and the development of more productive and reliable seed strains.

Substantial changes to the subsidy regime flowed from Britain's membership of the EU in 1973. The CAP worked through price supports. EU prices were set high to encourage domestic production and a variable tariff raised prices of imported foodstuffs to domestic levels. The CAP has been financed by consumers who pay the high food prices and tax-payers through the EU budgetary system (Chapter 11), transferring resources from food consumers to agricultural producers (Davenport 1982: 236). British food prices rose substantially between 1973 and 1979 as the CAP was phased in, despite manipulation of the 'green pound' to cushion British consumers (Grant 1981).

Agricultural production continued to expand, especially where the CAP subsidy regime was most favourable. Production of wheat and oilseed rape expanded particularly rapidly after 1973 in response to the pattern of subsidies (Table 12.4) with cereal growers switching into wheat from other grains and employing still more capital-intensive methods. The trend in livestock numbers has been generally stable. Prosperity brought new capital, notably from large financial institutions, into agriculture but produced speculation in land prices during the 1980s. Between 1974 and 1984, agricultural output and value added

*Table 12.4* Agricultural crop areas, production statistics and livestock numbers, 1961–93 (selected crops, averages of years stated)

|  | 1961–3 | 1971–3 | 1981–3 | 1991–3 |
|---|---|---|---|---|
| Total tillage (million hectares) | 4.48 | 4.94 | 5.11 | 4.82 |
| Temporary grass | 2.85 | 2.34 | 1.87 | 1.57 |
| Total arable | 7.33 | 7.22 | 6.98 | 6.44 |
| Permanent grass | 5.09 | 4.98 | 5.10 | 5.22 |
| Rough grazing | 7.34 | 6.66 | 4.98 | 4.66 |
| Total area | 19.8 | 19.1 | 18.8 | 18.5 |
| Wheat |  |  |  |  |
|   Area (thousand hectares) | 812 | 1,124 | 1,616 | 1,936 |
|   Yield (tonnes/hectare) | 4.0 | 4.3 | 6.2 | 7.1 |
|   Production (thousand tonnes) | 3,215 | 4,865 | 9,942 | 13,772 |
| Barley |  |  |  |  |
|   Area | 1,693 | 2,285 | 2,232 | 1,285 |
|   Yield | 3.5 | 3.9 | 4.7 | 5.5 |
|   Production | 5,882 | 8,936 | 10,378 | 7,053 |
| Oats |  |  |  |  |
|   Area | 614 | 320 | 127 | 99 |
|   Yield | 2.8 | 3.9 | 4.4 | 5.1 |
|   Production | 1,698 | 1,230 | 553 | 504 |
| Oilseed rape |  |  |  |  |
|   Area | — | 9 | 175 | 413 |
|   Yield | — | 2.1 | 2.8 | 2.78 |
|   Production | — | 18 | 494 | 1,152 |
| Sugar Beet |  |  |  |  |
|   Area | 171 | 192 | 204 | 197 |
|   Yield[a] | n.a. | 39.2 | 41.3 | 43.3 |
| Production[a] | n.a. | 7,171 | 8,299 | 8,508 |
| Total cattle and calves (thousand head) | 11,837 | 13,617 | 13,224 | 11,807 |
| Total sheep and lambs | 29,270 | 27,010 | 33,078 | 43,840 |
| Total pigs | 6,541 | 8,791 | 8,008 | 7,654 |
| Total fowls | 111,831 | 141,641 | 122,195 | 127,139 |

*Note*:
a In the 1960s and earlier sugar beet yields and production were recorded as sugar content, not as raw beet.
*Sources*: *Annual Review of Agriculture*, various years; *Agriculture in the United Kingdom*, various years.

in the industry doubled, but rent on tenanted land rose fourfold (MAFF 1985). As a result, farm income rose by only 42 per cent over the period as against retail prices, which rose by 166 per cent (Harvey and Thomson 1985: 6). Labour productivity rose by an average of 4 per cent per annum over the decade (MAFF 1985: 5). Prosperity was, however, built upon an increasingly exposed CAP system. The gap between world and EU prices widened after 1974, stimulating production but resulting in embarrassing surpluses in many products (McCormick 1988: 186). Despite mounting pressure, vested interests resisted reform of the CAP (Fennell 1987). Significant changes were introduced in 1984–5 when milk quotas marked the first shift from price to quantity regulation, and slow, painful steps were taken to reduce guaranteed price levels and cut production. In these circumstances, British agriculture has marked time. In real terms, agricultural output has increased but agriculture's share of GDP has fallen from 2.0 per cent (1982–4) to 1.3 per cent (1990–3) and both capital formation and the labour force have declined (MAFF 1994: 4,6). The pace of CAP reform has not satisfied critics and the Uruguay Round of GATT provided a convenient focus for primary producers in the USA and elsewhere to force the EU in the Blair House agreement of November 1992 to phase out some of the more protectionist aspects of the system.

Much more spectacular change has overtaken the energy sector. In 1950 coal was almost the sole domestically produced fuel and represented 90 per cent of all fuel consumed (Table 12.5). By the early 1990s, coal accounted for only one-quarter of production and a slightly larger proportion of consumption (Table 12.5). Oil and gas production, on the other hand, was insignificant until the 1960s when natural gas was discovered in commercial quantities. North Sea oil began to flow in 1975 and reached its peak rate in 1985–6, when it accounted for more than 50 per cent of domestic energy production.

Coal entered public ownership on 1 January 1947 and within weeks the country was paralysed by a fuel crisis. Coal supply had been precarious throughout the war (Chapter 8) and obvious problems were ducked in 1945–6 (Cairncross 1985: 354–84). The crisis was overcome but the industry persistently failed to realise its output and productivity goals before the late 1950s (Beacham 1958: 119). The huge backlog of investment remained and shortages of steel, timber and foreign currency before 1951 limited the National Coal Board to small-scale modernisation projects (Pryke 1971: 27,39). Persistent coal shortages drove the NCB to retain uneconomic pits and maximise short-run output until 1957 when an economic downturn and falling oil prices coincided (Ashworth 1986: 155–234). The first big colliery closure programme began. In the next ten years, the number of pits was more than halved, the labour force shrank by approximately 40 per cent and output by one-third (Table 12.6). The closure programme was accompanied by new investment in power-loading and self-advancing pit props and productivity growth accelerated (Pryke 1971: 63–5). New methods brought change in payment systems and work practices (Ashworth 1986: 295–301) but accelerating inflation after 1967 and narrowing pay differentials within the industry created discontent, erupting

Table 12.5 UK fuel production and consumption, 1950–92 (million tonnes of coal equivalent: mtce)

| | 1950 | | 1960 | | 1973 | | 1985 | | 1992 | |
|---|---|---|---|---|---|---|---|---|---|---|
| | mtce | % of total | mtce | % of total | mtce | % of total | mtce | % of total | mtce | % of total |
| Fuel Production: | | | | | | | | | | |
| Coal | 219 | 100 | 198 | 99 | 132 | 70 | 94 | 24 | 86 | 24 |
| Oil | 1 | — | 3 | 1 | 1 | 1 | 217 | 54 | 160 | 44 |
| Primary electricity[a] | — | — | — | — | 12 | 6 | 24 | 6 | 32 | 9 |
| Natural Gas | — | — | — | — | 43 | 23 | 63 | 16 | 81 | 23 |
| Total | 220 | 100 | 201 | 100 | 188 | 100 | 398 | 100 | 359 | 100 |
| Fuel Consumption:[b] | | | | | | | | | | |
| Coal | 204 | 90 | 199 | 74 | 133 | 38 | 105 | 32 | 102 | 29 |
| Oil | 23 | 10 | 68 | 25 | 164 | 46 | 115 | 35 | 122 | 35 |
| Primary electricity[c] | 1 | — | 3 | 1 | 12 | 4 | 24 | 8 | 39 | 11 |
| Natural gas | — | — | — | — | 44 | 12 | 82 | 25 | 89 | 25 |
| Total | 228 | 100 | 270 | 100 | 353 | 100 | 326 | 100 | 352 | 100 |

Notes:
a Nuclear, hydro-electricity, renewables other than hydro.
b Energy uses only. Small additional amounts of oil and coal are utilised for ships' bunkers and small amounts of oil are used as industrial raw materials.
c Nuclear, hydro-electricity, renewables other than hydro and imported electricity.
Source: Department of Energy, Digest of UK Energy Statistics, various issues.

in national strikes in 1971 and 1974 (McCormick 1979: 189–217). OPEC1 gave mineworkers a vision of a revitalised coal industry and a new ten-year investment programme was launched in 1974 with ambitious projections of future demand (Thomas 1988: 58). However productivity fell between 1971 and 1978 (Pryke 1981: 50) and optimism was undermined by North Sea oil and gas.

Britain had long produced tiny quantities of oil, but the discovery of natural gas off the Dutch coast in the early 1960s and international agreement on partitioning the continental shelf stimulated interest in large-scale exploration in the North Sea after 1964. Commercial quantities of gas were found in the British sector almost immediately, prompting exploration for oil in the deeper, colder and more turbulent northern waters. Extracting oil under such conditions is expensive (Robinson and Hann 1988: 33–5). By quadrupling the world oil price, OPEC1 made North Sea oil commercially attractive but even the big oil companies spread their risks by forming partnerships and consortia to bid for licences to drill. British governments have made frequent changes in the conditions for licences to explore, the tax treatment of oil revenues and the purchasing requirements of North Sea companies (Hann 1986; Jenkin 1981) but oil output rose rapidly and continuously from 1975 to its peak in 1985. The contribution of North Sea oil and gas to GDP rose from nothing in 1975 to 7 per cent in 1984 (Johnson 1991: 268) but, as noted in Chapter 11, there were adverse effects for manufacturing.

This enormous growth of North Sea output undermined the projections of coal demand made in the 1970s, leading to over-production and a new pit closure programme in 1984–5. The NUM struck to defend jobs but was completely defeated after a long, bitter conflict. There were strong political overtones to the coal dispute of 1984–5 and, as in the 1920s, the government enjoyed the spoils of victory (Kessler and Bayliss 1992: 125). The terms of electricity privatisation were deliberately unfavourable to the British Coal Corporation, as the NCB had become in 1987 (Roberts *et al.* 1991: 71–2). Government assisted BCC to develop its highly capital-intensive retreat-wall mining systems which gave pit managers much greater control over the pace and intensity of coalface work. The result of the contraction of the main market for coal and the introduction of more capital-intensive production has been enormous rises in productivity and accelerating pit closures since 1985; coal production has fallen by 50 per cent, the work-force by more than 90 per cent and productivity has more than trebled (Table 12.6). The long-term future of the industry is, however, uncertain even at the levels of efficiency achieved in 1994, with continuing competition from imported open-cast and drift-mined coal and electricity generators heavily committed to gas.

*Table 12.6* Coal statistics, 1947–93

|  | 1947 | 1957 | 1968–9 | 1974–5 | 1979–80 | 1985–6 | 1990–1 | 1991–2 | 1992–3 | 1993–4 |
|---|---|---|---|---|---|---|---|---|---|---|
| Output (million tonnes) | | | | | | | | | | |
| NCB deep-mined | 187.5 | 210.8 | 155.6 | 116.9 | 109.3 | 88.4 | 72.3 | 71.0 | 61.8 | 42.8 |
| Open-cast | 10.4 | 13.8 | 6.4 | 9.2 | 15.3 | 14.1 | 17.0 | 16.7 | 15.0 | 16.4 |
| Number of NCB pits at year end | 958 | 822 | 317 | 246 | 211 | 133 | 65 | 50 | 50 | 17 |
| Labour Force[a] ('000s) | 718 | 704 | 336 | 246 | 295 | 180 | 74 | 58 | 44 | 17 |
| Output per manshift[b] (tonnes) | 1.09 | 1.26 | 2.16 | 2.29 | 2.31 | 2.72 | 4.70 | 5.31 | 6.34 | 9.24 |

*Notes:*
a Before 1979–80 and 1993–4, 'average colliery manpower', 'total labour force' elsewhere.
b Overall output per manshift (i.e. output divided by total labour force rather than faceworkers or men on colliery books).
*Source: Annual Reports,* of National Coal Board (prior to March 5 1987) and British Coal Corporation thereafter; *Business Monitor* PQ 1113.

## THE MANUFACTURING SECTOR

The postwar period has seen the continuing decline of the old staples, and by the 1980s both shipbuilding and cotton textiles had been virtually eliminated. The decline of British shipbuilding has taken place against the background of the most rapid and sustained expansion in the history of world shipbuilding from 1945 to 1975 (Lorenz and Wilkinson 1986: 109). British shipbuilders had a head-start after the war. In 1950, Britain took 37 per cent of the market by tonnage launched and remained the world's largest shipbuilder until late 1955. However, in 1974, when new tonnage launched reached its postwar peak, Britain's share had slumped to 3.7 per cent (Hilditch 1988: 129). The British mercantile fleet remained large, and the total launchings for registration in the UK trebled between 1958 and 1973 (Williams et al. 1983: 193). British shipyards built a slowly declining proportion of these new British-registered vessels from the 1950s to the mid-1960s and after 1967 British ship owners ordered between 50 and 85 per cent of their ships from overseas. There was a demand-side problem in British shipbuilding. British yards looked primarily to supply the large but extremely fragmented British mercantile fleet leaving British shipyards competing for small-scale orders of individualistic designs. But British ship-owners, who rarely had interests in shipbuilding, were not committed to a buy-British policy (Williams et al. 1983: 191–6). The dwindling proportion of orders that they did place at home remained the core of the work of British shipyards; the industry had traditionally been comparatively uninterested in overseas markets. The main growth areas in the demand for ships were, on the one hand, oil tankers and bulk carriers, which could be prefabricated from standardised panels and, on the other, more specialised vessels which required more skilled labour and higher-value components. Prefabrication technology was highly capital-intensive and offered large productivity gains but favoured green-field sites, especially as tanker size increased rapidly in the 1960s, and did not require traditional shipbuilding crafts (Lorenz 1991: 96–101). This demand was satisfied initially from Japan, but latterly increasingly from the cheap labour yards of Brazil, Greece, Singapore, South Korea and Spain. British shipbuilders were equally unsuccessful in the market for more sophisticated, specialised vessels. They tended to produce general cargo vessels, the segment in which demand growth was slowest (Williams et al. 1983: 184–7). The fragmentation of the industry in Britain made specialisation difficult but mergers of any size were rare. Trade union organisation also helped perpetuate traditional British methods and added to competitive problems when the employers belatedly sought to increase the pace of work and substitute semi-skilled for skilled labour (Lorenz 1991: 114–22). Most British shipbuilders were, however, very reluctant to consider specialisation and expansionist investment programmes (Hilditch 1988: 130–7). Thus the industry suffered a slow and painful death, which was protracted by government efforts to reorganise where private enterprise had failed. The (Geddes) Committee of Inquiry on Shipbuilding proposed regional groupings of yards, to permit greater specialisation but restructuring had not been completed before financial problems multiplied. The bankruptcy of one of the Geddes groupings, Upper Clyde Shipbuilders, led to its nationalisation in 1973, and the majority of the industry followed in 1977. State control during a shipbuilding depression could not overcome the problems which private ownership had failed to resolve during expansion. Losses mounted despite cuts in capacity. At the first sign of an upswing in world shipbuilding demand, an anxious Conservative government sold the yards at bargain prices. British shipbuilding has all but disappeared outside the naval dockyards and even work for the navy has been severely curtailed since the 1960s by successive defence cuts.

The textile industry also emerged from war in a sellers' market, both at home and abroad (Furness 1958: 191–6). Government saw the export potential of cotton textiles and tried unsuccessfully to restructure the industry (Singleton 1990a). British textile firms feared renewed competition from low-wage economies and directed their efforts to price-fixing and lobbying government to prevent Japanese recovery rather than investment and reorganisation (Singleton 1990a: 66–71). The sellers' market peaked in 1951 and Lancashire competed unsuccessfully thereafter. Between 1950 and 1968 Britain's share of world cotton exports fell from 15.6 per cent to 2.8 per cent and employment in the spinning and weaving sections declined from 244,000 to 81,000 (Singleton 1990b: 130). Recovery was inhibited by fragmentation, specialisation, intense competition and low managerial quality (Lazonick 1983: 216–30). Success in textiles in the high-wage economies of Europe depended upon protection, highly capital-intensive methods and high volume production (Lazonick 1983: 219; Foreman-Peck 1983: 290). Government tried to push the industry in this direction with the Cotton Industry Act, 1959, providing financial aid to scrap excess capacity and install new equipment. Productivity rose rapidly as the industry's labour force fell, but even better performance was achieved by Britain's competitors (Pollard 1983: 295–6). As in shipbuilding, Britain declined as world demand grew.

When artificial fibre producers began to buy up Lancashire mills in the 1960s the long overdue restructuring began. The driving force was Courtaulds which had faced take-over by ICI in 1962 (Coleman 1980: 174–288). Courtaulds used its growing strength to modernise the textile industry, secure the market for its synthetic yarn, and press for protection (Singleton 1990a: 66–71). Protection increased in 1962 after a GATT agreement to limit imports of textiles from LDCs into richer countries (Foreman-Peck 1983: 304) and was formalised in the Multifibre Arrangement of 1974. The MFA aimed in principle to liberalise world trade in textiles, but in practice ratified protectionism and discrimination by the industrial countries (Green 1989: 191). The postwar artificial fibre industry had become global in scale. Inducements to locate in Northern Ireland proved particularly attractive to multinational firms, producing high levels of inward investment into Ulster from 1953 to 1963 (Ollerenshaw 1991: 76). These changes affected the regional balance of the British textile industry, but could not reverse decline. OPEC1 and 2 hit the artificial fibre industry particularly hard and overvaluation of sterling in the 1980s and 1990s made trading conditions exceptionally difficult at a time of excess capacity and increasing specialisation (Shaw and Simpson 1988: 131–2). Overcapacity again drew the state into the regulation of the industry, and the D'Avignon Agreement of 1978 proposed market sharing and planned reductions in capacity on a European level. Further agreements have followed as trading conditions deteriorated in the early 1980s, but the fate of the textile industry in all developed countries seems to have been sealed by the Uruguay Round of GATT under which the LDCs secured fundamental changes in the MFA and greater liberalisation.

The most important 'modern' industry has been motor vehicles which expanded rapidly after 1945, accounting in 1966 for 7.5 per cent of manufacturing output, 6 per cent of manufacturing employment and approximately 10 per cent of manufacturing investment (Armstrong 1967). The effects of war on Continental car-makers allowed UK and US firms to dominate world markets until the mid-1950s (Maxcy and Silberston 1959) when Britain still had the highest labour productivity outside North America (Cairncross et al. 1983: 72). British annual output was overtaken by West Germany in 1956, but British car-makers fell behind European efficiency levels after 1965 (Table 12.7). In 1973 The Economist revealed that British factories needed between 67 and 132 per cent more labour than German and Belgian producers to make apparently identical vehicles (Pollard 1983: 289). Britain's labour costs were lower than her European rivals but not by enough to offset the productivity differential. In cars, import penetration increased and Britain's share of export markets declined after 1968 (Prais 1981: 159). In commercial vehicles, similar processes began in the mid-1970s (Table 12.8). Production of both cars and commercial vehicles peaked in the late 1960s and with very substantial import penetration thereafter the motor industry balance of payments deteriorated rapidly (Table 12.8).

There is no consensus on the cause of this dramatic collapse (Church 1994). Among the most frequently-cited problems have been: inappropriate government policies – frequent variations in purchase tax and hire purchase terms, high interest and exchange rates and regional policies which took new factories to unsuitable sites (Bhaskar 1979; Dunnett 1980; Pollard 1982; Rhys 1988); trade union power – controlling the pace of work (Lewchuk 1986; CPRS 1975), producing high strike levels (Jones and Prais 1978) or multi-unionism (Prais 1981: 145–64); inadequate management – leading to low levels of investment (HMSO 1975; Lewchuk 1987), inability to identify market limitations (Williams *et al*. 1983) and failure to rationalise production and marketing (Turner 1971). No single answer can, however, fully explain the timing and pattern of the British slide (Church 1994: 115–24).

A comparison of Ford-UK and the British Motor Corporation, formed in 1952 by the merger of Morris and Austin, illuminates some of the issues. BMC held 38 per cent of the car market from 1953 to 1966 but fell behind Ford-UK's capital intensity. BMC specialised in small cars where profits were low, and its rudimentary cost controls damaged profitability further (Turner 1971: 182–3) producing inadequate funds for re-equipment (Church 1994: 72–82). Among other British car-makers in similar difficulties, Rootes was taken over by the US giant, Chrysler, in 1967 (Thoms and Donnelly 1985: 170–4). With all three major US producers (General Motors owned Vauxhall) involved in the UK, in 1968 the Labour government tried to create a 'national champion' by merging Leyland Trucks, owner of Standard-Triumph and Rover cars, and BMC into British Leyland (Turner 1971: 101–97). BL, probably then the world's fifth largest car-maker, unfortunately inherited 48 separate plants, a massive model range and an extremely unwieldy management structure (Church 1994: 88; Williams *et al*. 1983: 218). Market changes in the late 1960s did not help. Demand for smaller cars for private buyers, which BMC had traditionally dominated, declined relative to the fleet market of larger cars for business users, which Ford commanded with the Escort and Cortina, leaving no company with sufficiently large demand to produce on an internationally competitive scale or able to generate sufficient funds from the British market to finance new model development – a key element in competitive performance (Williams *et al*. 1983: 230–5). BL began badly; its first new models, the Marina and Allegro, were neither design nor commercial successes.

At the same time, Ford-UK's wages structure and industrial relations system were under pressure (Tolliday 1991) and real assets per worker fell between 1968 and 1973 (Church 1994: 72). These problems occurred when the parent company was beginning to plan production on a Europe-wide basis; Cologne rather than Dagenham became the effective centre of Ford Europe. Ford-UK increasingly imported cars and major sub-assemblies from Germany and Spain. In 1973, some 88 per cent of the value of all Ford cars sold in the UK had been produced in the UK; in 1983 the proportion was 22 per cent (Church 1994: 110). These problems

*Table 12.7* Comparative rates of growth of output and employment in the motor industry, selected countries (average annual rates of growth)

|  | 1960–4 | 1964–9 | 1969–73 | 1973–8 |
|---|---|---|---|---|
| Output by value (constant prices): | | | | |
| West Germany | 8.1 | 6.5 | 4.8 | 2.5 |
| France | 5.5[b] | 9.1 | 7.4 | 3.1 |
| UK | 5.6 | 2.2 | 0.4 | −2.4 |
| Italy[a] | n.a. | n.a. | 3.6[d] | 1.7 |
| Output of units produced: | | | | |
| West Germany | 9.1 | 4.4 | 2.3 | 1.2 |
| France | 4.2 | 8.8 | 7.0 | 1.7 |
| UK | 6.5 | −1.3 | −0.2 | −4.7 |
| Italy | 14.0 | 7.9 | 5.2 | −2.9 |
| Employment: | | | | |
| West Germany | 6.2 | 2.3 | 2.3 | 0.5 |
| France | 2.5 | 2.6 | 5.1 | 0.7[e] |
| UK | 6.5 | −1.3 | −0.2 | −4.7 |
| Italy | 4.9[c] | 6.8 | 1.5 | 1.4[e] |

*Notes:*
a  Relates to transport equipment, not just the motor industry.
b  1962–64.
c  1961–64.
d  1970–73.
e  1973–77.
*Source:* Jones 1981: Table 1.

were, however, minor compared with the catastrophes which befell BL. Profits were hit by poor sales of the Marina and Allegro and BL's failure to rationalise, producing insufficient resources for new model development (Williams *et al.* 1983: 239–66). Committed to preserving its national champion, the Labour government nationalised BL in 1975 and endorsed an overambitious investment programme, but labour unrest increased, especially when redundancy and reform of work practices became central issues (Church 1994: 101–3). The work-force was cut by 44 per cent from 1977 to 1982, raising labour productivity rapidly, and new model development was assured by a strategic link with Honda of Japan from 1979 (Wilks 1984: 215). BL's market share continued to decline (even after relaunching the company as Rover Group in 1985) producing insufficient revenue to service the cost of the capital equipment introduced since 1977 (Williams *et al.* 1987). Rover Group continued to require state finance which Conservative governments of the 1980s were increasingly reluctant to provide. Accordingly, Rover was sold cheaply, and how cheaply was hidden from scrutiny, to British Aerospace in 1988 and again to BMW in 1994. The company which had produced approxi-

Table 12.8 Motor industry: new registrations, production and foreign trade, 1947–89

| | Cars[a] | | | | Commercial vehicles[a] | | | | Motor industry balance of trade[a] |
|---|---|---|---|---|---|---|---|---|---|
| | Registrations (000) | Production (000) | Exports (000) | Import penetration[b] (%) | Registrations (000) | Production (000) | Exports (000) | Import penetration[b] (%) | (£m) |
| 1947 | 148 | 287 | 141 | 0.1 | 124 | 155 | 49 | 0.1 | +63.3 |
| 1951 | 138 | 476 | 368 | 2.7 | 87 | 258 | 137 | 0.2 | +126.0 |
| 1964 | 1,216 | 1,868 | 679 | 5.4 | 235 | 465 | 170 | 1.7 | +355.0 |
| 1973 | 1,648 | 1,747 | 632 | 30.6 | 295 | 417 | 197 | 12.5 | +804.0 |
| 1979 | 1,716 | 1,070 | 375 | 61.8 | 306 | 408 | 161 | 22.1 | −287.0 |
| 1985 | 1,832 | 1,048 | 226 | 58.5 | 287 | 266 | 70 | 40.0 | −2,758.0 |
| 1989 | 2,301 | 1,299 | 281 | 59.6 | 371 | 327 | 97 | 39.6 | −6,550.0 |

Notes:

a To 1964, figures relate to trade in cars and commercial vehicles. From 1973, the figures relate to the entire motor industry.
b The proportion of total new registrations accounted for by imports (complete vehicles plus chassis).
Source: Society of Motor Manufacturers and Traders, The Motor Industry of Great Britain (various issues).

mately 1 million vehicles in 1968, accounting for just under 40 per cent of total UK production held in 1991 barely 13 per cent of the UK market, representing an output of 0.4 million vehicles (Church 1994: 107). The only bright spot has been the establishment by Japanese car-makers (Nissan, Honda and Toyota) of their EU production bases in the UK during the 1980s and 1990s.

One of the few industries to have recorded continuously positive rates of growth since 1945 has been electrical engineering (Table 12.2). Its products are diverse (from power station equipment and weapons management systems to kitchen appliances and microchips) and the application of electronics to other industries has made it an important 'carrier' of technical change in the twentieth century (Soete 1985: 5). The industry performed creditably between the wars, but the gap between British and US productivity levels probably widened, despite the presence of many US firms in the UK (Caterall 1979: 266; Hannah 1976: 112). Price rings and market-share agreements spread in some sections of the industry in the 1930s (Jones and Marriott 1972: 188; Williams *et al.* 1983: 135) but in others intense competition eroded profits, R&D activity and investment levels (Caterall 1979: 263–4).

The war both brought rapid expansion (Wilson 1958: 145) and exposed weaknesses in production engineering and management (Barnett 1986: 166–81). After the war, British firms enjoyed expanding home and export markets until the mid-1950s when European manufacturers re-established themselves (Wilson 1958). The restrictive agreements of the 1930s remained until a highly critical Monopolies Commission report in 1957, just as competition was intensifying in key sectors. To consolidate British competitive strength, the Labour government of 1964–70 encouraged the formation by merger of another 'national champion' in GEC under Arnold (later Lord) Weinstock (Jones and Marriott 1972: 309–68). The new GEC had interests in most branches of this diverse industry. Unlike BL, GEC has prospered, especially in financial terms, with high profits throughout the 1970s (Williams *et al.* 1983: 153–7). In other ways, however, performance has been disappointing. It withdrew from TV-set production, where Weinstock made his original reputation, and faced enormous problems in domestic appliances (Williams *et al.* 1983: 164). From the mid-1970s, and increasingly in the 1990s in joint ventures with other European producers, GEC has concentrated instead on defence, power station and telecommunications equipment, the heavier end of the industry where home rather than export sales predominate and where government rather than the individual consumer is the main buyer. The main criticism of GEC has been its failure to channel its profits into R&D to resolve the problems of its consumer goods divisions (Williams *et al.* 1983), but it has survived the three recessions since 1973 in more robust health than equivalent European companies and with a clearer, but more specialised, strategic goal.

GEC was not the only British TV-set manufacturer to experience difficulties as Japanese competition increased from the early 1970s. Japanese strength derived from more efficient manufacturing processes and higher standards of quality and reliability (Cawson *et al.* 1990). In 1978, the average Japanese producer could make a TV-set for three-quarters of the sum required in the UK or Germany (NEDO 1979). Thorn Electrical Industries, the largest and most profitable TV-set maker in Britain, was hit hard by Japanese competition, resulting in merger (with EMI) in 1980 and sale of the TV-set business in 1987. By the 1990s, the only firms making TVs in the UK were Japanese.

The fate of the British computer industry is similar. The world's first computer (1948) and the first commercially delivered computer (1951) were British (Tweedale 1992: 98–9). However, British firms have lacked the resources and the domestic market necessary for long-run commercial viability. IBM, the dominant hardware-maker for much of the post-war period, received military contracts to the value of £350 million from the US government during the 1950s. In the same period, British government sponsorship of computing amounted to little more than £12 million (Campbell-Kelly 1989). British computer-makers (such as the remarkable case of J. Lyons, the catering firm, which marketed a complete computerised office system) found demand in the 1950s and 1960s small and segmented, very different conditions from those facing IBM in the USA (Hendry 1987). The Wilson government created another 'national champion' in 1968 by amalgamating British computer-makers into ICL and increasing development finance but research and market limitations remained. ICL also moved into and out of public ownership, reducing its commercial sights in the process. Its operations continue under the ownership since 1990 of the Japanese chip-maker Fujitsu, where it forms part of the world's second-largest computer-producer (Sarson 1993).

In sum, the electrical engineering sector has performed reasonably. Import penetration has increased but export sales have also expanded as the more successful domestic producers reaped the opportunities of trade liberalisation (Soete 1985: 77). In this industry, competitiveness depends heavily upon technological advantage which is in turn highly influenced by R&D activity and the availability of technical and managerial skills (Soete 1985: 14–32). Despite government attempts to promote national champions and channel funds into R&D, British-owned firms have found it difficult to compete and since the 1950s British governments have encouraged inward investment by US, Continental and Japanese multinationals (Sawyer 1989: 244–5). Whilst the results for employment, productivity and investment have been positive in the short-term (Booth 1995b: extract 2.15), the longer run consequences have yet to be established.

## SERVICES

In the space available, only two services, transport and retailing, will be considered in depth. Together they have accounted for approximately 15 per cent of total output in the postwar period (Matthews *et al.* 1982: 243–7) and have recorded consistently positive rates of growth of output during the postwar years (Table 12.9).

Under the Transport Act of 1947, the Attlee government nationalised the entire railway system and most of the road haulage industry (Gwilliam 1988: 257) and established the British Transport Commission (BTC) with wide responsibilities to provide an efficient, economical and integrated transport network (Gourvish 1991: 121, 354). However, parts of road haulage were excluded from nationalisation (Clegg 1952: 435) and the BTC lacked authority and clear terms of reference (Gourvish 1986: 106–7). After 1951, road haulage was largely de-nationalised (one of the first privatisations) and attempts at integration ceased (Gourvish 1986: 137–72).

British Railways managed to hold a roughly stable volume of passenger traffic, increasingly by concentrating its expenditure on those parts of the market (Inter-City and commuter services in the South East) where it has maintained a comparative advantage (Gwilliam 1988: 261). In freight, the rise of road transport has been less marked than in the passenger sector, but BR's loss of market share has been much steeper, involving a large absolute fall in traffic. The management of railway decline has been erratic and uneven. After wartime damage and disinvestment, the system needed rapid and extensive modernisation but the capital programme was delayed first by shortages (Gourvish 1986: 68–90) and then by management reorganisation in the early

*Table 12.9 Growth of output and productivity in transport and distribution, 1951–88 (% per annum).*

|  | 1951–64 | 1964–73 | 1973–9 | 1979–88 |
|---|---|---|---|---|
| Growth of Output: |  |  |  |  |
| Distribution | 2.9 | 2.8 | 0.4 | 2.6 |
| Transport and communications | 2.2 | 3.5 | 1.7 | 2.8 |
| Growth of Labour Productivity: |  |  |  |  |
| Distribution | 1.7 | 4.7 | n.a. | 2.0 |
| Transport and communications | 2.9 | 4.8 | n.a. | 3.6 |

*Sources*: Matthews *et al.* 1982: 243–7; Feinstein and Matthews 1990: 81.

1950s (Pryke 1971: 42–3). The Modernisation Plan of 1955 soon ran into difficulties; capital costs were higher and benefits accrued more slowly than anticipated. From the mid-1950s, BR began to accumulate large losses, exacerbated by difficulties, as with other nationalised industries, in raising prices (Gourvish 1991: 122). Increasing deficits led to management reorganisation (again) and the appointment of a businessman from ICI, Dr Richard Beeching, to bring commercial methods into railway management. Beeching's Report (1963) pointed out that half the route mileage carried only 5 per cent of the total traffic and that one-third of the stations generated only 1 per cent of traffic. He proposed to reduce the network by 5,000 miles and close 2,363 of the 4,293 passenger stations. The Beeching Report created a political storm, and government implemented only part of the cuts (Pryke 1971: 251–5). Since the mid-1960s, contraction has proceeded steadily (Table 12.10). Losses have continued and have been extremely cyclically sensitive (Gwilliam 1988: 267–9). Labour productivity has risen by 3.8 per cent per annum between 1948 and 1973 (Gourvish 1986: 612–3) and since 1950 total factor productivity has increased more rapidly than on US railroads (Smith *et al.* 1982: 145–6; Millward 1990: 432–5).

BR has retained its core passenger markets with a shrinking labour force; in 1992 the BR work-force was less than one-fifth of that in 1948 (Table 12.10). Some staff losses have resulted from privatisation in the 1980s which has had a major impact on the peripheral activities of the railways (engineering workshops, hotels, shipping, catering and the property portfolio) but political considerations kept BR's core activities within the public sector until deteriorating public finances in the mid-1990s brought privatisation of the rail network back to the forefront of the agenda.

With petrol rationing continuing to 1950, private motoring did not regain its prewar level until the early 1950s, but the number of motor vehicles has increased almost sevenfold since 1947, with huge increases in private car ownership (Table 12.10). Frequent and substantial changes in goods vehicle classification make it impossible to identify trends but heavy goods vehicles have undoubtedly become much more efficient; average load size has increased, speed has risen and maintenance requirements have fallen. The number of public-service vehicles (coaches and buses) grew rapidly from 1945 to 1952, and then stabilised until a second, less substantial, phase of growth occurred in the 1980s when bus and coach services were privatised and deregulated. The data must be treated with extreme care but appear to show continuing productivity growth in the industry (Table 12.9). International labour productivity comparisons suggest that both US and German road transport had higher productivity than Britain in the early 1970s, but the gap was much smaller than that between the respective manufactur-

*Table 12.10* Selected transport statistics, 1947–92

| | 1948 | 1953 | 1973 | 1979 | 1989 | 1992 | 1953 | 1992 |
|---|---|---|---|---|---|---|---|---|
| | | Percentage shares of total traffic | | | | | Actual traffic | |

**Changes in the distribution of passenger and freight traffic:**

| | | | | | | | Billion passenger-km | |
|---|---|---|---|---|---|---|---|---|
| **Passengers** | | | | | | | | |
| Railways | n.a. | 21 | 8 | 8 | 6 | 6 | 39 | 38 |
| Public road | n.a. | 43 | 12 | 11 | 7 | 6 | 82 | 43 |
| Private road | n.a. | 36 | 80 | 80 | 87 | 88 | 68 | 595 |
| Air | n.a. | – | 0.5 | 1 | 1 | 1 | – | 5 |
| **Freight** | | | | | | | Billion tonne-km | |
| Railways | n.a. | 44 | 18 | 12 | 8 | 7 | 37 | 16 |
| Road | n.a. | 38 | 65 | 60 | 62 | 61 | 32 | 127 |
| Canal & coastal shipping | n.a. | 18 | 15 | 22 | 26 | 26 | 15 | 55 |
| Pipeline | n.a. | – | 2 | 6 | 4 | 5 | 0.2 | 11 |

**Railway statistics:**

| | | | | | | | | |
|---|---|---|---|---|---|---|---|---|
| Network (000 km) | 31.5 | 30.9 | 18.2 | 17.7 | 16.6 | 16.5 | | |
| Staff (000) | 649 | 602 | 229 | 218 | 128 | 123 | | |

**The road system (000 km):**

| | | | | | | | | |
|---|---|---|---|---|---|---|---|---|
| Motorways | 0 | 0 | 1.1 | 2.5 | 3.0 | 3.1 | | |
| Trunk roads | 13.2 | 13.3 | 15.1 | 14.8 | 12.7 | 12.3 | | |
| Principal roads | 31.4 | 31.6 | 32.9 | 34.4 | 35.0 | 35.7 | | |
| Other roads | 250.0 | 256.3 | 280.4 | 286.3 | 305.9 | 311.2 | | |
| Total | 294.6 | 301.2 | 329.5 | 338.0 | 356.6 | 362.3 | | |

**Licensed motor vehicles[a] (millions)**

| | | | | | | | | |
|---|---|---|---|---|---|---|---|---|
| Private Cars and Light Goods[b] | 2.0 | 2.7 | 13.4 | 15.7 | 21.4 | 22.3 | | |
| Public Service Vehicles[c] | 0.12 | 0.12 | 0.11 | 0.11 | 0.12 | 0.11 | | |
| Goods[d] | 0.08 | 0.10 | 0.17 | 0.06 | 0.05 | 0.04 | | |
| Others | 1.5 | 2.4 | 3.3 | 2.7 | 2.6 | 2.4 | | |
| Total | 3.7 | 5.3 | 17.0 | 18.6 | 24.2 | 24.9 | | |

*Notes*:
[a] This part of the Table relates only to *licensed* motor vehicles. At the end of 1992, it was estimated that there were also 1.24 million unlicensed vehicles on the road, of which roughly two-thirds were in the private/light goods (PLG) categories. The extent of licence-evasion in previous years is unknown. There have been two major re-classifications within the period, in 1978 and 1991, which means that classes are not consistent over time.
[b] Private cars and light vans to 1973, but PLG thereafter.
[c] Includes taxis.
[d] The major change of classification occurred in 1978, when some vehicles previously classed as 'goods' were reclassified into PLG. In addition, agricultural vans and lorries were added to the goods class in 1978. In 1980, electric goods vehicles were exempted from licence duty and are excluded from the Table in 1989 and 1992.

*Source: Transport Statistics: Great Britain*, various issues.

ing sectors (Smith *et al.* 1982: 146–8). The road network has found it increasingly difficult to cope with the growth of traffic. Public expenditure on road building has risen steadily after a relatively slow beginning in the 1940s and 1950s (Pollard 1983: 300) and even the growth of the motorway network since 1959 has failed to provide a lasting answer to congestion. Government expenditure has favoured roadbuilding over the railways but increasing concern about congestion, pollution, wider environmental issues and the cost of roadbuilding, are the main issues facing road transport in the late twentieth century.

In distribution, one of the most important postwar changes has been the abolition of resale price maintenance (RPM) in the 1950s and 1960s (Eliot 1988: 252). By allowing manufacturers to insist that all retailers charged the same price for any given product, RPM prevented price competition and its removal paved the way for rapid expansion of the more efficient parts of the distributive trades (George and Joll 1981: 286–91). Measurement problems make it difficult to identify clear trends in individual retail markets, but there are signs that many branches of retailing have become increasingly dominated by large companies over the postwar period. In 1961 the top 100 retailers had 21 per cent of total sales, by 1980 the same percentage was in the hands of 12 companies and by 1984 the top 10 had 24 per cent (Eliot 1988: 240). Some sections of retailing had long been dominated by large businesses – footwear, men's clothing, furniture – but concentration ratios also grew in food-related retailing from the 1960s, with the growth of the major off-licence chains and the growing dominance of the major supermarkets (Sainsbury, Tesco, Asda, Safeway) (Eliot 1988: 241). A casualty has been the Co-operative movement, which has steadily lost market share since the late 1950s (Eliot 1983). Three factors have underpinned this growth of concentration. First, large retailers have been able to secure large economies of scale, especially in the discounts they have been able to obtain from manufacturers, which have been impossible for smaller businesses. In food retailing, smaller producers have responded by forming large, voluntary purchasing organisations (such as Spar and VG) but this has been a comparatively rare example of reaction by small-scale retailers. Second, the shift of retailing from the town centre to peripheral, suburban locations with excellent parking and access has encouraged concentration by increasing capital intensity. Finally, large multiples appear to have been better at exploiting changes in the labour market where ample supplies of (largely female) unskilled and part-time workers have become available. In sharp contrast with manufacturing, larger-scale units in retailing appear to be well managed, with good performance in the management of stocks, distribution, purchasing and marketing by the major chains, especially in food retailing (Eliot 1988: 243–52).

As in transport, there was a gap between British and US retailing productivity in the early 1970s, but it was less than that between the respective manufacturing sectors (Smith and Hitchens 1983). Some of the difference in productivity arose from the larger average size of US shops, but for any given shop size US productivity levels were higher than those of the UK because of greater capital intensity in the USA – more bricks, mortar and fittings per shop assistant (Smith and Hitchens 1983: 55). Since Smith and Hitchens published their findings, productivity in British retailing has undoubtedly risen but British retailing remained less capital-intensive than in the USA and comparatively slow to exploit new methods which offered productivity growth (Eliot 1988: 250).

Although international comparisons are very fragmentary and must be treated with extreme caution, they tend to confirm a widely held belief that Britain's comparative performance in the postwar period has been better (more exactly, less poor) in the service sector than in manufacturing, at least until the late 1970s. Since the mid-1970s the service sector appears to have absorbed resources and has underemployed them in many areas, just as in the interwar years, so that productivity has declined relative to manufacturing (Millward 1990: 428).

## SUPPLY-SIDE PROBLEMS

Chapter 10 listed the supply-side weaknesses identified by Crafts (1991a: 273–9; 1991b) as causes of Britain's relatively slow growth; poorly qualified managers making British companies inadequately organised and incapable of fully exploiting economies of scale; an adverse climate of industrial relations; insufficient attention to R&D; inadequate monitoring of company performance by the financial sector; and inappropriate government policies. Of course, these are not independent categories and weakness in one area may easily lead to problems elsewhere, but this catalogue is a useful way of organising the discussion of managerial and institutional failures.

Chandler (1962, 1977) has emphasised the importance in the USA of the emergence of large-scale, vertically integrated firms which pioneered mass production and developed deep managerial hierarchies and a multi-divisional form (separate product divisions subject to strategic control and monitoring by head office) to implement their strategy of growth and diversification. In his most recent study, Chandler (1990) has argued that this US pattern is critical for competitive success in the capital-intensive manufacturing industries which are crucial to twentieth century industrial development. The multi-divisional firm has developed much more slowly in the UK. In 1950 there were in Britain only a dozen multi-divisional firms, of which eight were subsidiaries of US parents, and by 1970 only one-third of British firms were so structured (Channon 1973: 67–9,238). Growing competition and low profits from the later 1960s made organisational change more urgent and by the mid-1970s three-quarters of British firms had adopted some form of multi-divisional organisation (Gospel 1992: 110). However, these changes need to be placed in perspective; there are good reasons for believing that the advantages of multi-divisional form did not always translate easily to other countries from the USA (Hannah 1991: 299). In postwar Britain, for example, there is no clear association between either organisational structure and market performance or even between organisational structure and managerial strategy (Gourvish 1987: 40). In Britain large-scale corporations tended to evolve from holding companies, making structures weaker than in their US counterparts, with smaller managerial hierarchies and weaker central planning organisations (Gospel 1992: 110).

British managers have been notably ill-qualified. Ackrill estimated that in the late 1980s, only 24 per cent of senior British managers were graduates, compared with 85 per cent in the USA and Japan (1988: 71). It has traditionally been easier to enter management without formal educational qualification in Britain than elsewhere (Swords-Isherwood 1980: 91–3) and British managers are only marginally more qualified than the general population (Crockett and Elias 1984: 36). In part, this situation has arisen from the inadequate supply of graduates from British higher education (Sanderson 1991: 171–82). But there have also been problems on the demand side, which were probably more significant. Most British firms did not recruit graduate managers before the mid-1950s (Ackrill 1988: 71). The engineering industry has been especially reluctant to recruit graduate engineers (Albu 1980) and there may be a deeply entrenched culture among British managers which identifies expertise in terms of personal characteristics rather than technical competence (Swords-Isherwood 1980: 95). However, the effects of the 'quality gap' in British management are unquantifiable. Ackrill suggests that British firms tended to be rather slow to embrace change as a result of the comparatively poor education of their senior managers (1988: 72). This is, however, unverifiable and measurement of social gains from graduate-level qualifications is unreliable (Shackleton 1992: 30–3).

Britain's comparative shortage of specific managerial skills in engineering and technology may however have weakened the ability to undertake a range of technological activities, such as design, R&D, and production engineering which help to establish technological leads in product markets, a critical factor in non-price competitiveness (Patel and Pavitt 1987: 72). R&D expenditure can be measured as can the establishment of the patents which should result from successful 'technological activity' by the firm (Pavitt 1981). The amount of research undertaken by British industry increased during the 1940s and 1950s but tended to be highly concentrated in a relatively small number of large firms in chemicals and electrical engineering (Edgerton 1987: 88–9). In 1967, Britain stood second among OECD countries in the proportion of GDP spent on R&D and fourth in that spent on civilian R&D. By 1983, it was sixth in total R&D spending and ninth in civilian R&D (Patel and Pavitt 1987). The statistics of international patenting show a similar decline. The British share of foreign patents taken out in the USA, a measure of R&D effectiveness, has fallen; in 1958, Britain had 23.4 per cent, Germany 25.6 per cent and Japan 1.9 per cent of all foreign patents, but by 1979 the percentages were 10.1, 23.9 and 27.7 per cent respectively (Pavitt and Soete 1980). Britain has consistently devoted too much of its R&D activity to defence-related projects in the aircraft and electronics industries, where the record of major blunders (the TSR2, Concorde, the Magnox nuclear reactors, the advanced gas-cooled reactors) is unenviable (Peck 1968; Pavitt 1980: 9). Mary Kaldor (1980) has argued that high levels of government-financed R&D weakens civilian innovation by pre-empting scarce supplies of qualified personnel and allowing bad habits (like the neglect of users' needs and poor awareness of market constraints) to persist. R&D financed by industry fell absolutely between 1963 and 1975 and may have been a cause of poor industrial performance in the 1970s or, more likely, a consequence of the profits crisis of 1964–75 (Glyn and Sutcliffe 1972; Flemming *et al.* 1976).

Widening profit margins after 1975 enabled industrial R&D expenditure to recover. Civilian research in pharmaceuticals has increased continuously whereas that undertaken by electronics companies expanded until the mid-1980s and then began to contract (Pavitt 1981: 92–3; Lister and Golland 1993: 101). The concerns over British 'technological activity' have continued. Studies in the early 1980s showed the British engineering industry relatively slow to diffuse key innovations and liable to lose many of its existing technological leads (Patel and Pavitt 1987: 73). The comparatively low levels of business R&D are known to be matched in many industries by inadequate design, inadequate marketing and inadequate production engineering (Pavitt 1981: 101). Within this very sluggish overall trend in 'technological activity', large British firms in chemicals, pharmaceuticals, aerospace, electronics and electrical engineering have performed well. There is however a significant gap when compared with other advanced countries – in automobiles, reflecting the problems noted above (Patel and Pavitt 1987: 78–82).

If the ability to undertake effective 'technological activity' is so uneven within British industry, why have the efficient not driven the weak out of business? In part, this is a question about industrial policy, considered below, but it also raises issues about the finance–industry links. Crafts has criticised the weak competitive pressures (considered in the next section) and feeble disciplines imposed by the financial system before the 1970s (1991a: 277–8). Agreed mergers have been common in Britain since the late nineteenth century, but the take-over bid was extremely rare before the 1950s. The pace of merger activity quickened in the 1950s and 1960s, not only in manufacturing (Hannah 1983: 144–5) but also in finance, transport and retailing (Wardley 1991). However, mergers and acquisitions have not yielded the anticipated gains. Firms appear to have been less, not more, efficient after merger (Meeks 1977: ch. 3) with stock market valuations below the sum of the previously separate parts (Firth 1979), perhaps because take-over targets are distinguished by size rather than profitability (Singh 1975). Stock market disciplines can be counter-productive for long-run growth. Firms have attempted to secure share-holder loyalty by maximising short-term profitability, often by cuts which endanger longer-term growth prospects (Finegold and Soskice 1988: 29). Moreover, despite rising concentrations of ownership before 1970, concentration of production simply did not occur; during the merger boom of the 1960s average plant size in the largest firms fell rather than increased. Stock market disciplines are not necessarily growth-enhancing. But the focus on financial disciplines misses a more fundamental point: efficient, energetic, ambitious managers did not drive out the inefficient within firms. Poor managerial quality, noted above, seems to be the more entrenched weakness.

Equally inconclusive has been the debate on the postwar influence of the banks on industry. Following the interwar Macmillan Committee Report, in the postwar period the Radcliffe Committee (1959), the Prices and Incomes Board (1967), the Bolton Committee (1971) and the Wilson Committee (1980) have all investigated the provision of bank finance for industry and have concluded that the cost and availability of finance have *not* been disadvantageous in Britain. Gaps in the supply of capital have been closed by the creation of new institutions; the Industrial and Commercial Finance Corporation in 1945 and the Unlisted Securities Market in 1980, for example (Capie and Collins 1992: 65–6). Firms have continued to rely on retained profits as the main source of invest-ment but the banks' high liquidity after 1945 encouraged lending to domestic industry and the existence of controls on capital exports until 1979 probably kept the cost of bank capital to domestic industry lower than it would otherwise have been (Capie and Collins 1992: 64). Industry certainly turned to banks for new finance in the mid-1970s when infla-tion rose and profitability declined (Thomas 1978: 198). A comparison of finance–industry links in Britain and Germany in the period 1970–88 found little difference in sources of funds, especially for larger firms (Mayer and Alexander 1990).

However, the criticism of banks' treatment of industry has persisted, and has focused on the costs to industry of the City's international role. Ingham, for example, points out that the City has developed a range of international commercial and banking services which did not depend for profitability upon the performance of the national productive economy (1984: 62–78). Thus, the interests of the City and domestic industry need not coincide, at least in the short term, as is clear in the debates about restoration of the gold standard (Chapter 6) and entrance into the EMS (Chapter 11). When such clashes occur, the City's critics argue that the voice of financial and commercial capital invariably prevails, often at great cost to domestic industry. Pollard, for example, has identified a 'contempt for production' at the centre of Britain's establishment as City interests have consistently prevailed over those of industry (1982: 71–101). The City's power has been very resilient and may be evident in economic policy – high interest and exchange rates, heavy international commitments, and failed efforts to mobilise City capital to restructure British industry (Pollard 1982; Ingham 1984; Newton and Porter 1988; Cain and Hopkins 1993b). The debates on the effects on industry of finance are thus far from resolution.

On closer investigation, therefore, the case for a catalogue of unambiguous supply-side weaknesses is rather less convincing. There has been a clear deficiency in the qualifications of British managers and the level of measurable 'technological activity' undertaken by British firms. In other areas, there is much less agreement about whether a problem has existed and the effectiveness of the most commonly proposed remedies. In the individual industries considered above there have been equally obvious demand-side problems: segmented and limited demand for ships, motor cars and computers. In all the manufacturing problem-cases, supply and demand factors interacted making it unlikely that supply-side explanations (note that the debates about the damaging impact of labour will be considered in Chapter 13) can carry the entire burden of poor performance since 1945. Nevertheless, governments have had to act on these very uncertain suppositions in formulating industrial policy, to which attention now turns.

## INDUSTRY, MARKETS AND THE STATE

The Attlee government came to power in 1945 committed to use state power to reform British industry. It nationalised the 'commanding heights' (coal, electricity, gas, transport) and less important interests (the Bank of England, Cable and Wireless) with little effective opposition (Chester 1975; Morgan 1984: 94–9). Although nationalisation had been advocated to cure almost every problem of British industry, Labour had come increasingly to emphasise its potential to reorganise management and increase technological activity (Tomlinson 1994: 162–7). Labour also had plans to use state power to reform old consumer industries (cotton, clothing, cutlery, furniture and pottery) where demand growth had slowed and excessive competition had diluted profits, weakened investment, reduced R&D activity and bred conservative management (Henderson 1952: 454–6). The government hoped to draw the rest of the private sector into planning in the tripartite machinery administering controls (Rogow and Shore 1955: 12–100). However, the only unambiguous industrial policy commitment was to control monopolies (Mercer 1992).

In the dire economic position after 1947 the government began to recognise the need to collaborate with powerful employers' associations to increase output, especially of dollar-earning exports. The government did not immediately appease industry (further nationalisation was planned), but opposition from employers' associations led to dilution of the government's original aims in key areas. The 1948 Monopolies and Restrictive Practices Act, for example, was much weaker than originally proposed, and the Development Councils for the old consumer industries were toothless (Tomlinson 1994: 178–82). The Federation of British Industry also campaigned effectively for the withdrawal of controls as shortages abated, to shift from government control to self-government for industry (Rogow and Shore 1955: 94–5). Instead of controlling industry, the Attlee government found itself working with business to raise output and productivity. Productivity growth was the only method of increasing output in a fully employed economy and the government undertook a massive propaganda campaign (Cairncross 1985: 499). Tomlinson has hinted that the Attlee government placed industrial efficiency at the centre of the political agenda (1994: 184) but its actual achievements were extremely limited. It established the British Institute of Management, the Anglo-American Council for Productivity and measures to improve joint consultation at the workplace (Tiratsoo and Tomlinson 1993: 65–152) but never forced the productivity issue, except in its dealings with the unions (Booth 1995a). In the nationalised industries, for example, ministers gave no guidance on how to raise efficiency while meeting other statutory targets (Gourvish 1991: 116–20). Most nationalised industries urgently required new investment, but all had their modernisation programmes delayed in the interests of the export drive (see the discussion of coal and railways above).

After 1947 industrial policy allowed employers' associations greater scope to regulate their own affairs in a context of limited market and ineffective state disciplines. The election of the Conservatives in 1951 reinforced the trend. Conservative industrial policy in the 1950s did not place a high premium on forcing competitiveness. The Conservatives denationalised steel and parts of road haulage (Burk 1988: Pryke 1971: 29–39) and continued to de-control industry, but did little to promote competition beyond freeing European trade and payments (Chapter 11). European industry was much slower to recover (as evident in all

the manufacturing industries considered above) and imposed few competitive pressures on British industry before the mid-1950s. The Monopolies Commission, however, after a slow start, began to illuminate the
extent of restrictive practices in British industry. The Conservative government, attempting to shield employers' associations from the full force
of the Monopoly Commission's scrutiny, introduced the Restrictive
Practices Act of 1956 which forced industrialists to register their restrictive agreements and deemed them illegal unless they satisfied specific
criteria to show that they were in the national interest (Mercer 1991).
This machinery proved far more liberalising than intended; by 1966,
some 83 per cent of all registered restrictive agreements had been
amended or discontinued (Walshe 1991: 363). Industry responded with
an accelerating merger movement which aroused public disquiet and
prompted a further, albeit weak, response from government (Roberts
1992). Weakness is apparent also in the limited change to the nationalised industries where, apart from managerial decentralisation, little was
done to alter existing structures or clarify public-sector goals (Dunkerley
and Hare 1991: 389). The modernisation programmes for coal and rail
were introduced in the 1950s and helped to accelerate public-sector
productivity growth after 1958 (Pryke 1971: 58–77) but no special credit
attaches to the Conservative government (see above).

However, problems mounted from the late 1950s. Competition from
Europe strengthened, evidence of Britain's slow growth accumulated,
the costs of 'world power status' were increasingly difficult to bear.
These factors stimulated British interest in 'indicative planning' as
undertaken in Europe (Chapter 14) but also prompted concern about
the structure of British industry in more open world manufacturing
markets. The Conservative government's preference for business self-
regulation limited industrial policy but Labour came to power in 1964
with firm ideas. A strengthened Monopolies Commission sharpened
competition policy but Labour also expanded selective support for
industry and established the Industrial Reorganisation Corporation to
facilitate mergers where economies of scale and balance of payments
concerns were potentially important. These two strategies were potentially inconsistent but in practice Labour gave much more emphasis to
intervention. Substantial assistance was given to shipbuilding, iron and
steel (involving selective re-nationalisation), aerospace, aluminium-
smelting, textiles and computing in the form of R&D, rationalisation
and modernisation grants to strengthen British performance. The high
point of interventionism was the creation of 'national champions' (see
motor cars and electrical engineering above). Early judgements of
Labour's industrial policy were very unenthusiastic (Graham 1972:
216–7) and the subsequent failure of BL and tortured progress of ICL
have only confirmed that view (Cairncross 1992: 173–4).

The inability of Labour's industrial policies in the 1960s to improve competitive performance helped to steer the Conservative government elected in 1970 towards anti-interventionism. However, the collapse of major firms in shipbuilding and aerospace left the Conservatives with little alternative but to intervene, nationalise its 'lame ducks' and increase the scale of government aid to industry. The Conservatives' Industry Act of 1972 permitted financial support for industry and acted as *carte blanche* for crisis-driven intervention (Tomlinson 1994: 301). These changes in industrial policy are at the core of the Heath 'U-turn' considered more fully in Chapter 14. The successor Labour government also arrived with radical commitments. During opposition, Labour had identified the power of multinational corporations and low levels of investment as the main cause of weak competitive performance. The remedies were a new National Enterprise Board, to take strategic equity stakes in manufacturing firms, and planning agreements, to make companies comply with government objectives in return for state financial assistance (Kirby 1991: 253–4). Although the governments of the 1970s had very different goals, they pursued similar policies. Both brought failed manufacturing companies into the public sector, with Labour completing the job of nationalising the shipbuilding and aerospace industries begun by the Conservatives (Sawyer 1991: 164–5). Both concentrated mainly on competitive failures, particularly in older industries (Tomlinson 1994: 301; Silberston 1981: 49–50) though some assistance went in the later 1970s to small high-technology firms (Sawyer 1991: 172; Kirby 1991: 254–5). Industrial policy clearly failed in the 1970s, though more blame must fall on industry for its inability to resolve its own problems (Silberston 1981; Cowling and Sugden 1993: 86).

The Conservative right and free-market economists saw in industrial policies of the 1960s and 1970s only proof that governments retarded economic growth by stifling the invigorating effects of competition (Walters 1986; Maynard 1988). The Thatcher government came to office determined to reverse interventionism and enhance the role of market forces. There were some continuities; support for high technology and R&D projects continued, though with shifting priorities (Shepherd 1987: 60). However, de-regulation and privatisation have been the most prominent aspects of industrial policy since 1979 (general macro-economic measures are considered in Chapter 14). De-regulation, or the ending of government and producer controls, has been applied in areas as diverse as the running of bus services to the award of degrees. The financial sector has been the main focus as Conservative governments have tried to strengthen the City of London in global financial markets (Coakley and Harris 1992). Exchange controls were lifted in 1979, direct limits on bank lending in 1980, hire-purchase restrictions in 1982 and major changes occurred in the stock exchange's rules with the 'big bang' of

October 1986. The second main objective of de-regulation has been to give producers of public services more freedom of action and consumers more freedom of choice (Cairncross 1992: 267–8). Thus, schools and hospitals have been encouraged to opt out of state control without loss of state financial support and both parents and patients have (in theory) been given greater choice.

The most spectacular change in industrial policy has however been privatisation, or the sale of public-sector assets. The preceding eighteen years had seen the emergence of much more precise performance guide-lines for nationalised industries (Dunkerley and Hare 1991: 396–400). However, public-sector efficiency growth slowed after 1968, with poor financial returns by coal and rail, as noted above (Pryke 1981). Public dissatisfaction with the nationalised industries multiplied (Chick 1987: 111; NEDO 1976) and by 1979 they were widely regarded as a problem (Holmes 1985b: 161–3) whose losses and investment needs seemed to threaten government control of public expenditure. The remedy was 'privatisation', but it began slowly. Receipts from asset sales reached £1 billion only in 1983–4, but the pace quickened considerably thereafter with disposal of all or parts of major nationalised industries (gas, water, electricity, British Airways) and the competitive failures of the 1970s (Austin-Rover, ICL, British Aerospace, British Steel, Britoil). By the late 1980s, proceeds exceeded £5 billion per annum (Hyman 1989: 197). Local government has followed, with more than one million publicly-owned houses sold and services put out to competitive tendering.

Conservative governments manipulated dissatisfaction with the natio-nalised industries skilfully and argued that these industries would per-form better if freed from public-sector rules (notably tight controls over investment) and exposed to market forces. In practice, however, these arguments did not apply to utilities and telecommunications. Govern-ment has been caught between the need to make privatisation issues attractive to share buyers (retaining monopoly status) and promoting competition (breaking up the monopolies). As privatisation receipts have been vital in capping the growth of public borrowing, the need for revenue has overridden the promotion of competition. The govern-ment has been forced to regulate the big utilities (through Ofgas, Oftel, Ofwat etc.) to protect the consumer at the same time as de-regulating other activities with the same end in view. As a result, the making of industrial policy has become more fragmented and the promise of much greater responsiveness to consumer needs has been slow to arrive (Fine and Polletti 1992).

Throughout the postwar period, British governments have implemen-ted a broad range of industrial policies – state control, self-government for industry, exposure to market forces, protectionism, discriminatory intervention – without finding convincing answers to fundamental questions about the effectiveness of markets or governments in regulating industrial performance. It is still possible for non-partisan, pragmatic economists to call for an interventionist industrial strategy (Cowling and Sugden 1993) and a basically free-market approach to industry (Crafts 1993: 64–74). It will be recalled that the problems of textiles, shipbuilding and motor vehicles were soluble neither by markets nor by governments. Neither approach could tackle the interrelated managerial and demand constraints on performance. Given the complexity of the problems and their deep historical roots (see Chapter 4), it is perhaps unsurprising that the main concern of industrial policy has been to ensure orderly contraction by the most expedient means.

## DE-INDUSTRIALISATION

A convenient way to conclude is by considering the debate on British **de-industrialisation**. This is an extremely difficult concept to define precisely; it implies a reversal of the process of industrialisation but British economists have taken a much less literal view focusing on shifts of resources between industry and services (Bacon and Eltis 1976) or the home and export performance of manufacturing (Singh 1977). These approaches have been received unenthusiastically (Cairncross 1978). A rise in the proportion of national income generated in the service sector and increasing import penetration are common to almost all OECD nations (Table 12.1, Chapter 11) with no signs of industrial collapse. Britain has been exceptional in the consistent relative slowness of its growth rate (see Chapter 1), the scale of the relative contraction of manufacturing and the large fall in its share of world manufactured trade. Slow growth is not a new problem, but it was given renewed impetus by the decline in British manufacturing employment beginning in 1966 and accelerating after 1970 (Thatcher 1978: 32). These figures were immensely disturbing and gave rise to the Bacon and Eltis hypothesis which, although almost certainly a red herring (Chapter 10), had the positive effect of broadening the debate on Britain's relative decline. Hitherto manufacturing had been the overwhelming focus of attention, but now the strengths, weaknesses and potential of the service sector were recognised almost for the first time, prompting new questions. Could transfer of resources into services be advantageous for long-term growth? Would the balance of payments be supported by exports of services? Did the size and competitive strength of the manufacturing sector actually matter? In some quarters the growth of the service sector has been welcomed as a sign of fundamental restructuring of the world economy wherein rich countries will tend increasingly to buy manufactures from poorer industrialising countries and supply in return sophisticated services such as banking and consultancy (Rowthorn 1994).

This 'post-industrial' perspective is built on two assumptions: that consumers' expenditure in developed countries has shifted from manufactures into services and that the trade patterns of rich countries are moving in a similar direction. There is certainly a strong upward trend in the proportion of current expenditure devoted to services from 1960 to the present (Wells 1989: 42), but expenditure in current prices cannot show the volume of services consumed. When the distribution of consumers' expenditure at constant prices is examined, no stable relationship emerges between real per capita income and the share devoted to services (Kravis *et al.* 1982). In postwar Britain, there is no underlying upward trend in expenditure at constant prices on services: the trend was downwards from 1952 to 1960 when it stabilised until the early 1980s before rising steadily to the end of the decade (Wells 1989: 42). The share (at constant prices) devoted to manufactures has been strongly upward throughout the postwar period and since the early 1980s has been growing at approximately the same rate as expenditure on services. There has been a relative price effect. Services have tended to become increasingly expensive relative to manufactures over time; rising consumer expenditure (at current prices) on services indicates not that consumers are opting for more services, but are paying more for the services they select (Wells 1989: 34). Services have tended to become more expensive over time because productivity growth is so much slower in this sector than in manufacturing (Mayes 1987: 53). The idea that Britain is leading the world towards post-industrial society is based on a misapprehension of the dynamics of postwar change.

The second assumption appears to be equally dubious. Rowthorn (1994) sees no evidence of the trade of rich nations becoming dominated by invisibles. The international division of labour which has emerged since the early 1970s is rather one in which developing countries specialise in types of manufacturing (such as assembly, clothing, textiles) which use their abundant supplies of cheap, unskilled labour, while advanced countries specialise in manufactures requiring superior physical and human capital. Rowthorn's analysis focuses attention again on recent trends in Britain's manufactured trade. Does the growing deficit on visible trade in the 1980s indicate failure to secure a competitive position in the new international division of labour? In a perceptive reappraisal of postwar trade performance, Rowthorn and Wells (1987) have argued that Britain's manufacturing trade balance has been shaped by autonomous changes in other parts of the trade account. In 1951, Britain was a major importer of food and raw materials when the terms of trade favoured primary producers. To finance essential primary imports at prevailing relative prices, Britain needed a large surplus in manufactured trade which was secured in the strong sellers' markets before 1955 by the devices and controls developed in the 1940s to give manufacturers priority in resource allocation and protect sterling area markets. As Britain became more agriculturally self-sufficient after 1950 and international trade in services revived, benefiting the City, the need lessened for a substantial surplus in manufactured trade. The huge swing in the balance of energy trade following the discovery of North Sea oil and gas also reduced the need for manufacturing trade surplus. Rowthorn and Wells argue that the weakness of British manufacturing is evident less in the trade statistics than in Britain's comparatively slow rate of growth (the slowest-growing economy in Western Europe since 1950 – Table 10.1), rising unemployment since the 1960s (Chapter 13) and relative decline in Britain's living standards (well above the OECD average in 1950, well below in 1989 – Maddison 1991: 6).

Relative weakness in manufacturing has existed and appears likely to continue. Postwar growth of consumers' expenditure has been dominated by five main items: cars, foreign holidays, electronic goods, domestic electrical appliances and clothes (Wells 1989: 43). These are areas of production in which Britain lacks an adequate volume of internationally competitive capacity; for intrinsic reasons in the case of foreign holidays but also in clothing and consumer durables, as the evidence surveyed in this chapter has demonstrated. There are no reasons to expect fundamental change in the patterns of either consumers' expenditure or world production, so Britain's heavy dependence on imports will almost certainly continue. As depressing have been the signs that weaknesses in the British capital goods industries have multiplied since the early 1970s with import penetration rising much faster than export shares (Kilpatrick and Moir 1988: 162–3). The discussion above suggests that future living standards and employment levels will rest upon the ability to produce capital- and skill-intensive manufactures, oil and, less certainly, services to finance the imports of consumer goods and services. The outlook for exports of sophisticated manufactures is more cheerful than might be anticipated. The visible import–export balance was most healthy in the late 1980s where 'strong' (rather than 'moderate' or 'weak') demand growth is expected and British high technology industries appear relatively competitive, although comprising a relatively small share of total manufacturing output (Crafts 1993: 55–62). The future of the oil balance is impossible to predict as much depends upon the highly volatile price of oil which is itself subject to manipulation by an unstable cartel, OPEC. The outlook for invisible exports appears relatively bright. In sharp contrast to performance in manufactured trade, Britain has been able to maintain its share of world trade in services though service sector trade, like manufacturing, has been hit by high exchange rates, notably in 1979–82 (Sargent 1978: 104; Wells 1989: 44). Financial service exports have expanded particularly strongly throughout the postwar period, and London has retained its position as one of the world's leading financial centres. There are, however, indications that market constraints may limit the potential for future growth of exports of financial services. The comparatively small size of Britain's merchant banks and the smallness of Britain's domestic economy and high average interest rates are disadvantageous when compared with the USA and Japan (Smith 1992: 107–8). Competition for the world market in services is certain to intensify and the smallness of Britain's domestic market may well be as inimical to competitiveness in services as in parts of manufacturing (though the Swiss financial sector appears to cope well with a small domestic market). Even without these problems, two points must be recalled from Chapter 11: the size of the service-sector surplus has been curbed by the growth of British expenditure on foreign tourism; and the service-sector surplus has been unable to finance the deterioration in the manufacturing deficit since the mid-1980s. A final and crushing consideration needs to be added; when North Sea oil runs out, the problems become immense (Keegan 1985; Godley 1988: 13). There is no real prospect of service-sector trade filling a gap of this size. The shrinkage of the manufacturing sector is therefore a real problem both for the present and for the future.

# Chapter 13

# The labour market

At the start of the postwar period, once demobilisation was complete, the British work-force was overwhelmingly male, working a 48-hour week, with approximately equal numbers involved in industry and the service sector. By the 1990s there was a significantly bigger, more diverse labour force. The hard core in heavy industry had substantially diminished, work patterns had changed with the enormous growth of part-time employment and there was a much more even balance between males and females. Unemployment, which had been at almost insignificant levels in the late 1940s, re-emerged in the 1970s and since 1979 has been at levels which compare with the interwar period.

## EMPLOYMENT

The main changes in employment can be seen in Figure 13.1. Total employment rose for two decades until 1966, after which there has been stagnation before a rapid fall in the early 1980s and strong recovery thereafter. Male employment also peaked in the mid-1960s but has not regained its previous peak. The number of women workers, on the other hand, has expanded strongly since 1948, having been checked only by the sharp downturns after 1979 and 1990. Women made up 32 per cent of the work-force in 1951, 38 per cent in 1971 and now comprise almost 45 per cent. The number of full-time women workers has changed little since 1950, but the number of female part-timers has grown rapidly. Almost half the female work-force is now employed on a part-time basis (Table 13.1) compared with 10 per cent in 1951. The number of male part-timers has also expanded, but to nothing like the same extent. The growth of part-time work for women is visible in other OECD nations but not on the same scale as Britain (Dex 1985: 5; Rubery 1992: 607).

At the sectoral level, the main changes in employment follow from the changes in output discussed in Chapter 12. The production industries (manufacturing, construction, gas, electricity and water) accounted for just under half total employment in the 1950s and 1960s but have

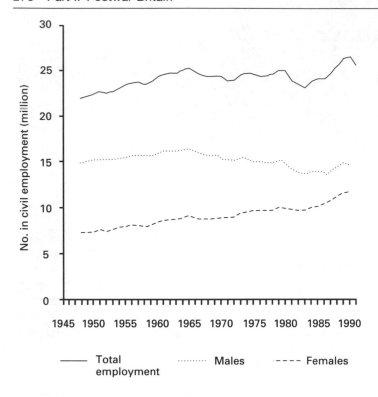

Figure 13.1 Changes in civilian employment, 1948–91
Source: Annual Abstract of Statistics, various issues.

Table 13.1 Growth of part-time employment in Britain, 1951–91 (employees in employment, all industries, thousands)

|  | Males | | | | Females | | | | All |
|---|---|---|---|---|---|---|---|---|---|
|  | Full-time | Part-time | All | % part-time | Full-time | Part-time | All | % part-time |  |
| 1951 | 13,438 | 45 | 13,483 | 0.3 | 5,752 | 754 | 6,506 | 11.6 | 19,989 |
| 1961 | 13,852 | 174 | 14,026 | 1.2 | 5,351 | 1,892 | 7,243 | 26.1 | 21,269 |
| 1971 | 12,840 | 584 | 13,424 | 4.4 | 5,467 | 2,757 | 8,224 | 33.5 | 21,648 |
| 1981 | 11,511 | 718 | 12,164 | 5.9 | 5,321 | 4,141 | 9,462 | 43.8 | 21,105 |
| 1991 | 10,432 | 1,015 | 11,447 | 8.9 | 5,962 | 4,738 | 10,664 | 44.4 | 22,112 |

Sources: Robinson 1988: 116; Employment Gazette, August 1993.

*Table 13.2* Proportions of the British work-force employed in different
sectors, 1931–91 (%)

|      | Primary$^a$ | Production$^b$ | Services | Not known |
|------|---------|------------|----------|-----------|
| 1931 | 11.9    | 37.0       | 50.6     | 0.5       |
| 1951 | 8.9     | 43.6       | 47.4     | 0.1       |
| 1961 | 6.6     | 44.3       | 48.7     | 0.4       |
| 1966 | 5.4     | 44.0       | 50.3     | 0.3       |
| 1971 | 4.3     | 42.9       | 52.8     | —         |
| 1976 | 3.3     | 39.5       | 57.2     | —         |
| 1981 | 3.2     | 35.3       | 61.5     | —         |
| 1986 | 2.6     | 30.6       | 66.8     | —         |
| 1991 | 1.9     | 26.9       | 71.2     | —         |

*Notes*:
a Before 1975: agriculture, forestry, fishing, mining and quarrying; after 1975:
   agriculture, forestry, fishing, coal, oil and natural gas extraction and processing.
b Manufacturing, gas, water, electricity, construction.
*Source*: *Annual Abstract of Statistics*, various issues.

contracted rapidly since 1966 (Table 13.2). The main cause has been the
loss of manufacturing jobs, which is illustrated in Table 13.3 (which is in
two parts because of major changes in the standard industrial classification). Between 1950 and 1965, employment grew in most heavier engineering industries, with shipbuilding and vehicles being the main
exceptions. After 1965, all manufacturing industries experienced job
losses, with the worst falls in the same heavier engineering sectors and
the 'older', lighter sectors like textiles, clothing, leather and footwear
which have long been in relative decline. Table 13.3 also illustrates the
spectacular contraction of employment in agriculture and coalmining
throughout the postwar period. In very broad terms, employment
appears to have been more resilient since 1965 in lighter industries
(like food, drink and tobacco; paper and printing; timber, rubber, plastics) than the heavier metal-bashing sectors but manufacturing employment as a whole has taken an enormous tumble (falling from 8.9 million
in the peak year of 1966 to 6.8 million in 1979 and 4.1 million in 1993). By
comparison, employment in the service sector has increased strongly,
with only minor falls in the slumps of the early 1980s and early 1990s
(Table 13.4). Only transport and communications has shown major job
losses in services over the postwar period. The impression that the
downswing of the early 1990s hurt the service sector is clearly a myth,
probably circulated by estate agents.

These very different trends of employment in the production and
service sectors help to explain the gender pattern with which we
began. Clearly, not all the jobs lost in the production industries were
of full-time, male workers but the declines in agriculture, coal-mining,
manufacturing and building are primarily responsible for the fall in male

*Table 13.3* Index numbers of employment in primary and production industries, 1950–91 (1975 = 100)

|  | 1950 | 1965 | 1975 |
|---|---|---|---|
| Agriculture, forestry, fishing | 314 | 123 | 100 |
| Mining and quarrying | 241 | 178 | 100 |
| Manufacturing | 110 | 122 | 100 |
| Food, drink, tobacco | 113 | 115 | 100 |
| Chemicals | 110 | 121 | 100 |
| Metal manufacture | 109 | 127 | 100 |
| Mechanical engineering | 92 | 137 | 100 |
| Electrical engineering | 74 | 115 | 100 |
| Shipbuilding and marine engineering | 167 | 119 | 100 |
| Vehicles | 135 | 115 | 100 |
| Other metal goods | 92 | 109 | 100 |
| Textiles | 191 | 154 | 100 |
| Leather | 188 | 144 | 100 |
| Clothing, footwear | 175 | 139 | 100 |
| Bricks, pottery, glass, cement | 120 | 130 | 100 |
| Timber, furniture | 120 | 114 | 100 |
| Paper, printing, publishing | 92 | 114 | 100 |
| Other manufacturing | 77 | 101 | 100 |
| Construction | 117 | 130 | 100 |
| Gas, electricity, water | 109 | 119 | 100 |
| Whole economy | 93 | 105 | 100 |

|  | 1975 | 1979 | 1982 | 1989 | 1991 |
|---|---|---|---|---|---|
| Agriculture, forestry, fishery | 100 | 93 | 87 | 72 | 69 |
| Coal, oil, gas | 100 | 99 | 92 | 47 | 42 |
| Energy, water | 100 | 99 | 95 | 80 | 78 |
| Manufacturing | 100 | 97 | 78 | 69 | 63 |
| Metal manufacture | 100 | 92 | 67 | 49 | 45 |
| Chemicals, fibres | 100 | 101 | 85 | 76 | 71 |
| Mechanical engineering | 100 | 98 | 80 | 73 | 65 |
| Office machines, electrical engineering, precision instruments | 100 | 98 | 84 | 75 | 68 |
| Motor vehicles and parts | 100 | 101 | 69 | 57 | 48 |
| Other transport equipment | 100 | 94 | 84 | 57 | 55 |
| Other metal goods | 100 | 96 | 73 | 63 | 54 |
| Food, drink, tobacco | 100 | 98 | 87 | 73 | 72 |
| Textiles, leather, footwear, clothing | 100 | 91 | 66 | 59 | 47 |
| Timber, furniture, rubber, plastics | 100 | 98 | 79 | 88 | 80 |
| Paper, printing, publishing | 100 | 98 | 89 | 88 | 83 |
| Construction | 100 | 100 | 86 | 87 | 80 |
| Whole economy | 100 | 102 | 86 | 87 | 80 |

*Source: Annual Abstract of Statistics*, various issues.

Table 13.4 Index numbers of employment in services, 1950–91[a] (1975 = 100)

|  | 1950 | 1965 | 1975 | 1979 | 1982 | 1989 | 1991 |
|---|---|---|---|---|---|---|---|
| Distribution | 70 | 99 | 100 | 105 | 101 | 112 | 111 |
| Hotels, catering | 83 | 77 | 100 | 113 | 116 | 145 | 150 |
| Transport, communications | 189 | 109 | 100 | 99 | 92 | 91 | 90 |
| Financial services | 30 | 44 | 100 | 110 | 121 | 177 | 179 |
| Public administration | 73 | 70 | 100 | 101 | 94 | 97 | 101 |
| Education | 37 | 75 | 100 | 105 | 100 | 112 | 111 |
| Medical and health services | 53 | 82 | 100 | 107 | 113 | 128 | 134 |
| Other services[b] | — | — | 100 | 114 | 118 | 152 | 151 |
| All services | 46 | 90 | 100 | 106 | 105 | 122 | 123 |
| Whole economy | 93 | 105 | 100 | 102 | 94 | 100 | 98 |

Notes:
a Data for the period 1975–91 are based on consistent definitions, but information for both 1950 and 1965 is subject to error arising from changes in classification.
b As this category is a residual, errors from changing classification would be concentrated here, so no figures have been given for 1950 and 1965 when errors are likely.
Sources: Annual Abstract of Statistics, various issues; Employment Gazette, August 1993.

employment. Although service-sector employment for males has increased over the postwar period, there has been substantial growth of female (often part-time) employment in distribution, hotel and catering, financial services, local authority and health service work, all of which have a very long history of employing women on low-paid, insecure work (Dex 1985: 95–9). Cost has been an important consideration for employers in both public and private sectors. Part-time workers have been cheap because until 1994 employers have paid lower statutory and occupational welfare contributions than for full-timers (Robinson 1988: 128–30) and employers have been able to expand the provision of services into weekends and evenings, without incurring the cost of overtime and premium payments to full-timers, especially in shops, banks, and the 'leisure industry'.

The growth of part-time work seems to have matched employers' demand for cheap and flexible workers with an increasing supply of women who have been unable or unwilling, because of child care or other responsibilities, to commit to a 'conventional' working week. The vast majority of part-time female workers have been married or single parents (Robinson 1988: 120). Unfortunately the reality is much less satisfactory. Part-time workers have low pay, minimal skills, few opportunities for training or promotion and little job security (Bruegel 1986;

Robinson 1988: 126–34). Employers of part-time workers want cheap labour which can be varied quickly and inexpensively.

An explanation of the main trends in the labour market may lie in the theories of the internal labour market (Doeringer and Piore 1971) and segmentation between primary and secondary labour markets (Doeringer and Bosanquet 1973). Firms with an internal labour market recruit their workers into a limited number of entry jobs and rely upon training and promotion to fill the majority of higher-level positions which tend to be arranged into something like a promotional hierarchy. The firm also tries to provide long-run stable employment for its core workers and fixes wages more according to internal administrative principles than to market forces. To meet fluctuations in demand, the firm will recruit peripheral workers who do not enjoy the same long-term continuity of employment or access to training and employment. Theories of labour market segmentation emphasise the distinction between a primary market which offers relatively high wages, good working conditions, job security and promotion prospects whereas jobs in the secondary market tend to be low-paid, with poor conditions, little chance of advancement and little job security (Piore 1975: 126). Movement towards internal labour markets has been slow and unsteady in comparison with the USA, Japan and Germany: in some firms recruitment procedures improved, internal promotion ladders were extended, and training was developed (Gospel 1992: 148–67). There is also some evidence of the development of primary and secondary markets with surveys showing that before 1979 60 per cent of male workers enjoyed long-run stability of employment (Main 1982) and that unemployment was concentrated on a relatively small section of the labour force (Disney 1979). A comparatively recent survey of British employers found relatively little trace of segmented labour markets, except in such large public sector institutions as hospitals and universities (MacInnes 1987). It has also become clear that segmented labour market theory is insufficiently refined to grasp the full implications of the growth and structure of female employment since 1950 (Dex 1985: 136–42).

## UNEMPLOYMENT

For three decades after the war there was widespread confidence in the ability of the government to deliver full employment. The 1944 Employment Policy white paper had been deliberately vague about targets, referring merely to 'high and stable employment' (Chapter 8), but in 1951 the Labour government committed itself publicly to keeping unemployment below 3 per cent (Tomlinson 1987: 122). Before 1975, that figure was exceeded only four times, and three of those were after

Table 13.5 The rate of unemployment in the UK, 1945–94 (annual averages, %)

| | Old basis of calculation[a] | |
|---|---|---|
| 1945–64 | 1.8 | |
| 1964–73 | 2.5 | |
| 1973–9 | 3.8 | |
| | Old basis[a] | Latest basis[a] |
| 1979 | 5.7 | 4.0 |
| 1980 | 7.4 | 5.1 |
| 1981 | 11.4 | 8.1 |
| 1982 | — | 9.5 |
| 1983 | — | 10.5 |
| 1984 | — | 10.7 |
| 1985 | — | 10.9 |
| 1986 | — | 11.1 |
| 1987 | — | 10.0 |
| 1988 | — | 8.1 |
| 1989 | — | 6.3 |
| 1990 | — | 5.8 |
| 1991 | — | 8.0 |
| 1992 | — | 9.8 |
| 1993 | — | 10.4 |
| 1994 | — | 9.8[b] |

Notes:
a Before 1982, the system of calculating unemployment was to count those who registered at Job Centres. The first change in the system was to count those who claimed benefit at Unemployment Benefit Centres. Since that time, numerous changes to the system have tended to exclude one group after another from the count of claimant unemployment. There have also been substantial changes to the way employment has been defined which have an obvious impact on statistics of the rate of claimant unemployment. The best guide to changes in both series is Johnson 1988: 81–104. The Employment Gazette of April 1989 produced in its Historical Supplement revised figures for the period down to 1971 using the latest definitions. The average rate of claimant unemployment for the period 1973–79 on this basis was 3.4 per cent, and should be contrasted with the figure in the Table.
b Average of first quarter, seasonally adjusted.
Sources: Annual Abstract of Statistics, various issues; Employment Gazette, Historical Supplement, April 1989; Employment Gazette, May 1994.

1970. From 1945 to the mid-1960s the average annual unemployment rate was 1.8 per cent, representing about 400,000 out of work (Table 13.5).

At the regional level, wide disparities continued with the highest rates of unemployment again recorded in the interwar 'depressed areas' (Table 13.6). But the extent of the all-round improvement before 1973 cannot be denied and on an international scale Britain had comparatively low unemployment during the long boom (Broadberry 1991: 228).

However, even before the mid-1970s there was a tendency for the

*Table 13.6* Regional unemployment rates, 1937–92 (annual averages, %)

|  | 1937 | 1951 | 1964 | 1973 | 1979 | 1986 | 1989 | 1992 |
|---|---|---|---|---|---|---|---|---|
| South East | { 5.4 | 0.9 | 1.0 } | 1.3 | 2.9 | 8.3 | 3.9 | 9.4 |
| East Anglia | { 5.4 | 0.9 | 1.0 } | 1.6 | 3.7 | 8.6 | 3.6 | 7.8 |
| South West | 6.8 | 1.2 | 1.5 | 2.1 | 4.6 | 9.6 | 4.5 | 9.4 |
| West Midlands | { 6.6 } | 0.4 | 0.9 | 1.7 | 4.7 | 12.7 | 6.7 | 10.6 |
| East Midlands | { 6.6 } | { 0.7 | 1.1 } | 1.8 | 3.8 | 10.2 | 5.5 | 9.1 |
| Yorks and Humber | 12.0 | { 0.7 | 1.1 } | 2.3 | 4.7 | 12.6 | 7.5 | 10.0 |
| North West | 12.8 | 1.2 | 2.1 | 2.9 | 5.9 | 14.1 | 8.6 | 10.8 |
| North | 16.7 | 2.2 | 3.3 | 3.9 | 7.3 | 15.3 | 10.2 | 11.3 |
| Wales | 20.7 | 2.7 | 2.6 | 3.0 | 6.3 | 13.9 | 7.5 | 10.0 |
| Scotland | 14.0 | 2.5 | 3.6 | 3.8 | 6.8 | 14.0 | 9.3 | 9.5 |
| N. Ireland | 21.7 | 6.1 | 6.6 | 4.9 | 9.7 | 18.6 | 14.5 | 14.2 |
| UK | 10.1 | 1.3 | 1.7 | 2.0 | 4.7 | 11.3 | 7.9 | 13.3 |

*Source*: *Annual Abstract of Statistics*, various issues.

unemployment level to rise slightly at each successive trough of the postwar economic cycle and the average rate of wage inflation began to creep upwards. In the late 1950s, Phillips (1958) claimed to have found a stable, long-standing link between annual changes in unemployment and the rate of change of money wages. The 'Phillips curve' implied that workers and their unions exploited tight labour markets to push up wages and that the remedy was higher unemployment or policy to restrain income growth. The Phillips curve aroused fierce debates (see Glynn 1991: 102) but by the mid-1960s many British economists believed that a new 'scientific' device permitted policy-makers to select the combination of inflation and unemployment which best suited their priorities. However, from 1960 the real world began to change in unpredictable ways. Unemployment and inflation began to rise together.

The seemingly inexorable rise of inflation and unemployment in the fifteen years after 1960 raised fundamental questions for the Keynesian orthodoxy and British economic policy, particularly in the early 1970s when unemployment approached one million for the first time since the 1930s. Unemployment and inflation were driven upwards by rising costs and shifts in the terms of trade and provoked an intense campaign from organised labour for government to honour its apparent commitment to full employment (Gourevitch *et al.* 1984: ch. 1). From the economic and political crises of the mid-1970s, new priorities began to emerge. Successive prime ministers, James Callaghan and Margaret Thatcher, tried to convince the British electorate that governments could not control the rate of unemployment. New ideas were beginning to influence the conduct of economic policy in Britain (see Chapters 9 and 14).

By the 1970s, it was already accepted that the main direct cause of Britain's postwar full employment had been the secular rise in investment after 1945 (Matthews 1968). The widespread belief that governments were committed to full employment had undoubtedly altered business expectations and indirectly contributed to expansion, but government policy had not been the cause of full employment. In the 1960s and 1970s, however, Friedman and others developed and refined the classical view to demonstrate that full employment could not be secured by governments. Friedman argued that unemployment was caused not by macroeconomic forces but by real market factors including labour force skills and flexibility, national levels of entrepreneurial talent, and the duration of job search as described in Chapter 5 (Friedman 1977). He defined the impact of these influences as 'the natural rate of unemployment' of the economy in equilibrium with non-accelerating inflation, usually termed the non-accelerating-inflation-rate-of-unemployment, or NAIRU. Government monetary expansion could push unemployment below this level but only for a short time and at the cost of rising inflation. Markets, basing their anticipations of future prices on past experience, would initially underestimate the inflationary impact of monetary expansion. This theory of 'adaptive expectations' has however met fierce criticism from other US economists working in the new classical tradition. The proponents of rational expectations analysis argue that markets adjust their price expectations on the basis of the most informed concepts. Thus, monetary expansion results only in higher inflation and unemployment does not budge from the natural rate. The natural rate itself is controversial because there is nothing 'natural' about labour market frictions and rigidities, especially if (as discussed below) they can be related to policy or institutions. But, as noted in Chapter 5, the idea of the NAIRU has become widely accepted by labour economists (see Layard *et al.* 1991).

The real market factors which affect the equilibrium rate of unemployment arise from two main sources: the benefit system and wage bargaining arrangements (Layard *et al.* 1991: 10–11). The benefit system affects unemployment by altering the duration of job search (see the comments on the analysis of Benjamin and Kochin in Chapter 5). The impact of the wage bargaining system depends on the strength of unions (powerful unions can force employers to pay higher wages than is justified by productivity levels, sacrificing competitiveness and jobs) and, more controversially, on the structure of bargaining organisations. Where wages are negotiated on a centralised basis (for the whole economy – as in Scandinavia) unions will be under enormous economic and political pressure to fix wages which will stabilise employment (Calmfors and Driffill 1988; Freeman 1988). In decentralised systems (wages fixed at the industry or firm level) labour economists have distinguished between 'insiders' and 'outsiders'. 'Insiders' are those in employment who will be concerned mainly about wage levels and comparatively little about the needs of the unemployed. If demand for the industry's or firm's products increases, insiders will press for higher wages for those in employment rather than additional jobs (Layard *et al*. 1991: 129–38). Thus, real wages will rise despite unemployment. The unemployed may lose their skills and become less attractive to potential employers; mass unemployment will persist and long-term unemployment will become an increasing problem. Thus, 'insider power' can lead to the combination of rising real wages for those in work and increasing duration of unemployment for those out of work.

The Thatcher government, much influenced by Friedmanite ideas, began an attack on equilibrium unemployment in the 1980s by reducing the relative level of state benefits (Chapter 10) and making access to those benefits more difficult – even though the evidence for benefit-induced unemployment has been extremely slim, especially since the 1960s (Broadberry 1991: 222–4) – and legal curbs on union power. The effect on the labour market was, however, swamped by the negative effects of the government's monetary policy which weakened competitiveness in home and export markets (Chapter 11). The reduction of demand was the primary cause of rising unemployment (Layard and Nickell 1986: 164). There was an enormous 'shake-out' of labour in 1980–1, as can be seen in the divergent paths of output and employment in the mid-1980s. Output began to pick up in 1982, but unemployment went on rising, as far as we can tell from the data, until the end of 1986. Despite the rise in unemployment during the slump of the early 1980s, real wages surged ahead, especially in manufacturing where job losses were most severe. Insider power apparently enabled those in employment to use the substantial rises in manufacturing productivity in the early 1980s (see below) to extract higher wages in unpropitious circumstances.

The second half of the 1970s saw a sea-change in British labour market history, marking the end of 'full employment' in both the operational and conceptual senses (Aldcroft 1984). The government's ability to meet its full employment target before 1975 was noted above (see also Table 13.5). In 1972, the Heath government was forced into a major reflationary stimulus as a result of rising unemployment (Blackaby 1987b: 63–4). The Labour governments which followed however relaxed their adherence to Keynesian policies (Jones 1987: 104) but attempted to support the labour market by subsidies to industry. In 1980–1, even these props to the labour market were withdrawn. Macro-economic policy was concerned solely with the conquest of inflation and industrial subsidies were pruned to restrain public spending (Johnson 1991: ch. 7). As jobless totals began to rise in the early 1980s, the political resonance of unemployment diminished. In 1983, the Conservatives won the first postwar general election to be held under mass unemployment by concentrating on foreign and defence policies following the Falklands War. Unemployment is no longer a major political issue; in 1992 the government won the first general election since 1931 to be held in the depths of a slump. As in the interwar years, the unemployed became a marginalised minority who were increasingly held to be responsible for their own condition, a perception unshaken by the rise of unemployment in London and the south east during the 1990s (Table 13.6). During the 1980s, political parties focused their attentions increasingly on the employed majority.

As unemployment has risen since the 1970s, so echoes of the interwar years have been heard ever more loudly. As in the 1920s, there have been frequent 'adjustments' of the official unemployment statistics as the government tried to deflect criticism of its economic policies. British official unemployment statistics had long been out of line with other OECD countries, so revision was required. However, the changes were piecemeal, frequent and invariably timed to ease political pressure on the government; of more than twenty revisions made since 1979, only one has added to the official count of the unemployed (Johnson 1988: 88–93). Unemployment has again been concentrated on manual and on unskilled non-manual workers such as shop assistants (Layard and Nickell 1986: 123); it has tended to be lower among females than males (Humphries and Rubery 1992) and again there is evidence of a 'discouraged worker effect' on women during the slump of the early 1980s (Owen and Joshi 1987). The high rates of company collapse in the slumps of the 1980s and 1990s have brought a rise in the number of managerial workers out of work, but manual workers in manufacturing accounted for the bulk of the increase in unemployment in both depressions. It is also likely that since 1980 unemployment has been comparatively high among older workers, as it was during the interwar years, but a number of the more substantial 'adjustments' of the unemployment statistics have taken the older unemployed off the register. The onset of mass unemployment in the 1980s has resulted in the re-emergence of long-term unemployment. Just as in the 1930s, as unemployment has risen so duration has increased (Table 13.7). In 1986, a higher proportion of the male unemployed (58 per cent) has been out of work for more than 12 months than was recorded at any time during the 1930s. However, manipulation of official statistics has been especially effective at removing the long-term unemployed, so the data after 1986 are worthless.

The most striking differences from the interwar pattern have been the emergence of a youth unemployment problem and very high rates of unemployment among some ethnic minorities in the 1980s. A 'juvenile

*Table 13.7* Duration of unemployment, 1974–93 (all workers, July figures, percentage of total unemployed in each category)

|  | > 4 weeks | 4–26 weeks | 26–52 weeks | 52 < weeks |
|---|---|---|---|---|
| 1974 | 31.9 | 34.3 | 12.1 | 21.6 |
| 1979 | 24.0 | 36.3 | 15.2 | 24.5 |
| 1982 | 12.2 | 33.1 | 21.2 | 33.6 |
| 1986 | 11.6 | 28.1 | 19.2 | 41.1 |
| 1989 | 14.0 | 29.8 | 18.1 | 38.1 |
| 1993 | 12.3 | 30.1 | 20.7 | 36.9 |

*Source Employment Gazette*, various issues.

unemployment problem' did not exist between the wars, though there was real concern about youngsters entering jobs which had no prospects (Chapter 5). In 1986, when official unemployment figures at last began to fall after the slump of 1980–2, the rate of unemployment for those in the first year after school was running at 30 per cent and was over 50 per cent in some areas (Walker and Barton 1986). Young people faced problems entering an oversupplied labour market in which many employers were uninterested in training or recruiting (White 1987). The rapidly expanding special measures for the young unemployed (see below) have had only limited impact; in 1992 the unemployment rate amongst 18–19 year olds is almost 20 per cent, despite the proliferation of training places (*Employment Gazette*, August 1993). It is also clear that unemployment rates are higher amongst some ethnic minorities at all ages. In the spring of 1992, the government's labour force survey revealed that unemployment was more than twice the white rate amongst blacks (Caribbean, African and other black people of non-mixed origin) and almost three times higher amongst those of Pakistani and Bangladeshi origin (*Social Trends* 1993). There is no reason to believe that these proportions are in any way atypical of postwar experience (Holmes 1991: 226).

## WAGES

Since the Second World War, economists have tried to understand and model the behaviour of wages but with limited success. The wage equation in most econometric models is not infrequently 'overridden' (a technical term used by econometricians when they cross out the predicted figures and write in what actually happened) whenever wages do anything even slightly unusual (Surrey 1985: 450). The main difficulty for economists is that the neo-classical tools of supply and demand are unhelpful because empirical studies persistently show a large dispersion of wages paid to individuals doing the same or comparable jobs (Brown and Nolan 1988). Pay is the outcome of a collective bargaining process which orthodox economics is ill-equipped to study.

There is however a long-standing theme in labour economics that trade unions' 'monopoly' control of labour supply is the principal factor determining wages. Surveys have consistently revealed a 'trade union mark up', with unionists receiving higher wages than non-unionists in the same industry (Layard *et al*. 1991: 26–7). But it is extremely rare to find two groups of workers identical in every respect – skill levels, industry, region – except that one group is unionised and the other is not (Parsley 1980). There is moreover evidence from the USA that unionised workers are more productive than their unorganised counter-parts and merit their higher pay (Freeman and Medoff 1984). Despite these warnings, neo-classical labour economists continue to be suspicious of those organisations, like trade unions, which seek collective representation in markets. Hines (1964; 1969), for example, blamed 'union pushfulness' for rising wages between 1948 and 1962, but his ideas have been largely discredited (Purdy and Zis 1974; Wilkinson and Burket 1973). Crude models of trade union power have more recently been supplanted by insider-outsider theories of the type considered above, but empirical support is equally unconvincing (Richardson 1991; 438–9). Attempts to portray inflation as a process driven by union power have been unsuccessful but, to anticipate the discussion of Chapter 14, so have explanations which see changes in money as the main cause of inflation.

Any account of actual movements of wages in the British economy since 1945 must begin with the institutional framework. In the late 1940s, the government gradually removed its wartime controls over pay bargaining and labour mobility and restored the *voluntary system of industrial relations*, that is a system in which the law plays a minor part in collective bargaining over wages, conditions and procedures for resolving disputes. During the long boom, most industries had multi-union and multi-employer bargaining over wages and conditions for certain classes of labour. But these national, industry-wide agreements were skeletal, leaving much to be decided at the workplace (Gospel 1992: 158–9). In the tight labour market, employers competed fiercely especially for skilled labour. Firms were less inhibited about the growth of wages than they had been in the interwar years because they could pass on higher costs to consumers. As a result, a gap ('wage drift') opened in some industries between pay set in industry-wide agreements and actual pay fixed at plant level. In the late 1940s, employers tried to drive productivity forward by using systems of payments-by-results, or piecework (Zweig 1951). However, piecework handed control over the pace of work to the work-force and during the long boom shopfloor workers raised pay rates in local bargaining while retaining control over the pace of work. Thus, pay began to rise more rapidly than underlying productivity, in sharp contrast to interwar experience. In a number of industries in the 1960s, industrial relations deteriorated, with increasing numbers of strikes over pay and control (Gospel 1992: 161), especially in motor car manufacture (Lewchuk 1986: 148–9).

Strikes, wage drift and disorderly industrial relations posed problems for governments as much as for employers. In 1965 the Labour government appointed a royal commission under Lord Donovan which reported that in the late 1960s Britain had two systems of industrial relations, a formal system based on industry-wide collective bargaining and an informal system at the workplace, which were in conflict

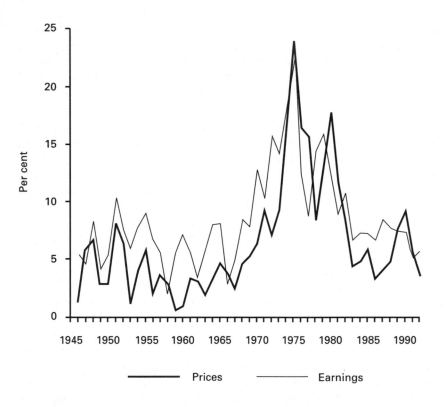

*Figure 13.2* Changes in prices[a] and earnings[b], 1946–92 (annual average percentage change)

Notes:
a Retail prices index.
b Average weekly earnings of male, full-time, manual workers.
Source: Annual Abstract of Statistics, various issues.

(Donovan 1968). Donovan proposed to strengthen workplace bargaining, encouraging firms to establish their own formal collective agreements and take responsibility for the pay, conditions and grievance procedures of their own workers. Structures have changed as Donovan had hoped; by 1978, two-thirds of all manual and three-quarters of all non-manual employees were covered by a formal bargaining structure of single-employer agreements (Robinson 1985: 334). But average earnings have risen faster than both retail prices and output per head (Hickling 1981: 82–3; *Employment Gazette* August 1993).

Rising prices and wages weaken international competitiveness. Direct price control is held to be inefficient, so attempts have been made to restrain wages. Direct control over wages has a high potential to create conflict, but incomes policy has been seen by many postwar governments as better than using unemployment to curb labour costs. Any method of restraining income growth raises important issues about the distribution of income, wealth and power, as well as efficiency and governments have frequently preferred to proceed by consent. Incomes policy has usually amounted to little more than exhortation, but accompanied by some form of threat. In the early 1950s, for example, Conservative ministers openly urged TUC leaders to restrain pay and, behind the scenes, hinted that statutory controls would follow if wage increases exceeded productivity growth (Booth 1995a). More vigorous policies have also been applied. A statutory limit to pay (and price) increases was imposed in both the mid-1960s and early 1970s and in the late 1940s and late 1970s there were 'voluntary' policies which differed little from the full statutory regime (Brittan and Lilley 1977: 154–5). Incomes policy is commonly seen as the archetypal corporatist measure, when leaders of government, employers and unions formulate policy without control from the formal political system (Panitch 1976). However, British statutory incomes policies have typically been very different, beginning with wage freezes, imposed by government without reference to unions or employers in the interest of short-term crisis management, usually prompted by the balance of payments. The British problem (visible in Figure 13.2 in the rising gap between earnings and prices in 1966–70 and 1978–9) has been to return to voluntary collective bargaining without undue disruption. Economists' studies of this 're-entry problem' tend to show that any deceleration in wage growth during the 'severe' phase is compensated when policy is relaxed (Parkin and Sumner 1972; Henry and Ormerod 1978). Incomes policies have engineered short-run falls in real wages in 1948–9, 1966–7, 1972–3 and 1976–7. Ministers were no doubt grateful for such small mercies. Only in the later 1970s did governments attempt to build a framework for longer-term control of incomes (Jones 1987: 110). This 'social contract' began with a tight, and successful, crisis period but the government miscalculated the politics of longer-term control. The resulting 'winter of discontent' dealt Labour government a political body-blow (Chapter 9) but has also terminated Britain's experiment with overt incomes policies, whether short- or long-term. Since 1979, Conservative governments have calculated that the political costs of incomes policy are unbearable and have turned to high unemployment, high exchange and interest rates to encourage employers to control wages. But even these governments have been unable to dispense entirely with incomes policies. Since the introduction in 1976 of cash limits on public expenditure, governments have needed to estimate the increase in public sector pay, and so informal pay guidelines have been imposed. Those guidelines have become formal in the 1990s as public spending has once more caused political concern.

There has been a substantial literature on wage restraint, but comparatively little on measures to raise the incomes of some of those in work, particularly the low-paid. Aid to the low-paid has followed three main routes – wage councils, family income supplement/family credit, and preferential treatment in incomes policies. Direct intervention in the wages of the low-paid began in 1909, with the establishment of 'trade boards' to fix minimum wages in the 'sweated trades'. In 1945, the boards were re-named wages councils and their coverage was extended so that by 1979 minimum wages were fixed in 47 industries. They were, however, widely regarded as ineffective (Atkinson 1975). Family income supplement was introduced in 1971 to provide means-tested benefits for those in work but receiving low incomes. However, total household income for recipients has remained below state benefit levels (Lowe 1993: 145). Statutory incomes policies have often been accompanied by provisions to give proportionately more help to the low-paid on grounds of 'fairness'. However, the economic effects were negligible (Dean 1978) and the political costs of miscalculation enormous, as the 'winter of discontent' revealed. Since 1979, government policy to the low-paid has virtually disappeared. The responsibilities of wage councils have been curtailed, and in 1993 all their functions in relation to adult workers have been abolished, causing falls in the relative pay of the low-paid. Only family credit, the successor to FIS, remains to support them.

The low-paid are disproportionately made up of female workers. At every level at which comparisons are made, male rates of pay tend to be higher than those for females, and earnings differentials are wider still because of the very high proportion of women workers employed on a part-time basis. As noted in Chapter 8, during the Second World War (and in the First) women factory workers performed tasks equal to those of the male workers who had been conscripted into the forces. At the same time, male-dominated craft unions did not want to see those jobs which had been assigned to women for the duration of the war permanently modified or redesignated as semi-skilled (Summerfield 1984: ch. 7). For short-term tactical reasons, unions rallied behind calls for equal pay for men and women but the achievements were very limited, in part because of the machinations of Churchill and Conservative traditionalists (Thane 1991: 184–91). Thereafter, the question of equal pay languished until the 1960s, when it was given new impetus by the combination of the rise of the feminist movement, strikes for equal pay in industry, and a growing sense that the actual and potential skills of women workers were being lost because of prejudice and discrimination. The Equal Pay Act of 1970 finally gave legal backing for equal pay for equal work and the Sex Discrimination Act of 1975 attempted to deal with the discriminatory processes which excluded women from higher earning occupations, establishing the first Equal Opportunities Commission (Thane 1991: 206–7). The anti-discriminatory momentum has been maintained during the 1980s in EU policy and legislation (Hoskyns 1986) and has blunted the British government's drive to encourage women to withdraw from paid labour to undertake tasks within the home which had formerly been provided by state welfare agencies (Hamnett *et al*. 1989: 189–93). There is some evidence to suggest that the Equal Pay Act has closed the gap between men and women's pay, with women's full-time earnings rising from approximately two-thirds to closer to three-quarters of the male rate (Tzannatos and Zabalza 1984). But women workers continue to have more difficulty than men in securing promotion.

Governments have also had limited success in reducing earnings differentials arising from differences in ethnic origin. The Race Relations Act of 1968 made it unlawful to discriminate on grounds of race, colour, ethnic or national origin in employment. But Blackaby (1976) has estimated that, other things being equal, non-white males earned approximately 9 per cent less than white males. But non-white males also find it much more difficult to enter occupations which have high wages, so the gap between average white and non-white male earnings is approximately twice this level (Brown 1984). The same problems confront black women in the labour market (Phizacklea 1982; Mama 1988). Thus there is widespread evidence of discrimination in the labour market on non-economic grounds.

## UNIONS

In previous sections, the trade unions have emerged, at least in the eyes of many social scientists, as villains of the postwar labour market, but villains who remain unconvicted because the evidence has never quite been strong enough. It might come as a surprise, therefore, to learn that the trade union movement emerged from the Second World War with high membership, density above even the best interwar year and very high public esteem after its role in wartime policy-making (Barnes and Reid 1982). But even under the Attlee government, trade union leaders complained that their influence had evaporated and in the 1950s rising industrial unrest and creeping inflation (which Conservative politicians were keen to blame on union greed) weakened the unions' standing in public opinion. In the 1960s, governments needed union co-operation when interventionist economic policies came back into fashion, but the unions' political decline continued. Divisions in union ranks were exacerbated by leadership participation in the making and implementation of incomes policies. The unfavourable impression created by disunity was aggravated in the 1970s by growing levels of industrial conflict (Figure 13.3), for which unions were blamed. Despite this deteriorating political position, union strength at the workplace continued to grow, especially under closed shop agreements (under which only union members could be employed) and with the rejuvenation of public sector unionism. However, politically weak trade unions were powerless to counter the reforming zeal of the Thatcher government which came to office in 1979 convinced that trade union power was a key component of the British disease. The government began a major legislative programme to weaken union institutions (in particular the closed shop) and eject them from the policy-making process. Rising unemployment in the 1980s decisively weakened trade unions and membership began to contract steadily (Figure 13.3).

Figure 13.3 also gives estimates of union density, defined here as the proportion of those in employment who belong to trade unions. Density can vary because of changes in employment or union membership. Aggregate density changed hardly at all from 1945 to 1969, whereupon it rose at a pace which was unprecedented in peacetime (Richardson 1991: 418). After 1979, there was an even sharper fall so that by 1990 density was below the levels of the 1960s. Clearly, the rise of unemployment, changes in the composition of employment (away from full-time male manual jobs in manufacturing which unions have traditionally found easy to organise towards the more difficult part-time, service-sector employment for females) and the impact of legislation all play a part in explaining the loss of members, though there is no agreement among labour economists about the exact influence of each of these factors (Carruth and Disney 1988; Green 1992).

If trade union guilt for restricting employment growth, raising unemployment and accelerating inflation is at best unproven, the argument that unions have undermined postwar labour productivity growth appears stronger: unions have been implicated in poor productivity performance before 1979; and since 1979 there have been claims for a 'productivity miracle' in British manufacturing caused by the declining

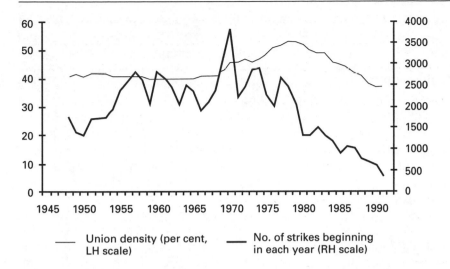

_Figure 13.3_ Changes in union density and strike activity, 1947–92
_Notes_: Union density is the proportion of those in civilian employment who are
    members of trade unions.
_Sources_: Department of Employment and Productivity 1971; _Annual Abstract of_
    _Statistics_, various issues.

union density noted above. The most forceful case that unions constrained productivity growth before 1979 has come from Pratten
(1976), Prais (1981) and Caves (1980). Pratten examined international
companies with plant in the UK, France, Germany or the USA and
found that labour productivity in the UK was consistently below levels
achieved by the same company in other countries. Half the shortfall was
due to what he termed 'behavioural factors' – the impact of unions and
different national attitudes to effort. Prais found that in six of the ten
industries he studied productivity increases had been retarded in the UK
by difficulties in negotiating manning levels with unions. He also found
that British large plant were very strike-prone in the 1970s, reinforcing
Caves's main finding that productivity shortfalls were most common in
the UK in industries where large plant size was the rule. Underpinning
these studies is Mancur Olson's (1982) study of the effects of institutions
on the pace of economic growth. Broadly, Olson argued that the longer a
country experiences social and political stability, the more likely it is to
produce a network of economic interest groups which inhibit the pace of
economic growth. He contends that economic interest groups will tend
to dissolve unless they can find ways of extracting an economic rent
from society (taking out of the economy more than is put in). Social and
political stability facilitates rent-seeking but these institutional strategies
retard the adjustments which are necessary for growth. Thus, politically

*Table 13.8* Institutional structures and labour productivity growth, 1950–79
(rates of growth of GDP per worker-hour)

|  | 1950–73 | 1973–9 |
|---|---|---|
| **High sclerosis:** | | |
| a) Broad scope, high sophistication | | |
| Netherlands | 4.4 | 3.3 |
| Norway | 4.2 | 3.9 |
| Sweden | 4.2 | 1.9 |
| Belgium | 4.4 | 4.2 |
| Mean | 4.3 | 3.3 |
| b) Narrow scope, low sophistication | | |
| Canada | 3.0 | 1.0 |
| USA | 2.6 | 1.4 |
| UK | 3.1 | 2.1 |
| Australia | 2.6 | 2.6 |
| Mean | 2.8 | 1.8 |
| c) Broad scope, low sophistication | | |
| Switzerland | 3.4 | 1.3 |
| d) Narrow scope, high sophistication | | |
| Denmark | 4.3 | 1.6 |
| **Low sclerosis:** | | |
| a) Broad scope, high sophistication | | |
| Austria | 5.9 | 3.8 |
| Finland | 5.2 | 1.7 |
| West Germany | 6.0 | 4.2 |
| Mean | 5.7 | 3.2 |
| b) Broad scope, low sophistication | | |
| Japan | 8.0 | 3.9 |
| France | 5.1 | 3.5 |
| Italy | 5.8 | 2.5 |
| Mean | 6.3 | 3.3 |

*Source*: Batstone 1986: 37.

stable nations are characterised by slow productivity growth. Batstone (1986) agreed that the ability of industrial relations systems to deliver fast productivity growth will depend upon the historical continuity of its institutions (the Olson effect which Batstone termed 'institutional sclerosis'), but also on other factors. Structural characteristics enable those labour market institutions which have wide coverage (broad scope) and the ability to make and enforce policy easily (high sophistication) to generate faster productivity growth than labour markets, like the British, which have sectional bargaining units (narrow scope) with little central control over policy (low sophistication). Batstone demonstrated

(Table 13.8) that countries with labour market institutions which had been reformed after 1945 (low sclerosis) tended to have faster productivity growth over the period 1950–73 than those with longer institutional continuity (high sclerosis).

Within both the high and low sclerosis group of countries, those with broad scope and high sophistication had faster labour productivity growth. Britain, with high sclerosis, narrow scope and low sophistication was among the most slowly growing. This would suggest strongly that institutions matter in determining the pace of labour productivity growth were it not for the breakdown of the relationship after 1973. Finally, radical analyses of shopfloor behaviour seemed to confirm that British unions had constrained productivity growth. Braverman's (1974) study of US managers' close control of the pace and methods of production (or the labour process) have stimulated studies of the very different conditions in British firms. Kilpatrick and Lawson (1980) explained the inability of British managers to pursue American-style mass production methods as the result of craft workers' retention of control over the labour process to an extent which has no parallels elsewhere. Most of their evidence is from the nineteenth century but Lewchuk's studies (1986; 1987) of the British motor car industry (Chapter 12) have illustrated similar problems in a key postwar manufacturing industry. Thus agreement has emerged from very different traditions that worker control over the pace of work has resulted in slow productivity growth.

This conclusion cannot however pass without some qualification. The work of Pratten, Prais and Caves has been subject to devastating criticism by Nichols (1986) who found misrepresentation, unquestioning acceptance of managerial views and determination to portray a British worker problem despite the evidence. The institutionalist literature cannot explain why very centralised bargaining systems were so good at producing fast productivity growth before 1973 (Table 13.8) but stable employment, and consequently slow productivity growth from 1973 to the late 1980s (see the discussion of insider–outsider influences above). Still less can it explain why a number of very centralised bargaining systems have disintegrated in the 1990s – we may know that institutions matter but not why. Finally, labour process studies are by their nature specific and do not allow broad conclusions to be drawn and Lewchuk's conclusions have been questioned (Church 1994: 60–75). The net result of all this is that labour probably retarded productivity growth in the motor car and newspaper industries, but even in motor cars the impact of labour/union intransigence on productivity was small when set against other, acknowledged problems (Williams *et al.* 1983: ch. 3).

The tendency to blame unions for slow postwar productivity growth has however increased during the 1980s. Manufacturing productivity growth surged from the early 1980s after disappointing performance in the 1970s (Chapter 10). As trade union strength moved inversely to productivity growth, it is not surprising that economists should investigate the possibility of causal links. Research has also benefited enormously from detailed information on wages, conditions and bargaining in the Workplace Industrial Relations Surveys (WIRS) undertaken in 1980, 1984 and 1990. Surveying the research findings, Metcalf (1989) argued that the industrial relations system, broadly defined, retarded productivity growth in the 1970s. The Donovan report increased union power, incomes policies of the 1970s offered no encouragement to productivity bargaining and industrial policy, by subsidising ailing firms, made it less likely that managers would control labour costs and productivity. The result, according to Metcalf, was that those firms with strongly unionised work-forces in the late 1970s also had relatively low productivity. In the first half of the 1980s, however, the new bargaining climate – with laws limiting trade union power, intense competitive pressure on manufacturing firms, and no state rescue for weak firms – made productivity improvement an absolute necessity, and the fastest growth was recorded in those unionised firms where managers had lost ground in the 1970s (Metcalf 1990). Indeed, Crafts (1991a; 1991b) has argued that the period of weak pressure on managers to control labour costs extends back to 1945 and helps explain the relatively slow postwar growth of British labour productivity. Only with the severe competition and market-orientated policies after 1979 were manufacturing firms induced to claw back control over the production process from their workers and accelerate efficiency gains.

This is a persuasive account if one looks only at the 1970s and 1980s. But manufacturing productivity growth in the 1980s only returned to the trend established in 1964–73 (Darby and Wren-Lewis 1988). In the 1960s the economy had full employment, interventionist governments seeking faster productivity growth and strong trade unions; it lacked completely the supposed advantages of a healthy climate of mass unemployment, a government antipathetic to the fate of manufacturing firms and a hobbled trade union movement, yet the rates of manufacturing productivity growth were remarkably similar. Moreover, if the new bargaining climate of the 1980s cowed the unions so successfully, why was productivity growth outside manufacturing, where unions had also been strong, so disappointing? Aggregate labour productivity growth in the acclaimed 1980s was little better than in the reviled 1970s and was below rates prevailing during the long boom (Table 10.6). In short, the 'productivity miracle' literature has not yet got to grips with all the issues involved. Social scientists' determination to blame unions for the ills of the British economy has outrun their powers of persuasion.

## SKILLS AND TRAINING

Economic historians have long argued that the British economy has suffered from deficiencies in its education and training systems. These arguments have, however, generally been loose and unpersuasive, especially when bound up with the idea of an 'anti-industrial culture' in Britain. Wiener (1981), for example, has explained Britain's relative decline in terms of the aristocracy's success in absorbing the wealthy entrepreneurial elite by opening up the public schools to sons of northern industrialists. He argues that the education provided by the leading public schools was ill-suited to industry but was geared to careers in finance, administration, the professions or the armed forces. The 'image' of 'Englishness' which public schools helped to invent in the late nineteenth century was backward-looking and rural and damaged industry, according to Wiener, because it steered those with ability away from manufacturing and traditionalism spread from the elite to the mass population, colouring attitudes and political debate until 1939. There are three main difficulties with this picture of the British elite, its culture and influence. The first, and by some way the most important, is that it is completely wrong at almost every level. Rubinstein's (1993) long and detailed researches on the wealthy in Britain have demonstrated that the sons of the wealthy were never seduced away from industry. Elite culture did not subvert an industrial spirit; the two co-existed. There is little evidence of sons abandoning family firms in favour of 'soft' professions. Nor have the public schools turned the able away from science; indeed, Britain's record of 66 Nobel prizes for scientific endeavour this century exceeds that of Germany (57). Second, the chronologies do not match. Relative economic decline accelerated after 1945, which is precisely when the public schools reformed themselves to eliminate imbalances against science and technology (Sanderson 1988). Finally, no reader would deduce from Wiener's book that British manufacturing remained one of the two or three most dynamic in the world for the vast bulk of his period. Wiener has simply ignored manufacturing. To be of lasting value, studies of culture, education and training have to recognise and explain economic strengths as well as weaknesses.

The education and skills of the elite may have a place in explaining relative economic performance, but a big research programme directed from the National Institute of Economic and Social Research since the early 1980s has concentrated instead on the abilities and training of ordinary workers and their supervisors (Prais 1985; Prais and Wagner 1983; Green and Steedman 1993). This is action-orientated research, geared to immediate problems and lacking any sense of historical development but it has identified a precise relationship between education, training and rates of growth of output and productivity which is so conspicuously absent from studies of the type undertaken by Wiener. This research into current problems of the British economy can help identify the right questions to ask about educational and training provision since 1945. One study investigated matched firms (type of product, size of firm, scale of production) in the German and British machine tool industries in the early 1980s (Daly *et al.* 1985). German productivity levels were 50–80 per cent higher than British. The gap owed nothing to more modern machinery in German firms; the average age of capital equipment was very similar in the two cases. German firms operated more sophisticated machines, but the simpler British machines broke down more often and required more maintenance workers. Finally, German machines were much more likely to have ancillary devices like automatic feeders which made it possible for the average German worker to look after more machines than his British counterpart. These are the problems, how did they relate to skills?

To take the last point first, German firms were better supplied with production engineers to design efficient work flows. A shortage of such high-level skills in the British firms contributed to lower output per worker. The second British shortfall concerned the quality of supervisory staff. The main cause of breakdown of simpler British machines was misuse; machines were used for the wrong tasks, were incorrectly set up or the operatives were not given all the necessary blueprints and working drawings. British foremen, with lower average levels of technical qualifications and almost no supervisory training, were simply much less good at these basic tasks than German supervisors. Finally, the German firms had proportionately twice as many skilled workers. German workers could more easily undertake basic cleaning and maintenance operations which were beyond the semi-skilled workers in the British firms, and the failure to clean British machines was a significant cause of breakdown. Similar findings emerged from an Anglo–German comparison of the production of kitchen units. German firms made higher quality products and enjoyed higher levels of productivity. Although firms in both countries had access to the same technology, the Germans utilised their more highly-qualified workers to operate more advanced machinery, adopt more complex production methods and, again, secure smoother operation and fuller exploitation of their capital equipment (Steedman and Wagner 1987). The higher qualifications possessed by German workers in this case had little to do with formal vocational training, but with higher levels of attainment in mathematics both at school and in continuing education. If fourteen-year-olds of average and below-average abilities in Britain and Germany are compared, the typical British child will already be two years behind the German in mathematical attainment (Prais and Wagner 1985). In the top third of the ability range, British children were better at mathematics than comparable German children, but British standards of learning (and teaching) at the lower levels of ability caused concern. These are small-scale studies at a specific point in time which have unknown relevance to manufacturing as a whole in the postwar period. But they demonstrate an unequivocal link between education and productivity performance which is unambiguous and free from airy generalisations and elite preoccupations. For an economic historian, however, these results are merely tantalising. There is no comparable research before the 1980s. But problem areas have at least been identified: the education and training needs of less able pupils; the output of skilled workers; the number of graduate engineers to supply industry with its production engineers.

For most of the postwar period, education policy has been governed by the Education Act of 1944, a cautious and conservative measure (Chapter 8). The Act divided compulsory education into two phases, primary and secondary, with the break at age eleven. Secondary education was made free for all and compulsory to age fifteen. Local education authorities (LEAs) were left to organise secondary education as they saw fit, but it was widely believed that grammar schools would continue for the most academically able (Lowe 1993: 196–203). For the remainder, the bulk of working class schoolchildren, interwar reports had recommended technical schools for those with industrial and commercial abilities and modern schools for the rest. However comparatively few secondary technical schools were established after 1945, leaving Britain as the only advanced industrial country which lacked a strong tradition of separate technical education (Barnett 1986: 201–3). Those technical schools which were established in the 1940s virtually disappeared in the educational reorganisation of the 1960s (Sanderson 1988). There have also been resourcing problems for the education of the working classes, as documented in a series of reports in the 1950s and 1960s. Inner city primary schools, for example, were shown to have staff with high turnover rates and low qualification levels and buildings in a poor average state of repair (Newsom 1963). Many of the 'new' secondary modern schools simply took over the buildings and staff of former elementary schools and certainly did not enjoy the 'parity of esteem' with grammar schools to which the 1944 Act had aspired. Educational expenditure rose rapidly in the 1950s and 1960s, but the lion's share went to the grammar schools and higher education (Lowe 1993: 206–7). Concern grew about the underperformance of many working class adolescents. Running through the entire postwar period is a consistent theme: British children stayed in secondary education in increasing numbers but whenever international comparisons are made, Britain emerges as the developed country with the lowest proportion of its children in post-compulsory education (Sanderson 1991; Green and Steedman 1993). The reform of secondary education into 'comprehensive' schools could have remedied some of the deficiencies, but the measure was over-hasty, under-funded and failed to tackle some of the key educational issues, such as curriculum design, the quality of teaching and teacher training and teaching practice (Lowe 1993: 213–25). The willingness of children to remain within the system after the minimum leaving age to gain academic, technical and vocational qualifications seems to depend upon the interaction of a host of factors, some relating to internal features of the education system (institutional structures, curriculum design, teaching methods, forms of assessment and certification) and others relating to broader social conditions (societal and parental attitudes and expectations, employment opportunities, the nature of the labour market) (Green and Steedman 1993: 14). Since the mid-1970s, the persistent turmoil imposed on the education system by politicians and the comparatively weak demand for new recruits to industry noted above have not provided the conditions to persuade sufficient numbers of working class children to 'stop on' to gain qualifications.

The comparative failure of schooling for the majority might have been less critical if training by employers had been more satisfactory. Shortage of skilled workers has however been a perennial problem in the postwar period. Second World War 'dilutees' (those semi- and un-skilled workers who undertook skilled work during the war) remained recognised as skilled craftsmen by agreement between unions and employers, but skill shortages were always acute. In 1961, there was a shortfall of 20,000 engineering craftsmen alone (Beveridge 1963) but even in the 1980s, with more than 3 million unemployed, 10–15 per cent of firms reported shortages of skilled workers as a constraint on output (Sanderson 1988). Apprenticeship remained the main system of training in the 1950s and 1960s, but was widely criticised for imparting low-grade skills, taking too long and inculcating defensive attitudes among craftsmen (Gospel 1992: 156–7). In 1964, the Labour government established industrial training boards which brought limited improvements but the benefits were soon swamped by the profits squeeze and competitive pressures which led firms in the 1970s to cut training, especially on apprenticeships.

The Thatcher government initially reduced state support for industrial training, arguing that private enterprise should take responsibility for equipping the work-force with skills. However, the dramatic rise of unemployment in 1981–2 led to the introduction of a series of measures to help take the unemployed off the jobless register. In the later 1980s, the school curriculum was reformed to standardise and monitor the effectiveness of what was taught and to ensure that 'education for industry' played a more substantial part. The new training initiatives were aimed primarily at the young to ensure that all those who left school at sixteen received at least one year of more or less compulsory vocational training. Much of this has been very helpful both to industry and new entrants into the labour market. The long-term unemployed have also been offered – with varying amounts of arm-twisting – training and re-training to assist them back into employment. But these schemes have also had a political goal – to reduce the official unemployment figures at low cost and lower the wage expectations of the young unemployed (Deakin 1992: 189). Training was thus provided as cheaply as possible and schemes were introduced in the shortest possible time to produce the maximum impact on rising unemployment. The creation in the late 1980s of local training and enterprise councils, led by local business interests, marks an effort to ensure that the provision of training meets the need of local employers, and a step away from the cheap and cheerful initiatives earlier in the decade. By common consent, it takes twenty years before changes in training have their full impact on industrial performance, but the interim judgement on the initiatives of the 1980s is 'not good enough' (Keep and Mayhew 1988; Finegold and Soskice 1988).

Britain's comparatively low output of graduate engineers is another problem which has failed to respond to treatment. International comparisons inevitably show Britain with a low proportion of qualified scientific and technical manpower in the work-force of key industries (Fulton 1990). Proposals to increase the supply have been made frequently (Barlow 1946; Finniston 1980), most recently in government efforts in 1993 to shift the balance of university students towards the sciences. The results have, however, been disappointing. Higher education was expanded after the Robbins Report (1963) but the fastest growth was in the relatively cheap arts and social science faculties, and even the new 'technological universities' of the 1960s have become less heavily biased towards science and technology than originally intended. The polytechnics which became the new universities of 1992 moved rapidly away from their prime concerns with science and industry as they expanded in the 1970s and 1980s (Sanderson 1991). But there is a reverse side to the coin. A severe shortage of engineers in British industry should lead to a relative rise in starting salaries for new engineers and technologists. No such change has been evident in the postwar period. In this gloomy picture, there is one bright spot. In the mid-1980s British employers began to learn how to recruit and value graduates in the way which had been common in competitor nations for many years (Fulton 1990). There is little doubt that the level of skills of the average British worker must be raised if Britain's industrial competitiveness is to be restored (Crafts 1991a: 281) but it is not clear that the three fundamental problems identified above have yet been tackled.

# Chapter 14

# Economic policy

Since 1945, economic policy has passed through three distinct phases. The period began with the election of a government committed to planning a 'socialist commonwealth' but which gradually allowed its more radical ambitions to lapse and become transformed into the 'postwar consensus'. This persisted until the 1970s and its essential elements were the welfare state, full employment, a more equal society, trade union consultation, the mixed economy and the Anglo-American alliance. This policy-making regime came under increasing pressure for its failure to reverse the processes of relative decline and eventually collapsed when the long postwar boom petered out amid the national and international turbulence of the 1970s. New approaches to the role of the state had begun to develop in the 1960s but it was unclear until the Thatcher government came to power in 1979 whether the postwar consensus would be toppled from the left or right. The 1979 result brought to office a government with radical new ideas in industrial, labour, monetary and welfare policies. The Conservative experiment has undoubtedly contained pragmatic and fortuitous elements, but its core has remained strong into the 1990s despite the departure from office of its leading propagandist and architect, Margaret Thatcher.

## THE TRANSITION FROM WAR TO PEACE

As noted in Chapter 8, wartime reconstruction planning began in 1943 and was determined to avoid the mistakes of the headlong decontrol after 1918. The scale of likely postwar shortages was frightening. A world food shortage was certain. British industry, having suffered extensive wartime disinvestment would be desperately short of all forms of capital equipment. Consumers needed to restock and the housing shortage would be horrifying. Foreign currency would be extremely scarce, severely limiting import capacity. In this context, there was broad agreement that controls would have to continue until shortages abated but there were wider strategic issues which were too politically contentious for the wartime coalition to resolve (Chapter 8). They were, however, settled when the electorate opted in July 1945 for Britain's first majority Labour government. Attlee's government came to power with a programme of economic and social reforms which embraced a broad commitment to economic planning, centred on a National Investment Board, and a major expansion of the public sector (Tomlinson 1994: 161). The goal was increased social security, with full employment, greater state control of private enterprise and the creation of a welfare state. Much of this programme derived from the 1930s but wartime developments had both advanced and undermined Labour plans. Labour's planners took heart from the wartime loss of faith in both free markets and the efficiency of private enterprise and from the creation of a system of economic controls which could be used for planning, but from mid-1944 the looming postwar economic and financial problems led civil servants and industrialists to view controls as merely a means of negotiating the transition from war to peace, whereupon industry would need to be free to exploit market opportunities to the full (Johnman 1991: 47).

Labour was, however, caught between the short and the long term in its core policies. As noted in Chapter 12, ministers emphasised the potential of state ownership to increase the efficiency of the basic industries, but were unable to translate these sentiments into effective policy for the nationalised industries (Tomlinson 1994: 196–8; Gourvish 1986: 71,100–1). The story was similar in planning. Apart from relaxing many of the controls over the labour market (Panitch 1976: ch. 1), the Attlee government made few changes to the wartime machinery of co-ordination and allocation and thought comparatively little about strategic economic goals. 'Planning' consisted mainly of using these inherited controls to regulate consumption and the balance of payments, under conditions of excess demand and inherited external weakness (Tomlinson 1990: 206). The National Investment Board was established, but was ineffectual and soon collapsed (Rogow and Shore 1955: 27–9, 61–2).

Initially, the Attlee government's preoccupation with the short-term produced success. During the first months of peace demobilisation proceeded smoothly and Labour also undertook a vigorous campaign to steer firms to new factories to prevent rising unemployment in the prewar 'depressed areas' (Booth 1982). A strong employment policy was also pursued from the centre. The Chancellor of the Exchequer, Hugh Dalton, had a simple vision of a socialist budgetary policy: deflation must be avoided and the burden of taxation should be shifted from the poor to the rich. If expansion threatened to accelerate inflation, the network of controls would contain price rises (Pimlott 1985: ch. 26). This programme appeared to work. Although there were difficulties in attracting workers to industries which had an important role in recovery (like coal-mining) or in strengthening the trade balance (like agriculture and textiles), signs of economic vigour multiplied in 1946. Industrial production rose and exports began to recover. Government finances appeared very healthy, with a large budget surplus (Dalton 1962: 223). External policy gave few indications of the troubles ahead in the balance of trade with the dollar area. The difficulties of obtaining supplies from the USA in 1946 kept overseas dollar expenditure to tolerable levels (Cairncross 1985: 130).

Early in 1947 recovery ground to a halt when coal supplies could not keep pace with demand (Chapter 12). Industry was put on short time, unemployment rose for a brief period and the government was in a state of disarray. Labour's *annus horrendus* continued during the summer when the first postwar balance-of-payments crisis, associated with the imposition of convertibility of sterling into dollars under the terms of the US loan agreement (Chapter 11), undermined government confidence further. The government lost its sense of direction and public confidence in planning was severely weakened. Although ministerial incompetence played its part in the crises of 1947, the problems were generated more by the processes of strong recovery in an economy with balance of payments weaknesses (Milward 1984: 1–55). When the financial crisis eased, significant changes were made to the machinery and techniques of planning which ensured that policy was conducted more rigorously but with the aim of resolving limited, short-term problems. Before 1947, responsibility for economic planning had fallen on three ministers; the overburdened Lord President, Herbert Morrison; the mercurial Chancellor, Hugh Dalton; and the dour President of the Board of Trade, Stafford Cripps. After the crisis, Cripps eventually became Chancellor and 'economic supremo' of the Cabinet. These changes improved co-ordination between economic and financial planning, which had been weak before 1947 (Booth 1989: 158–67). As a result, the Treasury regained the position, which it had lost in 1940, as the principal economic ministry. The status of the Economic Section, the group of academic economists brought into Whitehall during wartime, was also raised by the crisis of 1947 because it had a clear policy for short-term economic management. More generally, the influence of industrialists and their employers' associations also rose during 1947. They helped to administer the tighter coal rationing and distribution schemes and began to play a more forceful role in measures to stimulate exports and strengthen the balance of payments. Employers' associations had been the strongest wartime opponents of long-term planning to raise efficiency and were able to use their enhanced status to block industrial reorganisation (Tiratsoo and Tomlinson 1991: 81–4).

The crises of 1947 were a deep shock to the government and brought new measures (noted in Chapter 11) to discriminate against supplies from the dollar area and strengthen the balance of payments. Fear of the dollar deficit also led the government into unwise plans to develop sterling area resources. The groundnut scheme to produce peanuts in East Africa was a notable bungle (Ady 1952: 561–4). Nevertheless, with new attitudes in Washington towards Britain with the onset of the Cold War, Britain secured dollar aid and a steady improvement in its balance of payments, albeit after a major devaluation in 1949 (see Chapter 11). In domestic policy the main consequence of 1947 was the return of wages and prices as major (short-term) political and economic problems. Although the rate of inflation was low by international standards, it was beginning to rise and, to Treasury eyes, threaten the current account (Cairncross 1985: 40–1). The Economic Section, using Keynesian analysis, had been calling for cuts in public expenditure almost since the end of the war but without any great influence on Dalton. In the emergency budget of November 1947, however, Keynesian arithmetic helped to determine the broad size of public expenditure cuts (Booth 1983) and it remained a major influence for the rest of the government's period in office. With the budget restored to its wartime role of broadly matching purchasing power to the value at constant prices of goods and services coming onto the market in the year ahead, the pressure of excess demand was reduced, shortages began to abate, and the rationale for controls began to diminish. The 'bonfire of controls' in 1948 was possible because the Treasury was now budgeting for a surplus and was containing inflationary forces.

This certainly does not mean that all controls were removed. The food ration remained into the 1950s because world food supply remained precarious. Doubts also surrounded the accuracy of the Keynesian national income forecasts on which the Treasury's tax and spending judgements were based (Rollings 1985). The government did not remove excess demand completely (Cairncross 1985: 23). It was always fearful of a return to deflationary forces in the world economy and was determined to keep the domestic labour market tight (Tomlinson 1987: chs 6–7). The Attlee government could justifiably claim to have made real the 1944 promise of full employment (Morgan 1984: 180–4). There was a cost in running the economy with a small margin of excess demand and with a decreasing role for controls; inflation was a constant bogey even after the re-integration of Keynesian techniques into policy-making. Cripps stepped into this vacuum to lead by personal example. He was a sanctimonious, abstemious politician who did not lack self-righteousness (Churchill is said to have quipped, 'There but for the grace of God goes God') but had great personal integrity. He persuaded the British that after the privations of war continuing 'austerity' was essential; everyone must work harder and face real cuts in income (Morgan 1984: ch. 9; Middlemas 1986: ch. 5). His major success was the creation of

Britain's most successful peacetime incomes policy on the basis of voluntary agreement with the TUC (Jones 1987: 38–47). However, Cripps was uninterested in trying to convert this crisis initiative into the long-run integration of TUC leaders into policy-making. He made few concessions to the needs of working-class consumers and also lacked Dalton's redistributive zeal in budgetary strategy. The collapse of the Cripps voluntary pay policy in 1950 soured the already strained relationship between the unions and the government (Booth 1995a).

Paradoxically, Labour managed to establish strategic goals in one area, foreign economic policy, but almost certainly with short- and long-term costs to the economy. As noted in Chapter 11, driven by the vigorous nationalism and anti-communism of Ernest Bevin, Attlee's first Foreign Secretary, Britain pursued a foreign economic policy which was very costly for a country with such severe external problems (Chapter 11 above; Tomlinson 1991). The government which said so much about equality of sacrifice and the need for efficiency did not blanch at imposing substantial additional burdens on the domestic economy in the pursuit of power and influence in the world. In the process, Britain moved much closer to the USA and became a relentless opponent of the USSR. However, Bevin had the political establishment behind him and, after Marshall aid, even his critics on Labour's backbenches gave support (Morgan 1984: 276–8). The vast bulk of the electorate also seemed to expect Britain to act as a world power. No-one thought to count the cost. Thus, Labour negotiated the transition to peace successfully, but its initial driving zeal to transform British industry was blunted *en route*.

## STOP–GO AND BEYOND

On taking office in 1951, the Conservative government promised to set the people free. In the short term it needed controls and higher taxes to rearm for the Korean War. World-wide rearmament led to boom conditions, a shift in Britain's terms of trade and a huge current account deficit, leading to tougher controls over imports and prices of basic consumer goods. Price controls remained in force until 1952 and rationing ended only in 1954 (Hall 1962: 429–30) but the Conservatives quickly dismantled the machinery of planning after the Korean War, almost certainly at a faster pace than Labour would have contemplated. As de-regulation proceeded the government began to sound a new note in economic policy; Crippsian austerity was buried beneath a new emphasis on increased living standards. The Conservatives reintroduced an active monetary policy; interest rates were more flexible than at any time since the 1920s (Kennedy 1962: 301). The broad outlines of the public sector were left unaltered, despite some de-nationalisation.

The Conservatives had learned from their defeat in 1945 that they needed credible employment policies and Churchill also appointed a conciliator, Walter Monckton, as his first Minister of Labour and principal contact with the trade union movement (Harris 1972: chs 5–9). Conservative welfare policy had also changed since 1945. The new government set more ambitious house-building targets than Labour, though with more reliance on private building and owner-occupation than hitherto (Short 1982). More traditional Conservative themes also reappeared with pledges to reduce the 'burden' of personal taxation – the share of taxes in national income declined only slowly to 1954 and hardly at all thereafter (Little 1962: 295). In foreign economic policy the Conservatives continued to rebuild great power status through a strong sterling area and close Anglo-American co-operation. There were many continuities with Labour's economic strategy but also differences in emphasis and approach within the broad, shared framework. The existence of a postwar consensus on economic policy is far from axiomatic (see Chapter 9 above) but there are enough continuities to encourage many historians to argue the case (Middlemas 1979: chs 11–14; Kavanagh and Morris 1989).

Short-term macro-economic policy was comparatively easy in the 1950s, especially before 1956. The maintenance of full employment was made possible by the rapid growth of capital accumulation in Britain and the rest of the developed world (Matthews 1968). Balance of payments equilibrium was aided by the substantial devaluation of 1949 and the USA's persistent current account deficit (Chapter 11). Flows of destabilising short-term capital were still minute before the creation of the eurocurrency markets in the 1960s (Strange 1986: 6–7). Counter-inflationary policy benefited from co-operative industrial relations and strong memories of interwar unemployment. Inflation did rise in the Korean War crisis, but there was no evidence of workers trying to derive the maximum benefit from the tight labour market. Throughout the 1950s the marvel was that, in a fully employed economy where consumers were increasingly encouraged to buy on credit, there was so little inflation.

The annual budget remained the focus of economic policy and techniques of budgetary policy changed little. Official forecasts of the likely value at constant prices of supply and demand for the year ahead formed one of the key economic foundations of macro-economic policy. They were, however, slow, prone to inaccuracy and became, if anything, less reliable over time (Brittan 1971: 128–38). There were also political constraints on budgetary policy. Labour had been averse to raising interest rates, but Conservative Chancellors had ideological qualms about increasing income taxes and relied very heavily on the monetary policies which Labour had spurned. Monetary policy was not called upon often but the 'credit squeezes' of 1951–2 and 1955–8 revealed only how difficult it was to manage the domestic economy in this way. The impact of changes in interest rates tended to be slow and unpredictable but changes in the hire purchase controls acted very quickly, though with very severe effects on a small number of industries (Radcliffe 1959: 167–8). Faced by these logistical and political problems, the Treasury changed macro-economic policy according to simpler rules. Politicians believed that electoral difficulties were inevitable if unemployment climbed above 500,000 (650,000 in the 1960s). When the danger level was approached, an expansionary budget would follow. The pegged exchange rate system and Britain's weak reserves created the second stimulus to action. Confidence in sterling was fragile; any sign of weakness would lead the Treasury to implement a credit squeeze and cuts in the pressure of demand. To the casual observer, policy always appeared to be in a state of flux, with the Treasury responding to signals alternately from the foreign exchange and labour markets. Policy was guided more by political than economic judgements (Brittan 1971: 455) and those economic judgements may occasionally have been based on orthodox rather than Keynesian reasoning (Rollings 1988; Lowe 1993: 112).

This stop–go pattern led to the thesis that macro-economic policy had been 'de-stabilising'; in other words, that output would have grown more smoothly in the absence of policy changes (Dow 1964; Artis 1972). This view has been criticised (Bristow 1968) but the fuss about de-stabilisation seems to have been misplaced. The impact of demand management policies was usually quite small and equivalent to a change of hardly greater than one percentage point on the unemployment rate (Cairncross 1981: 374). The fluctuations in the British economy from 1950 to 1970 were much less than in the interwar years and less than in other OECD countries at the time (Whiting 1976). Stop–go seemed much more threatening to contemporaries and met very severe criticism from British industry, especially from those sectors relying on hire purchase (Blank 1973: 146–7). It was also blamed for the comparatively slow rate of growth in the British economy from the late 1950s (Kirby 1991: 243; Chapter 10). Once again, British governments were forced to consider long-term problems and policies. A few economists, the forerunners of the monetarist school, argued that faster output growth would result from slower growth of monetary demand (Paish 1962: 309–32). Similar ideas were held in the Bank of England and, briefly, in the Treasury in 1957–8 until the resignation of the Chancellor and his ministerial team in 1958. In the early 1960s, however, most economists believed that the government would be much more likely to achieve its various policy goals simultaneously if it had a wider range of policy instruments; a specific policy was needed for each goal; prices and incomes policies to cope with inflation, planning to accelerate growth and reappraisal of government overseas spending to support the balance of payments. After more than a decade in which short-term management of demand had been the priority of policy-makers, interest in the supply side of the economy and the longer-term began to revive.

The most dramatic innovation in supply-side policy was indicative planning, a method of encouraging industrialists to plan their firms' growth on the basis of consistent views of the medium-term outlook for the national economy. Indicative planning had operated in France since the late 1940s and by the late 1950s British opinion was very impressed with parts of the French system (Shonfield 1969: chs 1–5; Denton *et al*. 1968). In 1961, the Conservatives embraced a weak model of indicative planning by establishing the National Economic Development Council (NEDC), comprising representatives of government, industry and the unions, and a small administrative apparatus, NEDO, the National Economic Development Office, significantly outside the formal Whitehall machine. Discussions during 1961–2 resulted in a paper (NEDO 1963) which explored the possibility of raising the British growth rate to 4 per cent per annum (from around 2.7 per cent). The discontent with stop–go also bore fruit in reorganisation of Treasury control of public expenditure. Instead of annual cash limits, public spending projects were planned over a period of years, aiming to expand state expenditure in line with growth in the aggregate economy (Plowden 1961). The new methods of managing public spending came into operation when the government had committed itself to the NEDO plan, and under Maudling, Chancellor of the Exchequer from 1962 to 1964, public spending increased at a rate consistent with 4 per cent growth in the economy as a whole (Leruez 1975: 125).

The return of a new Labour government in 1964 led to a new enthusiasm for growth and a much stronger ideological commitment to planning. Labour retained the NEDC and NEDO, but also created within Whitehall a new Department of Economic Affairs (DEA) charged with drawing up a five-year plan for the British economy. The DEA was a counterweight in economic policy to the Treasury and its responsibility for sterling and the short term. Labour's 'National Plan' (DEA 1965) had the same growth target as Maudling's 'dash for growth' after 1962, a result more of Labour's political needs than of realistic appraisal of Britain's medium-term economic prospects (Opie 1972). Labour also established a new Ministry of Technology to expand the flow of government funds for civilian R&D (Tomlinson 1994: 264–7) and oversee links between government and the science-based industries (Leruez 1975: ch. 14). The most interesting of Labour's new agencies was the Industrial Reorganisation Corporation (IRC), established in 1966 to act as a state merchant bank. It promoted 'national champions' in key industries (see Chapter 12).

The rate of productivity growth certainly accelerated (from 2.2 per cent per annum in 1955–60 to 4.5 per cent per annum in 1969–73: Jones 1976) during this burst of creative energy in policy-making but it would be rash to propose a causal link. New policies for growth were developed at the same time as the current account was showing ominous signs of deterioration, raising the familiar clash between short- and long-term perspectives. Measures taken to defend the exchange rate without compromising the growth strategy (an IMF credit, higher bank rate, a temporary surcharge on imports, reduction of overseas commitments) failed and by mid-1966, the Treasury's short-term concern with the balance of payments had obviously triumphed over the DEA's growth perspective. The growth target was buried under large public expenditure cuts which began in 1965 and were repeated annually until 1968; stop–go became stop. The government might have had more chance of reconciling growth and the balance of payments if it had launched its growth strategy with a devaluation, as the French had done so successfully in 1958. Labour's first decision in economic policy was, however, to defend the value of sterling (Pimlott 1992: 350–1) but it is not clear that devaluation in 1964 would have made so very much difference. Current account weakness had much to do with poor non-price competitiveness and when devaluation did come in 1967 it needed a huge disinflationary package to restore confidence in sterling (Chapter 11 above).

Just as economic planning failed to achieve faster growth, so prices and incomes policy did not deliver lower wage inflation for more than a short period. Incomes policy has been discussed extensively in the previous chapter and we need only note here that it was only after 1961 when planning for growth was introduced that governments began to establish 'guiding lights' or 'norms' for wage growth (Jones 1985: ch. 5; Brittan and Lilley 1977). After 1964 incomes policy became still more sophisticated, with a productivity dimension. Labour's National Board for Prices and Incomes tried to induce firms seeking permission to raise prices to raise productivity instead (Mitchell 1972). Wage increases were also allowed to breach the pay 'norm' if they were accompanied by measures to improve labour productivity. Ultimately, however, the incomes policies of the 1960s followed the established, short-term, crisis-management pattern: a brief period of toughness followed by a longer period of relaxation and eventual collapse in 1969.

Thus, the 1960s began with professional criticism of stop–go and a search for new policy instruments to permit simultaneous achievement of full employment, fast growth, stable prices and external equilibrium. Innovative policies were developed during the 1960s, but had to co-exist with, and quickly became subordinate to, traditional short-term policies to defend sterling. The commitment of the government to its new measures was always half-hearted as the early and over-riding decision to defend the parity of sterling demonstrated. By 1969, unemployment rates were higher, growth was slower, inflation was rising and the balance of payments had improved only after devaluation and deflationary budgets. Productivity growth accelerated after 1964, but remained below the OECD average. It was the wrong time to launch a half-hearted drive to modernise British industry and policy-making structures. Britain's international competitiveness continued to deteriorate and, as the Bretton Woods system began to disintegrate, it was ever more difficult to manage the weak external account. At the same time, the British electorate demanded faster growth. A weak supply-side growth policy was an unfortunately predictable response to these pressures. The failures of the 1960s began to convince sections of both main political parties that the basic policy programme needed reform. The search for fundamentally different approaches had begun.

## PROBLEMS OF THE 1970s

The 1970s have been seen both by contemporaries and in retrospect as a decade of national and international economic crisis. The long postwar boom came to an end, new political and economic strategies were developed and the electorate became increasingly volatile as social consensus began to fray. By 1979, the way had been prepared for Thatcherism. Economic policy-makers became less concerned with achieving the goals set out in 1944 and more preoccupied by the need to reconcile the electorate to the obvious signs of Britain's postwar relative economic decline. Instability in the world economy provided a very testing environment for national policy-making. The decade began with the collapse of Bretton Woods and a huge shift in terms of trade which both accelerated inflation and exerted a deflationary pressure on economic activity. Efforts to organise a simultaneous, co-ordinated reflation of the OECD countries came to nothing. Just as more settled conditions began to appear in the late 1970s, OPEC again raised oil prices (Chapter 11 for a fuller survey). This was not the ideal environment in which to solve the competitive problems of the British economy; crisis management had to be the priority as both Conservative and Labour governments came, belatedly, to appreciate.

The Conservative government which came to power in 1970 had experienced a particularly formative period in opposition. The increase of inflation and unemployment after 1965 and the failure of the Wilson governments to modernise the British economy sharpened the critique of postwar policy from the anti-interventionist wing of the Conservative Party. After two general election defeats in 1964 and 1966, plans were laid for the next Conservative government to 'disengage' from the economy (Seldon 1991: 245–6). This 'Selsdon programme' embraced reform of industrial relations, industrial policy and foreign economic policy with the goal of sharpening market disciplines on British industry. In industrial relations, the Conservatives viewed trade union power as a destabilising force and introduced an Industrial Relations Act of 1971 to constrain union action. The main change in industrial policy was the withdrawal of state support from firms in financial difficulty. In the rather confused metaphor of the time, 'lame duck' firms would be allowed to 'go to the wall'. A number of the 'quangos' which gave trade unions access to key areas of policy-making were terminated. Underpinning this strategy was the application to join the EU to give British industry access to a much bigger 'domestic' market, but one in which competitive pressures were stronger. Competition was also extended in the financial sector where regulation in the 1960s had produced growing signs of distortion and instability (Moran 1984).

Unfortunately the plan did not work as intended. Wage inflation, which had accelerated in 1969–70, continued to rise (Figure 13.2). Unemployment also climbed and approached the politically sensitive total of one million. Major British companies (Rolls-Royce and Upper Clyde Shipbuilders) were in severe financial difficulty. Rising unemployment made the unions even more hostile to industrial relations law. Confrontational politics were evident on all sides. The government reversed course with Heath's celebrated 'U-turn'. The direction of industrial policy switched from non-intervention to intervention (Chapter 12). Above all, the government turned from its anti-inflationary bias to undertake another 'dash for growth' (in effect, to launch a major Keynesian reflationary package) to reduce unemployment but, in contrast to 1962–4, sterling was allowed to float free from its Bretton Woods pegged bands (see Chapter 11). Far from expelling the unions from policy-making, the government returned to the tripartite approaches which had characterised the 1960s (Holmes 1982) and, in the hope of minimising the impact of expansion on inflation, began to court the unions and search for a workable incomes policy (Jones 1987: 86). Output and employment expanded as intended, but the government appeared to have lost control, especially of prices (Cairncross 1992: 190–1) and public expenditure (Heald 1983). The government's incomes policy, which contained automatic indexation of wages to prices, seemed to exacerbate rather than cure the problem (Jones 1987: 92–8). The impression of a rudderless government increased with OPEC 1 and a major industrial dispute in coal mining which led directly to rationing of electricity supplies and a three-day-week for British industry. The government's loss of authority was confirmed by its failure in the February 1974 general election.

To the Conservative right, the 'U-turn' in 1972 and the debacle thereafter was a betrayal of market economics. In all quarters of the party, the
role of the unions in bringing down the government and the mistimed
and mismanaged dash for growth helped increase the determination to
break union strength and discredit Keynesian demand management. The
rapid acceleration of inflation helped to shift priorities away from
employment, despite or because of Heath's overriding concern with
unemployment levels (Holmes 1982). This Conservative rejection of
Keynesian, interventionist policies took place against a background of
new interest in alternatives to Keynesian doctrine. The simultaneous rise
of unemployment and inflation after 1965 posed problems with which
Keynesian analysis was ill-equipped to cope (Bleaney 1985: 131–2).
However, other authorities drawing on a much older tradition claimed
that analytical tools were available. This analysis was termed 'monetarism' but was essentially a revival and redevelopment of nineteenth
century neo-classical economics. Monetarism was associated above all
with the US economist Milton Friedman who had developed the quantity theory in ways which led to empirical testing and refinement of the
model (1956; 1969). Friedman argued that there was a clear and stable
relationship between changes in economic activity and money stock and
that changes in the money stock did not simply result from changes in
economic activity but, on the contrary, were the major influences on
economic activity (Friedman and Schwartz 1963).

Friedman's work also coincided with the rise of the 'new right' in US
political thought, which began to question the notion that the state was
an altruistic agency which could be relied upon to correct market failure
in the public interest; politicians were individuals subject to maximising
behaviour which could be analysed in neo-classical economic terms
(Buchanan and Tullock 1962). The activities of government reflect the
selfish interests of pressure groups and power brokers which frequently
fail to represent national interests. In short, 'government failure' is
possible and may even be likely. These new political ideas, when combined with the neo-classical belief that the market economy will tend to
return to stability at full employment, created a critique of Keynesian
political economy which had enormous resonance in the disturbed
international economic conditions of the mid-1970s. Keynesian efforts
to preserve full employment would result only in accelerating inflation
(Hayek 1972; Buchanan *et al.* 1978). New free market theorists (the
rational expectations school noted in Chapter 13) argued there was *no*
economic role for government other than control of the money supply
and ensuring that the supply side of the economy, and in particular the
labour market, was subject to the disciplines of competition. These views
made much more headway in the USA than in Britain, but Alan Walters
at the LSE was a great supporter of Friedman's early work and was

joined by significant groups in Manchester and Liverpool universities. Faith in the self-righting properties of market economies had been kept alive in Britain by Hayek and was given new emphasis at the Institute of Economic Affairs (IEA).

Labour's radicals were, of course, on the interventionist left and had committed the party during its period of opposition to more extensive public ownership and control of private industry (Grant 1982). For the third time in thirty years, Labour arrived in office apparently committed to planning as a means of modernising British industry, but this time the goal was not technocratic but socialist planning involving a major expansion of the public sector. As noted in Chapter 12, the main agencies of Labour's planning in the mid-1970s were the National Enterprise Board (NEB), planning agreements and the tripartite sector working parties under the aegis of NEDC. The 1964–70 Labour government had believed that scale was the route to competitive success (Tomlinson 1994: 299) but in opposition the Labour left came to see control as the key issue, and both planning agreements and the NEB were designed to force industry to comply with government policies (Tomlinson 1990: 308). The second long-term element of the Labour government's programme was its 'social contract' with the unions which had been devised in opposition to establish a framework for long-run collaboration between the TUC and a Labour government over wages (Fishbein 1984: 115–32). The government hoped that union leaders would moderate wage demands; the TUC hoped to regain the influence over economic policy which it had lost in the immediate postwar period. But, like its predecessors, this government also quickly abandoned its radical strategy and resorted to short-term crisis avoidance, much to the relief of the leadership which had always distrusted the radical programme (Pimlott 1992: 666–74). But the effective neutering of industrial policy in 1975, when Tony Benn was moved from the Department of Trade and Industry, did not end Labour's difficulties.

Financial markets had been concerned about rising inflation and deteriorating public finances since 1972–3. The public sector borrowing requirement (PSBR) was rising, apparently out of control. In intellectual circles there were arguments from left (O'Connor 1973; Habermas 1975) and right (Bacon and Eltis 1976) about the causes and consequences of rising public expenditure. It was widely believed that electoral pressures led to spending programmes which the economy could not satisfy (Brittan 1975), producing 'overload' of the public sector (King 1975). As noted in Chapter 11, the City was reluctant to fund the PSBR until the government brought spending back under control – by deep cuts, notably in radical policies for state support of industry (Wilks 1984: 52–4) and by introducing cash limits on expenditure programmes. This change in direction was consolidated by the request to the IMF for a substantial line of credit (Chapter 11 above). The deep rifts within Cabinet made the politics of public spending particularly byzantine and contorted (Burk and Cairncross 1992) but there was no doubt at all that Treasury ministers and officials had regained control of economic strategy and refocused attention on the short-term.

But Labour's reappraisal of policy went far beyond the successful attempts to neuter radical industrial policy and to regain control over public spending and inflation. In a very famous speech to the 1976 Labour Party conference, the new Prime Minister, James Callaghan, renounced Keynesian approaches to economic policy. He argued that the Keynesian option of spending our way out of recession 'no longer exists, and in so far as it ever did exist it only worked on each occasion since the war by injecting bigger doses of inflation into the economy' (Labour Party 1976: 188). A permanent rise in employment could be achieved only if British industry was made more competitive. The speech, written by his son-in-law, Peter Jay, was aimed primarily at the City and probably should not be regarded as a barometer of opinion even within the Labour leadership, but it illustrates very clearly the diminishing resonance of full employment and the pressure on the government to send Friedmanite signals to the markets.

As has been noted above, the essence of Friedmanite monetarism was that an expansion of the money supply would lead inevitably to a proportionate rise in the rate of inflation after a predictable time-lag. In Britain, the annual changes in the money supply, as measured by £M3, in the five years 1971–6 predicted the increase in inflation from 1973 to 1978 (that is to say, two years later) with remarkable precision (Kaldor 1982: 83). This 'relationship' (which has since disappeared completely) was noted by Samuel Brittan in the *Financial Times* and by Peter Jay and William Rees-Mogg in *The Times*, in early 1976 and had a major impact in the City. Monetarist ideas were given circulation among the chattering classes in what were then regarded as authoritative broadsheet newspapers. Friedmanite analysis had begun to spread far beyond its 'natural' home on the right of the Conservative Party.

There were also good practical grounds reassessing policy in the mid-1970s. The goals established at the end of the war were becoming increasingly difficult to achieve at all, much less simultaneously. Balance of payments stability had emerged over the preceding decades as the biggest problem and even allowing sterling to float had given only temporary respite from persistent external crises (Chapter 11 above). To defend the current account, successive British governments had drastically curbed great power pretensions, borrowed, devalued sterling inside and outside the rules of the IMF, encouraged exports and discouraged imports inside and outside the rules of GATT and in domestic policy, state direction, liberalisation and tripartite arrangements had all been enlisted to help strengthen the current account. The balance of payments had improved from the dire straits of 1945, but the external position was never strong enough to permit governments to pursue full employment and faster growth in a consistent way. New strategies had to be considered, and three options presented themselves in the later 1970s. The first was to recognise that a solution to the external problem was virtually impossible without reversing the process of Britain's integration into the world economy. Protectionism had enjoyed little political favour since the mid-1940s, but it was championed by the Labour left in the 1970s because it appeared the only method of arresting higher import penetration and the long-run decline in Britain's share of world manufactured trade. A full employment level of output would be impossible without import quotas; the tariff would be much less effective and in the medium term would raise inflation rather than permit external balance (Gamble 1981: 181–97; CEPG 1975; Godley 1978). The second was to renounce Keynesian analysis, back Friedmanite monetarism and withdraw government from intervention in the market economy and concentrate on the control of the money stock to reduce inflation (Gamble 1981: 143–64). This strategy had traditional appeal to the Conservative right but support for parts of this programme were spreading in the 1970s, as noted above. The final option was to eschew ideological and theoretical approaches and take pragmatic steps until North Sea oil flowed in sufficient quantities to return the current account to the black and create a more favourable environment in which to tackle poor industrial competitiveness.

The 1974–9 Labour government opted for pragmatism. In its monetary policy, the imposition of cash limits, control of the PSBR and sales of public assets to raise revenue without affecting the PSBR (by the sale of BP shares) point to Thatcherism. But the government also pursued a vigorous 'Keynesian' incomes policy. After a lax first year, the social contract target for wage growth tightened dramatically and helped bring about a substantial fall in real wages in 1976–7 (Jones 1987: 110). It remained tight until 1978–9 (Fishbein 1984: 175–8) but ministers increasingly lost sight of the longer-term goals and used incomes policy to exert maximum short-term pressure on union leaders to hold down wage demands. Industrial policy and nationalisation were shorn of their radical aims but were used to preserve British industrial capacity as underlying unemployment began to rise (Ormerod 1991: 68–9). Labour's policies have been roundly criticised (Holmes 1985a; Coates 1980) but Artis and Cobham (1991a) have controversially given a measured defence of macro-economic policy, noting that inflation was lower in 1979 than 1974, growth had been resumed, unemployment (though higher) was falling and both the balance of payments and the exchange rate were stronger. In the very difficult international climate of the late-

1970s and the absence of any clear understanding about how the economy worked, these may have been substantial achievements. On the other hand, the government did not tackle poor industrial competitiveness and it miscalculated its handling of the social contract, helping to provoke the 'winter of discontent' (Ormerod 1991). After this debacle with the unions, the Labour government appeared tired, demoralised and unconvincing (Seldon 1991: 240). The electorate was now prepared to back new approaches to economic policy.

## CONSERVATIVE STOP–GO REVISITED: THATCHERISM AND MAJORITIS

The Conservatives came to power in 1979 with a new leader, Margaret Thatcher, and the outlines of a new philosophy. Mrs Thatcher came from the 'new right' of the party, but her populist appeal crossed traditional boundaries. In opposition in the late–1970s, the Conservative party developed a programme which had anti-inflationary and anti-union policies to the fore and which tapped popular discontent with economic policy by promising to 'roll back' the state, reduce unemployment and reduce taxes. The election manifesto skilfully addressed the worries of ordinary people with remedies derived from 'new right' thinking. This was the third Conservative government in almost thirty years to promise to set the people free, but the Thatcher government combined a modernising zeal and a determination not to be diverted. The essence of its appeal was to provide greater stability in economic policy and to create both the space and the culture which would allow British industry to prosper.

The centrepiece of policy was the medium-term financial strategy (MTFS), the creation of Nigel Lawson, the Financial Secretary to the Treasury. The MTFS aimed to force down the rate of inflation by establishing clear, stable targets for financial policy over the medium term. The Treasury produced targets for the rate of growth of broad money (£M3 – which had so accurately predicted the rate of inflation since 1973) for four years. To keep broad money within the target range, government proposed to use interest rates and reduction of the PSBR. The exchange rate, on the other hand, would be allowed to float according to market pressures (Cairncross 1992: 241–2). Although the government made much during the election campaign of the rise of unemployment under the Wilson–Callaghan government, it also expected a short-term rise in unemployment until unions and firms accommodated to the new monetary policy. Economic agents would soon learn that the government meant business and measures to weaken the trade unions would make the labour market more flexible. Above all, the government must not be deflected by rising unemployment; it had to avoid a Heath U-turn.

The MTFS was a disastrous failure. The authorities failed to achieve control over the rate of growth of the money stock. Table 14.1 shows that the actual growth of both the PSBR and £M3 consistently exceeded the rates set out in the first MTFS. As a result, the targets were revised upwards in 1982 and 1986, which destroyed even the semblance of the stable framework which the policy was intended to provide (Coakley and Harris 1992: 42). Even these revised targets were overshot, as is evident from Table 14.1. To make matters still worse, there were very unpleasant side effects of the MTFS. Interest rates were raised from 12 to 17 per cent in the government's first six months and helped accelerate the rise in the exchange rate (Chapter 11 above). Sterling rose by about 25 per cent between 1979–81, to the apparent relief of the government because import prices eased considerably. But these same relative price effects made it much harder for British producers to compete with imports and retain export markets. British firms could not absorb these competitive pressures. In the second half of 1980 GDP fell by 4 per cent and by a further 1.2 per cent in 1981 (Cairncross 1992: 239). Many manufacturing firms, and not necessarily the least efficient, went into liquidation (Chapter 12 above) or became distress borrowers from the banks. Distress borrowers need to borrow to survive; the rate of interest is immaterial. Banks preferred to offer lifelines rather than closure to major customers; credit (and, hence, £M3) continued to expand. The rapid rise of unemployment in 1980–1 increased government expenditure on benefits and reduced revenue from taxes and pushed the growth of the PSBR outside its target range. The disastrous impact of policy can be measured by the large fall in British GDP despite the enormous expansion of oil output at a time when other OECD countries experienced significant growth in GDP (Table 14.2).

Inflation did fall, but not immediately in part because the new government's decision to switch the burden of taxation from direct to indirect sources led to a big rise in VAT with an adverse impact on prices (Woodward 1991: 205). RPI inflation reached a peak of 18 per cent in 1980, but was reduced to single figures in 1982 and to around 5 per cent throughout the mid-1980s (Figure 13.2). The government's monetary policy may have contributed to the fall of inflation but the main cause in Britain and other OECD countries in the mid-1980s was the collapse of primary product prices (Beckerman and Jenkinson 1986). The sharp rise in unemployment from 5 to 12.5 per cent between 1979 and 1983 must also have had some impact, but wages continued to rise steadily, especially in manufacturing, where job losses were most severe (Muellbauer 1986: xvi; Tomlinson 1990: 340; Chapter 13).

The willingness of government to countenance such a huge rise in the

Table 14.1 The medium-term financial strategy and monetary growth, 1979/80–88/89

| Date set | Projections and out-turns (annual % changes) | | | | | | | | | |
|---|---|---|---|---|---|---|---|---|---|---|
| | 1979/80 | 1980/81 | 1981/82 | 1982/83 | 1983/84 | 1984/85 | 1985/86 | 1986/87 | 1987/88 | 1988/89 |
| Targets for £M3: | | | | | | | | | | |
| June 1979 | 7–11 | | | | | | | | | |
| March 1980 | | 7–11 | (6–10) | (6–9) | (4–8) | | | | | |
| March 1981 | | | 6–10 | (6–9) | (4–8) | | | | | |
| March 1982 | | | | 8–12 | (7–11) | (6–10) | | | | |
| March 1983 | | | | | 7–11 | (6–10) | (5–9) | (4–8) | (3–7) | (2–6) |
| March 1984 | | | | | | 6–10 | (5–9) | (4–8) | (3–7) | (2–6) |
| March 1985 | | | | | | | 5–9 | | | |
| March 1986 | | | | | | | | 11–15 | | |
| Out-turn | 16.2 | 19.4 | 12.8 | 11.2 | 9.4 | 11.9 | 16.9 | 19.0 | | |
| PSBR targets in the first MTFS (% of GDP): | | | | | | | | | | |
| Target | | 3.75 | 3.0 | 2.25 | 1.5 | | | | | |
| Out-turn | | 5.4 | 3.3 | 3.1 | 3.2 | | | | | |

Source: National Institute Economic Review, various issues.

*Table 14.2* Annual changes in real GDP, 1979–85, selected countries

|         | 1979 | 1980 | 1981 | 1982 | 1983 | 1984 | 1985 |
|---------|------|------|------|------|------|------|------|
| France  | 3.3  | 1.1  | 0.5  | 1.8  | 0.7  | 1.5  | 1.1  |
| Germany | 4.2  | 1.4  | 0.2  | −0.6 | 1.5  | 2.7  | 2.6  |
| Japan   | 5.2  | 4.4  | 3.9  | 2.8  | 3.2  | 5.0  | 4.5  |
| UK      | 2.2  | −2.3 | −1.2 | 1.0  | 3.8  | 2.2  | 3.7  |
| USA     | 2.0  | 0.0  | 3.7  | −2.5 | 4.0  | 6.7  | 3.0  |

Source: *OECD Economic Outlook*, various issues.

unemployment rate with apparent equanimity was the most significant development in economic policy in the 1980s. The Thatcher government shrewdly deflected criticism of economic policy by blaming the unions and previous governments for high unemployment and emphasising the government's success in reducing inflation. Although there were fierce rows in cabinet, the government was not pushed into expansionary policies by fear of unemployment. But the experiences of 1979–82 had a significant impact on policy-making. Lawson, who succeeded to the post of Chancellor of the Exchequer in 1983, duly abandoned sole reliance on the broad money supply (£M3) to guide monetary policy. In 1984, targets were established for narrow money (M0) as well as £M3, and in 1985 the government recognised the costs of sterling's float during 1979–82 and began to manage the exchange rate actively as noted in Chapter 11 above. However, the managed rates of the later 1980s were almost as costly as floating exchanges had been earlier in the decade. The currency markets, driven by euphoric government news management, overestimated the strength of the British economy in the later 1980s. As funds flowed into London, the Treasury was forced to lower interest rates to maintain sterling's pegged level against the Dmark. Interest rates were driven down further by a stock market crash in 1987 when, as in 1929, share values across the world were marked down. On this occasion, there was no general slump because financial authorities across the world had learned not to raise interest rates. Lower interest rates enabled the British recovery, which had been gathering momentum since 1982 to become a feverish, uncontrolled boom. Property prices rose by 75 per cent in three years (1985–8) and RPI inflation approached double figures at the end of the 1980s.

   The most disturbing feature of the Lawson boom was the huge rise in imports in the late 1980s. There were remarkable changes in consumer behaviour during the 1980s which helped initiate, sustain and then burst the boom. The savings ratio (the proportion of personal income saved) stood at 13.5 per cent in 1980, fell to the historically low level of 8.2 per cent in 1986, but fell further to 5.4 per cent in 1988. Consumers believed themselves to be suddenly richer as a result of rising property prices and began to borrow much more heavily to finance current consumption. Consumer spending rose faster than GDP in 1988, with imports rising by almost as much as total GDP (Cairncross 1992: 229). The surge of imports in 1987–9, growing concern about rising inflation and indebtedness put pressure on the Treasury to raise interest rates. Higher interest rates contributed to the steep fall in asset values (especially property) and a rise in the savings ratio, to 10.9 per cent in 1990. The forces which had driven the boom made the slump very severe.

The downturn was always going to be difficult because of the overhang of debt from the late 1980s, but was made deeper by further policy mistakes. As noted in Chapter 11, the decision to join the EMS at an overvalued rate of exchange led to interest rates being held higher than conditions in the real economy merited. The slump was therefore deeper and more prolonged than it need have been. The costs were similar to those which flowed from high interest and exchange rates in the early 1980s: a fall in output, accelerated relative decline, higher unemployment, permanent loss of productive capacity, particularly from the manufacturing sector and a big increase in social insecurity for the most vulnerable. The only positive outcome from the second slump in a decade was the squeezing of inflation, so that in the early 1990s, Britain's inflation rate was below the OECD average. Inflation may now be under control, though experience of the 1980s suggests that predictions are very foolhardy. This is, however, the only positive outcome of the new monetary policies since 1979. The priority for monetary management throughout has been to create a stable and predictable macro-economic environment. The government has, however, presided over the biggest bust–boom–bust cycle in the postwar period and has made the 1980s a rival to the 1920s as the most turbulent decade in British macro-economic history. In the 1920s, instability originated in the world economy but since 1979 mistakes of domestic policy have been largely to blame. The unprecedented changes in consumer behaviour, which underwrote the boom of the later 1980s, may have been difficult to predict, but consumers were only reacting to signals around them – loose monetary conditions and excessive official optimism about a British productivity miracle – to demand what the weakened productive base could not supply. The greatest weakness of macro-economic policy since 1979 has been the failure to utilise the opportunities offered by North Sea oil. The balance of payments constraint which had dogged British economic policy-making since 1945 should have receded almost from view. Oil revenues were, however, used to bribe the electorate with tax cuts, boosting consumer spending, exacerbating the balance-of-payments problem and may have weakened Britain's long-term ability to generate current account balance (Chapter 12).

In the early 1980s, when the government began to realise the problems confronting its monetary policy, there was a change of emphasis in the way ministers presented the Thatcherite economic project. The preoccupation with the money supply waned and the core, distinctive feature became liberalisation of the supply side of the economy. Much effort was directed to making the labour market more flexible (see Chapter 13) but the government also tried to 'get on top of' public spending, roll back the frontiers of the state, and release enterprise and initiative. Deep cuts in public expenditure were essential for success, but the record since 1979 has been mixed. Five broad programmes – health and social services, social security, defence, education and the Scottish, Welsh and Northern Irish Offices – consume three-quarters of all government spending (Tomlinson 1990: 321). The scope for cuts here has been very limited (at least until the early 1990s when defence spending became more vulnerable with the end of the cold war). The main retrenchment has been in housing and subsidies to industry, but the volume of resources consumed by the NHS has increased between 1979 and 1990 (Rowthorn 1992: 274). Thus, public spending as a whole has risen in real terms over the period 1979–93 and as a proportion of GDP has fluctuated around the levels established in the 1970s. The PSBR has fluctuated even more wildly, with a big rise in both slumps as expenditure on unemployment rose and revenue contracted while the frenetic boom, oil revenues and sales of public assets in the late 1980s produced a negative PSBR (revenue exceeded expenditure in the public sector as a whole). Public spending has been a more difficult target than anticipated because unemployment has been much higher than anticipated throughout the Conservatives' period of office.

Other aspects of 'rolling back' the state have been more successful. As was seen in Chapter 12, both de-regulation and privatisation have made significant progress since the mid-1980s. As the Labour Party has seen nationalisation as a quick cure for most of the ailments of private enterprise, so the Conservatives have had very broad expectations of privatisation. Tomlinson (1994: 207) has identified eight objectives in official statements on privatisation since 1979. If the most important in practice seem to have been the raising of revenue and reducing the PSBR (Chapter 12), the political rhetoric has emphasised the potential for increased productivity gains which can be made by industries freed from government involvement in decisions, able to respond quickly to consumer pressures and able to plan investment programmes without the constraining effects of PSBR targets. Privatisation has become the leading edge of the government's commitment to market forces and the promotion of enterprise (Bishop and Kay 1988). The evidence that privatisation has improved business performance is undeniable, but the hoped for effects on productivity are less easily identifiable. Table

14.3 shows productivity growth in the nationalised/privatised sector since 1978 and shows no obvious pattern. Three industries (steel, coal, postal services) have experienced a substantial improvement in labour productivity, but only one, steel, has been privatised and the improvements in labour productivity in coalmining rest on a capital programme which has almost certainly earned too low a rate of return to have been justified under private ownership. In other industries, productivity growth has tended to be lower in the 1980s than the 1970s. Insufficient time has elapsed to judge the impact of new policies (tighter budget controls and new management methods as well as changing ownership) on performance. There is, though, no obvious evidence for the broadly held belief that public-sector industries performed badly and that substantial efficiency gains have flowed from policy changes.

If the efficiency gains from the flagship policy have been so uncertain, what can be said about the effects of Conservative policies on relative decline? Growth of output and productivity have risen since 1979 but there still has been no British 'economic miracle' (Crafts 1993: 40). Productivity growth in manufacturing certainly has accelerated, but manufacturing's relative decline has not been halted, and may even have accelerated (Tables 10.6 and 12.1 above). The intensification of market forces has apparently had no more beneficial effects on either output or productivity than the failed interventionism of the later 1960s. Whatever gains have accrued have been small and have been concentrated in areas, such as the creation of an enterprise culture, which are unquantifiable and have an uncertain impact on aggregate economic performance.

The Conservative governments since 1979 have not been alone in their

Table 14.3 Labour productivity growth rates in the UK nationalised/ privatised sector, 1968–88 (% per annum)

|  | 1968–78 | 1978–88 |
| --- | --- | --- |
| Nationalised Sector: | | |
| Coal | −0.7 | 6.2 |
| Railways | 0.8 | 0.8 |
| Postal | −1.3 | 2.2 |
| | | |
| Privatised Sector: | | |
| Steel | −0.2 | 9.4 |
| Electricity | 5.3 | 3.2 |
| Gas | 8.5 | 5.2 |
| Telecommunications | 8.2 | 5.6 |
| Airways | 6.4 | 4.2 |
| National freight | 2.7 | 3.7 |

Source: Crafts 1993: 48.

failure to get to grips with Britain's fundamental economic problems. The previous four chapters have suggested that most OECD countries have experienced fast growth since 1945 based upon the creation of conditions for successful 'technological activity' as described in Chapter 12. Technological and competitive success was based in the early post-war period on the capacity to absorb and adapt US methods of production and organisation. In more recent times, however, competitive success has meant the ability to create and maintain a technological lead in product areas in an increasingly integrated international economy. The best British firms (and foreign-owned companies operating in Britain) have been able to succeed in this highly competitive environment, but many domestically owned companies have been handicapped by the poor quality of their managers, the comparative shortage of technological expertise within British industry and the low skill levels, broadly defined, of British workers. There may also have been weaknesses in company organisation and finance-industry linkages, but these are more uncertain and the potential remedies have never been without problems of their own. Supplementing and reinforcing these supply-side weaknesses have been demand-side constraints. In many cases British markets have been too small or too segmented to justify the volume of production and profit upon which successful technological activity must be based. In addition, the costs of Britain's misguided pretensions to great power status, especially early on in the postwar period, resulted in curbs to the growth of aggregate demand in the interests of external stability. A government wishing to tackle Britain's underlying economic problems has thus been faced with a formidable task, not least because the stock of managerial, technological and workplace skills will be little affected by short-term changes and market segmentation has arisen from consumer choices which governments are naturally reluctant to reshape. Governments have certainly attempted to address these problems throughout the postwar period, there have been a series of measures to improve training, education, R&D activity and even to restructure industries in the hope of breaking demand and supply constraints. The focus has however been intermittent; for much of the postwar period, governments have been thrown off course by the need to attend to short-term problems, particularly on external account. This inability to tackle underlying weaknesses for more than brief interludes between financial crises is especially unfortunate as the time horizons before tangible benefits flow from training initiatives, for example, are very long; reform will not have its maximum impact until accommodating changes are made in 'the interlocking network of societal institutions' (Finegold and Soskice 1988: 26). In this respect, the governments with the largest 'policy space' to tackle deeply entrenched supply- and demand-side weaknesses have been those since the late 1970s when

North Sea oil flows should have removed the external constraint. The full test of economic policy since 1977–8 has yet to be seen, but current evidence suggests that this breathing space was not used to best advantage.

# Bibliography

The place of publication is London unless otherwise indicated.

Abel-Smith, B. and Townsend, P. (1965) *The Poor and the Poorest*, Bell.

Abramovitz, M. (1986) 'Catching up, forging ahead and falling behind', *Journal of Economic History* 46: 385–406.

Abrams, P. (1963) 'The failure of social reform: 1918–20', *Past and Present* 24: 43–64.

Ackrill, M. (1988) 'Britain's managers and the British economy, 1870s to the 1980s', *Oxford Review of Economic Policy* 4: 59–73.

Addison, J.T. and Barnett, A.H. (1982) 'The impact of unions on productivity', *British Journal of Industrial Relations* 20: 145–62.

Addison, P. (1977) *The Road to 1945: British Politics and the Second World War*, Quartet Books.

Adkin, N. (1994) 'Characteristics of the bottom 20 per cent of the income distribution', *Social Trends* 24: 13–20.

Ady, P.H. (1952) 'Britain and overseas development', in G.D.N. Worswick and P.H. Ady (eds), *The British Economy, 1945–1950*, Oxford: Oxford University Press.

Albu, A. (1980) 'British attitudes to engineering education: a historical perspective', in K. Pavitt (ed.), *Technological Innovation and British Economic Performance*, Macmillan.

Aldcroft, D.H. (1967) 'Economic growth in the inter-war years: a re-assessment', *Economic History Review* XX: 311–326.

—— (1970) *The Inter-war Economy: Britain, 1919–1939*, Batsford.

—— (1978) *From Versailles to Wall Street 1919–1929*, Allen Lane.

—— (1984) *Full Employment: The Elusive Goal*, Brighton: Wheatsheaf.

—— (1986) *The British Economy. Volume 1: The Years of Turmoil, 1920–1951*, Brighton: Wheatsheaf.

Aldcroft, D.H. and Fearon, P. (eds) (1969) *Economic Growth in Twentieth Century Britain*, Macmillan.

Alford, B.W.E. (1972) *Depression and Recovery? British Economic Growth, 1918–1939*, Macmillan.

—— (1981) 'British industry between the wars', in R.C. Floud and D.N. McCloskey (eds), *The Economic History of Britain since 1700*, Cambridge: Cambridge University Press, vol. 2.

—— (1988) *British Economic Performance, 1945–1975*, Macmillan.

Allen, G.C. (1951) 'The concentration of production policy', in D.N. Chester (ed.), *Lessons of the British War Economy*, Cambridge: Cambridge University Press.

—— (1959) *British Industries and their Organisation*, Longman.

Allsopp, C.J. (1985) 'Economic growth', in D. Morris (ed.), *The Economic System in the UK*, Oxford: Oxford University Press.

Andrejewski, S. (1954) *Military Organisation and Society*, Routledge.

Armstrong, A.G. (1967) 'The motor industry and the British economy', *District Bank Review* 163: 19–40.

Armstrong, H.W. and Taylor, J. (1985) *Regional Economics and Policy*, Oxford: Philip Allen.

Armstrong, W.A. (1988) *Farmworkers: A Social and Economic History 1770–1988*, Batsford.

Arndt, H.W. (1944) *Economic Lessons of the 1930s, a Report*, 2nd edn, 1963, Cass.

Artis, M. (1972) 'Fiscal policy for stabilisation', in W. Beckerman (ed.), *The Labour Government's Economic Record, 1964–1970*, Duckworth.

—— (ed.) (1989) *Prest and Coppock's The UK Economy: A Manual of Applied Economics*, Weidenfeld & Nicolson, 12th edn.

Artis, M. and Cobham, D. (1991a) 'Summary and appraisal', in M. Artis and D. Cobham (eds), *Labour's Economic Policies, 1974–79*, Manchester: Manchester University Press.

Artis, M. and Cobham, D. (eds) (1991b) *Labour's Economic Policies, 1974–79*, Manchester: Manchester University Press.

Ashworth, W. (1953) *Contracts and Finance*, HMSO and Longman.

—— (1986) *The History of the British Coal Industry, Volume 5, 1946–1982: The Nationalised Industry*, Oxford: Clarendon Press.

Atkinson, A.B. (1969) *Poverty in Britain and the Reform of Social Security*, Cambridge: Cambridge University Press.

—— (1975) *The Economics of Inequality*, Oxford: Oxford University Press.

Atkinson, A.B., Gordon, J.P.F. and Harrison, A.J. (1989) 'Trends in shares of top wealth-holders in Britain, 1923–1981', *Oxford Bulletin of Economics and Statistics* 51: 315–32.

Atkinson, A.B. and Harrison, A.J. (1978) *Distribution of Personal Wealth in Britain*, Cambridge: Cambridge University Press.

Atkinson, A.B. and Micklewright, J. (1989) 'Turning the screw: benefits for the unemployed, 1979–1988', in A.W. Dilnot and I. Walker (eds) *The Economics of Social Security*, Oxford: Oxford University Press.

Austin, B. and Lloyd, W.F. (1926) *The Secret of High Wages*, Unwin.

Bacon, R. and Eltis, W.A. (1976) *Britain's Economic Problem: Too Few Producers*, Macmillan, 2nd edn, 1978.

Bagwell, P.S. (1988) *The Transport Revolution from 1770*, Routledge, 2nd edn.

Baines, D. (1981) 'The labour supply and the labour market 1860–1914'. in R.C. Floud and D.N. McCloskey (eds), *The Economic History of Britain since 1700*, Cambridge: Cambridge University Press, vol. 2.

—— (1985) *Migration in a Mature Economy; Emigration and Internal Migration in England and Wales, 1961–1900*, Cambridge: Cambridge University Press.

Balassa, B. (1979) 'Export composition and export performance in industrial countries', *Review of Economics and Statistics* 61: 604–7.

Balfour Committee (1926–30) *Reports of the Committee on Industry and Trade*, HMSO.

Barker, T. and Dunne, P. (eds) (1988) *The British Economy After Oil: Manufacturing or Services?*, Croom Helm.

Barker, T.C. and Robbins, M. (1974) *A History of London Transport: Passenger Travel and the Development of the Metropolis*, vol. 2., Allen & Unwin.

Barlow Report (1946) *Report of the Committee on Scientific Manpower*, HMSO.

Barnes, D. and Reid, E. (1982) 'A new relationship: trade unions in the Second

World War', in B. Pimlott and C. Cook (eds) *Trade Unions in British Politics*, Longman.

Barnett, C. (1986) *The Audit of War: The Illusion and Reality of Britain as a Great Nation*, Macmillan.

Barr, N.A. (1981) 'Empirical definitions of the poverty line', *Policy and Politics* 9: 1–21.

Barr, N.A. and Coulter, F. (1990) 'Social security: solution or problem?', in J. Hills (ed.), *The State of Welfare: The Welfare State in Britain since 1974*, Oxford: Clarendon Press.

Batchelor, R.A., Major, R.L. and Morgan, A.D. (1980) *Industrialisation and the Basis for Trade*, Cambridge: Cambridge University Press.

Batstone, E. (1986) 'Labour and productivity', *Oxford Review of Economic Policy* 2: 32–43.

Baumol, W.J. (1986) 'Productivity growth, convergence and welfare: what the long-run data show', *American Economic Review* 76: 1072–85.

Beacham, A. (1958) 'The coal industry', in Burn (ed.), *The Structure of British Industry: A Symposium*, Cambridge: Cambridge University Press.

Bean, C., Layard, P.R.G. and Nickell, S. (eds) (1986) *The Rise in Unemployment*, Oxford: Blackwell.

Beckerman, W. (ed.) (1965) *The British Economy in 1975*, Cambridge: Cambridge University Press.

—— (ed.) (1972) *The Labour Government's Economic Record 1964–1970*, Duckworth.

—— (ed) (1979) *Slow Growth in Britain: Causes and Consequences*, Heinemann.

Beckerman, W. and Jenkinson, T. (1986) 'What stopped inflation: unemployment or commodity prices?', *Economic Journal* 96: 39–54.

Beeching, R. (1963) *The Reshaping of British Railways* (the Beeching Report), British Railways Board.

Beenstock, M.F., Capie, F. and Griffiths, B. (1984) 'Economic recovery in the United Kingdom in the 1930s', *Bank of England Panel of Academic Consultants, Panel Paper*, No.23: 57–85.

Beer, S. (1965) *Modern British Politics*, Faber.

Benjamin, D.K. and Kochin, L.A. (1979) 'Searching for an explanation of unemployment in interwar Britain', *Journal of Political Economy*, 87: 441–78.

Benwell Community Development Project (1979) *The Making of a Ruling Class*, Newcastle-upon-Tyne: Benwell CDP.

Beveridge, A. (1963) *Apprenticeship Now*, Chapman Hall.

Beveridge, W.H. (1942) *Social Insurance and Allied Services*, Cmd 6404, HMSO.

—— (1944) *Full Employment in a Free Society: A Report*, Allen & Unwin, 2nd edn. 1960.

Bhaskar, K. (1979) *The Future of the British Motor Industry*, Kogan Page.

Bienefeld, M.A. (1972) *Working Hours in British Industry: An Economic History*, Weidenfeld & Nicolson.

Bird, D., Beatson, M. and Butcher, S. (1993) 'Membership of trade unions', *Employment Gazette* May 1993: 189–96.

Bishop, M. and Kay, J.A. (1988) *Does Privatization Work?*, London Business School.

Black, D. (1980) *Inequalities in Health: Report of a Research Working Group* (the Black Report), DHSS.

Blackaby, D. (1986) 'An analysis of the male racial earnings differential in the UK', *Applied Economics* 18: 1233–42.

Blackaby, F. (ed.) (1978a) *De-industrialisation*, Heinemann.

—— (ed.) (1978b) *British Economic Policy, 1960–1974*, Cambridge: Cambridge University Press.

Blank, S. (1973) *Industry and Government in Britain: The Federation of British Industries in Politics*, Farnborough: Saxon House.

Bleaney, M. (1976) *The Rise and Fall of Keynesian Economics: An Investigation of its Contribution to Capitalist Development*, Macmillan.

Boltho, A. (ed.) (1982) *The European Economy: Growth and Crisis*, Oxford: Oxford University Press.

Bolton Committee (1971) *Small Firms: Report of the Committee of Inquiry on Small Firms*, HMSO, Cmnd 4811.

Booth, A. (1978) 'An administrative experiment in unemployment policy in the thirties', *Public Administration* 56: 139–57.

—— (1982) 'The Second World War and the origins of modern regional policy', *Economy and Society* 11: 1–21.

—— (1983) 'The Keynesian revolution in economic policy making', *Economic History Review* 26: 103–23.

—— (1987a) 'Britain in the 1930s: a managed economy?', *Economic History Review* XL: 499–522.

—— (1987b) 'Unemployment and interwar politics', in S. Glynn and A. Booth (eds), *The Road to Full Employment*, Allen & Unwin.

—— (1987c) 'The war and the white paper', in Glynn and Booth (eds), *The Road to Full Employment*, Allen & Unwin.

—— (1989) *British Economic Policy, 1931–49: Was there a Keynesian Revolution?* Hemel Hempstead: Harvester.

—— (1995a) 'Corporate politics and the quest for productivity: the TUC and the politics of industrial productivity, 1947–1960' in J.L. Melling and A. McKinlay (eds) *Work, Management and Authority in Modern Europe*, Aldershot: Edward Elgar.

—— (ed.) (1995b) *British Economic Development since 1945*, Manchester: Manchester University Press.

Booth, A. and Glynn, S. (1975) 'Unemployment in the interwar period: a multiple problem', *Journal of Contemporary History* 10: 611–36.

Booth, A. and Pack, M. (1985) *Employment, Capital and Economic Policy in Great Britain 1918–1939*, Oxford: Blackwell.

Boyd-Orr, J. (1936) *Food, Health and Income: Report on a Survey of Adequacy of Diet in Relation to Income*, Macmillan.

Braverman, H. (1974) *Labour and Monopoly Capital*, New York: Monthly Review Press.

Brett, E.A. (1985) *The World Economy since the War: The Politics of Uneven Development*, Macmillan.

Bristow, J.A. (1968) 'Taxation and income stabilisation', *Economic Journal* 78: 299–311.

British Association for the Advancement of Science (1935) *Britain in Depression, a Record of British Industries since 1929*, Pitman.

Brittan, S. (1971) *Steering the Economy: The Role of the Treasury*, Harmondsworth: Penguin.

—— (1975) *Second Thoughts on Full Employment Policy*, Centre for Policy Studies.

Brittan, S. and Lilley, P. (1977) *The Delusion of Incomes Policy*, Temple Smith.

Broadberry, S.N. (1980) 'Purchasing power parity and the pound–dollar rate in the 1930s', *Economica* 54: 69–78.

—— (1986) *The British Economy between the Wars. A Macroeconomic Survey*, Oxford: Oxford University Press.

—— (1988) 'The impact of the wars on the long-run performance of the British economy', *Oxford Review of Economic Policy* 4: 25–37.

—— (1990) 'The emergence of mass unemployment: explaining macroeconomic trends in Britain during the trans-world war I period', *Economic History Review* XLIII, 71–82.

—— (1991) 'Unemployment', in N.F.R. Crafts and N.W.C. Woodward (eds), *The British Economy since 1945*, Oxford: Oxford University Press.

—— (1993) 'Manufacturing and the convergence hypothesis: what the long-run data show', *Journal of Economic History* 53: 772–95.

Broadberry, S.N. and Crafts, N.F.R. (1990) 'Explaining Anglo-American productivity differences in the mid-twentieth century', *Oxford Bulletin of Economics and Statistics* 52: 375–402.

Broadberry, S.N. and Crafts, N.F.R. (1992) 'Britain's productivity gap in the 1930s: some neglected factors', *Journal of Economic History* 52: 531–58.

Broadberry, S.N. and Fremdling, R. (1990) 'Comparative productivity in British and German industry, 1907–1937', *Oxford Bulletin of Economics and Statistics* 52: 403–21.

Brown, C. (1984) *Black and White in Britain: The Third PSI Survey*, Heinemann.

Brown, J. (1987) *Agriculture in England: A Survey of Farming, 1870–1947*, Manchester: Manchester University Press.

Brown, W. and Nolan, P. (1988) 'Wages and productivity: the contribution of industrial relations research to the understanding of pay determination', *British Journal of Industrial Relations* 26: 339–61.

Bruegel, I. (1986) 'The reserve army of labour, 1974–1979' in Feminist Review (ed.), *Waged Work: A Reader*, Virago.

Buchanan, J.M. and Tullock, G. (1962) *The Calculus of Consent: Logical Foundations of Constitutional Democracy*, Ann Arbor: University of Michigan Press.

Buchanan, J.M., Burton, J. and Wagner, R.E. (1978) *The Consequences of Mr. Keynes*, Institute of Economic Affairs.

Bullen, R. and Pelley, M.E. (1986) *Documents on British Foreign Policy Overseas, Series I, Volume III: Britain and America: Negotiation of the United States Loan*, HMSO.

Bullock, A. (1967) *The Life and Times of Ernest Bevin, Volume II: Minister of Labour, 1940–1945*, Heinemann.

—— (1983) *Ernest Bevin: Foreign Secretary, 1945–51*, Heinemann.

Burk, K. (ed.) (1982) *War and the State*, Allen & Unwin.

—— (1988) *The First Privatisation: Politicians, the City and the De-nationalisation of Steel*, Historians' Press.

Burk, K. and Cairncross, A.K. (1992) *Good-bye Great Britain: The 1976 IMF Crisis*, New Haven, CT: Yale University Press.

Burn, D. (ed.) (1958) *The Structure of British Industry: A Symposium*, 2 vols, Cambridge: Cambridge University Press.

Burnham, T.H. and Hoskins, G.O. (1943) *Iron and Steel in Britain, 1870–1930*, Allen & Unwin.

Buxton, N.K. and Aldcroft, D.H. (1979) *British Industry between the Wars: Instability and Industrial Development, 1919–1939*, Scolar Press.

CEPG (1975) Cambridge Economic Policy Group *Britain's Economic Crisis*, Nottingham: Spokesman.

CPRS (1975) Central Policy Review Staff *The Future of the British Car Industry*, HMSO.

CSO (1990) Central Statistical Office 'The effects of taxes and benefits on household income, 1987', *Economic Trends* 439: 84–118.

—— (1994) 'The effects of taxes and benefits on household income, 1992', *Economic Trends* 483: 100–32.

Cain, P.J. and Hopkins, A.G. (1993a) *British Imperialism: Innovation and Expansion 1688–1914*, Longman.

Cain, P.J. and Hopkins, A.G. (1993b) *British Imperialism: Crisis and Deconstruction, 1914–1990*, Longman.

Cairncross, A.K. (1978) 'What is de-industrialisation?', in F. Blackaby (ed.), *De-industrialisation*, Heinemann.

—— (1981) 'The postwar years, 1945–77', in R.C. Floud and D.N. McCloskey (eds), *The Economic History of Britain since 1700*, Cambridge: Cambridge University Press, vol. 2.

—— (1985) *Years of Recovery: British Economic Policy 1945–51*, Methuen.

—— (1992) *The British Economy since 1945: Economic Policy and Performance, 1945–1990*, Oxford: Blackwell.

Cairncross, A.K. and Eichengreen, B. (1983) *Sterling in Decline: The Devaluations of 1931, 1949 and 1967*, Oxford: Blackwell.

Cairncross, A.K., Kay, J.A. and Silberston, Z.A. (1983) 'The regeneration of manufacturing industry' in R.C.O. Matthews and J.R.Sargent (eds) *Contemporary Problems of Economic Policy: Essays from the CLARE Group*, Methuen.

Calder, A. (1965) *The Peoples' War*, Cape.

Calmfors, L. and Driffil, J. (1988) 'Bargaining structure, corporatism and macroeconomic performance', *Economic Policy* 6: 13–61.

Campbell, J. (1993) *Edward Heath: A Biography*, Cape.

Campbell-Kelly, M. (1989) *ICL: A Business and Technical History*, Oxford: Clarendon Press.

Capie, F. (1980) 'The pressure for tariff protection in Britain, 1917–1931', *Journal of European Economic History* 9: 431–48.

—— (1983) *Depression and Protectionism: Britain between the Wars*, Allen & Unwin.

—— (1987) 'Unemployment and real wages', in S. Glynn and A. Booth (eds), *The Road to Full Employment*, Allen & Unwin.

Capie, F. and Collins, M. (1992) *Have the Banks Failed British Industry?*, Institute of Economic Affairs.

Carew, A. (1987) *Labour under the Marshall Plan: The Politics of Productivity and the Marketing of Management Science*, Manchester: Manchester University Press.

Carr, J.C. and Taplin, W.A. (1962) *History of the British Steel Industry*, Oxford: Blackwell.

Carr-Saunders, A.M. (1937) *A Survey of Social Structure in England and Wales*, Oxford: Clarendon Press, revised edition.

Carruth, A. and Disney, R. (1988) 'Where have two million trade union members gone?', *Economica* 55: 1–19.

Carter, C. (ed.) (1981) *Industrial Policy and Innovation*, Heinemann.

Caterall, R.E. (1979) 'Electrical engineering', in N.K. Buxton and D.H. Aldcroft (eds), *British Industry between the Wars: Instability and Industrial Development, 1919–1939*, Scolar Press.

Caves, R.E. (ed.) (1968) *Britain's Economic Prospects*, Washington, DC: Brookings Institute.

—— (1980) 'Productivity differentials among industries', in R.E. Caves and L.B. Krause (eds), *Britain's Economic Performance*, Washington, DC: Brookings Institute.

Caves, R.E. and Krause, L.B. (eds) (1980) *Britain's Economic Performance*, Washington, DC: Brookings Institute.

Cawson, A., Morgan, K., Webber, D., Holmes, P. and Stevens, A. (1990) *Hostile*

*Brothers: Competition and Closure in the European Electronics Industry*, Oxford: Clarendon Press.

Cd 4499 (1909) *Royal Commission on the Poor Laws, Minority Report*, HMSO.

Cd 9182 (1918) *Committee on Currency and Foreign Exchanges after the War. First Interim Report*, HMSO.

Ceadel, M. (1991) 'Labour as a governing party: balancing left and right' in T. Gourvish and A. O'Day (eds), *Britain since 1945*, Macmillan.

Chalmers, M. (1985) *Paying for Defence*, Pluto.

Champernowne, D.G. (1937–8 and 1938–9) 'The uneven distribution of unemployment in the United Kingdom, 1929–36', *Review of Economic Studies*, 5: 93–106; and 6: 111–24.

Chandler, A.D. (1962) *Strategy and Structure: Chapters in the History of Industrial Enterprise*, Cambridge, MA: Harvard University Press.

—— (1977) *The Visible Hand: The Managerial Revolution in American Business*, Cambridge, MA: Harvard University Press.

—— (1990) *Scale and Scope: The Dynamics of Industrial Capitalism*, Cambridge, MA: Harvard University Press.

Channon, D.F. (1973) *The Strategy and Structure of British Enterprise*, Macmillan.

Chapman, A.L. and Knight, R. (1953) *Wages and Salaries in the UK, 1920–38*, Cambridge, Cambridge University Press.

Charles, R. (1973) *The Development of Industrial Relations in Britain, 1911–1939: Studies in the Evolution of Collective Bargaining at the National and Industry Level*, Hutchinson.

Chatterji, M. and Wickens, M.R. (1982) 'Productivity, factor transfers and economic growth in the UK', *Economica* 49: 21–38.

Chester, D.N. (1951a) 'The central machinery for economic policy', in Chester (ed.), *Lessons of the British War Economy*, Cambridge: Cambridge University Press.

—— (ed.) (1951b) *Lessons of the British War Economy*, Cambridge: Cambridge University Press.

—— (1975) *The Nationalisation of British Industry*, HMSO.

Chick, M. (1987) 'Privatisation: the triumph of past practice over current requirements', *Business History* 29: 104–16.

Chrystal, A. and Alt, J. (1983) *Political Economics*, Brighton, Wheatsheaf.

Church, R. (1979) *Herbert Austin. The British Motor Car Industry to 1941*, Europa.

—— (1994) *The Rise and Decline of the British Motor Industry*, Macmillan.

Clark, C. (1937) *National Income and Outlay*, Cass (reprinted 1965).

—— (1951) *The Conditions of Economic Progress*, Macmillan, 2nd edn.

Clarke, R.W.B. (1982) *Anglo-American Collaboration in War and Peace* (ed. A. Cairncross), Oxford: Oxford University Press.

Cleary, M.N. and Hobbs, G.D. (1983) 'The fifty year cycle: a look at the empirical evidence', in C. Freeman (ed.) *Long Waves in the World Economy*, Butterworth.

Clegg, H.A. (1954) 'Some consequences of the general strike', *Transactions of the Manchester Statistical Society*, 10: 1–28.

—— (1970) *The System of Industrial Relations in Great Britain*, Oxford: Blackwell.

Clegg, H.A., Fox, A. and Thompson, A. (1985) *A History of British Trade Unions since 1889, vol.2. 1911–1933*, Oxford: Clarendon Press.

Cmd 2600 (1926) *Report of the Royal Commission on the Coal Industry* (1925) (The Samuel Commission), vol.1. *Report*, HMSO.

Cmd 3282 (1929) *Final Report of the Committee on Industry and Trade* (Balfour Report), HMSO.

Cmd 3331 (1929) *Memoranda on Certain Proposals Relating to Unemployment*, HMSO.

Cmd 3897 (1931) *Committee on Finance and Industry: Report and Minutes of Evidence* (Macmillan Committee), HMSO.

Cmd 6527 (1944) *Employment Policy*, HMSO.

Cmd 7695 (1948) *Report of the Royal Commission on Population* (Barlow Commission), HMSO.

Cmd 7695 (1949) *Papers*, vol.1, *Report of an Inquiry into Family Limitation and its Influence on Human Fertility in the Past Fifty Years* (by J. Lewis-Fanning), HMSO.

Coakley, J. and Harris, L. (1992) 'Financial globalisation and deregulation', in J. Michie (ed.), *The Economic Legacy, 1979–1992*, Academic Press.

Coates, D. (1980) *Labour in Power? A Study of the Labour Government, 1974–9*, Longman.

—— (1994) *The Question of UK Decline. State, Society and Economy*, Hemel Hempstead: Harvester Wheatsheaf.

Coleman, D.C. (1969) *Courtaulds, an Economic and Social History*, 3 vols, Oxford: Clarendon Press.

Compton, M. and Bott, E.H. (1940) *British Industry: Its Changing Structure in Peace and War*, Drummond.

Congdon, T. (1988) *The Debt Threat: The Dangers of High Real Interest Rates for the World Economy*, Oxford: Blackwell.

Conservative Central Office (1992) *The Best Future for Britain. The Conservative Manifesto 1992*, Conservative Party.

Cottrell, P.L. (1975) *British Overseas Investment in the Nineteenth Century*, Macmillan.

Court, W.H.B. (1945) 'Problems of the British coal industry between the wars', *Economic History Review*, 15: 1–24.

—— (1951) *Coal*, HMSO and Longman.

Coutts, K. and Godley, W. (1992) 'Does Britain's balance of payments matter any more?', in J. Michie (ed.), *The Economic Legacy, 1979–1992*, Academic Press.

Cowling, K. and Sugden, R. (1993) 'Industrial strategy: a missing link in British economic policy', *Oxford Review of Economic Policy* 9: 83–100.

Crafts, N.F.R. (1981) 'The eighteenth century: a survey', in R.C. Floud and D.N. McCloskey (eds), *The Economic History of Britain since 1700*, Cambridge: Cambridge University Press.

—— (1985) *British Economic Growth during the Industrial Revolution*, Oxford: Clarendon Press.

—— (1987) 'Long-term unemployment in Britain in the 1930s', *Economic History Review*, XL: 418–32.

—— (1988) 'The assessment: British economic growth over the long run', *Oxford Review of Economic Policy*, 4: i–xxi.

—— (1991a) 'Economic growth', in N.F.R. Crafts and N.W.C. Woodward (eds), *The British Economy since 1945*, Oxford: Oxford University Press.

—— (1991b) 'Reversing economic decline?', *Oxford Review of Economic Policy*, 7: 81–98.

—— (1992) 'Productivity growth reconsidered', *Economic Policy*, 15: 387–426.

—— (1993) *Can De-industrialisation Seriously Damage your Wealth? A Review of Why Growth Rates Differ and How to Improve Economic Performance*, Institute of Economic Affairs.

Crafts, N.F.R., and Thomas, M. (1986), 'Comparative advantage in UK manufacturing trade 1910–1936', *Economic Journal*, 96, 629–45.

Crafts, N.F.R. and Woodward, N.W.C. (eds) (1991) *The British Economy since 1945*, Oxford: Oxford University Press.

Crocket, G. and Elias, P. (1984), 'British managers: a study of their education, training and earnings', *British Journal of Industrial Relations* 22: 34–46.

Croft, S. (1986) 'Women, caring and the necessity of need: a feminist reappraisal', *Critical Social Policy* 16: 23–39.

Crofts, W. (1986) 'The Attlee government's pursuit of women', *History Today* 36: 29–35.

Cronin, J.E. (1984) *Labour and Society in Britain 1918–1979*, Batsford.

Crosland, S. (1982) *Tony Crosland*, Cape.

Crouch, C. (ed.) (1979) *State and Economy in Contemporary Capitalism*, Croom Helm.

Crowther, M.A. (1988) *Social Policy in Britain 1914–1938*, Macmillan.

Cutler, T., Haslam, C., Williams, K. and Williams, J. (1989) *1992 – The Struggle for Europe: A Critical Evaluation of the European Community*, Oxford: Berg.

Cutler, T., Williams, K. and Williams, J. (1986) *Keynes, Beveridge and Beyond*, Routledge.

DEA (1965) Department of Economic Affairs *The National Plan*, HMSO Cmnd 2764.

DHSS (1984) Department of Health and Social Security *Population, Pension Costs and Pensioners' Incomes*, HMSO.

Dalton, H. (1962) *Memoirs, 1945–1960: High Tide and After*, Frederick Muller.

Daly, A., Hitchens, D.M.W.N., and Wagner, K. (1985) 'Productivity, machinery and skills in a sample of British and German manufacturing plants', *National Institute Economic Review* 111: 48–61.

Darby, J. and Wren-Lewis, S. (1988) *UK Manufacturing in an International Perspective*, National Institute of Economic and Social Research.

Davenport, M. (1982) 'The economic impact of the EEC' in A. Boltho (ed.), *The European Economy: Growth and Crisis*, Oxford: Oxford University Press.

Deakin, S. (1992) 'Labour law and industrial relations' in J. Michie (ed.) *The Economic Legacy, 1979–1992*, Academic Press.

Dean, A.J.H. (1978) 'Incomes policies and differentials', *National Institute Economic Review* 85: 40–8.

Dell, E. (1991) *A Hard Pounding: Politics and Economic Crisis, 1974–76*, Oxford: Oxford University Press.

Denison, E.F. (1967) *Why Growth Rates Differ*, Washington DC: Brookings Institute.

Dennison, S.R. (1939) *The Location of Industry and the Depressed Areas*, Oxford: Oxford University Press.

Denton, G., Forsyth, M. and MacLennan, M. *Economic Planning and Policies in Britain, France and Germany*, Allen & Unwin.

Department of Employment and Productivity (1971) *British Labour Statistics: Historical Abstract 1886–1968*, HMSO.

Dex, S. *The Sexual Division of Work*, Brighton: Wheatsheaf.

Diamond (1976) Royal Commision on the Distribution of Income and Wealth (Diamond Commision) *Second Report on the Standing Reference* (Report 4), HMSO, Cmnd 6626.

—— (1978) *Lower Incomes* (Report 6), HMSO, Cmnd 7175.

—— (1979) *Fourth Report on the Standing Reference* (Report 7), HMSO, Cmnd 7595.

Digby, A. (1989) *British Welfare Policy, Workhouse to Workfare*, Faber.

Dilnot, A.W. and Walker, I. (eds) (1989) *The Economics of Social Security*, Oxford: Oxford University Press.

Dilnot, A.W., Kay, J.A., and Morris, C.N. (1984) *The Reform of Social Security*, Oxford: Clarendon Press.

Dimsdale, N.H. (1981) 'British monetary policy and the exchange rate 1920–1938', *Oxford Economic Papers* 33: 306–49.

—— (1984) 'Employment and real wages in the inter-war period', *National Institute Economic Review* 110: 94–103.

Disney, R. (1979) 'Recurrent spells and the concentration of unemployment in Great Britain', *Economic Journal* 89: 109–19.

Dobson, A. (1986) *US Wartime Aid to Britain, 1940–1946*, Croom Helm.

Doeringer, P.B. and Bosanquet, N. (1973) 'Is there a dual labour market in Great Britain?', *Economic Journal* 83: 421–35.

Doeringer, P.B. and Piore, M.J. (1971) *Internal Labor Markets and Manpower Analysis*, Lexington, MA: D.C.Heath.

Donnelly, T. and Thoms, D. (1990) 'Trade unions, management and the search for production in the Coventry motor car industry, 1939–75', *Business History* 31: 98–113.

Donovan (1968) Royal Commission on Trade Unions and Employers' Associations (Donovan Commission), *Report*, HMSO, Cmnd 3623.

Dornbusch, R. and Fischer, S. (1980) 'Sterling and the external balance' in R.E. Caves and L.B. Krause (eds), *Britain's Economic Performance*, Washington, DC: Brookings Institute.

Dow, J.C.R. (1964) *The Management of the British Economy, 1945–60*, Cambridge: Cambridge University Press.

Dowie, J.A. (1968) 'Growth in the inter-war period: some more arithmetic', *Economic History Review* XXI: 93–112.

—— (1975) '1919–20 is in need of attention', *Economic History Review* XXVIII: 94–103.

Dreisziger, N.F. (ed.) (1981) *Mobilization for Total War: The Canadian, American and British Experience, 1914–18, 1939–45*, Waterloo, Ontario.

Drummond, I.M. (1972) *British Economic Policy and the Empire, 1919–1939*, Allen & Unwin.

—— (1974) *Imperial Economic Policy, 1917–1939: Studies in Expansion and Protection*, Allen & Unwin.

—— (1981) *The Floating Pound and the Sterling Area, 1931–1939*, Cambridge: Cambridge University Press.

—— (1987) *The Gold Standard and the International Monetary System 1900–1939*, Macmillan.

Duff, P. (1949) *British Ships and Shipping: A Survey of Modern Ship Design and Shipping Practice*, Harrap.

Dumke, R.H. (1990) 'Reassessing the *Wirtschaftswunder*: reconstruction and post-war growth in West Germany in an international context', *Oxford Bulletin of Economics and Statistics* 52: 451–91.

Dunkerley, J. and Hare, P.G. (1991) 'Nationalised industries', in N.F.R. Crafts and N.W.C. Woodward (eds), *The British Economy since 1945*, Oxford: Oxford University Press.

Dunleavy, P. (1980) *Urban Political Analysis*, Macmillan.

Dunnett, P.J.S. (1980) *The Decline of the British Motor Industry: The Effects of Government Policy, 1945–1979*, Croom Helm.

Dyos, H.J. and Aldcroft, D.H. (1969) *British Transport. An Economic Survey*, Leicester: Leicester University Press.

Edelstein, H. (1982) *Overseas Investment in the Age of High Imperialism: The United Kingdom 1850–1914*, Methuen.

Edgerton, D.E.H. (1987) 'Science and technology in British business history' *Business History* 29: 84–103.

Edwards, R.C. (ed.) (1975) *Labor Market Segmentation*, Lexington, MA: D.C. Heath.

Eichengreen, B. (ed.) (1985) *The Gold Standard in Theory and History*, Methuen.

Eichengreen, B. and Portes, R. (1981) *Sterling and the Tariff, 1929–1932*, Princeton: Princeton University Press.

Eichengreen, B. and Portes, R. (1989) 'Debt and default in the 1930s: causes and consequences', *European Economic Review*, 30.

Elbaum, B. and Lazonick, W. (eds) (1986) *The Decline of the British Economy*, Oxford: Oxford University Press.

Eliot, S.J. (1983) 'The crisis of the co-operative movement', *Retail and Distribution Management* 11: 8–14.

—— (1988) 'Retailing', in P. Johnson (ed.), *The Structure of British Industry*, Unwin Hyman, 2nd edn.

Ermisch, J.F. (1983) *The Political Economy of Demographic Change: Causes and Implications of Population Trends in Great Britain*, Heinemann.

Falkingham, J. (1989) 'Dependency and ageing in Britain: a re-examination of the evidence', *Journal of Social Policy* 18: 211–33.

Fearon, P. (1974) 'The British airframe industry and the state, 1918–35', *Economic History Review* XXII: 236–51.

—— (1979) 'Aircraft manufacturing', in N.R. Buxton and D.H. Aldcroft (eds), *British Industry between the Wars: Instability and Industrial Development, 1919–1939*, Scolar Press.

Feinstein, C.H. (1972a) *National Income, Expenditure and Output of the United Kingdom, 1855–1965*, Cambridge: Cambridge University Press.

—— (1972b) *Statistical Tables of National Income, Expenditure and Output of the U.K. 1855–1965*, Cambridge: Cambridge University Press.

—— (1988) 'Economic growth since 1870: Britain's performance in international perspective', *Oxford Review of Economic Policy* 4:1–13.

—— (1990a) 'What really happened to real wages?: trends in wages, prices and productivity in the UK, 1880–1913', *Economic History Review* XLIII: 329–55.

—— (1990b) 'Benefits of backwardness and costs of continuity', in A. Graham and A. Seldon (eds), *Government and Economies in the Postwar World: Economic Policies and Comparative Performance 1945–85*, Routledge.

Feinstein, C.H. and Matthews, R.C.O. (1990) 'The growth of output and productivity in the UK: the 1980s as a phase in the postwar period', *National Institute Economic Review* 133: 78–90.

Feminist Review (ed.) (1986) *Waged Work: A Reader*, Virago.

Fenelon, K.G. (1935) 'The road transport industry', in British Association for the Advancement of Science, *Britain in Depression*, Pitman.

Fennell, R. (1987) 'Reform of the CAP: shadow or substance?', *Journal of Common Market Studies* 26: 61–77

Ferguson, N.A. (1975) 'Women's work: employment opportunities and economic roles 1918–1939', *Albion* 7.

Field, A.J. (1984) 'A new interpretation of the onset of the great depression', *Journal of Economic History* 44: 489–98.

Field, F. (ed.) (1983) *The Wealth Report – 2*, Routledge.

Field, F., Meacher, M. and Pond, C. (1977) *To him who hath: a Study of Poverty and Taxation*, Harmondsworth: Penguin.

Fine, B. and Poleti, C. (1992) 'Industrial prospects in the light of privatisation', in J. Michie (ed.), *The Economic Legacy, 1979–1992*, Academic Press.

Finegold, D. and Soskice, D. (1988) 'The failure of training in Britain: analysis and prescription', *Oxford Review of Economic Policy* 4: 21–53.

Finer, S.E. (ed.) (1975) *Adversary Politics and Electoral Reform*, Wigram.

Finniston, M. (1980) *Engineering our Future* (the Finniston Report), HMSO, Cmnd 7794.

Firth, M. (1979) 'The profitability of takeovers and mergers', *Economic Journal* 89: 316–28.

Fishbein, W.H. (1984) *Wage Restraint by Consensus: Britain's Search for an Incomes Policy Agreement, 1965–79*, Routledge.

Fisher, S. (ed.) (1988) *Lisbon as a Port Town, the Seaman and Other Maritime Themes*, Exeter: Exeter University Press.

Flemming, J.S., Price, L.D.D. and Ingram, D.H.A. (1976) 'Trends in company profitability', *Bank of England Quarterly Bulletin* 16: 36–52.

Floud, R.C. (1981) 'Britain 1860–1914: a survey', in R.C. Floud and D.N. McCloskey (eds), *The Economic History of Britain since 1700*, Cambridge: Cambridge University Press, vol. 2.

Floud R.C. and McCloskey, D.N. (eds) (1981) *The Economic History of Britain since 1700*, Cambridge: Cambridge University Press, 2 vols.

Ford, A.G. (1962) *The Gold Standard: Britain and Argentina 1890–1914*, Oxford: Clarendon Press.

Foreman-Peck, J. (1981) 'The British tariff and industrial protection in the 1930s: an alternative model', *Economic History Review* XXXIV: 132–9.

—— (1983) *A History of the World Economy, International Economic Relations since 1850*, Brighton: Wheatsheaf.

—— (1991) 'Trade and the balance of payments', in N.F.R. Crafts and N.W.C. Woodward (eds), *The British Economy since 1945*, Oxford: Oxford University Press.

Forrester, J.W. (1976) 'New perspectives for growth over the next thirty years' *Middle- and Long-Term Energy Policies and Alternatives*, US House of Representatives, Sub-Committee on Energy and Power, 94th Congress, 2nd Session, Part I.

Fox, D.M. (1986) 'The National Health Service and the Second World War: the elaboration of consensus', in N.L. Smith (ed.), *War and Social Change: British Society in the Second World War*, Manchester: Manchester University Press.

Freeman, C. (ed.) (1983) *Long Waves in the World Economy*, Butterworth.

Freeman, C., Clark, J. and Soete, L. (1982) *Unemployment and Technical Innovation: A Study of Long Waves and Economic Development*, Pinter.

Freeman, R. (1988) 'Labour markets', *Economic Policy* 6: 63–80.

Freeman, R. and Medoff, J. (1984) *What do Unions do?*, New York: Basic Books.

Friedman, M. (1956) *Studies in the Quantity Theory of Money*, Chicago: Harper and Row.

—— (1969) *The Optimum Quantity of Money and Other Essays*, Macmillan.

—— (1977) *Inflation and Unemployment: The New Dimension in Politics*, Institute of Economic Affairs.

Friedman, M. and Schwartz, A.J. (1963) *A Monetary History of the United States 1857–1960*, Princeton: Princeton University Press.

Frielander, D. and Roshier, R.J. (1966) 'A study of internal migration in England and Wales. Part I: geographical patterns of internal migration, 1851–1951', *Population Studies* 19, 239–79.

Fulton, O. (1990) 'Higher education and employment: pressures and responses since 1960', in P. Summerfield and E.J. Evans (eds) *Technical Education and the*

*State since 1850: Historical and Contemporary Perspectives*, Manchester: Manchester University Press.

Furness, G.W. (1958) 'The cotton and rayon textile industry', in D. Burn (ed.), *The Structure of British Industry: A Symposium*, Cambridge: Cambridge University Press.

Galbraith, J.K. (1961) *The Great Crash, 1929*, Harmondsworth: Penguin.

Gamble, A. (1974) *The Conservative Nation*, Routledge.

—— (1981) *Britain in Decline: Economic Policy, Political Strategy and the British State*, Macmillan.

—— (1988) *The Free Economy and the Strong State*, Macmillan.

Gamble, A. and Walkland, S. (1984) *The British Party System and Economic Policy 1945–1983: Studies in Adversary Politics*, Oxford: Clarendon Press.

Gardner, J.W. (1972) 'Historical series of the Index of Industrial Production', *Economic Trends*, 223: vi–xxiii.

Gardner, R.N. (1956) *Sterling–Dollar Diplomacy: Anglo-American Collaboration in the Reconstruction of Multilateral Trade*, Oxford: Clarendon Press.

Garside, W.R. (1980) *The Measurement of Unemployment: Methods and Sources in Great Britain 1850–1979*, Oxford: Blackwell.

—— (1990) *British Unemployment 1919–1939: a Study in Public Policy*, Cambridge: Cambridge University Press.

Garside, W.R. and Hatton, T.J. (1985) 'Keynesian policy and British unemployment in the 1930s', *Economic History Review*, XXXVIII: 83–8.

George, K.D. and Joll, C. (1981) *Industrial Organisation*, Allen & Unwin, 3rd edn.

George, V. and Miller, S. (1994) *Social policy towards 2000, Squaring the Welfare Circle*, Routledge.

Gerschenkron, A. (1962) *Economic Backwardness in Historical Perspective: a Book of Essays*, Cambridge, MA: Harvard University Press.

Gilbert, B.B. (1970) *British Social Policy 1914–39*, Batsford.

Gillie, A. (1991) 'Redistribution', in M. Artis and D. Cobham (eds), *Labour's Economic Policies, 1974–79*, Manchester: Manchester University Press.

Glennerster, H. and Low, W. (1990) 'Education and the welfare state: does it all add up?', in J. Hills (ed.), *The State of Welfare: The Welfare State in Britain since 1974*, Oxford: Clarendon Press.

Glyn, A. and Sutcliffe, B. (1972) *British Capitalism, Workers and the Profits Squeeze*, Harmondsworth: Penguin.

Glynn, S. (1987) 'Real policy options', in S. Glynn and A. Booth (eds), *The Road to Full Employment*, Allen & Unwin.

—— (1991) *No Alternative? Unemployment in Britain*, Faber.

Glynn, S. and Booth, A. (1983a) 'Unemployment in interwar Britain: a case for re-learning the lessons of the 1930s?', *Economic History Review* XXXVI: 329–348.

Glynn, S. and Booth, A. (1983b) *British Unemployment in the Interwar Period: Survey and Perspective*, Canberra: Australian National University Press.

Glynn, S. and Booth, A. (eds) (1987) *The Road to Full Employment*, Allen & Unwin.

Glynn, S. and Howells, P.G. (1980) 'Unemployment in the 1930s: the "Keynesian solution" reconsidered', *Australian Economic History Review* 20: 28–45.

Glynn, S. and Oxborrow, J. (1976) *Interwar Britain: An Economic and Social History*, Allen & Unwin.

Glynn, S. and Shaw, S. (1981) 'Wage bargaining and unemployment', *Political Quarterly* 52.

Godley, W. (1978) 'Britain's chronic recession: can anything be done?', in W. Beckerman (ed.), *Slow Growth in Britain: Causes and Consequences*, Heinemann.

—— (1988) 'Manufacturing and the future of the British economy', in T. Barker and P. Dunne (eds), *The British Economy After Oil: Manufacturing or Services?*, Croom Helm.

Goldthorpe, J.H. (1979) *Social Mobility and Class Structure in Modern Britain*, Oxford: Clarendon Press.

Gomulka, S. (1979) 'Britain's slow economic growth: increasing inefficiency versus low rate of technical change', in W. Beckerman (ed.), *Slow Growth in Britain: Causes and Consequences*, Heinemann.

Goodman, A. and Webb, S. (1994) *For Richer or Poorer: The Changing Distribution of Income in the UK*, Institute of Fiscal Studies.

Gordon, R.J. (1992) 'Discussion', *Economic Policy* 15: 414–21.

Gorz, A. (1982) *Farewell to the Working Class*, Pluto.

Gospel, H.F. (1992) *Markets, Firms, and the Management of Labour in Modern Britain*, Cambridge: Cambridge University Press.

Gould, F. and Rowett, B. (1980) 'Public spending and social policy: the UK, 1950–77', *Journal of Social Policy* 9: 337–57.

Gourevitch, P., Martin, A., Ross, G., Bornstein, S., Markovits, A. and Allen, C. *Unions and Economic Crisis: Britain, West Germany and Sweden*, Allen & Unwin.

Gourvish, T.R. (1979) 'The standard of living, 1890–1914', in A. O'Day (ed.) *The Edwardian Age: Conflict and Stability, 1900–1914*, Macmillan.

—— (1986) *British Railways, 1948–1973: A Business History*, Cambridge: Cambridge University Press.

—— (1987) 'British business and the transition to a corporate economy: entrepreneurship and management structures', *Business History* 29: 18–45.

—— (1991) 'The rise (and fall?) of state-owned enterprise', in T. Gourvish and A. O'Day (eds), *Britain since 1945*, Macmillan.

Gourvish, T. and O'Day, A. (eds) (1991) *Britain since 1945*, Macmillan.

Gowing, M.M. (1972) 'The organisation of manpower in Britain during the Second World War', *Journal of Contemporary History* 7: 147–67.

Graham, A. (1972) 'Industrial policy', in W. Beckerman (ed.), *Slow Growth in Britain: Causes and Consequences*, Heinemann.

Graham, A. and Seldon, A. (1990) *Government and Economics in the Postwar World: Economic Policies and Comparative Performance 1945–85*, Routledge.

Grant, W. (1981) 'The politics of the green pound, 1974–79', *Journal of Common Market Studies* 19: 313–29.

—— (1982) *The Political Economy of Industrial Policy*, Butterworth.

Green, A. and Steedman, H. (1993) *Educational Provision, Educational Attainment and the Needs of Industry: A Review of Research for Germany, France, Japan and Britain*, National Institute of Economic and Social Research.

Green, C. (1989) 'The balance of payments', in M. Artis (ed.), *Prest and Coppock's the UK Economy: A Manual of Applied Economics*, Weidenfeld & Nicolson, 12th edn.

Green, F. (ed.) (1989) *The Restructuring of the UK Economy*, Hemel Hempstead: Harvester.

—— (1992) 'Recent trends in British trade union density: how much of a compositional effect?', *British Journal of Industrial Relations* 30: 445–58.

Gwilliam, K. (1988) 'Rail transport', in P. Johnson (ed.), *The Structure of British Industry*, Unwin Hyman, 2nd edn.

*Guardian* (1992) 'Pound drops out of the ERM', The *Guardian*, 17 Sept. 1992.

HMSO (1975) *The Motor Vehicle Industry*, Fourteenth Report from the Expenditure Committee (Trade and Industry Sub-Committee), Session 1974/5, HMSO.

Habermas, J. (1976) *Legitimation Crisis*, Heinemann.

Hacche, G. and Townsend, J. (1981) 'A broad look at exchange rate movements for eight countries, 1972–80', *Bank of England Quarterly Bulletin* 21: 489–509.

Hall, M. (1962) 'The consumer, capital and labour markets', in G.D.N. Worswick and P.H. Ady (eds), *The British Economy with Nineteen-Fifties*, Oxford: Oxford University Press.

Halsey, A.H. (ed.) (1972) *Trends in British Society since 1900: A Guide to the Changing Social Structure of Britain*, Macmillan.

—— (1978) *Change in British Society: Based on the Reith Lectures*, Oxford: Oxford University Press.

Halsey, A.H., Heath, A.F. and Ridge, J.M. (1980) *Origins and Destinations: Family, Class and Education in Modern Britain*, Oxford: Clarendon Press.

Hamnet, C. McDowell, L. and Sarre, P. (1989) (eds) *The Changing Social Structure*, Sage.

Hancock, W.K. and Gowing, M.M. (1949) *British War Economy*, HMSO.

Hann, D. (1986) *Government and North Sea Oil*, Macmillan.

Hannah, L. (1974) 'Takeover bids in Britain before 1950: an exercise in business pre-history', *Business History* 16: 65–77.

—— (1979) *Electricity before Nationalisation: A Study of the Development of the Electricity Supply Industry in Britain to 1948*, Macmillan.

—— (1983) *The Rise of the Corporate Economy*, Methuen, 2nd edn.

—— (1986) *Inventing Retirement: The Development of Occupational Benefits in Britain*, Cambridge: Cambridge University Press.

—— (1991) 'Scale and scope: towards a European visible hand?', *Business History* 33: 297–309.

Harris, J. (1972) *Unemployment and Politics: A Study in English Social Policy 1886–1914*, Oxford: Clarendon Press.

—— (1981) *William Beveridge: A Biography*, Oxford: Oxford University Press.

Harris, L. (1984) 'State and economy in the Second World War', in G. McLennan, D. Held and S. Hall (eds) *State and Society in Contemporary Britain: A Critical Introduction*, Cambridge: Polity Press.

Harris, N. (1972) *Competition and the Corporate Society: British Conservatives, the State and Industry, 1945–1964*, Methuen.

Harrison, M. (1988) 'Resource mobilisation for world war II: the USA, UK, USSR and Germany, 1938–1945', *Economic History Review* XLI: 171–92.

Harrod, R.F. (1972) *The Life of John Maynard Keynes*, Harmondsworth: Penguin.

Harte, P.E. and Clarke, R. (1980) *Concentration in British Industry, 1935–1975*, Cambridge: Cambridge University Press.

Harvey, D.R. and Thomson, K.J. (1985) 'Costs, benefits and the future of the Common Agricultural Policy', *Journal of Common Market Studies* 24: 1–20.

Hatton, T.J. (1983) 'Unemployment benefits and the macroeconomics of the interwar labour market: a further analysis', *Oxford Economic Papers* 35: 486–505.

Hay, D.A. (1985) 'International trade and development', in D. Morris (ed.), *The Economic System in the UK*, Oxford: Oxford University Press.

Hayek, F.A. (1972) *A Tiger by the Tail*, Institute of Economic Affairs.

Heald, D. (1983) *Public Expenditure: Its Defence and Reform*, Oxford: Oxford University Press.

Heath, A. and McDonald, S.K. (1987) 'Social change and the future of the left', *Political Quarterly* 58: 364–77.

Henderson, P.D. (1952) 'Development councils: an industrial experiment', in G.D.N. Worswick and P.H. Ady (eds), *The British Economy, 1945–50*, Oxford: Oxford University Press.

Hendry, J. (1987) 'The teashop computer manufacturer: J. Lyons, Leo and the potential and limits of high-tech diversification', *Business History* 29: 73–102.

Henry, S. and Ormerod, P. (1978) 'Incomes policy and wage inflation', *National Institute Economic Review* 85: 31–9.

Hewer, A. (1980) 'Manufacturing industry in the seventies: an assessment of import penetration and export performance', *Economic Trends* 320: 97–109.

Hickling, A. (1981) 'Movements in UK costs and prices, 1973–79', *Economic Trends* 334: 82–93.

Hilditch, P. (1988) 'The decline of British shipbuilding since the Second World War', in S. Fisher (ed.) *Lisbon as a Port Town, the British Seaman and Other Maritime Themes*, Exeter: Exeter University Press.

Hill, T.P. (1964) 'Growth and investment according to international comparisons'. *Economic Journal* 74: 287–304.

Hills, J. (ed.) (1990) *The State of Welfare: The Welfare State in Britain since 1974*, Oxford: Clarendon Press.

Hills, J. and Mullings, B. (1990) 'Housing: a decent home for all within their means?', in J. Hills (ed.), *The State of Welfare: The Welfare State in Britain since 1974*, Oxford: Clarendon Press.

Hines, A.G. (1964) 'Trade unions and wage inflation in the UK, 1893–1961', *Review of Economic Studies* 31: 221–52.

—— (1969) 'Wage inflation in the UK, 1948–62: a disaggregated study', *Economic Journal* 79: 66–89.

Hinton, J. (1980) 'Coventry communism: a study of factory politics in the Second World War', *History Workshop Journal* 10: 90–118.

Hirsch, F. (1977) *The Social Limits to Growth*, Routledge.

Hirsch, F. and Goldthorpe, J.H. (eds) (1978) *The Political Economy of Inflation*, Oxford: Martin Robertson.

Hobbs, G.D. (1985) 'Long waves of economic activity' in D. Morris (ed.), *The Economic System in the UK*, Oxford: Oxford University Press.

Hobsbawm, E. (1978) 'The long march of labour halted?', *Marxism Today* Sept.: 279–86.

—— (1983) 'Labour's lost millions', *Marxism Today* Oct.: 7–13.

—— (1987) 'Out of the wilderness', *Marxism Today* Oct.: 12–19.

Hobson, J.A. (1896) *The Problem of the Unemployed: An Enquiry and an Economic Policy*, Methuen.

Hogan, M. (1987) *The Marshall Plan: America, Britain and the Reconstruction of Europe, 1947–1952*, Cambridge: Cambridge University Press.

Holmes, C. (1991) 'Immigration' in T. Gourvish and A. O'Day (eds), *Britain since 1945*, Macmillan.

Holmes, C. and Booth, A. (eds) (1991) *Economy and Society: European Industrialisation and its Social Consequences. Essays Presented to Sidney Pollard*, Leicester: Leicester University Press.

Holmes, M. (1982) *Political Pressure and Economic Policy: British Government, 1970–74*, Butterworth.

—— (1985a) *The Labour Government, 1974–79: Political Aims and Economic Reality*, Macmillan.

—— (1985b) *The First Thatcher Government, 1979–83: Contemporary Conservatism and Economic Change*, Brighton: Wheatsheaf.

Hoskyns, C. (1986) 'Equality and the European Community', in Feminist Review (ed.), *Waged Work: A Reader*, Virago.

House of Lords (1985) *Report from the Select Committee on Overseas Trade*, HMSO.

Houthakker, H.S. (1980) 'The use and management of North Sea oil', in R.E.

Caves and L.B. Krause (eds), *Britain's Economic Performance*, Washington, DC: Brookings Institute.

Houthakker, H.S. and Magee, S.P. (1969) 'Income and price elasticities in world trade', *Review of Economics and Statistics* 51: 111–25.

Howson, S. (1975) *Domestic Monetary Management in Britain, 1919–38*, Cambridge: Cambridge University Press.

—— (1980a) 'The management of sterling 1932–1939', *Journal of Economic History* 40: 53–60.

—— (1980b) *Sterling's Managed Float: The Operation of the Exchange Equalisation Account 1932–39*, Princeton: Princeton University Press.

Howson, S. and Winch, D. (1977) *The Economic Advisory Council, 1930–1939: A Study in Economic Advice during Depression and Recovery*, Cambridge: Cambridge University Press.

Hughes, J.J. and Thirlwall, A.P. (1977) 'Trends and cycles in import penetration in the UK', *Oxford Bulletin of Economics and Statistics* 39: 301–17.

Humphries, J. and Rubery, J. (1992) 'The legacy for women's employment: integration, differentiation and polarisation', in J. Michie (ed.), *The Economic Legacy, 1979–1992*, Academic Press.

Hutchison, T.W. (1977) *Keynes versus the 'Keynesians'?: An Essay in the Thinking of J.M. Keynes and the Accuracy of its Interpretation by his Followers*, Institute of Economic Affairs.

Hyman, H. (1989) 'Privatisation: the facts', in C. Veljanovski (ed.) *Privatisation and Competition: A Market Prospectus*, Institute of Economic Affairs.

Inman, P. (1957) *Labour in the Munitions Industries*, HMSO and Longman.

Ingham, G. (1984) *Capitalism Divided? The City and Industry in British Social Development*, Macmillan.

Isserlis, L. (1935) 'Shipping', in British Association, *Britain in Depression*, Pitman.

Jackson, P.M. (1991) 'Public Expenditure', in M. Artis and D. Cobham (eds), *Labour's Economic Policies, 1974–79*, Manchester: Manchester University Press.

James, E. (1962) 'Women at work in twentieth century Britain', *Manchester School of Economic and Social Studies* XXX: 283–300.

Jay, D. (1985) *Sterling: Its Use and Misuse: A Plea for Moderation*, Oxford: Oxford University Press.

Jefferys, K. (1987) 'British politics and social policy during the Second World War', *Historical Journal* 30: 123–44.

Jenkin, M. (1981) *British Industry and the North Sea: State Intervention in a Developing Industrial Sector*, Macmillan.

Johnman, L. (1991) 'The Labour Party and industrial policy, 1940–45' in N. Tiratsoo (ed.) *The Attlee Years*, Pinter.

Johnson, C. (1988) *Measuring the Economy*, Harmondsworth: Penguin.

—— (1991) *The Economy under Mrs Thatcher 1979–1990*, Harmondsworth: Penguin.

Johnson, P. (ed.) (1988) *The Structure of British Industry*, Unwin Hyman, 2nd edn.

Jones, D.T. (1976) 'Employment and productivity in Europe since 1955', *National Institute Economic Review* 77: 72–85.

—— (1981) *Maturity and Crisis in the European Car Industry: Structural Change and Public Policy*, Brighton: Sussex European Research Centre.

Jones, D.T and Prais, S.J. (1978) 'Plant size and productivity in the motor industry: some international comparisons', *Oxford Bulletin of Economics and Statistics* 40: 131–51.

Jones, G. and Kirby, M. (eds) (1991) *Competitiveness and the State*, Manchester: Manchester University Press.

Jones, L. (1957) *Shipbuilding in Britain between the Two World Wars*, Cardiff: University of Wales Press.

Jones, R. (1987) *Wages and Employment Policy 1936-1985*, London: Allen & Unwin.

Jones, R. and Marriott (1972) *Anatomy of a Merger: A History of GEC, AEI and English Electric*, Pan.

Jones, S.G. (1986) *Workers at Play. A Social and Economic History of Leisure 1918–1939*, Routledge and Keegan Paul.

*Journal of Political Economy* (1982) Special issue on *Unemployment in Interwar Britain*.

Kaldor, M. (1980) 'Technical change in the defence industry', in K. Pavitt (ed.), *Technological Innovation and British Economic Performance*, Macmillan.

Kaldor, N. (1966) *Causes of the Slow Rate of Growth of the United Kingdom*, Cambridge: Cambridge University Press.

—— (1971) 'Conflicts in national economic objectives', *Economic Journal* 81: 1–16.

—— (1982) *The Scourge of Monetarism*, Oxford: Oxford University Press.

Kavanagh, D. (1992) 'The postwar consensus', *Twentieth Century British History* 3: 175–90.

Kavanagh, D. and Morris, P. (1989) *Consensus Politics*, Oxford: Blackwell.

Keegan, W. (1984) *Mrs Thatcher's Economic Experiment*, Allen Lane.

—— (1985) *Britain Without Oil*, Harmondsworth: Penguin.

Keep, E. and Mayhew, K. (1988) 'The assessment: education, training and economic performance', *Oxford Review of Economic Policy* 4: i-xv.

Kennedy, C. (1962) 'Monetary policy', in Worswick and Ady (eds), *The British Economy in the Nineteen-Fifties*, Oxford: Oxford University Press.

Kennedy, P. (1988) *The Rise and Fall of the Great Powers*, Unwin Hyman.

Kennedy, W.P. (1973–74) 'Foreign investment, trade and growth in the United Kingdom, 1870–1913', *Explorations in Economic History* XI: 415–44.

—— (1987) *Industrial Structure, Capital Markets and the Origins of British Economic Decline*, Cambridge: Cambridge University Press.

Kenwood, A.G. and Lougheed, A.L. (1971) *The Growth of the International Economy, 1820–1980; An Introductory Text*, Allen and Unwin, revised edn, 1983.

Keynes, J.M. (1923) *A Tract on Monetary Reform*, vol.4. of *The collected writings*.

—— (1925) *The Economic Consequences of Mr. Churchill*, reprinted in (1989) *Collected Writings of John Maynard Keynes*, vol.IX., Macmillan.

—— (1936) *The General Theory of Employment, Interest and Money*, Macmillan.

—— (1979) *The Collected Writings of John Maynard Keynes: vol.XXIV: Activities 1944–46: The Transition to Peace*, Macmillan.

Kessler, S. and Bayliss, F. (1992) *Contemporary Industrial Relations*, London: Macmillan.

Kilpatrick, A. and Lawson, T. (1980) 'On the nature of industrial decline in the UK', *Cambridge Journal of Economics* 4: 85–102.

Kilpatrick, A. and Moir, C. (1988) 'Developments in the UK's international trading performance', in T. Barker and P. Dunne (eds), *The British Economy After Oil: Manufacturing or Services?*, Croom Helm.

Kindleberger, C.P. (1973) *The World in Depression 1929–1939*, Allen Lane.

King, A. (ed.) (1976) *Why is Britain Becoming Harder to Govern?*, BBC.

Kirby, M.W. (1981) *The Decline of British Economic Power since 1870*, Allen & Unwin.

—— (1987) 'Industrial policy', in S. Glynn and A. Booth (eds), *The Road to Full Employment*, Allen & Unwin.

—— (1991) 'Supply-side management', in N.F.R. Crafts and N.W.C. Woodward (eds), *The British Economy since 1945*, Oxford: Oxford University Press.

Kitson, M. and Solomou, S. (1989) 'The macroeconomics of protectionism', *Cambridge Journal of Economics* 13: 155–70

Kock, K. (1969) *International Trade Policy and the GATT, 1947–67*, Stockholm: Almquist & Wicksell.

Kolko, G. (1968) *The Politics of War: The World and United States Foreign Policy, 1943–1945*, New York: Random House.

Kolko, J. and Kolko, G. (1972) *The Limits of Power: The World and United States Foreign Policy, 1945–1954*, New York: Harper and Row.

Kondratiev, N. (1926) 'Die langen Wellen der Konjunktur', *Archiv fur Sozialwissenschaft und Sozialpolitik* LXVI: 573–609.

—— (1935) 'Long waves in economic life', *Review of Economics and Statistics* XVII: 105–15.

Kravis, I.B. (1976) 'A survey of international comparisons of productivity', *Economic Journal* 86: 1–44.

Kravis, I.B. (ed.) (1982) *World Product and Income*, UN.

Kuczynski, J. (1991) 'A note on the structure of the world economy, 1850–1987' in C. Holmes and A. Booth (eds), *Economy and Society: European Industrialisation and its Social Consequences. Essays Presented to Sidney Pollard*, Leicester: Leicester University Press.

Kuznets, S.S. (1966) *Modern Economic Growth: Rate, Structure and Spread*, New Haven: Yale University Press.

LCES (London and Cambridge Economic Service) (n.d.) *The British Economy. Key Statistics 1900–1970*, Times Newspapers Ltd.

Labour Party (1976) *Report of the Annual Conference of the Labour Party*, The Labour Party.

Laidler, D. and Purdy, D. (eds) (1974) *Inflation and Labour Markets*, Manchester: Manchester University Press.

Lambert, P. (1964) *Nutrition in Britain, 1950–60*, Bell.

Landesmann, M. and Snell, A. (1989) 'The consequences of Mrs Thatcher for UK manufacturing exports', *Economic Journal* 99: 1–27.

Lawson, N. (1992) *The View from No. 11: Memoirs of a Tory Radical*, Bantam.

Layard, P.R.G. (1986) *How to Beat Unemployment*, Oxford: Oxford University Press.

Layard, P.R.G. and Nickell, S. (1986) 'Unemployment in Britain' in C. Bean, P.R.G. Layard and S. Nickell (eds) *The Rise in Unemployment*, Oxford: Blackwell.

Layard, P.R.G., Nickell, S. and Jackman, R. (1991) *Unemployment: Macroeconomic Performance and the Labour Market*, Oxford: Oxford University Press.

Lazonick, W. (1983) 'Industrial organisation and technical change: the decline of the British cotton industry', *Business History Review* LVII: 195–236.

—— (1986) 'The cotton industry' in B. Elbaum and W. Lazonick (eds), *The Decline of the British Economy*, Oxford: Oxford University Press.

Lee, R.D. (1977) (ed.) *Population Patterns in the Past*, Academic Press.

Le Grand, J., Winter, D. and Woolley, F. (1990) 'The National Health Service: safe in whose hands?', in J. Hills (ed.), *The State of Welfare: The Welfare State in Britain since 1974*, Oxford: Clarendon Press.

Leruez, J. (1975) *Economic Planning and Politics in Britain*, Oxford: Martin Robertson.

Levine, A.M. (1967) *Industrial Retardation in Britain*, Weidenfeld & Nicolson.

Lewchuk, W. (1986) 'The motor vehicle industry', in B. Elbaum and W. Lazonick (eds), *The Decline of the British Economy*, Oxford: Oxford University Press.

—— (1987) *American Technology and the British Vehicle Industry*, Cambridge: Cambridge University Press.

Lewis, J. (1984) *Women in England, 1870–1950; Sexual Divisions and Social Change*, Brighton: Wheatsheaf.

Lewis, W.A. (1949) *Economic Survey, 1919–1939*, Allen & Unwin.

Liberal Industrial Inquiry (1928) *Britain's Industrial Future*, Benn.

Liberal Party (1929) *We Can Conquer Unemployment. Mr Lloyd George's Pledge*, Liberal Party.

Lister, W. and Golland, J. (1993) 'Research and development in the United Kingdom in 1991', *Economic Trends* 478: 90–106.

Little, I.M.D. (1962) 'Fiscal policy', in Worswick and Ady (eds), *The British Economy in the Nineteen-Fifties*, Oxford: Oxford University Press.

Llewellyn Smith, H. (ed.) (1934) *The New Survey of London Life and Labour*, P.S. King.

—— (1964) 'Growth and productivity in the UK', *Productivity Measurement Review*, 38: 5–22.

Lorenz, E.H. (1991) *Economic Decline in Britain: The Shipbuilding Industry, 1890–1970*, Oxford: Clarendon Press.

Lorenz, E.H. and Wilkinson, F. (1986) 'The shipbuilding industry, 1880–1965' in B. Elbaum and W. Lazonick (eds), *The Decline of the British Economy*, Oxford: Oxford University Press.

Lovell, J.C. (1977) *British Trade Unions 1875–1933*, Macmillan.

Lovell, J.C. and Roberts, B.C. (1968) *A Short History of the T.U.C.*, Macmillan.

Lowe, R. (1993) *The Welfare State in Britain since 1945*, Macmillan.

Lundberg, E. (1968) *Instability and Economic Growth*, New Haven: Yale University Press.

Lyman, R.W. (1957) *The First Labour Government, 1924*, Chapman & Hall.

MAFF (1985) Ministry of Agriculture, Fisheries and Food *Annual Review of Agriculture, 1985*, London: HMSO, Cmnd 9423.

—— (1994) *Agriculture in the United Kingdom, 1993*, London: HMSO.

McLennan, G., Held, D. and Hall, S. (eds) (1984) *State and Society in Contemporary Britain: A Critical Introduction*, Cambridge: Polity Press.

McCloskey, D.N. (1970) 'Did Victorian Britain fail?', *Economic History* Review, XXIII: 446–459.

—— (ed.) (1981) *Enterprise and Trade in Victorian Britain: Essays in Historical Economics*, Allen & Unwin.

McCombie, J. and Thirlwall, A.P. (1992) 'The re-emergence of the balance of payments constraint', in J. Michie (ed.), *The Economic Legacy, 1979–1992*, Academic Press.

McCormick, B.J. (1979) *Industrial Relations in the Coal Industry*, Macmillan.

—— (1988) *The World Economy: Patterns of Growth and Change*, Oxford: Philip Allan.

McCrone, G. (1969) *Regional Policy in Britain*, Allen & Unwin.

McDonald, G.W. and Gospel, H.F. (1973) 'The Mond–Turner talks 1927–1933', *Historical Journal* 20: 807–29.

McGuire, E.B. (1939) *The British Tariff System*, Methuen.

MacInnes, J. (1987) *Thatcherism at Work*, Milton Keynes: Open University Press.

McLaine, I. (1979) *Ministry of Morale: Home Front Morale and the Ministry of Information in the Second World War*, Allen & Unwin.

Macmillan, H. (1973) *At the End of the Day: Memoirs, 1961–1963*, Macmillan.

Macnicol, J. (1980) *The Movement for Family Allowances, 1918–1945, A Study in Social Policy Development*, Heinemann.

MacRae, C.D. (1977) 'A political model of the business cycle', *Journal of Political Economy* 85: 239–64.

Mack, J. and Lansley, S. (1985) *Poor Britain*, Allen & Unwin.

Maddison, A. (1982) *Phases of Capitalist Development*, Oxford: Oxford University Press.

—— (1987) 'Growth and slowdown in advanced capitalist economies: techniques of quantitative assessment', *Journal of Economic Literature* XXV: 649–98.

—— (1989) *The World Economy in the Twentieth Century*, Paris: OECD.

—— (1991) *Dynamic Forces in Capitalist Development: A Long-Run Comparative View*, Oxford: Oxford University Press.

Main, B.G.M. (1982) 'The length of job in Great Britain', *Economica* 49: 325–33.

Mama, A. (1986) 'Black women and the economic crisis' in Feminist Review (ed.), *Waged Work: A Reader*, Virago.

Mandel, E. (1972) *Late Capitalism*, Frankfurt: Suhrkampf.

Maroof, F. and Rajan, A. (1976) 'UK and West German trade in manufactures' in M. Panic (ed.), *The UK and West German Manufacturing Industry*, NEDO.

Marshall, G., Newby, H., Rose, D. and Vogler, C. (1988) *Social Class in Modern Britain*, Hutchinson.

Martin, A. (1979) 'The dynamics of change in a Keynesian political economy: the Swedish case and its implications', in C. Crouch (ed.) *State and Economy in Contemporary Capitalism*, Croom Helm.

Marwick, A. (1967) *The Deluge: British Society and the First World War*, Harmondsworth: Penguin.

—— (1970) *Britain in the Century of Total War: War, Peace and Social Change, 1900–1967*, Harmondsworth: Penguin.

—— (1974) *War and Social change in the Twentieth Century: A Comparative Study of Britain, France, Germany, Russia and the United States*, Macmillan.

—— (1981) 'Problems and consequences of organizing society for total war' in N.F. Dreisziger (ed.) *Mobilization for Total War: The Canadian, American and British Experience, 1914–18, 1939–45*, Waterloo, Ontario.

—— (1982) *British Society since 1945*, Harmondsworth: Penguin.

Matthews, R.C.O. (1968) 'Why has Britain had full employment since the war?', *Economic Journal* 78: 555–69.

Matthews, R.C.O., Feinstein, C.H., and Odling-Smee, J. (1982) *British Economic Growth, 1856–1973*, Stanford, CA: Stanford University Press.

Matthews, R.C.O. and Sargent, J.R. (eds) *Contemporary Problems of Economic Policy: Essays from the CLARE Group*, Methuen.

Maxcy, G. and Silberston, A. (1959) *The British Motor Industry*, Allen & Unwin.

Mayer, C. and Alexander, I. (1990) 'Banks and securities markets: corporate financing in Germany and the UK', *Centre for Economic Policy Research, Discussion Paper 117*.

Mayes, D.G. (1987) 'Does manufacturing matter?', *National Institute Economic Review* 122: 47–58.

Maynard, G. (1988) *The Economy under Mrs. Thatcher*, Oxford: Blackwell.

Meeks, G. (1977) *Disappointing Marriage: A Study of the Gains from Merger*, Cambridge: Cambridge University Press.

Melling, J.L. and McKinlay, A. (eds) (1995) *Work, Management and Authority in Modern Europe*, Aldershot: Edward Elgar.

Mensch, G. (1975) *Stalemate in Technology: Innovations Overcome the Depression*, New York: Ballinger.

Mercer, H. (1991) 'The Monopolies and Restrictive Practices Commission: a study in regulatory failure' in G. Jones and M. Kirby (eds) *Competitiveness and the State*, Manchester: Manchester University Press.

—— (1992) 'Anti-monopoly policy' in H. Mercer, N. Rollings and J. Tomlinson (eds) *Labour Governments and the Private Sector: The Experience of 1945–51*, Edinburgh: Edinburgh University Press.

Mercer, H., Rollings, N. and Tomlinson, J. (eds) (1992) *Labour Governments and the Private Sector: the Experience of 1945–51*, Edinburgh: Edinburgh University Press.

Metcalf, D. (1989) 'Water notes dry up: the impact of the Donovan reform proposals and Thatcherism at work on labour productivity in British manufacturing industry', *British Journal of Industrial Relations* 27: 1–31.

—— (1990) 'Union presence and labour productivity in British manufacturing industry: a reply to Nolan and Marginson', *British Journal of Industrial Relations* 28: 249–66.

Metcalf, D., Nickell, S. and Floros, N. (1982) 'Still searching for a solution to unemployment in inter-war Britain', *Journal of Political Economy* 90: 386–99.

Metcalf, J.S. (1984) 'Foreign trade and payments' in A.R. Prest and D.J. Coppock (eds) *The UK Economy: A Manual of Applied Economics*, Weidenfeld & Nicolson, 10th edn.

Michie, J. (ed.) (1992) *The Economic Legacy, 1979–1992*, Academic Press.

Middlemas, R.K. (1979) *Politics in Industrial Society. The British Experience of the System since 1911*, Deutsch.

—— (1986) *Power, Competition and the State, Volume I: Britain in Search of Balance, 1940–61*, Macmillan.

Middlemas, R.K. and Barnes, A.J.L. (1969) *Baldwin: A Biography*, Weidenfeld & Nicolson.

Middleton, R. (1985) *Towards the Managed Economy: Keynes, the Treasury and the Fiscal Policy Debate of the 1930s*, Methuen.

—— (1987) 'Treasury policy on unemployment', in S. Glynn and A. Booth (eds), *The Road to Full Employment*, Allen & Unwin.

Millar, J. and Glendinning, C. (1989) 'Gender and poverty', *Journal of Social Policy* 18: 363–81.

Millward, R. (1990) 'Productivity in the UK services sector: historical trends 1856–1985 and comparisons with the USA, 1950–85', *Oxford Bulletin of Economics and Statistics* 52: 423–36.

Milward, A.S. (1970) *The Economic Effects of the World Wars on Britain*, Macmillan.

—— (1984) *The Reconstruction of Western Europe, 1945–51*, Methuen.

Ministry of Fuel and Power (1945) *Coal Mining: Report of the Technical Advisory Committee* (the Reid Report), HMSO, Cmd 6610.

Mitchell, B.R. and Deane, P. (1962) *Abstract of British Historical Statistics*, Cambridge: Cambridge University Press.

Mitchell, J. (1972) *The National Board for Prices and Incomes*, Secker and Warburg.

Mitchison, R. (1977) *British Population Change since 1860*, Macmillan.

Moggridge, D.E. (1969) *The Return to Gold: The Formulation of Economic Policy*, Cambridge: Cambridge University Press.

—— (1972) *British Monetary Policy 1924–1931: The Norman Conquest of $4.86*, Cambridge: Cambridge University Press.

—— (ed.) (1989) *The Collected Writings of John Maynard Keynes*, London: Macmillan.

Mokyr, J. (ed.) (1985) *The Economics of the Industrial Revolution*, Allen & Unwin.

Moran, M. (1984) *The Politics of Banking: The Strange Case of Competition and Credit Control*, Macmillan.

Morgan, A.D. (1978) 'Commercial policy' in F. Blackaby (ed), *British Economic Policy, 1960–1974*, Cambridge: Cambridge University Press.

Morgan, E.V. (1953) *Studies in British Financial Policy, 1914–25*, Macmillan.

Morgan, K.O. (1984) *Labour in Power, 1945–51*, Oxford: Oxford University Press.

Morris, D. (ed.) (1985) *The Economic System in the UK*, Oxford: Oxford University Press.

Morris, M. (1976) *The General Strike*, Harmondsworth: Penguin.

Mosley, P. (1984) *The Making of Economic Policy: Theory and Evidence from Britain and the US since 1945*, Brighton: Wheatsheaf.

Mowat, C.L. (1955) *Britain Between the Wars, 1918–1940*, Methuen.

Muellbauer, J. (1986) 'The assessment: productivity and competitiveness in British manufacturing', *Oxford Review of Economic Policy* 2: i–xxv.

Murray, K.A.H. (1955) *Agriculture*, HMSO and Longman.

Musson, A.E. (1978) *The Growth of British Industry*, Batsford.

NEDO (1963) *Conditions Favourable to Faster Growth*, NEDO.

—— (1979) *Electronic Consumer Goods Industry: Report of the Sector Working Party*, NEDO.

Newsom, J. (1963) *Half our Future: A Report of the Central Advisory Council for Education (England)* (the first Newsom Report), Ministry of Education.

Newton, S. and Porter, D. (1988) *Modernisation Frustrated: The Politics of Industrial Decline in Britain since 1900*, Unwin Hyman.

Nichols, T. (1986) *The British Worker Question: A New Look at Workers and Productivity in Manufacturing*, Routledge.

Nolan, P. (1989) 'The productivity miracle?', in F. Green (ed.), *The Restructuring of the UK Economy*, Hemel Hempstead, Harvester.

Nordhaus, W. (1975) 'The political business cycle', *Review of Economic Studies* 42: 169–90.

OECD (1982) *OECD Historical Statistics, 1960–1980*, Paris: OECD.

—— (1988) *OECD Historical Statistics, 1960–1987*, Paris: OECD.

—— (1991) *OECD Historical Statistics, 1960–1989*, Paris: OECD.

—— (1993) *OECD National Accounts, Volume II: Detailed Tables, 1979–1991*, Paris: OECD.

OPCS (1990) *Birth Statistics, 1990*, HMSO.

O'Connor, J. (1973) *The Fiscal Crisis of the State*, New York: St. Martin's Press.

O'Day, A. (ed.) (1979) *The Edwardian Age: Conflict and Stability, 1900–1914*, Macmillan.

Offer, A. (1991) 'Farm tenure and land values in England, c.1750–1950', *Economic History Review* XLIV: 1–20.

Ojala, E.M. (1952) *Agriculture and Economic Progress*, Oxford: Oxford University Press.

Ollerenshaw, P. (1991) 'Textiles and regional economic decline: Northern Ireland, 1914–1970' in C. Holmes and A. Booth (eds), *Economy and Society: European Industrialisation and its Social Consequences. Essays Presented to Sidney Pollard*, Leicester: Leicester University Press.

Olson, M. (1982) *The Rise and Decline of Nations: Economic Growth, Stagnation and Social Rigidities*, New Haven, Conn: Yale University Press.

Opie, R. (1972) 'Economic planning and growth', in W. Beckerman (ed.), *The Labour Government's Economic Record 1964–1970*, Duckworth.

Ormerod, P. (1991) 'Incomes policy', in M. Artis and D. Cobham (eds), *Labour's Economic Policies, 1974–79*, Manchester: Manchester University Press.

—— (1992) 'Waiting for Newton', *New Statesman and Society* 28 Aug. 1992: 12–13.

Overy, R.J. (1976) *William Morris Viscount Nuffield*, Europa.

Owen, S.J. and Joshi, H.E. (1987) 'Does elastic retract: the effect of recession on women's labour force participation', *British Journal of Industrial Relations* 26: 125–43.

PEP (Political and Economic Planning) (1939) *Report on the Location of Industry*, PEP.

Page, R.M. (1991) 'Social welfare since the war', in N.F.R. Crafts and N.W.C. Woodward (eds), *The British Economy since 1945*, Oxford: Oxford University Press.

Paish, F. (1962) *Studies in an Inflationary Economy*, Macmillan, 2nd edn.

Panic, M. (ed.) (1976) *The UK and West German Manufacturing Industry, 1954–72*, NEDO.

—— (1992) 'Comment: UK monetary policy in the 1980s', in J. Michie (ed.), *The Economic Legacy, 1979–1992*, Academic Press.

Panitch, L. (1976) *Social Democracy and Industrial Militancy: The Labour Party, the Trade Unions and Incomes Policy, 1945–74*, Cambridge: Cambridge University Press.

Parkin, M. and Sumner, M.T. (eds) *Incomes Policy and Inflation*, Manchester: Manchester University Press.

Parsley, C.J. (1980) 'Labor union effects on wage gains: a survey of recent literature', *Journal of Economic Literature* XVIII: 1–31.

Patel, P. and Pavitt, K. (1987) 'The elements of British technological competitiveness', *National Institute Economic Review* 122: 72–83.

Pavitt, K. (1980a) 'Introduction and summary', in K. Pavitt (ed.), *Technological Innovation and British Economic Performance*, Macmillan.

—— (ed.) (1980b) *Technological Innovation and British Economic Performance*, Macmillan.

—— (1981) 'Technology in British industry: a suitable case for improvement' in C. Carter (ed.), *Industrial Policy and Innovation*, Heinemann.

Pavitt, K. and Soete, L. (1980) 'Innovative activities and export shares: some comparisons between industries and countries' in K. Pavitt (ed.), *Technological Innovation and British Economic Performance*, Macmillan.

Peck, M.J. (1968) 'Science and technology', in R.E. Caves (ed.) *Britain's Economic Prospects*, Washington, DC: The Brookings Institute.

Peden, G.C. (1983) 'Sir Richard Hopkins and the "Keynesian revolution" in employment policy, 1929–1945', *Economic History Review* XXXVI: 281–96.

—— (1984) 'The "Treasury view" on public works and employment in the interwar period', *Economic History Review* XXXVII: 167–81.

—— (1988) *Keynes, the Treasury and Economic Policy*, Macmillan.

—— (1991) *British Economic and Social Policy: Lloyd George to Margaret Thatcher*, Hemel Hempstead: Phillip Allan, 2nd edn.

Pelling, H. (1970) *Britain and the Second World War*, Collins.

—— (1991) *A Short History of the Labour Party*, Macmillan, 9th edn.

Phelps Brown, E.H. (1988) *Egalitarianism and the Generation of Inequality*, Oxford: Oxford University Press.

Phillips, A.W. (1958) 'The relationship between unemployment and the rate of change of money wage rates in the United Kingdom', *Economica* 25: 283–99.

Phillips, G.A. (1976) *The General Strike: The Politics of Industrial Conflict*, Weidenfeld and Nicolson.

Phizacklea, A. (1982) 'Migrant women and wage labour: the case of West Indian women in Britain', in J. West (ed.) *Work, Women and the Labour Market*, London: Routledge.

Piachaud, D. (1978) 'Inflation and income distribution', in F. Hirsch and J.H. Goldthorpe (eds) *The Political Economy of Inflation*, Oxford: Martin Robertson.
—— (1987) 'Problems in the definition and measurement of poverty', *Journal of Social Policy* 16: 147–64.
—— (1988) 'Poverty in Britain, 1899–1983', *Journal of Social Policy* 17: 335–49.
Pimlott, B. (1985) *Hugh Dalton*, Cape.
—— (1989) 'Is the "postwar consensus" a myth?', *Contemporary Record* 2: 12–14
—— (1992) *Harold Wilson*, HarperCollins.
Pinchbeck, I. (1981) *Women Workers and the Industrial Revolution 1750–1850*, Virago, 3rd edn.
Piore, M.J. (1975) 'Notes for a theory of labour market stratification' in R.C. Edwards (ed.) *Labor Market Segmentation*, Lexington, MA: D.C. Heath.
Playford, C. and Pond, C. (1983) 'The right to be unequal: inequality of incomes' in F. Field (ed.) *The Wealth Report – 2*, Routledge.
Pliatzky, L. (1984) *Getting and Spending: Public Expenditure, Employment and Inflation*, Oxford: Blackwell, 2nd edn.
Plowden (1961) *Control of Public Expenditure: The Plowden Report on the Machinery of Government*, HMSO, Cmnd 1432.
Plummer, A. (1937) *New British Industries in the Twentieth Century: A Survey of Development and Structure*, Pitman.
Pollard, S. (ed.) (1970) *The Gold Standard and Employment Policies between the Wars*, Methuen.
—— (1982) *The Wasting of the British Economy: British Economic Policy 1945 to the Present*, Croom Helm, 2nd edn.
—— (1983) *The Development of the British Economy*, Edward Arnold, 3rd edn.
Pollard, S. and Robertson, P. (1979) *The British Shipbuilding Industry 1870–1914*, Cambridge, MA: Harvard University Press.
Posner, M. and Steer, A. (1978) 'Price competitiveness and the performance of manufacturing industry', in F. Blackaby (ed.), *De-industrialisation*, Heinemann.
Prais, S.J. (1981) *Productivity and Industrial Structure: A Statistical Study of Manufacturing Industry in Britain, Germany and the United States*, Cambridge: Cambridge University Press.
—— (1985) 'What can we learn from the German system of education and training?', in G.D.N. Worswick (ed.) *Education and Economic Performance*, Aldershot: Gower.
Prais, S.J. and Wagner, K. (1983) *Schooling Standards in Britain and Germany*, National Institute of Economic and Social Research.
Prais, S.J. and Wagner, K. (1985) 'Schooling standards in England and Germany: some summary comparisons bearing on economic performance', *National Institute Economic Review* 112: 53–76.
Pratten, C.F. (1976) *Labour Productivity Differentials within International Companies*, Cambridge: Cambridge University Press.
Pressnell, L. (1986) *External Economic Policy, Volume I: The Postwar Financial Settlement*, HMSO.
Prest, A.R. and Coppock, D.J. (eds) (1984) *The UK Economy: A Manual of Applied Economics*, Weidenfeld & Nicolson, 10th edn.
Price, R. (1986) *Labour in British Society: An Interpretive History*, Croom Helm.
Prices and Incomes Board (1967) *Bank Charges* (Report 34), HMSO. Cmnd 3292.
Priestley, J.B. (1934) *English Journey*, Heinemann, Jubilee edition 1984.
Pryke, R. (1971) *Public Enterprise in Practice: The British Experience of Nationalisation over Two Decades*, MacGibbon & Kee.

—— (1981) *The Nationalised Industries: Policies and Performance since 1968*, Oxford: Martin Robertson.

Purdy, D. and Zis, G. (1974) 'Trade unions and wage inflation in the UK: a reappraisal', in D. Laidler and D. Purdy (eds) *Inflation and Labour Markets*, Manchester: Manchester University Press.

Radcliffe (1959) *Committee on the Working of the Monetary System, Report* (the Radcliffe Report), HMSO, Cmnd 827.

Ramsden, J. (1991) 'Thatcher and Conservative history', *Contemporary Record* 4: 2–3.

Ranki, G. (1988) 'Economy and the Second World War: a few comparative issues', *Journal of European Economic History* 17: 303–47.

Reader, W.J. (1975) *Imperial Chemical Industries: A History. vol.2. The First Quarter Century. 1926–1952*, Oxford: Oxford University Press.

Redmond, J. (1980) 'An indication of the effective exchange rate of the pound in the nineteen-thirties', *Economic History Review* XXXIII: 83–91.

—— (1984) 'The sterling overvaluation in 1925: a multilateral approach', *Economic History Review* XXXVII: 520–31.

Renshaw, P. (1975) *The General Strike*, Eyre Methuen.

Rhodes J. and Tyler, P. (1993) 'Time to manufacture growth?' *The Guardian*, 21 June 1993.

Rhys, G. (1988) 'Motor vehicles', in Johnson (ed.), *The Structure of British Industry*, Unwin Hyman, 2nd edn.

Richardson, H.W. (1965) 'Overcommitment in Britain before 1930', *Oxford Economic Papers*, 17.

—— (1967) *Economic Recovery in Britain, 1932–9*, Weidenfeld & Nicolson.

Richardson, H.W. and Aldcroft, D.H. (1968) *Building in the British Economy between the Wars*, Allen & Unwin.

Richardson, K. and O'Gallagher, C.N. (1977) *The British Motor Industry 1896–1939*, Macmillan.

Robbins (1963) *Higher Education* (the Robbins Report), HMSO, Cmnd 2154.

Roberts, B.C. (1958) *The Trades Union Congress*, Allen & Unwin.

Roberts, J., Elliott, D. and Houghton, T. (1991) *Privatising Electricity: The Politics of Power*, Bellhaven.

Roberts, R. (1971) *The Classic Slum. Salford Life in the First Quarter of the Century*, Manchester: Manchester University Press.

Roberts, R. (1984) 'The administrative origins of industrial diplomacy: an aspect of government-industry relations', in Turner (ed.), *Businessmen and Politics: Studies of Business Activity in British Politics 1900–1945*, Heinemann.

—— (1992) 'Regulatory responses to the rise of the market for corporate control in Britain in the 1950s', *Business History* 34: 183–200.

Robertson, A.J. (1982) 'Lord Beaverbrook and the supply of aircraft, 1940–1941' in A. Slaven and D.H. Aldcroft (eds) *Business, Banking and Urban History: Essays in Honour of S.G. Checkland*, Edinburgh: John Donald.

Robinson, C. and Hann, D. (1988) 'North Sea oil and gas', in P. Johnson (ed.), *The Structure of British Industry*, Unwin Hyman.

Robinson, D. (1985) 'Government and pay', in O. Morris (ed.), *The Economic System in the UK*, Oxford: Oxford University Press.

Robinson, E.A.G. (1951) 'The overall allocation of resources', in D.N. Chester (ed.), *Lessons of the British War Economy*, Cambridge: Cambridge University Press.

Robinson, O. (1988) 'The changing labour market: growth of part-time employment and labour market segmentation in Britain' in S. Walby (ed.) *Gender Segregation at Work*, Milton Keynes: Open University Press.

Robson, W.A. (ed.) (1937) *Public Enterprise: Developments in Social Ownership and Control in Great Britain*, Allen & Unwin.

Rogow, A.A. and Shore, P. (1955) *The Labour Government and British Industry, 1945–51*, Ithaca, NY: Cornell University Press.

Rollings, N. (1988) 'British budgetary policy, 1945–54: a "Keynesian revolution"?', *Economic History Review* XLI: 283–98.

Rooth, T. (1984) 'Limits of leverage: the Anglo-Danish agreement of 1933', *Economic History Review* XXXVII: 211–28.

—— (1986) 'Trade and bargaining: Anglo-Scandinavian economic relations in the 1930s', *Scandinavian Economic History Review* 34: 54–71.

Rose, R. (1980) *Do Parties Make a Difference?*, Macmillan.

Rostas, L. (1948) *Comparative Productivity in British and American Industry*, Cambridge: Cambridge University Press.

Rostow, W.W. (1971) *The Stages of Economic Growth: A Non-communist Manifesto*, Cambridge: Cambridge University Press.

—— (1975) 'Kondratieff, Schumpeter and Kuznets: trend periods revisited', *Journal of Economic History* XXXV: 719–53.

—— (1978) *The World Economy: History and Prospect*, Macmillan.

Routh, G. (1965) *Occupation and Pay in Great Britain*, Cambridge: Cambridge University Press.

Rowbotham, S. (1977) *Hidden From History: 300 Years of Women's Oppression and the Fight against it*, Pluto Press.

Rowntree, B.S. (1941) *Poverty and Progress*, Longman.

Rowthorn, R.E. (1975) 'What remains of Kaldor's law?', *Economic Journal* 85: 10–19.

—— (1992) 'Government spending and taxation in the Thatcher era', in J. Michie (ed.), *The Economic Legacy, 1979–1992*, Academic Press.

—— (1994) 'Brave new world of services exports is folly'; *The Guardian*, 23 May 1994.

Rowthorn, R.E. and Wells, J.R. (1987) *De-industrialisation and Foreign Trade*, Cambridge: Cambridge University Press.

Rubery, J. (1992) 'Pay, gender and the social dimension to Europe' *British Journal of Industrial Relations* 30: 605–21.

Rubinstein, W.D. (1981) *Men of Property: The very Wealthy in Britain since the Industrial Revolution*, Croom Helm.

—— (1986) *Wealth and Inequality in Britain*, Faber.

—— (1993) *Capitalism, Culture and Decline in Britain, 1750–1990*, Routledge.

Rutter, M. and Madge, N. (1976) *Cycles of Disadvantage: A Review of Research*, Heinemann.

Sandberg, L. (1974) *Lancashire in Decline: A Study in Entrepreneurship, Technology, and International Trade*, Columbus: Ohio State University Press.

Sanderson, M. (1988) 'Education and economic decline, 1890 to the 1990s', *Oxford Review of Economic Policy* 4: 38–50.

—— (1991) 'Social equity and industrial need: a dilemma of English education since 1945', in T. Gourvish and A. O'Day (eds), *Britain since 1945*, Macmillan.

Sargent, J.R. (1952) 'Britain and the sterling area', in G.D.N. Worswick and P.H. Ady (eds), The British Economy, 1945–50, Oxford: Oxford University Press.

—— (1978) 'UK performance in services', in F. Blackaby (ed.), *De-industrialisation*, Heinemann.

Sarson, R. (1993) 'Firm grasp on the future', The *Guardian*, 8 July 1993.

Saville, J. (1990) 'Britain, the Marshall Plan and the cold war', *International Socialism* 46: 143–52.

Sawyer, M. (1989) 'Industry', in M. Artis (ed.), *Prest and Coppock's the UK Economy: A Manual of Applied Economics*, Weidenfeld & Nicolson, 12th edn.

—— (1991) 'Industrial policy', in M. Artis and D. Cobham (eds), *Labour's Economic Policies, 1974–79*, Manchester: Manchester University Press.

Sayers, R.S. (1950) 'The springs of technical progress in Britain, 1919–39', *Economic Journal*, 60.

—— (1956) *Financial Policy, 1939–1945*, HMSO and Longman.

—— (1976) *The Bank of England 1891–1944*, Cambridge: Cambridge University Press.

Schumpeter, J. (1939) *Business Cycles: A Theoretical, Historical and Statistical Analysis of the Capitalist Process*, New York: McGraw-Hill, 2 vols.

Scott, J. and Griff, C. (1984) *Directors of Industry: The British Corporate Network, 1904–76*, Cambridge: Polity Press.

Scott, M. (1962) 'The balance of payments crises', in G.D.N. Worswick and P.H. Ady (eds), *The British Economy in the Nineteen-Fifties*, Oxford: Oxford University Press.

Seers, D. (1949) *Changes in the Cost of Living and the Distribution of Income since 1938*, Oxford: Blackwell.

—— (1951) *The Levelling of Incomes since 1938*, Oxford: Blackwell.

Seldon, A. (1991) 'The Conservative Party since 1945', in T. Gourvish and A. O'Day (eds), *Britain since 1945*, Macmillan.

Shackleton, J.R. (1992) *Training too Much? A Sceptical Look at the Economics of Skill Provision in the UK*, Institute of Economic Affairs.

Shaw, G.K. (1992) 'Policy implications of endogenous growth theory', *Economic Journal* 102: 611–21.

Shaw, R. and Simpson, P. (1988) 'Synthetic fibres', in P. Johnson (ed.), *The Structure of British Industry*, Unwin Hyman.

Shepherd, J. (1987) 'Industrial support policies', *National Institute Economic Review* 122: 59–71.

Shonfield, M. (1969) *Modern Capitalism: The Changing Balance of Public and Private Power*, Oxford: Oxford University Press.

Short, J.R. (1982) *Housing in Britain: The Postwar Experience*, Methuen.

Silberston, Z.A. (1981) 'Industrial policies in Britain', in C. Carter (ed.), *Industrial Policy and Innovation*, Heinemann.

Simmons, I.G. (1993) *Environmental History. A Concise Introduction*, Oxford: Blackwell.

Singh, A. (1975) 'Takeovers, natural selection and the theory of the firm: evidence from postwar experience', *Economic Journal* 85: 497–515.

—— (1977) 'UK industry and the world economy: a case of de-industrialisation?', *Cambridge Journal of Economics*, 1: 113–36.

Singleton, J. (1990a) 'Planning for cotton, 1945–1951', *Economic History Review* XLIII: 62–78.

—— (1990b) 'Showing the white flag: the Lancashire cotton industry, 1945–65', *Business History* 32: 129–49.

Skidelsky, R. (1967) *Politicians and the Slump: The Labour Government of 1929–1931*, Macmillan.

—— (ed.) (1988) *Thatcherism*, Chatto and Windus.

Slaven, A. and Aldcroft, D.H. (eds) (1982) *Business, Banking and Urban History: Essars in Honour of S.G. Checkland*, Edinburgh: John Donald.

Smith, A.D. (1992) 'Britain's performance in international financial markets', *National Institute Economic Review* 141: 106–9.

Smith, A.D. and Hitchens, D.M.W.N. (1983) 'Comparative British and American productivity in retailing', *National Institute Economic Review* 104: 45–57.

Smith, A.D., Hitchens, D.M.W.N., and Davies, S.W. (1982) *International Industrial Productivity: A Comparison of Britain, America and Germany*, Cambridge: Cambridge University Press.

Smith, H.L. (1981) 'The problem of "equal pay for equal work" in Great Britain', *Journal of Modern History* 53: 652–72.

—— (1984) 'The womanpower problem in Britain during the Second World War', *Historical Journal* 27: 925–45.

—— (1986a) 'The effect of war on the status of women', in H.L. Smith (ed.), *War and Social Change: British Society in the Second World War*, Manchester: Manchester University Press.

—— (ed.) (1986b) *War and Social Change: British Society in the Second World War*, Manchester: Manchester University Press.

Soete, L. (1985) *Technological Trends and Employment, 3: Electronics and Communications*, Aldershot: Gower.

Solomou, S. (1988) *Phases of Economic Growth 1850–1973*, Cambridge: Cambridge University Press.

Spero, J. (1982) *The Politics of International Relations*, Allen & Unwin.

Stanworth, P. and Giddens, A. (eds) (1974) *Elites and Power in British Society*, Cambridge: Cambridge University Press.

Stark, T. (1977) *The Distribution of Income in Eight Countries* (Royal Commission on the Distribution of Income and Wealth, Background Paper 4), London: HMSO.

Stedman Jones, G. (1971) *Outcast London: A Study of the Relationship between Classes in Victorian Society*, Oxford: Oxford University Press.

Steedman, A. and Wagner, K. (1987) 'A second look at productivity, machinery and skills in Britain and Germany', *National Institute Economic Review* 122: 84–95.

Stevenson, J. (1977) *Social Conditions in Britain between the Wars*, Harmondsworth: Penguin.

—— (1984) *British Society 1914–45*, Harmondsworth: Penguin.

Stewart, M. (1967) *Keynes and After*, Harmondsworth: Penguin.

—— (1972) 'The distribution of income', in W. Beckerman (ed.), *The Labour Government's Economic Record, 1964–1970*, Duckworth.

—— (1977) *The Jekyll and Hyde Years: Politics and Economic Policy since 1964*, Dent.

Stout, D.K. (1976) *International Price Competitiveness, Non-price Factors in International Trade*, NEDO.

Strange, S. (1971) *Sterling and British Policy: A Political Study of an International Currency in Decline*, Oxford: Oxford University Press.

—— (1986) *Casino Capitalism*, Oxford: Blackwell.

Sturmey, S.G. (1962) *British Shipping and World Competition*, Athlone Press.

Summerfield, P. (1984) *Women Workers in the Second World War: Production and Patriarchy in Conflict*, Croom Helm.

—— (1986) 'The levelling of class', in H.L. Smith (ed.), *War and Social Change: British Society in the Second World War*, Manchester: Manchester University Press.

Summerfield, P. and Evans, E.J. (eds) (1990) *Technical Education and the State since 1850: Historical and Contemporary Perspectives*, Manchester: Manchester University Press.

*Sunday Times*, 'Secret report shows shocking state of British industry', 14 March 1993.

Supple, B. (1988) 'The political economy of demoralisation: the state and the coalmining industry in America and Britain between the wars', *Economic History Review* XLI: 566–91.

—— (1987) *The History of the British Coal Industry, vol.4: 1913–1946: The Political Economy of Decline*, Oxford: Clarendon Press.

Surrey, M.J.C. (1985) 'Modelling the economy', in D. Morris (ed.), *The Economic System in the UK*, Oxford: Oxford University Press.

Svennilson, I. (1954) *Growth and Stagnation in the European Economy*, Geneva: League of Nations.

Swords-Isherwood, N. (1980) 'British management compared', in K. Pavitt (ed.), *Technological Innovation and British Economic Performance*, Macmillan.

Tew, B. (1970) *International Monetary Co-operation, 1945–70*, Hutchinson, 10th edn.

Thane, P. (1982) *Foundations of the Welfare State*, Longman.

—— (1991) 'Towards equal opportunities? Women in Britain since 1945', in T. Gourvish and A. O'Day (eds), *Britain since 1945*, Macmillan.

Thatcher, A.R. (1978) 'Labour supply and employment trends', in Blackaby (ed.), *De-industrialisation*, Heinemann.

Thirwall, A.P. (1986) *Balance of Payments Theory and United Kingdom Experience*, Macmillan, 3rd edn.

Thom, D. (1986) 'The 1944 Education Act: "the art of the possible"?', in H.L. Smith (ed.), *War and Social Change: British Society in the Second World War*, Manchester: Manchester University Press.

Thomas, B. (1937) 'The influx of labour to London and the south-east, 1920–1936', *Economica*, N.S. IV.

Thomas, B. (1988) 'Coal', in P. Johnson (ed.), *The Structure of British Industry*, Unwin Hyman, 2nd edn.

Thomas, M. (1983) 'Rearmament and economic recovery in the late 1930s', *Economic History Review* 36.

Thomas, T. (1981) 'Aggregate demand in the United Kingdom 1918–45', in R.C. Floud and D.N. McCloskey (eds), *The Economic History of Britain since 1700*, Cambridge: Cambridge University Press, vol. 2.

Thomas, W.A. (1978) *The Finance of British Industry, 1918–1976*, Methuen.

Thoms, D. and Donnelly, T. (1985) *The Motor Car Industry in Coventry since the 1890s: Origins, Development, Structure*, Croom Helm.

Thompson, F.M.L. (1963) *English Landed Society in the Nineteenth Century*, Routledge & Kegan Paul.

Tiratsoo, N. (ed.) (1991) *The Attlee Years*, Pinter.

Tiratsoo, N. and Tomlinson, J. (1993) *Industrial Efficiency and State Intervention: Labour, 1939–1951*, Routledge.

Titmuss, R.M. (1950) *Problems of Social Policy*, Longman.

—— (1958) *Essays on The Welfare State*, Allen & Unwin.

Tolliday, S. (1987) *Business, Banking and Politics: The Case of British Steel, 1918–1939*, Cambridge, MA: Harvard University Press.

—— (1991) '"Ford" and "Fordism" in postwar Britain: enterprise management and the control of labour, 1937–1987', in S. Tolliday and J. Zeitlin (eds) *The Power to Manage: Employers and Industrial Relations in Comparative-Historical Perspective*, Routledge.

Tolliday, S. and Zeitlin, J. (eds) (1991) *The Power to Manage: Employers and Industrial Relations in Comparative-Historical Perspective*, Routledge.

Tomlinson, J. (1987) *Employment Policy: The Crucial Years, 1939–1955*, Oxford: Clarendon Press.
—— (1990) *Public Policy and the Economy since 1900*, Oxford: Clarendon Press.
—— (1991) 'The Attlee government and the balance of payments', *Twentieth Century British History* 2: 47–66.
—— (1994) *Government and the Enterprise since 1900*, Oxford: Clarendon Press.
Tout, H. (1938) *The Standard of Living in Bristol*, Bristol: Bristol University Press.
Townsend, P. (1957) *Family Life of Old People*, Routledge.
—— (1979) *Poverty in the United Kingdom*, Harmondsworth: Penguin.
Townsend, P. and Davidson, N. (1982) *Inequalities in Health: The Black Report*, Harmondsworth: Penguin.
Treasury (1957) *The European Free Trade Area*, HMSO, Cmnd 72.
Turner, G. (1971) *The Leyland Papers*, Eyre and Spotiswoode.
Turner, J. (ed.) (1984) *Businessmen and Politics: Studies of Business Activity in British Politics 1900–1945*, Heinemann.
Tweedale, G. (1992) 'Marketing the second industrial revolution: a case study of the Ferranti Computer Group, 1949–63', *Business History* 34: 96–127.
Tyszynsky, H. (1951) 'World trade in manufactured commodities 1899–1950', *Manchester School of Economic and Social Studies* XIX: 272–304.
Tzannatos, P.Z. and Zabalza, A. (1984) 'The anatomy of the rise of British female relative wages in the 1970s: evidence from the New Earnings Survey', *British Journal of Industrial Relations* 22: 177–94.
van der Wee, H. (1987) *Prosperity and Upheaval: The World Economy, 1945–1980*, Harmondsworth: Penguin.
van Slooten, R. and Coverdale, A.G. (1977) 'The characteristics of low-income households', *Social Trends* 7: 26–39.
Veit-Wilson, J. (1987) 'Consensual approaches to poverty lines and social security', *Journal of Social Policy* 16: 183–211.
—— (1992) 'Muddle or mendacity? The Beveridge committee and the poverty line', *Journal of Social Policy* 21: 269–301.
Veljanovski, C. (ed.) (1989) *Privatisation and Competition: A Market Prospectus*, Institute of Economic Affairs.
von Tunzelmann, N. (1981) 'Britain 1900–45: a survey', in R.C. Floud and D.N. McCloskey (eds) *The Economic History of Britain since 1700*, Cambridge: Cambridge University Press.
Walby, S. (ed.) (1988) *Gender Segregation at Work*, Milton Keynes: Open University Press.
Walker, G.J. (1947) *Road and Rail: An Enquiry into the Economics of Competition and State Control*, Allen & Unwin, 2nd edn.
Walker, S. and Barton, L. (1986) *Youth Unemployment and Schooling*, Milton Keynes: Open University Press.
Walshe. J.G. (1991) 'Industrial organisation and competition policy', in N.F.R. Crafts and N.W.C. Woodward (eds), *The British Economy since 1945*, Oxford: Oxford University Press.
Walters, A. (1986) *Britain's Economic Renaissance*, Oxford: Oxford University Press.
—— (1988) 'Britain does best outside the EMS', *The Times* 6 April 1988.
Wardley, P. (1991) 'The anatomy of big business: aspects of corporate development in the twentieth century', *Business History* 33: 268–96.
Webb, S. and Webb, B. (eds) (1920) *The History of Trade Unionism, 1666–1920*, printed by the authors.
Webster, C. (1982) 'Healthy or hungry thirties', *History Workshop Journal* 10: 110–29.

—— (1985) 'Health, welfare and unemployment during the depression', *Past and Present* 109: 204–30.

—— (1988) *The Health Services since the War, Volume I: Problems of Health Care, the National Health Service before 1957*, HMSO.

Wells, J. (1989) 'Uneven development and de-industrialisation in the UK since 1979', in F. Green (ed.), *The Restructuring of the UK Economy*, Hemel Hempstead: Harvester.

Wells, J.D. and Imber, J.C. (1977) 'The home and export performance of UK industries', *Economic Trends* 286: 78–89.

West, J. (ed.) (1982) *Work, Women and the Labour Market*, Routledge.

Westergaard, J. and Resler, H. (1976) *Class in a Capitalist Society: A Study of Contemporary Britain*, Harmondsworth: Penguin.

White, M. (ed.) (1987) *The Social World of the Young Unemployed*, Policy Studies Institute.

Whiteside, N. (1987) 'The social consequences of interwar unemployment', in S. Glynn and A. Booth (eds), *The Road to Full Employment*, Allen & Unwin.

Whiteside, N. and Gillespie, J.A. (1991) 'Deconstructing unemployment: developments in Britain in the interwar years', *Economic History Review* XLIV: 665–82.

Whiting, A. (1976) 'An international comparison of the instability of economic growth', *Three Banks Review* 109: 26–46.

Wiener, M.J. (1981) *English Culture and the Decline of the Industrial Spirit, 1850–1980*, Cambridge: Cambridge University Press.

Wigham, E. (1973) *The Power to Manage: A History of the Engineering Employer's Federation*, Macmillan.

Wilkinson, R. and Burkitt, B. (1973) 'Wage determination and trade unions', *Scottish Journal of Political Economy* 20: 107–22.

Wilkinson, R.G. (1989) 'Class mortality differentials, income distribution and trends in poverty, 1921–1981', *Journal of Social Policy* 18: 307–35.

Wilks, S. (1984) *Industrial Policy and the Motor Industry*, Manchester: Manchester University Press.

Williams, A. (1992) *Trading with the Bolshevics*, Manchester: Manchester University Press.

Williams, D. (1963) 'London and the 1931 financial crisis', *Economic History Review* XV: 513–28.

Williams, K., Williams, J. and Thomas, D. (1983) *Why are the British Bad at Manufacturing?*, Routledge.

Williams, K., Williams, J. and Haslam C. (1987) *The Breakdown of Austin-Rover: A Case Study in the Failure of Business Strategy and Industrial Policy*, Leamington Spa: Berg.

Willmott, P. and Young, M. (1960) *Family and Class in a London Suburb*, Routledge.

Wilson (1980) *Committee to Review the Functioning of Financial Institutions* (the Wilson Committee), HMSO, Cmnd 7937 (2 vols.).

Wilson, T. (1958) 'The electronics industry', in D. Burn (ed.), *The Structure of British Industry: A Symposium*, Cambridge: Cambridge University Press.

Winch, D. (1969) *Economics and Policy: A Historical Study*, Hodder and Stoughton.

Winter, J.M. (1986a) *The Great War and the British People*, Macmillan.

—— (1986b) 'The demographic consequences of the war' in H.L. Smith (ed.), *War and Social Change: British Society in the Second World War*, Manchester: Manchester University Press.

Woodward, N.W.C. (1991) 'Inflation', in N.F.R. Crafts and N.W.C. Woodward (eds), *The British Economy since 1945*, Oxford: Oxford University Press.

Worswick, G.D.N. (1952) 'The British economy, 1945–50', in G.D.N. Worswick and P.H. Ady (eds), *The British Economy, 1945–50*, Oxford: Oxford University Press.
—— (1984) 'The sources of recovery in the UK in the 1930s', *National Institute Economic Review* : 85–93
—— (ed.) (1985) *Education and Economic Performance*, Aldershot: Gower.
Worswick, G.D.N. and Ady P.H. (eds) (1952) *The British Economy, 1945–50*, Oxford: Oxford University Press.
—— (1962) *The British Economy in the Nineteen-Fifties*, Oxford: Oxford University Press.
Wright, J.F. (1981) 'The inter-war experience', *Oxford Economic Papers*, 33 (Supplement).
Wrigley, C. (1976) *David Lloyd George and the British Labour Movement: Peace and War*, Brighton: Harvester Press.
—— (ed.) (1987) *A History of British Industrial Relations*, vol.II, *1914–1939*, Brighton: Harvester.
Yates, M.L. (1937) *Wages and Labour Conditions in British Engineering*, Unwin.
Young, J.W. (1993) *Britain and European Unity 1945-1992, Macmillan.*
Young, M. and Willmott, P. (1973) *The Symmetrical Family*, Routledge.
Zeitlin, J. (1986) *From Labour History to the History of Industrial Relations*, London: Centre for Economic Policy Research. Discussion paper 145.
Zeitlin, J. and Tolliday, S. (1986) *The Automobile Industry and its Workers*, Cambridge: Cambridge University Press.
Zweig, F. (1951) *Productivity and Trade Unions*, Oxford: Oxford University Press.

# Index

budget 132–3, 306, 309–10; *see also* PSBR, Treasury
building industry *see* construction
building materials industry 72, 81, 82; employment 60, 68, 145, 280; output 58, 68, 243
Butler, R.A. 186

Cabinet 39, 101, 102, 135, 159, 162, 179, 230, 322; and the general strike 106; and the gold standard 116, 129; splits 120, 160–1
Cable and Wireless 268
Calder, R. 92
Callaghan, J. 284, 317
Canada 122, 217
canals 21, 77
cancer 173
Capie, F. 96, 139
car ownership 202–3; *see also* motor vehicles
Caradog Jones, D. 31, 32
Caribbean 175–6
Caves, R. 295, 297
census of 1931 86
Chamberlain, N. 143, 151
Chancellor of the Exchequer 305, 306, 310, 311, 322
Chandler, A.D. 75, 264
chapel 29
Chapman, A. 86
cheap money *see* monetary policy
chemicals industry 57, 65, 69, 244, 266; employment 60, 68, 145, 280; exports 61; output 58, 59, 68, 243; productivity 68; synthetic dyestuffs 65; unemployment in 90
Child Benefit Act 1975 212
Child Support Agency 183
Chrysler Corporation 255
Churchill, W.S. 106, 143, 159, 185, 293, 307, 309; and return to the gold standard 130–1
cinema 10, 29
Citrine, W. 109
City and Guilds 76
City of London 94, 131–2, 230, 232, 267–8, 271, 275–6, 317, 322; inflow of funds into after devaluation in 1931 120–1; influence on economic policy 137, 267–8; reliance on short-term funds in 1920s 119; short-term liabilities post-1914 116
civil service 17, 54
Clark, C. 17

class conflict 39, 101, 177–80
Cleator Moor 92
Clegg, H.A. 97
clerical work 46, 177–8, 179
clothing industry: employment 60, 68, 145, 280; of females 46; exports 61; output 58, 59, 68, 243; productivity 68
Clydebank 92
coal industry 3, 56, 61–2, 77, 92, 272, 306; coal mining communities 176; cost structure interwar 62; crisis 1947 306; employment 62, 251; exports 61; industrial relations 62, 100, 104–5, 144, 149; strikes 104, 105, 106–7, 250, 314; *see also* general strike; investment 248–50; disinvestment 1939–45 149; Kent coalfield 92; policy 105: modernisation plan 270; nationalisation 104, 105, 248, 268; official inquiries 71, 104, 105, 164; rationalisation 62, 74; production 61–3, 146, 148–9, 249, 251; open cast 149; and rearmament 140; unemployment in 90
Coal Mines Act 1930 62–3
coalition government 1940–45 159–60
cold war 184, 221, 222, 307
collusion by industrialists 72, 164
Cologne 255
commerce 46, 145, 243
commodity prices 228; *see also* OPEC
Commonwealth 175, 237; New Commonwealth and Pakistan 175–6; *see also* British empire
Commonwealth Immigrants Act 1962, 175
comparative advantage 70, 111
competitive forces 72
comprehensive schools 302
computer industry 259, 268, 270
Concorde 266
Conservative governments: interwar 47–8; 1951–64 210, 269–70, 309; 1970–74 227, 271, 286, 313–16; since 1979 179, 187, 196, 213–5, 232, 240, 256, 286, 294, 319–27: economic policies 308–11; education and training policies 302; and income distribution 213–14; incomes policy 292; industrial policy 271–2;